computing ESSENTIALS

Making IT work for you

INTRODUCTORY 2011

·The O'Leary Series

Computing Concepts

- *Computing Essentials 2006* Introductory & Complete Editions
- *Computing Essentials 2007* Introductory & Complete Editions
- *Computing Essentials 2008* Introductory & Complete Editions
- *Computing Essentials 2010* Introductory & Complete Editions

Microsoft Office Applications

- *Microsoft Office 2007*
- *Microsoft Office Word 2007* Introductory & Brief Editions
- *Microsoft Office Excel 2007* Introductory & Brief Editions
- *Microsoft Office Access 2007* Introductory & Brief Editions
- *Microsoft Office PowerPoint 2007* Brief Edition

computing ESSENTIALS

Making IT work for you

INTRODUCTORY 2011

Timothy J. O'Leary

Professor Emeritus
Arizona State University

Linda I. O'Leary

McGraw Hill

Connect
Learn
Succeed™

COMPUTING ESSENTIALS 2011 INTRODUCTORY: MAKING IT WORK FOR YOU
Published by McGraw-Hill, a business unit of The McGraw-Hill Companies, Inc., 1221 Avenue of the Americas, New York, NY, 10020. Copyright © 2011 by The McGraw-Hill Companies, Inc. All rights reserved. No part of this publication may be reproduced or distributed in any form or by any means, or stored in a database or retrieval system, without the prior written consent of The McGraw-Hill Companies, Inc., including, but not limited to, in any network or other electronic storage or transmission, or broadcast for distance learning.

Some ancillaries, including electronic and print components, may not be available to customers outside the United States.

This book is printed on acid-free paper.

2 3 4 5 6 7 8 9 0 DOW/DOW 1 0 9 8 7 6 5 4 3 2 1 0

ISBN   978-0-07-733139-9
MHID   0-07-733139-7

Vice president/Editor in chief: *Elizabeth Haefele*
Vice president/Director of marketing: *John E. Biernat*
Publisher: *Kenneth S. Kasee Jr.*
Senior sponsoring editor: *Scott Davidson*
Freelance developmental editor: *Craig Leonard*
Editorial coordinator: *Alan Palmer*
Marketing manager: *Tiffany Wendt*
Lead digital product manager: *Damian Moshak*
Digital developmental editor: *Kevin White*
Director, Editing/Design/Production: *Jess Ann Kosic*
Project manager: *Marlena Pechan*
Senior production supervisor: *Janean A. Utley*
Senior designer: *Srdjan Savanovic*
Senior photo research coordinator: *Jeremy Cheshareck*
Photo researcher: *Keri Johnson*
Digital production coordinator: *Brent dela Cruz*
Cover design: *Daniel Drueger*
Interior design: *Laurie Entringer*
Typeface: *10/12 New Aster*
Compositor: *Laserwords Private Limited*
Printer: *R. R. Donnelley*
Cover credit: © *Louie Psihoyos/CORBIS*
Credits: The credits section for this book begins on page 377 and is considered an extension of the copyright page.

Library of Congress Cataloging-in-Publication Data

O'Leary, Timothy J., 1947-
    Computing essentials 2011 : making IT work for you/Timothy J. O'Leary, Linda I. O'Leary. — Introductory ed.
        p. cm. — (The O'Leary series)
    Includes index.
    ISBN-13: 978-0-07-733139-9 (alk. paper)
    ISBN-10: 0-07-733139-7 (alk. paper)
    1. Computers. 2. Electronic data processing. I. O'Leary, Linda I. II. Title.
QA76.5.O4285 2011
004—dc22   2009049578

The Internet addresses listed in the text were accurate at the time of publication. The inclusion of a Web site does not indicate an endorsement by the authors or McGraw-Hill, and McGraw-Hill does not guarantee the accuracy of the information presented at these sites.

www.mhhe.com

Dedication

We dedicate this edition to our parents Irene Perley Coats, Jean L. O'Leary, and Charles D. O'Leary for all that they have sacrificed for us.

Brief Contents

Contents

Preface

The 20th century brought us the dawn of the digital information age and unprecedented changes in information technology. There is no indication that this rapid rate of change will be slowing—it may even be increasing. As we begin the 21st century, computer literacy is undoubtedly becoming a prerequisite in whatever career you choose.

The goal of *Computing Essentials* is to provide you with the basis for understanding the concepts necessary for success. *Computing Essentials* also endeavors to instill an appreciation for the effect of information technology on people and our environment and to give you a basis for building the necessary skill set to succeed in this the 21st century.

Times are changing, technology is changing, and this text is changing too. As students of today, you are different from those of yesterday. You put much effort toward the things that interest you and the things that are relevant to you. Your efforts directed at learning application programs and exploring the Web seem, at times, limitless. On the other hand, it is sometimes difficult to engage in other equally important topics such as personal privacy and technological advances.

In this text, we present practical tips related to key concepts through the demonstration of interesting applications that are relevant to your lives and by focusing on outputs rather than processes. Then, we discuss the concepts and processes.

Motivation and relevance are the keys. This text has several features specifically designed to engage and demonstrate the relevance of technology in your lives. These elements are combined with a thorough coverage of the concepts and sound pedagogical devices.

Hands-On

ENVIRONMENTAL FACTS

New "Environmental Facts" boxes appear in each chapter and focus on technology and how it can be used to reduce environmental impact.

TIPS

Tips appear within nearly every chapter and provide advice on chapter-related issues, such as how to efficiently locate information on the Web, how to speed up computer operations, and how to protect against computer viruses. Tips assist you with common technology-related problems or issues and motivate you by showing the relevance of concepts presented in the chapter to everyday life. Additional tips can be found on the O'Leary Web site at www.computing 2011.com by entering the keyword **tips.**

ON THE WEB EXPLORATIONS

At least two On the Web Explorations appear within the margins of nearly every chapter. These explorations ask you to search specific Web sites for additional information on key topics, encouraging you to expand your knowledge through Web resources.

Learning Tools

MAKING IT WORK FOR YOU

Special-interest topics are presented in the Making IT Work for You section found within nearly every chapter. These topics include protecting against computer viruses, downloading music from the Internet, and using the Internet to place free long-distance telephone calls.

Reinforcing Key Concepts

CONCEPT CHECKS

Located at points throughout each chapter, the Concept Check cues you to note which topics have been covered and to self-test your understanding of the material already discussed.

☑ **CONCEPT CHECK**

What is system software? What are the four kinds of system software programs?

What is an operating system? Discuss operating system functions and features.

Describe each of the three categories of operating systems.

KEY TERMS

KEY TERMS

access speed (221)
Blu-ray Disc (BD) (230)
capacity (220)
CD (compact disc) (227)
CD-R (CD-recordable) (227)
CD-ROM (compact disc–read-only memory) (227)
CD-RW (compact disc rewriteable) (227)
cylinder (221)
density (221)
direct access (232)
disk caching (223)
DVD (digital versatile disc or digital video disc) (227)
DVD player (227)
DVD−R (DVD recordable) (230)
DVD+R (DVD recordable) (230)
DVD-RAM (DVD random-access memory) (230)
DVD-ROM (DVD-read-only memory) (227)
DVD−RW (DVD rewriteable) (230)
DVD+RW (DVD rewriteable) (230)
enterprise storage system (233)
erasable optical disc (227)
external hard drive (223)
file compression (223)
file decompression (223)
file server (233)
flash drive (225)
flash memory card (224)
floppy disk (231)
floppy disk drive (FDD) (231)
hard disk (221)
head crash (221)

hi def (high definition) (230)
high-capacity floppy disk (232)
internal hard disk (222)
land (227)
magnetic tape (232)
magnetic tape reel (232)
magnetic tape streamer (232)
mass storage (232)
mass storage devices (233)
media (220)
network attached storage (NAS) (233)
online storage service (231)
optical disc (225)
optical disc drive (227)
organizational online storage (233)
pit (227)
platter (221)
primary storage (220)
RAID system (233)
redundant array of inexpensive disks (RAID) (223)
secondary storage (220)
secondary storage device (220)
sector (221)
sequential access (232)
software engineer (234)
solid-state drive (SSD) (224)
solid-state storage (224)
storage area network (SAN) (234)
storage device (220)
tape cartridge (232)
tape library (233)
track (221)
traditional floppy disk (231)
USB drive (225)

To test your knowledge of these key terms with animated flash cards, visit our Web site at www.computing2011.com and enter the keyword terms8.

Throughout the text, the most important terms are presented in bold and are defined within the text. You will also find a list of key terms at the end of each chapter and in the glossary at the end of the book.

CHAPTER REVIEW

Following the Visual Summary, the chapter review includes material designed to review and reinforce chapter content. It includes a Key Terms list that reiterates the terms presented in the chapter, Multiple Choice questions to help test your understanding of information presented in the chapter, Matching exercises to test your recall of terminology presented in the chapter, and Open-Ended questions or statements to help review your understanding of the key concepts presented in the chapter.

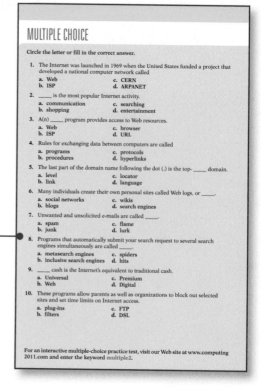

MULTIPLE CHOICE

Circle the letter or fill in the correct answer.

1. The Internet was launched in 1969 when the United States funded a project that developed a national computer network called
   a. Web   c. CERN
   b. ISP   d. ARPANET

2. _____ is the most popular Internet activity.
   a. communication   c. searching
   b. shopping   d. entertainment

3. A(n) _____ program provides access to Web resources.
   a. Web   c. browser
   b. ISP   d. URL

4. Rules for exchanging data between computers are called
   a. programs   c. protocols
   b. procedures   d. hyperlinks

5. The last part of the domain name following the dot (.) is the top-_____ domain.
   a. level   c. locator
   b. link   d. language

6. Many individuals create their own personal sites called Web logs, or _____.
   a. social networks c. wikis
   b. blogs   d. search engines

7. Unwanted and unsolicited e-mails are called _____.
   a. spam   c. flame
   b. junk   d. lurk

8. Programs that automatically submit your search request to several search engines simultaneously are called _____.
   a. metasearch engines   c. spiders
   b. inclusive search engines d. hits

9. _____ cash is the Internet's equivalent to traditional cash.
   a. Universal   c. Premium
   b. Web   d. Digital

10. These programs allow parents as well as organizations to block out selected sites and set time limits on Internet access.
    a. plug-ins   c. FTP
    b. filters   d. DSL

For an interactive multiple-choice practice test, visit our Web site at www.computing2011.com and enter the keyword multiple2.

The Future of Information Technology

CAREERS IN IT

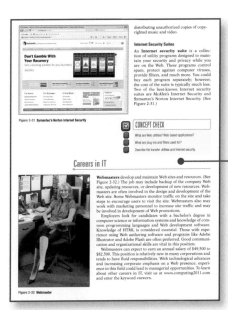

Some of the fastest-growing career opportunities are in information technology. Each chapter highlights one of the most promising careers in IT by presenting job titles, responsibilities, educational requirements, and salary ranges. Among the careers covered are Webmaster, software engineer, and database administrator. You will learn how the material you are studying relates directly to a potential career path.

A LOOK TO THE FUTURE

Each chapter concludes with a brief discussion of a recent technological advancement related to the chapter material, reinforcing the importance of staying informed.

Unique End-of-Chapter Materials

APPLYING TECHNOLOGY

In each chapter, Applying Technology presents questions designed to help you gain a better understanding of how technology is being used today. One question typically relates to the chapter's Making IT Work for You topic. Other questions focus on interesting applications of technology that relate directly to you. Topics include online auctions, online Personal Information Managers, and desktop and notebook computers.

EXPANDING YOUR KNOWLEDGE

In each chapter, Expanding Your Knowledge presents questions that help you gain a deeper understanding of select topics. Typically, one question relates to a topic presented at the book's Web site, www.computing 2011.com, such as How Instant Messaging Works, How Streaming Media Works, and How Virus Protection Works. Other questions in Expanding Your Knowledge typically require Web research into carefully selected topics including robotics, multimedia, HDTV, and Internet hard drives.

WRITING ABOUT TECHNOLOGY

In each chapter, Writing About Technology presents questions relating to security, privacy, and ethical issues. The issues presented include HTML source code, antitrust legislation, RFIDs, CD-R and music files, and electronic monitoring. One objective of the Writing About Technology feature is to help you develop critical thinking and writing skills. Another objective is to help you recognize, understand, and analyze key privacy, security, and ethical issues relating to technology.

Support Materials

The Instructor's Manual offers lecture outlines with teaching notes and page references. It provides definitions of key terms and solutions to the end-of-chapter material, including multiple-choice, matching, and open-ended questions. It also offers summaries of the concept checks in each chapter. A selection of G4techTV video clips accompany this text, as do summaries for each clip.

The PowerPoint slides are designed to provide instructors with a comprehensive resource for lecture use. The slides include a review of key terms and definitions, artwork taken from the text, as well as new illustrations to further explain concepts covered in each chapter. Comprehensive teaching notes are provided for each slide.

The testbank contains over 2,200 questions categorized by level of learning (definition, concept, and application). This is the same learning scheme that is introduced in the text to provide a valuable testing and reinforcement tool. Text page references have been provided for all questions, including a level-of-difficulty rating. The testbank is offered in Word files, as well as in EZ Test format.

The instructor support materials can be downloaded at www.mhhe.com/ce2011.

G4TECHTV VIDEOS

G4techTV videos offer instructors and students video content directly related to computing that enhances the classroom or lab experience with technology programming from business and society. Video selections include "The Screen Savers" and "Pulse," which provide edgy and informative discussion. Use of these videos will help students understand how computing interacts with and contributes to business and society and will also offer an advance look at emerging technology and devices.

THE O'LEARY WEB SITE

The O'Leary Web site can be found at www.computing2011.com. Students can find a host of additional resources on the Web site, including animations of key concepts, videos relating to select Making IT Work for You applications, and in-depth coverage of select topics. Look for the Web icon throughout the text to indicate where additional related materials can be found on the Web site.

O'LEARY SERIES

The O'Leary Application Series for Microsoft® Office is available separately or packaged with *Computing Essentials*. The O'Leary Application Series offers a step-by-step approach to learning computer applications and is available in both brief and introductory versions. The introductory books are MCAS Certified and prepare students for the Microsoft Office User Certification Exam.

SIMNET® ASSESSMENT FOR OFFICE APPLICATIONS

SimNet Assessment for Office Applications provides a way for you to test students' software skills in a simulated environment. SimNet is available for Microsoft Office 2007 and provides flexibility for you in your applications course by offering:

Pre-testing options

Post-testing options

Course placement testing

Diagnostic capabilities to reinforce skills

Web delivery of test

MCAS preparation exams

Learning verification reports

For more information on skills assessment software, please contact your local sales representative, or visit us at www.mhhe.com.

Acknowledgments

We would like to extend our thanks to the professors who took time out of their busy schedules to provide us with the feedback necessary to develop the 2011 edition of this text. The following professors offered valuable suggestions on revising the text:

Ping Chen,
University of Houston

Ric Calhoun,
Gordon College

Rhonda Simms,
Dallas County Community College

Kin Lam,
Medgar Evers College

Rick Kendrick,
Antonelli College

Bill Barge,
Trine University

Shane Stevens,
Bridgewater College

Wolfgang Pelz,
The University of Akron

Kevin Halvorson,
Ridgewater College

John Jemison,
Dallas Baptist University

Rose LaMuraglia,
San Diego Community College

Dave Fitzgerald,
Jackson Community College

Terry Rigsby,
Hill College

Jackie Armstrong,
Hill College, Hillsboro Campus

Bobby Thrash,
Pearl River Community College

Mary Lou Malone,
Ohio University

Sue Vanboven,
Maricopa Community College

Wayne Machuca,
Mt. Hood Community College

Diana Hill,
Chesapeake College

Michelle Parker,
Indiana University–Purdue University Indianapolis

Diane Stark,
Maricopa Community College

Cheryl Jordan,
San Juan College

Bill Holmes,
Maricopa Community College

Cindi Nadelman,
Granite State College

Louis Berzai,
University of Notre Dame

Our thanks also go to Linda Mehlinger for all her work on revising the PowerPoint presentations and Instructor's Manual to accompany the text. We are grateful to Triad Interactive for their work in revising the testbank.

Finally, we would like to thank Robyn Ness and John Ray, who helped out with this edition. They made significant contributions to several chapters. Also thanks to Carol and Steve Willis for their indispensible contributions to this and previous editions.

About the Authors

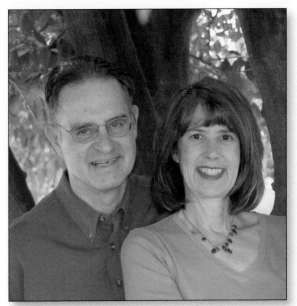

Tim and Linda O'Leary live in the American Southwest and spend much of their time engaging instructors and students in conversation about learning. In fact, they have been talking about learning for over 25 years. Something in those early conversations convinced them to write a book, to bring their interest in the learning process to the printed page. Today, they are as concerned as ever about learning, about technology, and about the challenges of presenting material in new ways, in terms of both content and method of delivery.

A powerful and creative team, Tim combines his 25 years of classroom teaching experience with Linda's background as a consultant and corporate trainer. Tim has taught courses at Stark Technical College in Canton, Ohio, and at Rochester Institute of Technology in upstate New York, and is currently a professor emeritus at Arizona State University in Tempe, Arizona. Linda offered her expertise at ASU for several years as an academic advisor. She also presented and developed materials for major corporations such as Motorola, Intel, Honeywell, and AT&T, as well as various community colleges in the Phoenix area.

Tim and Linda have talked to and taught numerous students, all of them with a desire to learn something about computers and applications that make their lives easier, more interesting, and more productive.

Each new edition of an O'Leary text, supplement, or learning aid has benefited from these students and their instructors who daily stand in front of them (or over their shoulders). *Computing Essentials* is no exception.

computing ESSENTIALS

Making IT work for you

INTRODUCTORY 2011

Information Technology, the Internet, and You

Competencies

After you have read this chapter, you should be able to:

1 Explain the five parts of an information system: people, procedures, software, hardware, and data.

2 Distinguish between system software and application software.

3 Discuss the three kinds of system software programs.

4 Distinguish between basic and specialized application software.

5 Identify the four types of computers and the six types of microcomputers.

6 Describe the different types of computer hardware including the system unit, input, output, storage, and communication devices.

7 Define data and describe document, worksheet, database, and presentation files.

8 Explain computer connectivity, the wireless revolution, and the Internet.

Just a few years ago, the computer was a device you might have used seated at a desk for work or school. Today computers go with us, connecting us to a world of information, our friends, and even our work. The speed of technological developments makes it easy to imagine a world where we are always connected to the Internet.

Some experts predict the Web will become seamlessly integrated into our lives. Connectivity will mean connections to our documents and data, our friends and family, and facts and figures gathered the world over. Imagine a world where the mobile device in your hand is like an expert personal assistant with access to all of these resources. Your calendar might remind you of a friend's birthday, provide suggestions for a gift, and provide a map to the store where you might want to shop on your way home from work.

chapter **1**

3

Introduction

The purpose of this book is to help you become competent with computer technology. **Computer competency** refers to acquiring computer-related skills—indispensable tools for today. They include how to effectively use popular application packages and the Internet.

In this chapter, we present an overview of an information system: people, procedures, software, hardware, and data. It is essential to understand these basic parts and how connectivity through the Internet and the Web expands the role of information technology in our lives. Later, we will describe these parts of an information system in detail.

Fifteen years ago, most people had little to do with computers, at least directly. Of course, they filled out computerized forms, took computerized tests, and paid computerized bills. But the real work was handled by specialists. Then microcomputers came along and changed everything. Today it is easy for nearly everybody to use a computer.

- Microcomputers are common tools in all areas of life. Writers write, artists draw, engineers and scientists calculate—all on microcomputers. Students and businesspeople do all this, and more.

- New forms of learning have developed. People who are homebound, who work odd hours, or who travel frequently may take Web courses. A college course need not fit within a quarter or a semester.

- New ways to communicate, to find people with similar interests, and to buy goods are available. People use electronic mail, electronic commerce, and the Internet to meet and to share ideas and products.

People are end users who use computers to make themselves more productive

Software provides step-by-step instructions for computer hardware

Procedures specify rules or guidelines for computer operations

Figure 1-1 The five parts of an information system

To be competent with computer technology, you need to know the five parts of an information system: people, procedures, software, hardware, and data. You also need to understand connectivity, the wireless revolution, the Internet, and the Web and to recognize the role of information technology in your personal and professional life.

Information Systems

When you think of a microcomputer, perhaps you think of just the equipment itself. That is, you think of the monitor or the keyboard. Yet, there is more to it than that. The way to think about a microcomputer is as part of an information system. An **information system** has five parts: *people, procedures, software, hardware,* and *data.* (See Figure 1-1.)

- **People:** It is easy to overlook people as one of the five parts of an information system. Yet this is what microcomputers are all about—making **people, end users** like you, more productive.
- **Procedures:** The rules or guidelines for people to follow when using software, hardware, and data are **procedures.** These procedures are typically documented in manuals written by computer specialists. Software and hardware manufacturers provide manuals with their products. These manuals are provided in either printed or electronic form.

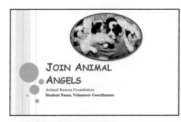

Data
consists of unprocessed facts including text, numbers, images, and sounds

Hardware
includes keyboard, mouse, monitor, system unit, and other devices

Connectivity
allows computers to share information and to connect to the Internet

- **Software:** A **program** consists of the step-by-step instructions that tell the computer how to do its work. **Software** is another name for a program or programs. The purpose of software is to convert **data** (unprocessed facts) into **information** (processed facts). For example, a payroll program would instruct the computer to take the number of hours you worked in a week (data) and multiply it by your pay rate (data) to determine how much you are paid for the week (information).
- **Hardware:** The equipment that processes the data to create information is called **hardware.** It includes the keyboard, mouse, monitor, system unit, and other devices. Hardware is controlled by software.
- **Data:** The raw, unprocessed facts, including text, numbers, images, and sounds, are called data. Processed data yields information. Using the previous example of a payroll program, the data (number of hours worked and pay rate) is processed (multiplied) to yield information (weekly pay).

Almost all of today's computer systems add an additional part to the information system. This part, called **connectivity,** typically uses the Internet and allows users to greatly expand the capability and usefulness of their information systems.

In large computer systems, there are specialists who write procedures, develop software, and capture data. In microcomputer systems, however, end users often perform these operations. To be a competent end user, you must understand the essentials of **information technology (IT),** including software, hardware, and data.

CONCEPT CHECK

 What are the five parts of an information system?

 What is the difference between data and information?

 What is connectivity?

People

People are surely the most important part of any information system. Our lives are touched every day by computers and information systems. Many times the contact is direct and obvious, such as when we create documents using a word processing program or when we connect to the Internet. Other times, the contact is not as obvious. Consider just the four examples in Figure 1-2.

Throughout this book you will find a variety of features designed to help you become computer competent and knowledgeable. These features include Making IT Work for You, Environmental Facts, Tips, Careers in IT, On the Web Exploration, and the Computing Essentials Web site.

- **Making IT Work for You.** In the chapters that follow, you will find Making IT Work for You features that present interesting and practical IT applications. Using a step-by-step procedure, you are provided with specific instructions on how to use each application. Figure 1-3 presents a list of these applications.
- **Environmental Facts.** Today it is more important than ever that we be aware of our impact on the environment. In this chapter and the following ones, you will find Environmental Facts boxes in the margin that present important relevant environmental information.

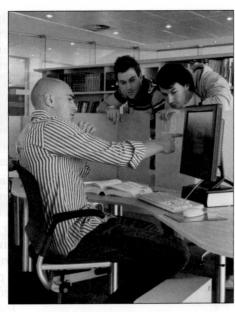

Figure 1-2 Computers in entertainment, business, education, and medicine

Application	Description
Sharing Large Files	Have you found it inconvenient or impossible to share large files with others. Perhaps you have found some video and other types of files are just too large to send as an e-mail attachment. An easy solution is to use free file-sharing services. See page 36.
Speech Recognition	Tired of using your keyboard to type term papers? Have you ever thought about using your voice to control application software? Perhaps speech recognition is just what you are looking for. See page 68.
Digital Video Editing	Do you want to make your own movie? Would you like to edit some home movies and distribute them to family and friends on DVDs? It's easy with the right equipment and software. See page 106.
Virus Protection and Internet Security	Worried about computer viruses? Did you know that others could be intercepting your private e-mail? It is even possible for them to gain access and control of your computer system. Fortunately, Internet security suites are available to help ensure your safety while you are on the Internet. See page 140.
TV Tuner Cards and Video Clips	Want to watch your favorite television program while you work? Perhaps you would like to include a video clip from a television program or from a DVD in a class presentation. It's easy using a TV tuner card. See page 168.
Web Cams and Instant Messaging	Do you enjoy chatting with your friends? Are you working on a project and need to collaborate with others in your group? What if you could see and hear your group online? Perhaps instant messaging is just what you're looking for. See page 196.
iPods and Video from the Internet	Want to use the Internet to find and play movies and television shows? Would you prefer to play the movies or shows on a digital media player? All you need is the right software, hardware, and a connection to the Internet. See page 226.
Home Networking	Computer networks are not just for corporations and schools anymore. If you have more than one computer, you can use a wireless home network to share files and printers, to allow multiple users access to the Internet at the same time, and to play interactive computer games. See page 262.
Spyware Removal	Are you concerned about maintaining your privacy while you are surfing the Web? Did you know that programs known as spyware could be monitoring your every move? Fortunately, these programs are relatively easy to detect and remove. See page 290.
Locating Job Opportunities Online	Did you know that you can use the Internet to find a job? You can browse through job openings, post your resume, and even use special programs that will search for the job that's just right for you. See page 320.

Figure 1-3 Making IT Work for You applications

Figure 1-6 Internet Explorer browser

Type	Description
Browser	Connect to Web sites and display Web pages
Word processor	Prepare written documents
Spreadsheet	Analyze and summarize numerical data
Database management system	Organize and manage data and information
Presentation graphics	Communicate a message or persuade other people

Figure 1-7 Basic applications

Hardware

Computers are electronic devices that can follow instructions to accept input, process that input, and produce information. This book focuses principally on microcomputers. However, it is almost certain that you will come in contact, at least indirectly, with other types of computers.

Types of Computers

There are four types of computers: supercomputers, mainframe computers, minicomputers, and microcomputers.

- **Supercomputers** are the most powerful type of computer. These machines are special high-capacity computers used by very large organizations. IBM's Blue Gene is one of the fastest computers in the world. (See Figure 1-8.)

- **Mainframe computers** occupy specially wired, air-conditioned rooms. Although not nearly as powerful as supercomputers, mainframe computers are capable of great processing speeds and data storage. For example, insurance companies use mainframes to process information about millions of policyholders.

- **Minicomputers,** also known as **midrange computers,** are refrigerator-sized machines. Medium-sized companies or departments of large companies typically use them for specific purposes. For example, production departments use minicomputers to monitor certain manufacturing processes and assembly-line operations.

- **Microcomputers** are the least powerful, yet the most widely used and fastest-growing type of computer. There are six types of micro-computers: *desktop, media center, notebook, netbook, tablet PC,* and *handheld computers.* (See Figure 1-9.) **Desktop computers** are small enough to fit on top of or alongside a desk yet are too big to carry around. **Media centers** blur the line between desktop computers and dedicated entertainment devices. **Notebook**

Figure 1-8 IBM's Blue Gene supercomputer

computers, also known as *laptop computers,* are portable, lightweight, and fit into most briefcases. **Netbooks** are smaller, lighter, and less expensive than notebook computers. A **tablet PC** is a type of notebook computer that accepts your handwriting. This input is digitized and converted to standard text that can be further processed by programs such as a word processor. **Handheld computers** are the smallest and are designed to fit into the palm of one hand. These systems contain an entire computer system, including the electronic components, secondary storage, and input and output devices. **Personal digital assistants (PDAs)** and **smartphones** are the most widely used handheld computers.

Figure 1-9 Microcomputers

Microcomputer Hardware

Hardware for a microcomputer system consists of a variety of different devices. See Figure 1-10 for a typical desktop system. This physical equipment falls into four basic categories: system unit, input/output, secondary storage, and communication. Because we discuss hardware in detail later in this book, here we will present just a quick overview of the four basic categories.

- **System unit:** The **system unit** is a container that houses most of the electronic components that make up a computer system. Two important components of the system unit are the *microprocessor* and *memory*. (See Figure 1-11.) The **microprocessor** controls and manipulates data to produce information. **Memory** is a holding area for data, instructions, and information. One type, **random-access memory (RAM)** holds the program and data that is currently being processed. This type of memory is sometimes referred to as *temporary storage* because its contents will typically be lost if the electrical power to the computer is disrupted.

- **Input/output: Input devices** translate data and programs that humans can understand into a form that the computer can process. The most common input devices are the **keyboard** and the **mouse. Output devices** translate the processed information from the computer into a form that humans can understand. The most common output devices are **monitors** (see Figure 1-12) and **printers.**

- **Secondary storage:** Unlike memory, **secondary storage** holds data and programs even after electrical power to the computer system has been turned off. The most important kinds of secondary media are *hard disks, solid-state storage,* and *optical disks.* **Hard disks** are typically used to

Monitor to display information

Speakers to play sounds and music

Optical disk drive to store and transport large amounts of data

Printer to produce output on paper

Keyboard to input instructions

Mouse to select items

Figure 1-10 Microcomputer system

Microprocessor

Memory

Figure 1-11 **System unit**

Figure 1-12 **Monitor**

Figure 1-13 **Optical disc**

store programs and very large data files. Using rigid metallic platters and read/write heads that move across the platters, data and information are stored using magnetic charges of the disk's surface. In contrast, **solid-state storage** does not have any moving parts, is more reliable, and requires less power. It saves data and information electronically similar to RAM except that it is not volatile. Three types are **solid-state drives (SSDs)** that are used much the same way as an internal hard disk, **flash memory cards** that are widely used in portable devices, and **USB drives** that are a widely used compact storage medium for transporting data and information between computers and a variety of specialty devices. **Optical discs** use laser technology and have the greatest capacity. (See Figure 1-13.)

On the Web Explorations

To learn more about one of the leaders in the development of DVD technology, visit our Web site at **www.computing2011.com and enter the keyword dvd.**

Three types of optical discs are **compact discs (CDs)**, **digital versatile** (or **video**) **discs (DVDs)**, and **high-definition (hi def) discs.**

- **Communication:** At one time, it was uncommon for a microcomputer system to communicate with other computer systems. Now, using **communication devices,** a microcomputer can communicate with other computer systems located as near as the next office or as far away as halfway around the world using the Internet. The most widely used communication device is a **modem,** which modifies telephone communications into a form that can be processed by a computer. Modems also modify computer output into a form that can be transmitted across standard telephone lines.

CONCEPT CHECK

What are the four types of computers? *Super, mainframe, mini, micro*

Describe the six types of microcomputers. *pg. 11*

Describe the four basic categories of microcomputer hardware. *system, I/O, temp storage, communication*

Data

Data is raw, unprocessed facts, including text, numbers, images, and sounds. As we have mentioned earlier, processed data becomes information. When stored electronically in files, data can be used directly as input for the system unit.

Four common types of files (see Figure 1-14) are

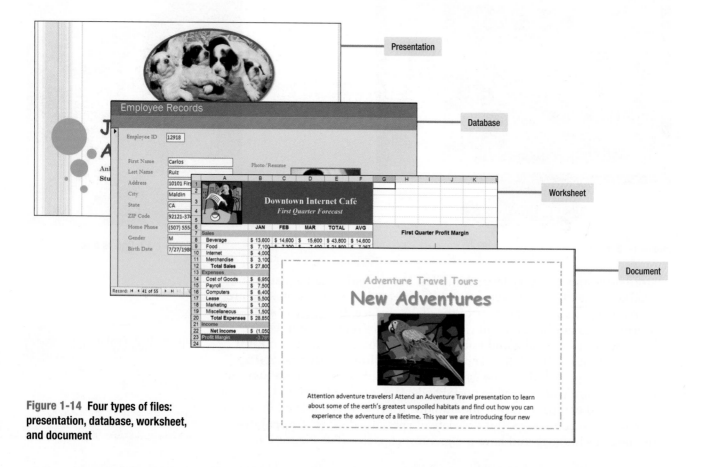

Figure 1-14 Four types of files: presentation, database, worksheet, and document

- **Document files,** created by word processors to save documents such as memos, term papers, and letters.
- **Worksheet files,** created by electronic spreadsheets to analyze things like budgets and to predict sales.
- **Database files,** typically created by database management programs to contain highly structured and organized data. For example, an employee database file might contain all the workers' names, social security numbers, job titles, and other related pieces of information.
- **Presentation files,** created by presentation graphics programs to save presentation materials. For example, a file might contain audience handouts, speaker notes, and electronic slides.

Connectivity, the Wireless Revolution, and the Internet

Connectivity is the capability of your microcomputer to share information with other computers. The single most dramatic change in connectivity in the past five years has been the widespread use of mobile or wireless communication devices. For just a few of these devices, see Figure 1-15. Many experts

Figure 1-15 Wireless communication devices

predict that these wireless applications are just the beginning of the **wireless revolution,** a revolution that will dramatically affect the way we communicate and use computer technology.

Central to the concept of connectivity is the **network.** A network is a communications system connecting two or more computers. The largest network in the world is the **Internet.** It is like a giant highway that connects you to millions of other people and organizations located throughout the world. The **Web** provides a multimedia interface to the numerous resources available on the Internet.

CONCEPT CHECK

 Define data. List four common types of files.

 Define connectivity and the wireless revolution.

 What is a network? Describe the Internet. What is the Web?

Careers in IT

As mentioned previously, each of the following chapters highlights a specific career in information technology. (See Figure 1-16.) Each provides specific job descriptions, salary ranges, advancement opportunities, and more. For a partial list of these careers, see Figure 1-17. For a complete list, visit our Web site at www.computing2011.com and enter the keyword **careers.**

Figure 1-16 Software engineer

Career	Description
Webmaster	Develops and maintains Web sites and Web resources. See page 52.
Computer support specialist	Provides technical support to customers and other users. See page 143.
Technical writer	Prepares instruction manuals, technical reports, and other scientific or technical documents. See page 207.
Software engineer	Analyzes users' needs and creates application software. See page 234.
Network administrator	Creates and maintains computer networks. See page 269.

Figure 1-17 Careers in information technology

A LOOK TO THE FUTURE

Using and Understanding Information Technology Means Being Computer Competent

The purpose of this book is to help you use and understand information technology. We want to help you become computer competent in today's world and to provide you with a foundation of knowledge so that you can understand how technology is being used today and anticipate how technology will be used in the future. This will enable you to benefit from six important information technology developments.

The Internet and the Web

The Internet and the Web are considered by most to be the two most important technologies for the 21st century. Understanding how to efficiently and effectively use the Internet to browse the Web, communicate with others, and locate information are indispensable computer competencies. These issues are presented in Chapter 2, The Internet, the Web, and Electronic Commerce.

Powerful Software

The software now available can do an extraordinary number of tasks and help you in an endless number of ways. You can create professional-looking documents, analyze massive amounts of data, create dynamic multimedia Web pages, and much more. Today's employers are expecting the people they hire to be able to effectively and efficiently use a variety of different types of software. Basic and specialized applications are presented in Chapters 3 and 4. System software is presented in Chapter 5.

Powerful Hardware

Microcomputers are now much more powerful than they used to be. New communication technologies such as wireless networks are dramatically changing the ways to connect to other computers, networks, and the Internet. However, despite the rapid change of specific equipment, their essential features remain unchanged. Thus, the competent end user should focus on these features. Chapters 6 through 9 explain what you need to know about hardware. A Buyer's Guide and an Upgrader's Guide are presented at the end of this book for those considering the purchase or upgrade of a microcomputer system.

Security and Privacy

What about people? Experts agree that we as a society must be careful about the potential of technology to negatively impact our personal privacy and security. Additionally, we need to be aware of potential physical and mental health risks associated with using technology. Finally, we need to be aware of negative effects on our environment caused by the manufacture of computer-related products. Thus, Chapter 10 explores each of these critical issues in detail.

Changing Times

Are the times changing any faster now than they ever have? Most people think so. Whatever the answer, it is clear we live in a fast-paced age. The Evolution of the Computer Age section presented at the end of this book tracks the major developments since computers were first introduced.

After reading this book, you will be in a very favorable position compared with many other people in industry today. You not only will learn the basics of hardware, software, connectivity, the Internet, and the Web, but you also will learn the most current technology. You will be able to use these tools to your advantage.

INFORMATION SYSTEMS

The way to think about a microcomputer is to realize that it is one part of an **information system.** There are five parts of an information system:

1. **People** are an essential part of the system. The purpose of information systems is to make people, or **end users** like you, more productive.
2. **Procedures** are rules or guidelines to follow when using software, hardware, and data. They are typically documented in manuals written by computer professionals.
3. **Software (programs)** provides step-by-step instructions to control the computer to convert **data** into **information.**
4. **Hardware** consists of the physical equipment. It is controlled by software and processes data to create information.
5. **Data** consists of unprocessed facts including text, numbers, images, and sound. **Information** is data that has been processed by the computer.

Connectivity is an additional part to today's information systems. It allows computers to connect and share information. To be **computer competent,** end users need to understand **information technology (IT).**

PEOPLE

People are the most important part of an information system. This book contains several features to demonstrate how people just like you use computers. These features include the following:

- **Making IT Work for You** presents several interesting and practical applications. Topics include using digital video editing and locating job opportunities.
- **Environmental Facts** discuss important and relevant environmental issues. The impact of computers and other technologies is more critical today than ever before.
- **Tips** offer a variety of suggestions on such practical matters as how to improve slow computer performance and how to protect your privacy while on the Web.
- **Careers in IT** presents job descriptions, employment demands, educational requirements, salary ranges, and advancement opportunities.
- **On the Web Explorations** direct you to important information and Web sites that relate to computers and technology.
- **Computing Essentials Web site** integrates the textbook with information on the Web including animations, career information, tips, test review materials, and much more.

To prepare for your future as a competent end user, you need to understand the basic parts of an information system: people, procedures, software, hardware, and data. Also you need to understand connectivity through the Internet and the Web and to recognize the role of technology in your professional and personal life.

SOFTWARE

Software, or **programs**, consists of system and application software.

System Software

System software enables application software to interact with computer hardware. It consists of a variety of programs:

- **Operating systems** coordinate resources, provide an interface for users and computer hardware, and run applications. Windows 7 and Mac OS X are the best-known microcomputer operating systems.
- **Utilities** perform specific tasks to manage computer resources.
- **Device drivers** are specialized programs to allow input and output devices to communicate with the rest of the computer system.

Application Software

Application software includes basic and specialized applications.

- **Basic applications** are widely used in nearly all career areas. Programs include browsers, word processors, spreadsheets, database management systems, and presentation graphics.
- **Specialized applications** focus on specific disciplines and occupations. These programs include graphics, audio, video, multimedia, Web authoring, and artificial intelligence programs.

HARDWARE

Hardware consists of electronic devices that can follow instructions, accept input, process, and produce information.

Types of Computers

Supercomputer, mainframe, minicomputer (midrange), and **microcomputer** are four types of computers. Microcomputers can be **desktop, media center, notebook, netbook, tablet PC,** or **handheld** (**PDAs** and **smartphones** are most widely used handheld microcomputers).

Microcomputer Hardware

There are four basic categories of hardware devices.

- **System unit** contains electronic circuitry, including the **microprocessor** and **memory. Random-access memory (RAM),** holds the program and data currently being processed.
- **Input/output devices** are translators between humans and computers. **Input devices** include the **keyboard** and **mouse. Output devices** include **monitors** and **printers.**
- **Secondary storage** holds data and programs. Typical media include **hard disks, solid-state storage (solid-state drives, flash memory cards,** and **USB drives),** and **optical discs (CD, DVD,** and **hi def).**
- **Communication devices** connect system units computers and the Internet. **Modems** modify output for transmission.

DATA

Data is the raw facts unprocessed about something. Common file types include

- **Document files** created by word processors.

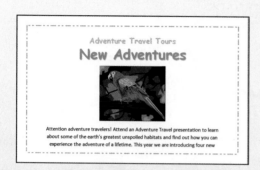

- **Worksheet files** created by spreadsheet programs.

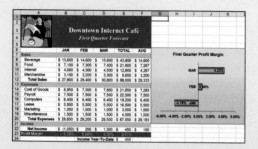

- **Database files** created by database management programs.

- **Presentation files** created by presentation graphics programs.

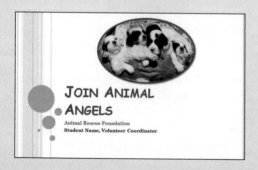

CONNECTIVITY AND THE INTERNET

Connectivity

Connectivity is a concept describing the ability of end users to tap into resources well beyond their desktops. **Networks** are connected computers that share data and resources.

The Wireless Revolution

The **wireless revolution** is the widespread and increasing use of mobile (wireless) communication devices.

Internet

The **Internet** is the world's largest computer network. The **Web** provides a multimedia interface to resources available on the Internet.

CAREERS IN IT

Career	Description
Webmaster	Develops and maintains Web sites and Web resources. See page 52.
Computer support specialist	Provides technical support to customers and other users. See page 143.
Technical writer	Prepares instruction manuals, technical reports, and other scientific or technical documents. See page 207.
Software engineer	Analyzes users' needs and creates application software. See page 234.
Network administrator	Creates and maintains computer networks. See page 269.

KEY TERMS

application software   (9)
basic application   (9)
communication device   (14)
compact disc (CD)   (14)
computer competency   (4)
connectivity   (6,15)
data   (6)
database file   (15)
desktop computer   (11)
device driver   (9)
digital versatile disc (DVD)   (14)
digital video disc (DVD)   (14)
document file   (15)
end user   (5)
flash memory card   (13)
handheld computer   (11)
hard disk   (12)
hardware   (6)
high definition (hi def) disc   (14)
information   (6)
information system   (5)
information technology (IT)   (6)
input device   (12)
Internet   (16)
keyboard   (12)
mainframe computer   (10)
media centers   (11)
memory   (12)
microcomputer   (11)
microprocessor   (12)
midrange computer   (10)
minicomputer   (10)

modem   (14)
monitor   (12)
mouse   (12)
netbook   (11)
network   (16)
notebook computer   (11)
operating system   (9)
optical disc   (13)
output device   (12)
people   (5)
personal digital assistant (PDA)   (11)
presentation file   (15)
printer   (12)
procedures   (5)
program   (6)
random access memory (RAM)   (12)
secondary storage   (12)
smartphone   (11)
software   (6)
solid-state drive (SSD)   (13)
solid-state storage   (13)
specialized application   (9)
supercomputer   (10)
system software   (8)
system unit   (12)
tablet PC   (11)
USB drive   (13)
utility   (9)
Web   (16)
wireless revolution   (16)
worksheet file   (15)

To test your knowledge of these key terms with animated flash cards, visit our Web site at www.computing2011.com and enter the keyword terms1.

MULTIPLE CHOICE

Circle the letter or fill in the correct answer.

1. People, procedures, software, hardware, and data are the five parts of a(n)

    a. competency system
    b. computer system
    c. information technology
    d. software system

2. Procedures are typically documented in manuals written by

    a. computer specialists
    b. end users
    c. Microsoft
    d. service providers

3. Which of the following is an example of connectivity?

    a. data
    b. hard disk
    c. Internet
    d. power cord

4. Windows 7 is an example of a(n)

    a. application software
    b. browser
    c. operating system
    d. shareware

5. The most powerful type of computer.

    a. mainframe computers
    b. microcomputers
    c. minicomputers
    d. supercomputers

6. The system component that controls and manipulates data in order to produce information is called the

    a. keyboard
    b. microprocessor
    c. monitor
    d. mouse

7. These devices translate data and programs that humans can understand into a form that the computer can process.

    a. display
    b. input
    c. output
    d. pointer

8. A DVD is an example of a(n)

    a. hard disk
    b. optical disc
    c. output device
    d. solid-state storage device

9. This type of file is created by word processors.

    a. worksheet
    b. document
    c. database
    d. presentation

10. Many experts are predicting that this revolution is expected to dramatically affect the way we communicate and use computer technology.

    a. graphics
    b. input
    c. memory
    d. wireless

For an interactive multiple-choice practice test, visit our Web site at www.computing2011.com and enter the keyword multiple1.

MATCHING

Match each numbered item with the most closely related lettered item. Write your answers in the spaces provided.

a. microcomputer
b. optical discs
c. output device
d. PDA
e. procedures
f. program
g. secondary storage
h. supercomputer
i. system software
j. the Internet

1. Guidelines people follow when using software. _____
2. Consists of the step-by-step instructions that tell the computer how to do its work. _____
3. Software that enables the application software to interact with the computer hardware. _____
4. The most powerful type of computer. _____
5. The least powerful and most widely used type of computer. _____
6. Translates the processed information from the computer into a form that humans can understand. _____
7. Holds data and programs even after electrical power to the system has been turned off. _____
8. Uses laser technology. _____
9. A type of handheld computer. _____
10. The largest network in the world. _____

For an interactive matching practice test, visit our Web site at www.computing2011.com and enter the keyword matching1.

OPEN-ENDED

On a separate sheet of paper, respond to each question or statement.

1. Explain the five parts of an information system. What part do people play in this system?
2. What is system software? What kinds of programs are included in system software?
3. Define and compare basic and specialized application software. Describe some different types of basic applications. Describe some types of specialized applications.
4. Describe the different types of computers. What is the most common type? What are the types of microcomputers?
5. What is connectivity? How are the wireless revolution and connectivity related? What is a computer network? What is the Internet? What is the Web?

WRITING ABOUT TECHNOLOGY

The ability to think critically and to write effectively is essential to nearly every profession. Writing about Technology questions are designed to help you develop these skills by posing thought-provoking questions about computer privacy, security, and/or ethics.

Regardless of your career path, critical thinking, analysis, and writing are essential skills. In each of the following chapters, the Writing about Technology feature presents questions about privacy, security, and ethics. These questions are designed to help you develop critical thinking, analysis, and writing skills. Some of the topics are listed below. Select two that you find the most interesting and then describe why they are of interest to you.

1 DIGITAL PHOTO MANIPULATION

Image editing software has made it easy to alter photographs, which in the past were accepted as visual records of real events. In some cases, the purpose of digital editing is humor and exaggeration, while other times subtle changes are used to alter a photo's deeper meaning. Some caution "seeing is believing" needs to be reconsidered for the digital age and argue that ethical standards need to be clearly established for photo manipulation. See page 124.

2 WEBCAMS

WebCams are almost everywhere, from dorm rooms to parking lots. They are used to communicate face-to-face with friends and family, to catch car thieves, and for any number of other applications. While acknowledging the many very positive applications of WebCams, some argue that their widespread and uncontrolled use has too many cases involving the loss of personal privacy. See page 217.

3 ELECTRONIC MONITORING

Surveillance of individuals occurs more frequently today than ever before. For example, the FBI has proposed the widespread use of a technology known as Carnivore to help them track terrorists. This technology supports widespread monitoring of individual Internet activity and e-mail. Privacy advocates claim that this would be an unnecessary and unneeded invasion of personal privacy. Others believe electronic surveillance is essential to protect national security. See page 279.

NOTES

The Internet, the Web, and Electronic Commerce

Competencies

After you have read this chapter, you should be able to:

1 Discuss the origins of the Internet and the Web.

2 Describe how to access the Web using providers and browsers.

3 Discuss Internet communications, including e-mail, instant messaging, social networking, blogs, microblogs, and wikis.

4 Describe search tools, including search engines, metasearch engines, and specialized search engines.

5 Evaluate the accuracy of information presented on the Web.

6 Discuss electronic commerce, including B2C, C2C, B2B, and security issues.

7 Describe these Web utilities: Web-based applications, plug-ins, filters, file transfer utilities, and Internet security suites.

Many of the earliest Web sites were digital versions of traditional resources like the dictionary, encyclopedia, or phone book. These sites made it possible to access information more easily, but they did not customize information for the user. Today it is possible to filter through this information more easily, and some Web sites are tailoring their content for each user.

Some experts predict that in the future your browser will act more like your personal assistant. Your computer will not only be capable of retrieving information from the Web, it will be able to understand and process it on your behalf. Imagine a world where your computer is like your trusted friend, able to make suggestions because it truly knows you. It may scan the Web for you and predict which of the latest films and new restaurants you might like and suggest openings on your calendar for a night out.

chapter 2

Introduction

Want to communicate with a friend across town, in another state, or even in another country? Looking for a long-lost friend? Looking for travel or entertainment information? Perhaps you're researching a term paper or exploring different career paths. Where do you start? For these and other information-related activities, most people use the Internet and the Web.

The Internet is often referred to as the Information Superhighway. In a sense, it is like a highway that connects you to millions of other people and organizations. Unlike typical highways that move people and things from one location to another, the Internet moves your ideas and information. The Web provides an easy-to-use, intuitive, multimedia interface to resources available on the Internet. It has become an everyday tool for all of us to use.

Competent end users need to be aware of the resources available on the Internet and the Web. Additionally, they need to know how to access these resources, to effectively communicate electronically, to efficiently locate information, to understand electronic commerce, and to use Web utilities.

The Internet and the Web

The **Internet** was launched in 1969 when the United States funded a project that developed a national computer network called **Advanced Research Project Agency Network (ARPANET).** The Internet is a large network that connects together smaller networks all over the globe. The **Web** was introduced in 1991 at the **Center for European Nuclear Research (CERN)** in Switzerland. Prior to the Web, the Internet was all text—no graphics, animations, sound, or video. The Web made it possible to include these elements. It provided a multimedia interface to resources available on the Internet. From these early research beginnings, the Internet and the Web have evolved into one of the most powerful tools of the 21st century.

It is easy to get the Internet and the Web confused, but they are not the same thing. The Internet is the actual network. It is made up of wires, cables, satellites, and rules for exchanging information between computers connected to the network. Being connected to this network is often described as being **online.** The Internet connects millions of computers and resources throughout the world. The Web is a multimedia interface to the resources available on the Internet. Every day over a billion users from nearly every country in the world use the Internet and the Web. What are they doing? The most common uses are the following:

- **Communicating** is by far the most popular Internet activity. You can exchange e-mail with your family and friends almost anywhere in the world. You can join and listen to discussions and debates on a wide variety of special-interest topics.

- **Shopping** is one of the fastest-growing Internet applications. You can window shop, look for the latest fashions, search for bargains, and make purchases.

- **Searching** for information has never been more convenient. You can access some of the world's largest libraries directly from your home computer. You can find the latest local, national, and international news.

- **Entertainment** options are nearly endless. You can find music, movies, magazines, and computer games. You will find live concerts, movie previews, book clubs, and interactive live games. (See Figure 2-1.)

- **Education** or **e-learning** is another rapidly emerging Web application. You can take classes on almost any subject. There are courses just for fun

On the Web Explorations

Many individuals and institutions played a part in the development of the Internet and the Web.

To learn more about the history of the Internet and Web, visit our site at www.computing2011.com and enter the keyword history.

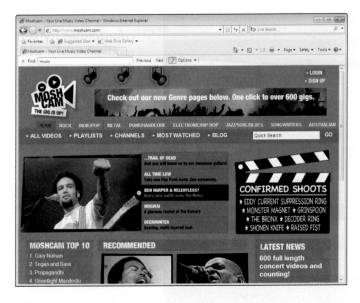

Figure 2-1 Entertainment site

and there are courses for high school, college, and graduate school credit. Some cost nothing to take and others cost a lot.

The first step to using the Internet and the Web is to get connected, or to gain access to the Internet.

CONCEPT CHECK

Describe how the Internet and the Web started.

What is the difference between the Internet and the Web?

List and describe five of the most common uses of the Internet and the Web.

Access

The Internet and the telephone system are similar—you can connect a computer to the Internet much like you connect a phone to the telephone system. Once you are on the Internet, your computer becomes an extension of what seems like a giant computer—a computer that branches all over the world. When provided with a connection to the Internet, you can use a browser program to search the Web.

Providers

The most common way to access the Internet is through an **Internet service provider (ISP).** The providers are already connected to the Internet and provide a path or connection for individuals to access the Internet. Your college or university most likely provides you with free access to the Internet either through its local area networks or through a **dial-up** or telephone connection. There are also some companies that offer free Internet access.

The most widely used commercial Internet service providers are national and wireless providers.

- **National service providers** like America Online (AOL) are the most widely used. They provide access through standard telephone or cable connections. Users can access the Internet from almost anywhere within the country for a standard fee without incurring long-distance telephone charges.

Communication

As previously mentioned, communication is the most popular Internet activity, and its impact cannot be overestimated. At a personal level, friends and family can stay in contact with one another even when separated by thousands of miles. At a business level, electronic communication has become a standard, and many times preferred, way to stay in touch with suppliers, employees, and customers. Some popular types of Internet communication are e-mail, instant messaging, social networking, blogs, and wikis.

E-mail

E-mail or **electronic mail** is the transmission of electronic messages over the Internet. At one time, e-mail consisted only of basic text messages. Now e-mail routinely includes graphics, photos, and many different types of file attachments. People all over the world send e-mail to each other. You can e-mail your family, your co-workers, and even your senator. All you need to send and receive e-mail is an e-mail account, access to the Internet, and an e-mail program. Two of the most widely used e-mail programs are Microsoft's Outlook Express and Mozilla Thunderbird.

A typical e-mail message has three basic elements: header, message, and signature. (See Figure 2-6.) The **header** appears first and typically includes the following information:

- **Addresses:** Addresses of the persons sending, receiving, and, optionally, anyone else who is to receive copies. E-mail addresses have two basic parts. (See Figure 2-7.) The first part is the user's name and the second part is the domain name, which includes the top-level domain. In our example e-mail, *dcoats* is Dan's user name. The server providing e-mail service for Dan is *usc.edu*. The top-level domain indicates that the provider is an educational institution.

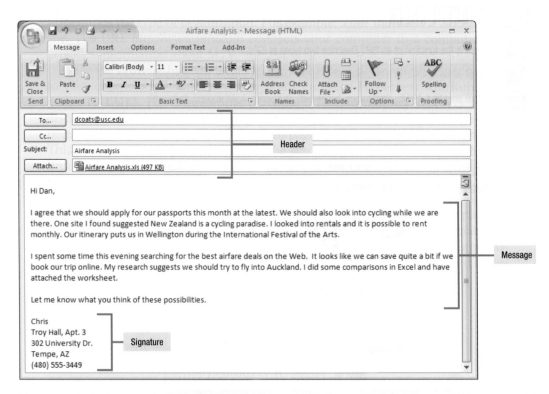

Figure 2-6 Basic elements of an e-mail message

Figure 2-7 **Two parts of an e-mail address**

- **Subject:** A one-line description, used to present the topic of the message. Subject lines typically are displayed when a person checks his or her mailbox.
- **Attachments:** Many e-mail programs allow you to attach files such as documents and image files. If a message has an attachment, the file name appears on the attachment line. If you are sending a large file, however, there are more efficient ways to send the file. To learn more about how you can send large files, see Making IT Work for You: Sharing Large Files on pages 36 and 37.

The letter or **message** comes next. Finally, the **signature** provides additional information about the sender. Typically, this information includes the sender's name, address, and telephone number.

E-mail can be a valuable asset in your personal and professional life. However, like many other valuable technologies, there are drawbacks too. Americans receive billions of unwanted and unsolicited e-mails every year. This unwelcome mail is called **spam.** While spam is indeed a distraction and nuisance, it also can be dangerous. For example, **computer viruses** or destructive programs are often attached to unsolicited e-mail. Computer viruses and ways to protect against them will be discussed in Chapter 5.

In an attempt to control spam, anti-spam laws have been added to our legal system. For example, the CAN-SPAM Act of 2003 requires that every marketing-related e-mail provide an opt-out option. When the option is selected, the recipient's e-mail address is to be removed from future mailing lists. Failure to do so results in heavy fines. This approach, however, has had minimal impact since over 50 percent of all spam originates from servers outside the United States. A more effective approach has been the development and use of **spam blockers.** (See Figure 2-8.) These programs use a variety of different approaches to identify and eliminate spam. To learn about these approaches, visit our Web site at www.computing2011.com and enter the keyword **spam.**

tips

Are you tired of sorting through an inbox full of spam? Americans receive over 200 billion spam e-mails every year. Here are a few simple tips to help ensure that your inbox is spam-free:

1. **Choose a complex address.** sally_smith@hotmail.com is much more likely to get spam than 4it3scoq2@hotmail.com. Consider using a more complicated, and less personal, user name.

2. **Keep a low profile.** Many spammers collect e-mail addresses from personal Web sites, chat rooms, and message boards. Use caution when handing out your address and be sure to read the privacy policy of a site before you hand over your address.

3. **Don't ever respond to spam.** Once you respond to spam, either in interest or to opt out of a list, you have confirmed the address is valid. Valid addresses are worth more to spammers, who then sell the addresses to others.

4. **Use e-mail filter options.** Most e-mail programs have a filter option that screens incoming e-mail based on a set of preferences you choose. You can set up your inbox to accept only mail from certain addresses or to block mail from others.

5. **Use spam blockers.** There are plenty of programs available to help protect your inbox. For example, MailWasher provides an effective and free program available at www.mailwasher.com.

To see other tips, visit our Web site at www.computing2011.com and enter the keyword tips.

Spam Blocker	Site
OnlyMyEmailPersonal	www.onlymymail.com
CA Anti-Spam Plus	www.qurb.com
Vanquish vqME	www.vanquish.com

Figure 2-8 **Spam blockers**

Instant Messaging

Instant messaging (IM) allows two or more people to contact each other via direct, live communication. To use instant messaging, you register with an instant messaging server and then specify a list of **friends.** Whenever you connect to the Internet, special software informs your messaging server that you are online. In response, the server will notify you if any of your friends are online. At the same time, it notifies your friends that you are online. You can then send messages directly back and forth to one another. Most instant messaging programs also include video conferencing features, file sharing, and remote assistance. Many businesses routinely use these instant messaging features. To see how instant messaging works, visit our Web site at www.computing2011.com and enter the keyword **im**.

The most widely used instant messaging services are AOL's Instant Messenger, Microsoft's MSN Messenger, and Yahoo Messenger. One limitation, however, is that many instant messaging services do not support communication with other services. For example, at the time of this writing, a user registered with AOL cannot use AOL's Instant Messenger software to communicate with a user registered with Yahoo Messenger. Recently, however, some software companies have started providing **universal instant messenger** programs that overcome this limitation. For example, Gain, Odigo, and Trillian provide instant messaging services that do support communication with other services.

Social Networking

One of the fastest-growing uses of the Internet is **social networking,** or connecting individuals to one another. Three basic categories of social networking sites are reuniting, friend-of-a-friend, and common interest.

- **Reuniting sites** are designed to connect people who have known one another but have lost touch; for example, an old high school friend that you have not seen for several years. You join a social network by connecting to a reuniting site and providing profile information such as your age, gender, name of high school, and so forth. This information is added to the reuniting site's member database. Members are able to search the database to locate individuals. Many of the sites will even notify you whenever a new individual joins that matches some parts of your profile (such as high school class). Two of the best-know reuniting sites are Classmates Online and Facebook.

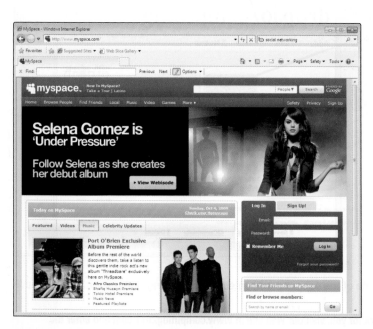

Figure 2-9 Friend-of-a-friend site

- **Friend-of-a-friend sites** are designed to bring together two people who do not know one another but share a common friend. The theory is that, if you share a common friend, then it is likely that you would become friends. For example, a network could be started by one of your acquaintances by providing profile information on him- or herself and a list of friends. You could visit your acquaintance's site to connect to a friend(s) of your acquaintance. You could even join the list of friends provided at the site. Two well-known friend-of-a-friend sites are Friendster and MySpace. (See Figure 2-9.)

- **Common interest sites** bring together individuals that share common interests or hobbies. You select a networking site based on a particular interest. For example, if you wanted to share images, you might join Flickr. If you are looking for business contacts, you might join LinkedIn. If you wanted to locate or create a special interest group, you might join Meetup.

Before providing any information to a social networking site or to any individual, consider carefully what you are disclosing. Do not provide inappropriate or overly personal information. For a list of some popular social networking sites, see Figure 2-10. To learn more about Twitter, one of the most widely used social networking sites, see Making IT Work for You: Twitter on pages 40 and 41.

Site	Description
Classmates.com	Reuniting, primarily for school, work, military
Facebook.com	Reuniting, primarily for college and high school students
Flickr.com	Common interest, image sharing
Friendster.com	Friend-of-a-friend, general
MySpace.com	Friend-of-a-friend, general
Twitter.com	Friend-of-a-friend, general
LinkedIn.com	Common interest, business
Meetup.com	Common interest, interest group meeting

Figure 2-10 Social networking sites

Blogs, Microblogs, and Wikis

In addition to social networking sites, there are other types of sites that help ordinary people communicate across the Web.

- Many individuals create personal Web sites, called **Web logs** or **blogs,** to keep in touch with friends and family. Blog postings are timestamped and arranged with the newest item first. Often, readers of these sites are allowed to comment. Some blogs are like online diaries with personal information; others focus on information about a hobby or theme, such as knitting, electronic devices, or good books. Although most are written by individual bloggers, there are also group blogs with multiple contributors. Some businesses and newspapers also have started blogging as a quick publishing method. Several sites provide tools to create blogs. Two of the most widely used are Blogger and WordPress. (See Figure 2-11.)

- A **microblog** publishes short sentences that only take a few seconds to write, rather than long stories or posts like a traditional blog. Microblogs are designed to keep friends and other contacts up-to-date on your interests and activities. The most popular microblogging site, **Twitter,** enables

Figure 2-11 Blog creation site

The Internet, the Web, and Electronic Commerce   **39**

Making IT work for you

TWITTER

Would you like your own microblog? A microblog can help you stay in touch with friends and family, or coordinate a project with other students. It's easy using the free Twitter microblogging service.

Sign Up   To create a new Twitter account:

1. ● Visit http://www.twitter.com.

   ● Click the *Sign up now* button.

2. ● Follow the on-screen instructions to create an account.

The username you select for your new account will be used to create a custom blog address where your posts can be viewed by others. For example, tweets posted by the user **comp_essentials** can be seen at **http://twitter.com/comp_essentials**.

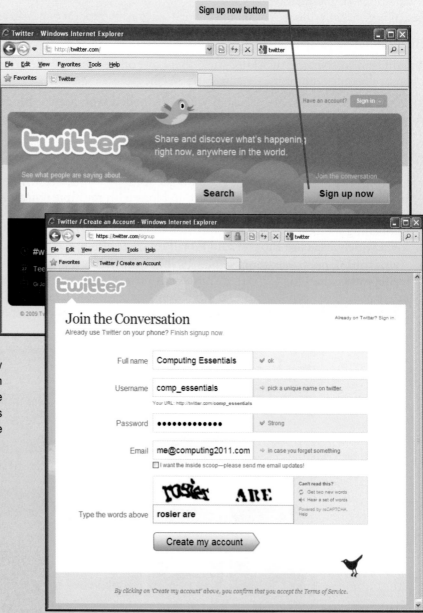

Posting and Following   Using Twitter involves posting short messages about your current status. Following others allows you to see their messages each time they post an update. To post an update to Twitter:

1
- **Enter a short message in the *What are you doing?* text box.**
- **Click the *update* button.**

Your text is immediately visible at your custom Twitter page. In addition to tweeting directly from the Twitter Web site, there are also options to tweet by sending a text message from a mobile phone, or using other software such as instant messaging applications.

Short message to post

Update button

Posts by others you are following

To follow updates by other people, simply visit their custom blog address and click the *Follow* button.

Follow button

The Web is continually changing, and some of the specifics presented in Making IT Work for You may have changed.
To learn about other ways to make information technology work for you, visit our Web site at www.computing2011.com and enter the keyword miw.

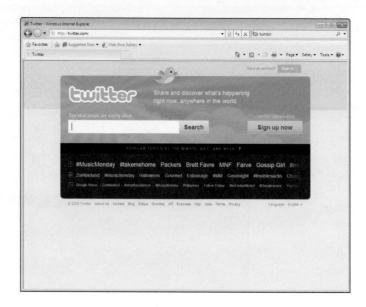

Figure 2-12 Microblog site

you to add new content from your browser, instant messaging application, or even a mobile phone. (See Figure 2-12.)

- A **wiki** is a Web site specially designed to allow visitors to fill in missing information or correct inaccuracies. "Wiki" comes from the Hawaiian word for fast, which describes the simplicity of editing and publishing through wiki software. Wikis support collaborative writing in which there isn't a single expert author, but rather a community of interested people that builds knowledge over time. Perhaps the most famous example is Wikipedia, an online encyclopedia, written and edited by anyone who wants to contribute, that has millions of entries in over 20 languages. (See Figure 2-13.)

Creating blogs and wikis are examples of Web authoring. We will discuss Web authoring software in detail in Chapter 4. To learn more about creating your own personal Web site, visit us at www.computing2011.com and enter the keyword **blog.**

Figure 2-13 Wikipedia

Search Tools

The Web can be an incredible resource, providing information on nearly any topic imaginable. Are you planning a trip? Writing an economics paper? Looking for a movie review? Trying to locate a long-lost friend? Information sources related to these questions, and much, much more, are available on the Web.

With over 20 billion pages and more being added daily, the Web is a massive collection of interrelated pages. With so much available information, locating the precise information you need can be difficult. Fortunately, a number of organizations called **search services** operate Web sites that can help you locate the information you need. They maintain huge databases relating to information provided on the Web and the Internet. The information stored at these databases includes addresses, content descriptions or classifications, and keywords appearing on Web pages and

Are you going to use a search tool to locate some information? Here are a few tips that might help.

1 **Start with the right approach.** For general information, use a direct search. For specific information, use a keyword search.

2 **Be as precise as possible.** Use specific keywords that relate directly to the topic.

3 **Use multiple words.** Use quotation marks to identify key phrases.

4 **Use Boolean operators.** Typically, these include words such as "and," "not," and "or."

5 **Check your spelling.** Misspelling is one of the most common problems.

6 **Keep moving.** Look only at the first page of search results. If necessary, try another search using different keywords.

To see other tips, visit our Web site at www.computing2011.com and enter the keyword tips.

other Internet informational resources. Special programs called **spiders** continually look for new information and update the search services' databases. Additionally, search services provide special programs called *search engines* that you can use to locate specific information on the Web.

Search Engines

Search engines are specialized programs that assist you in locating information on the Web and the Internet. To find information, you go to a search service's Web site and use its search engine. For example, see Figure 2-14 for Yahoo's search engine. This search engine, like most others, provides two different search approaches.

- **Keyword search:** In a **keyword search,** you enter a keyword or phrase reflecting the information you want. The search engine compares your entry against its database and returns a list of **hits,** or sites that contain the keywords. Each hit includes a hyperlink to the referenced Web page (or other resource) along with a brief discussion of the information contained at that location. Many searches result in a large number of hits. For

Keyword search

Directory search

Figure 2-14 Yahoo's search engine provides keyword and directory search

example, if you were to enter the keyword *travel*, you would get thousands of hits. Search engines order the hits according to those sites that most likely contain the information requested and present the list to you in that order, usually in groups of 10.

- **Directory search:** Most search engines also provide a directory or list of categories or topics such as Autos, Finance, and Games. In a **directory search,** you select a category or topic that fits the information that you want. Another list of subtopics related to the topic you selected appears. You select the subtopic that best relates to your topic and another subtopic list appears. You continue to narrow your search in this manner until a list of Web sites appears. This list corresponds to the hit list previously discussed.

As a rule, if you are searching for general information, use the directory search approach. For example, to find general information about rock music, use a directory search beginning with the category Music and then select the subtopic Rock. If you are searching for specific information, use the keyword approach. For example, if you were looking for a specific music file, you would use a keyword search that includes the album title and/or the artist's name.

A recent study by the NEC Research Institute found that any one search engine includes only a fraction of the informational sources on the Web. Therefore, it is highly recommended that you use more than one search engine when researching important topics. See Figure 2-15 for a list of some of the most widely used search engines. Or you could use a special type of search engine called a metasearch engine.

Metasearch Engines

One way to research a topic is to visit the Web sites for several individual search engines. At each site, you would enter the search instructions, wait for the hits to appear, review the list, and visit selected sites. This process can be quite time-consuming and duplicate responses from different search engines are inevitable. Metasearch engines offer an alternative.

Search Service	Site
AOL Search	search.aol.com
Ask	www.ask.com
Google	www.google.com
MSN Search	search.msn.com
Yahoo!	www.yahoo.com

Figure 2-15 Search engines

Metasearch engines are programs that automatically submit your search request to several search engines simultaneously. The metasearch engine receives the results, eliminates duplicates, orders the hits, and then provides the edited list to you. See Figure 2-16 for a list of several metasearch engines available on the Web. One of the best known is Dogpile; see Figure 2-17.

Metasearch Service	Site
Dogpile	www.dogpile.com
Ixquick	www.ixquick.com
MetaCrawler	www.metacrawler.com
Search	www.search.com
Clusty	www.clusty.com

Figure 2-16 Metasearch sites

Specialized Search Engines

Specialized search engines focus on subject-specific Web sites. Specialized sites can potentially save you time by narrowing your search. For a list of just a few selected specialized search engines, see Figure 2-18. For example, let's say you are researching a paper about the fashion industry. You could begin with a general search engine like Yahoo! Or you could go to a search engine that specializes specifically in fashion, such as infomat.com.

Content Evaluation

Search engines are excellent tools to locate information on the Web. Be careful, however, how you use the information you find. Unlike most published material found in newspapers, journals, and textbooks, not all the information you find on the Web has been subjected to strict guidelines to ensure accuracy. In fact, anyone can publish content on the Web. Many sites, such as Wikipedia.com, allow anyone to post new material, sometimes anonymously and without critical evaluation. To learn how you can publish on the Web, visit our Web site at www.computing2011.com and enter the keyword **blog**.

To evaluate the accuracy of information you find on the Web, consider the following:

- **Authority.** Is the author an expert in the subject area? Is the site an official site for the information presented, or is the site an individual's personal Web site?
- **Accuracy.** Has the information been critically reviewed for correctness prior to posting on the Web? Does the Web site provide a method to report inaccurate information to the author?

Figure 2-17 Dogpile metasearch site

Topic	Site
Environment	www.eco-web.com
Fashion	www.infomat.com
History	www.historynet.com
Law	www.lawcrawler.com
Medicine	www.medscape.com

Figure 2-18 Select specialized search engines

- **Objectivity.** Is the information factually reported or does the author have a bias? Does the author appear to have a personal agenda aimed at convincing or changing the reader's opinion?
- **Currency.** Is the information up to date? Does the site specify the date when the site was updated?

CONCEPT CHECK

What are search services, search engines, and spiders?

What is the difference between a keyword and a directory search?

Compare search, metasearch, and specialized search engines.

What are the four considerations for evaluating Web site content?

Electronic Commerce

Electronic commerce, also known as **e-commerce,** is the buying and selling of goods over the Internet. Have you ever bought anything over the Internet? If you have not, there is a very good chance that you will within the next year or two. Shopping on the Internet is growing rapidly and there seems to be no end in sight.

The underlying reason for the rapid growth in e-commerce is that it provides incentives for both buyers and sellers. From the buyer's perspective, goods and services can be purchased at any time of day or night. Traditional commerce is typically limited to standard business hours when the seller is open. Additionally, buyers no longer have to physically travel to the seller's location. For example, busy parents with small children do not need to coordinate their separate schedules or to arrange for a baby sitter whenever they want to visit the mall. From the seller's perspective, the costs associated with owning and operating a retail outlet can be eliminated. For example, a music store can operate entirely on the Web without an actual physical store and without a large sales staff.

Another advantage is reduced inventory. Traditional stores maintain an inventory of goods in their stores and periodically replenish this inventory from warehouses. With e-commerce, there is no in-store inventory and products are shipped directly from warehouses.

While there are numerous advantages to e-commerce, there are disadvantages as well. Some of these disadvantages include the inability to provide immediate delivery of goods, the inability to "try on" prospective purchases, and questions relating to the security of online payments. Although these issues are being addressed, very few observers suggest that e-commerce will replace bricks-and-mortar businesses entirely. It is clear that both will coexist and that e-commerce will continue to grow.

Just like any other type of commerce, electronic commerce involves two parties: businesses and consumers. There are three basic types of electronic commerce:

- **Business-to-consumer (B2C)** involves the sale of a product or service to the general public or end

tips Have you ever bought anything online? If not, it's likely that in the future you will join the millions that have. Here are a few suggestions on how to shop online:

1 **Consult product review sites.** To get evaluations or opinions on products, visit one of the many review sites on the Web such as www.consumersearch.com and www.epinions.com.

2 **Use a shopping bot.** Once you have selected a specific product, enlist a shopping bot or automated shopping assistants to compare prices. Two well-known shopping bots are located at www.mysimon.com and www.pricegrabber.com.

3 **Consult vendor review sites.** Of course, price is not everything. Before placing an order with a vendor, check their reputation by visiting vendor review sites such as www.resellerratings.com and www.bizrate.com.

To see other tips, visit our Web site at www.computing2011.com and enter the keyword tips.

users. Oftentimes this arrangement eliminates the wholesaler by allowing manufacturers to sell directly to customers. Other times, existing retail stores use B2C e-commerce to create a presence on the Web as another way to reach customers.

- **Consumer-to-consumer (C2C)** involves individuals selling to individuals. This often takes the form of an electronic version of the classified ads or an auction.
- **Business-to-business (B2B)** involves the sale of a product or service from one business to another. This is typically a manufacturer–supplier relationship. For example, a furniture manufacturer requires raw materials such as wood, paint, and varnish.

Business-to-Consumer E-Commerce

The fastest-growing type of e-commerce is business-to-consumer. It is used by large corporations, small corporations, and start-up businesses. Whether large or small, nearly every existing corporation in the United States provides some type of B2C support as another means to connect to customers. Because extensive investments are not required to create traditional retail outlets and to maintain large marketing and sales staffs, e-commerce allows start-up companies to compete with larger established firms.

The three most widely used B2C applications are for online banking, financial trading, and shopping.

- **Online banking** is becoming a standard feature of banking institutions. Customers are able to go online with a standard browser to perform many banking operations. These online operations include accessing account information, balancing check books, transferring funds, paying bills, and applying for loans.
- **Online stock trading** allows investors to research, buy, and sell stocks and bonds over the Internet. While e-trading is more convenient than using a traditional full-service broker, the greatest advantage is cost.
- **Online shopping** includes the buying and selling of a wide range of consumer goods over the Internet. (See Figure 2-19.) There are thousands of e-commerce applications in this area. Fortunately, there are numerous

Figure 2-19 Online shopping site

Support	Site
Product comparisons	www.shopping.com
Locating closeouts	www.overstock.com
Finding coupons	www.ebates.com

Figure 2-20 Consumer support sites

Web sites that provide support for consumers looking to compare products and to locate bargains. (See Figure 2-20.)

Consumer-to-Consumer E-Commerce

A recent trend in C2C e-commerce is the growing popularity of Web auctions. **Web auctions** are similar to traditional auctions except that buyers and sellers seldom, if ever, meet face-to-face. Sellers post descriptions of products at a Web site and buyers submit bids electronically. Like traditional auctions, sometimes the bidding becomes highly competitive and enthusiastic. There are two basic types of Web auction sites:

- **Auction house sites** sell a wide range of merchandise directly to bidders. The auction house owner presents merchandise that is typically from a company's surplus stock. These sites operate like a traditional auction, and bargain prices are not uncommon. Auction house sites are generally considered safe places to shop.

- **Person-to-person auction sites** operate more like flea markets. The owner of the site provides a forum for numerous buyers and sellers to gather. While the owners of these sites typically facilitate the bidding process, they are not involved in completing transactions or in verifying the authenticity of the goods sold. (See Figure 2-21.) As with purchases at a flea market, buyers and sellers need to be cautious.

For a list of the most popular Web auction sites, see Figure 2-22.

Figure 2-21 Person-to-person Web auction site

Organization	Site
Amazon	www.auctions.amazon.com
WeBidz	www.webidz.com
eBay	www.ebay.com
Overstock	auctions.overstock.com

Figure 2-22 Auction sites

Security

The single greatest challenge for e-commerce is the development of fast, secure, and reliable payment methods for purchased goods. The three basic payment options are check, credit card, and digital cash.

- Checks are the most traditional. Unfortunately, check purchases require the longest time to complete. After selecting an item, the buyer sends a check through the mail. Upon receipt of the check, the seller verifies that the check is good. If it is good, then the purchased item is sent out.

- Credit card purchases are faster and more convenient than check purchases. Credit card fraud, however, is a major concern for both buyers and sellers. Criminals known as **carders** specialize in stealing, trading, and using stolen credit cards over the Internet. We will discuss this and other privacy and security issues related to the Internet in Chapter 10.

- **Digital cash** is the Internet's equivalent to traditional cash. Buyers purchase digital cash from a third party (a bank that specializes in electronic currency) and use it (see Figure 2-23) to purchase goods. Sellers convert the digital cash to traditional currency through the third party.

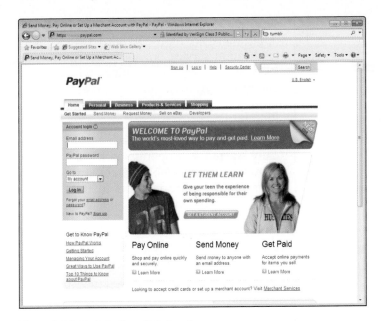

Figure 2-23 PayPal offers digital cash

Organization	Site
ECash	www.ecash.com
Google	checkout.google.com
Internet Cash	www.internetcash.com
PayPal	www.paypal.com

Figure 2-24 Digital cash providers

Although not as convenient as credit card purchases, digital cash is more secure. For a list of digital cash providers, see Figure 2-24.

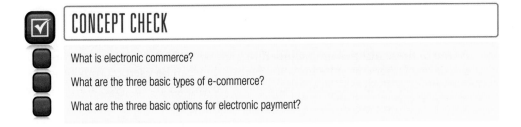

CONCEPT CHECK

What is electronic commerce?

What are the three basic types of e-commerce?

What are the three basic options for electronic payment?

Web Utilities

Utilities are programs that make computing easier. **Web utilities** are specialized utility programs that make using the Internet and the Web easier and safer. Some of these utilities are Internet services for connecting and sharing resources over the Internet. Others are browser-related programs that either become part of your browser or are executed from your browser. File transfer utilities allow you to copy files to and from your computer across the Internet.

Web-Based Applications

Typically, application programs are owned by individuals or organizations and stored on their computer system's hard disks. An emerging trend, however, is to free users from owning and storing applications. The most widely used **Web-based applications** are free using **Web-based services** that provide access to programs that run within your browser window. For example, Google Apps provides free access to programs with capabilities similar to Microsoft's Word, Excel, and PowerPoint. (See Figure 2-25.)

Another type of Web-based application typically runs on your desktop like a traditional application program. To use one of these, you connect to the Web site of an **application service provider (asp),** copy the application program to your computer system's memory, and then run the application. Unlike Web-based

Figure 2-25 Web-based service (Google Apps)

services, access is typically not free and the applications are more specialized. To see how application service providers work, visit our Web site at www.computing2011.com and enter the keyword **asp.**

Plug-ins

Plug-ins are programs that are automatically started and operate as a part of your browser. Many Web sites require you to have one or more plug-ins to fully experience their content. Some widely used plug-ins include

- Acrobat Reader from Adobe—for viewing and printing a variety of standard forms and other documents saved in a special format called PDF.
- Windows Media Player from Microsoft— for playing audio files, video files, and much more.
- QuickTime from Apple—for playing audio and video files. (See Figure 2-26.)
- RealPlayer from RealNetworks—for playing audio and video files.
- Shockwave from Adobe—for playing Web-based games and viewing concerts and dynamic animations.

Some of these utilities are included in many of today's browsers and operating systems. Others must be installed before they can be used by your browser. To learn more about plug-ins and how to download them, visit some of the sites listed in Figure 2-27.

Filters

Filters block access to selected sites. The Internet is an interesting and multifaceted arena. But one of those facets is a dark and seamy one. Parents, in particular, are concerned about children roaming unrestricted across the Internet. (See Figure 2-28.) Filter programs allow parents as well as

Figure 2-26 QuickTime movie at Apple.com

Plug-in	Source
Acrobat Reader	www.adobe.com
Media Player	www.microsoft.com
QuickTime	www.apple.com
RealPlayer	www.service.real.com
Shockwave	www.adobe.com

Figure 2-27 Plug-in sites

Figure 2-28 Parents play an important role in Internet supervision

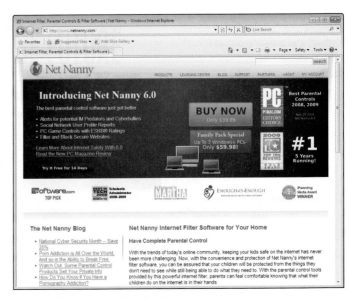

Figure 2-29 Net Nanny is a Web filter

organizations to block out selected sites and set time limits. (See Figure 2-29.) Additionally, these programs can monitor use and generate reports detailing the total time spent on the Internet and the time spent at individual Web sites, chat groups, and newsgroups. For a list of some of the best-known filters, see Figure 2-30.

On the Web Explorations

Some privacy groups object to the use of Web filtering programs on the grounds that they accidentally censor valuable Web content.

To learn more about this issue, visit our Web site at www.computing2011.com and enter the keyword filter.

File Transfer Utilities

Using file transfer utility software, you can copy files to your computer from specially configured servers. This is called **downloading.** You also can use file transfer utility software to copy files from your computer to another computer on the Internet. This is called **uploading.** Three popular types of file transfer are FTP, Web-based, and BitTorrent.

- **File transfer protocol (FTP)** and **secure file transfer protocol (SFTP)** allow you to efficiently copy files to and from your computer across the Internet, and are frequently used for uploading changes to a Web site hosted by an Internet service provider. FTP has been used for decades and still remains one of the most popular methods of file transfer.

- **Web-based file transfer services** make use of a Web browser to upload and download files. This eliminates the need for any custom software to be installed. A popular Web-based file transfer service is drop.io. (See Making IT Work for You: Sharing Large Files on pages 36 and 37 to learn more about how this service works.)

- **BitTorrent** distributes file transfers across many different computers for more efficient downloads, unlike other transfer technologies where a file is copied from one computer on the Internet to another. A single file might be located on dozens of individual computers. When you download the file, each computer sends you a tiny piece of the larger file, making BitTorrent well-suited for transferring very large files. Unfortunately, BitTorrent technology often has been used for

Filter	Site
CyberPatrol	www.cyberpatrol.com
Cybersitter	www.cybersitter.com
iProtectYou Pro Web Filter	www.softforyou.com
Net Nanny	www.netnanny.com
Safe Eyes Platinum	www.safeeyes.com

Figure 2-30 Filters

INTERNET AND WEB

Internet

Launched in 1969 with **ARPANET,** the **Internet** consists of the actual physical network made up of wires, cables, and satellites. Being connected to this network is often described as being **online.**

Web

Introduced in 1991 at **CERN,** the **Web** provides a multimedia interface to Internet resources.

Common Uses

The most common uses of the Internet and the Web include

- Communication—the most popular Internet activity.
- Shopping—one of the fastest-growing Internet activities.
- Searching—access libraries and local, national, and international news.
- Entertainment—music, movies, magazines, and computer games.
- Education—**e-learning** or taking online courses.

ACCESS

Once connected to the Internet, your computer seemingly becomes an extension of a giant computer that branches all over the world.

Providers

Internet service providers are connected to the Internet. The most widely used **ISPs** are **national** and **wireless.** Connection technologies include **DSL, cable,** and **wireless modems.**

Browsers

Browsers access the Web allowing you to **surf** or explore. Some related terms are

- **URLs**—**locations** or **addresses** to Web resources; two parts are **protocol** and **domain name; top-level domain (TLD)** identifies type of organization.
- **HTML**—commands to display **Web pages; hyperlinks (links)** are connections.
- **JavaScript**—a scripting language that adds basic interactivity and form checking to Web pages. **AJAX** allows rapid response time.
- **Applets**—special programs linked to Web pages; typically written in **Java.**
- **Mobile browsers**—run on portable devices; display on very small screens; provide special navigational tools.

To be a competent end user, you need to be aware of resources available on the Internet and Web, to be able to access these resources, to effectively communicate electronically, to efficiently locate information, to understand electronic commerce, and to use Web utilities.

COMMUNICATION

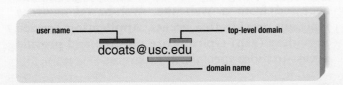

E-mail

E-mail (electronic mail) is the transmission of electronic messages. Basic elements: **header** (including **addresses**, **subject**, and **attachments**), **message**, and **signature**. **Spam** is unwanted and unsolicited e-mail that may include a **computer virus**. **Spam blockers** are programs that identify and eliminate spam.

Instant Messaging

Instant messaging (IM) supports live communication with **friends**. **Universal instant messengers** support communication with other services.

Social Networking

Social networks connect individuals to one another. Three types are

- **Reuniting sites** connect people who have lost touch with one another.
- **Friend-of-a-friend sites** bring together two people who share a common friend.
- **Common interest sites** connect individuals who share common interests or hobbies.

Blogs, Microblogs, and Wikis

A **Web log** or **blog** is an online journal with chronological postings. A **microblog** publishes short sentences; **Twitter** is the most popular microblogging site. A **wiki** is a Web site that allows people to edit or contribute to it by directly editing the pages.

SEARCH TOOLS

Search Service	Site
AOL Search	search.aol.com
Ask	www.ask.com
Google	www.google.com
MSN Search	search.msn.com
Yahoo!	www.yahoo.com

Search services maintain huge databases relating to Web site content. **Spiders** are programs that update these databases.

Search Engines

Search engines locate information on the Web. Two approaches are **keyword search** (enter keyword, and it returns a list of **hits**; good for locating specific information) and **directory search** (select from a list of topics; good for locating general information).

Metasearch Engines

Metasearch engines submit to several search engines simultaneously. Duplicate sites are eliminated, hits are ordered, and composite hits are presented.

Specialized Search Engines

Specialized search engines focus on subject-specific Web sites.

Content Evaluation

Consider the following criteria to evaluate the accuracy of information on the Web: authority, accuracy, objectivity, and currency.

MULTIPLE CHOICE

Circle the letter or fill in the correct answer.

1. The Internet was launched in 1969 when the United States funded a project that developed a national computer network called
   - **a.** Web
   - **b.** ISP
   - **c.** CERN
   - **d.** ARPANET

2. _____ is the most popular Internet activity.
   - **a.** Communication
   - **b.** Shopping
   - **c.** Searching
   - **d.** Entertainment

3. A(n) _____ program provides access to Web resources.
   - **a.** Web
   - **b.** ISP
   - **c.** browser
   - **d.** URL

4. Rules for exchanging data between computers are called
   - **a.** programs
   - **b.** procedures
   - **c.** protocols
   - **d.** hyperlinks

5. The last part of the domain name following the dot (.) is the top- _____ domain.
   - **a.** level
   - **b.** link
   - **c.** locator
   - **d.** language

6. Many individuals create their own personal sites called Web logs, or _____.
   - **a.** social networks
   - **b.** blogs
   - **c.** wikis
   - **d.** search engines

7. Unwanted and unsolicited e-mails are called _____.
   - **a.** spam
   - **b.** junk
   - **c.** flame
   - **d.** lurk

8. Programs that automatically submit your search request to several search engines simultaneously are called _____.
   - **a.** metasearch engines
   - **b.** inclusive search engines
   - **c.** spiders
   - **d.** hits

9. _____ cash is the Internet's equivalent to traditional cash.
   - **a.** Universal
   - **b.** Web
   - **c.** Premium
   - **d.** Digital

10. These programs allow parents as well as organizations to block out selected sites and set time limits on Internet access.
    - **a.** plug-ins
    - **b.** filters
    - **c.** FTP
    - **d.** DSL

For an interactive multiple-choice practice test, visit our Web site at www.computing2011.com and enter the keyword **multiple2**.

MATCHING

Match each numbered item with the most closely related lettered item. Write your answers in the spaces provided.

a. carders
b. wikis
c. e-commerce
d. header
e. hits
f. metasearch engine
g. plug-in
h. reuniting
i. URLs
j. Web auction

1. Addresses of Web resources. _____
2. Part of an e-mail message that includes the subject, address, and attachments. _____
3. Program that starts and operates as part of a browser. _____
4. The list of sites that contain the keywords of a keyword search. _____
5. Program that automatically submits a search request to several search engines simultaneously. _____
6. Buying and selling goods over the Internet. _____
7. Type of social networking site that reconnects people who have lost touch with one another. _____
8. Similar to a traditional auction, but buyers and sellers typically interact only on the Web. _____
9. Criminals that specialize in stealing, trading, and using stolen credit cards over the Internet. _____
10. Sites that allow visitors to easily contribute or correct content. _____

For an interactive matching practice test, visit our Web site at www.computing 2011.com and enter the keyword matching2.

OPEN-ENDED

On a separate sheet of paper, respond to each question or statement.

1. Discuss the uses of the Internet. Which activities have you participated in? Which one do you think is the most popular?
2. Explain the differences between the two most common types of providers.
3. What are the basic elements of an e-mail message?
4. What is social networking? Describe the three basic categories of social networking sites.
5. Describe the different types of search engines. Give an example of the type of search each engine is best for.

APPLYING TECHNOLOGY

The following questions are designed to demonstrate ways that you can effectively use technology today. The first question relates directly to this chapter's Making IT Work for You feature.

1 SHARING LARGE FILES

Do you ever need to share large files with others? Perhaps you have found that many video and other types of files can be too large to effectively send as an e-mail attachment. To learn how to share large files, review Making IT Work for You: Sharing Large Files on pages 36 and 37. Then complete the following: (a) Describe how the drop.io file-sharing service works. (b) What is a custom address and how is it used? (c) Describe how and why you might use a file-sharing service.

2 ONLINE SHOPPING

Connect to our Web site at www.computing2011.com and enter the keyword shopping to link to a popular shopping site. Once there, try shopping for one or two products, and answer the following questions: (a) What product(s) did you shop for? Could you find the product(s) at the site? If not, then search for another product that you can locate at the site. (b) Describe your experience. Was the site easy to use? Did you find it easy to locate the product(s)? What are the pros and cons of shopping online versus at a traditional store?

3 WEB AUCTIONS

Connect to our Web site at www.computing2011.com and enter the keyword auction to link to a popular online auction. Once there, read about how the auction works and check out a few of the items up for bid. Answer the following questions: (a) What are the advantages of using a Web auction to purchase items? What are the disadvantages? (b) What are the advantages and disadvantages to selling an item on an online auction, as opposed to a traditional method (such as a classified ad in the newspaper)? (c) Have you ever bought or sold an item at an online auction? If you have, describe what you bought and how you bought it. If you have not, do you think that you will in the near future? Why or why not?

EXPANDING YOUR KNOWLEDGE

The following questions are designed to add depth and detail to your understanding of specific topics presented within this chapter. The questions direct you to sources other than the textbook to obtain this knowledge.

1 HOW SPAM FILTERS WORK

Spam is an ongoing problem for e-mail users everywhere. Spam is cheap, easy to send, and difficult to track, so the problem is unlikely to disappear soon. Fortunately, spam-blocking software is available. To learn "How Spam Filters Work," visit our Web site at www.computing2011.com and enter the keyword spam. Then answer the following questions: (a) Briefly describe an advantage and a disadvantage to using each of the three types of filters to stop spam. (b) Choose one of the filters and draw a diagram depicting a spam e-mail going through this filter. Be sure to label each step. (c) Modify the diagram to show an e-mail from a friend.

2 HOW INSTANT MESSAGING WORKS

One of the fastest-growing applications on the Internet is instant messaging. This extension to e-mail provides a way for friends and colleagues to communicate and share information from almost anywhere in the world. To learn "How Instant Messaging Works," visit our Web site at www.computing2011.com and enter the keyword im. Then answer the following:

As described in Step 4: Communicate, Linda, Steve, and Chris agree to meet for a movie. Then Chris tells them that he has to leave for school and disconnects. Linda and Steve continue talking, with Linda asking Steve, "Have you seen any good movies lately?" On a single page of paper, create a drawing based on the animation that describes these events beginning with Step 5 when Chris says, "Bye for now—I have to leave for school."

3 DOMAIN REGISTRATION

Individuals and businesses do not *own* domain names. Instead, names such as "yahoo.com" are *registered* with a domain name registrar for an annual fee. Conduct a Web search to locate a domain name registrar site. Review the process for registering a domain name and address the following questions: (a) List the steps involved in registering a domain name. (b) What is the cost for registering a domain name? (c) How long can a domain name be registered for?

WRITING ABOUT TECHNOLOGY

The ability to think critically and to write effectively is essential to nearly every profession. The following questions are designed to help you develop these skills by posing thought-provoking questions about computer privacy, security, and/or ethics.

1 FREE SPEECH ONLINE

Some feel that there is too much objectionable material allowed on the Internet, whereas others argue that the Internet should be completely uncensored. Consider these two viewpoints and answer the following questions in a one-page paper: (a) Should religious groups be allowed to distribute information over the Internet? What about groups that advocate hatred or oppression? (b) Is there any material you feel should not be freely available on the Web? What about child pornography? (c) If you think some regulation is required, who should determine what restrictions should be imposed? (d) The Internet is not owned by a particular group or country. What limitations does this impose on enforcement of restrictions?

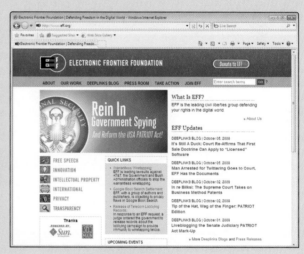

2 DIGITAL DIVIDE

The phrase "digital divide" describes the gap between people who have access to digital information via the Internet and people who lack effective access. Lack of access may stem from a physical lack of technology or from an inability to use available technology. Research two or three articles about the digital divide and address the following items in a one-page paper: (a) Summarize some factors that influence unequal Internet access for some members of society. Which ones seem the hardest to overcome and why? (b) What are some social or economic benefits brought by access to the Internet? (c) Make a prediction about the severity of the digital divide. Will it increase or decrease as new Internet-related technologies become available? Explain your answer.

On the Web Explorations

Microsoft is one of the leaders in creating software applications.

To learn more about the company, visit our Web site at www.computing2011 .com and enter the keyword microsoft.

Introduction

Not long ago, trained specialists were required to perform many of the operations you can now do with a microcomputer. Secretaries used typewriters to create business correspondence. Market analysts used calculators to project sales. Graphic artists created designs by hand. Data processing clerks created electronic files to be stored on large computers. Now you can do all these tasks—and many others—with a microcomputer and the appropriate application software.

Think of the microcomputer as an electronic tool. You may not consider yourself very good at typing, calculating, organizing, presenting, or managing information. However, a microcomputer can help you do all these things and much more. All it takes is the right kinds of software.

Competent end users need to understand the capabilities of basic application software, which includes word processors, spreadsheets, database management systems, and presentation programs. They need to know about integrated packages and software suites.

Application Software

As we discussed in Chapter 1, there are two kinds of software. **System software** works with end users, application software, and computer hardware to handle the majority of technical details. **Application software** can be described as end-user software and is used to accomplish a variety of tasks.

Application software, in turn, can be divided into two categories. One category, **basic applications,** is the focus of this chapter. These programs are widely used in nearly every discipline and occupation. They include word processors, spreadsheets, database management systems, and presentation graphics. The other category, **specialized applications,** includes thousands of other programs that are more narrowly focused on specific disciplines and occupations. Specialized applications are presented in Chapter 4.

Common Features

A **user interface** is the portion of the application that allows you to control and to interact with the program. Most applications use a **graphical user interface (GUI)** that displays graphical elements called **icons** to represent familiar objects and a mouse. The mouse controls a **pointer** on the screen that is used to select items such as icons. Another feature is the use of windows to display information. A **window** is simply a rectangular area that can contain a document, program, or message. (Do not confuse the term *window* with the various versions of Microsoft's Windows operating systems, which are programs.) More than one window can be opened and displayed on the computer screen at one time.

Traditionally, most software programs, including those in Microsoft Office 2003, use a system of menus, toolbars, dialog boxes, and buttons. (See Figure 3-1.) **Menus** present commands that are typically displayed in a **menu bar** at the top of the screen. When one of the menu items is selected, an additional list of menu options or a **dialog box** that provides additional information and requests user input may appear. **Toolbars** typically appear below the menu bar. They contain small graphic elements called **buttons** that provide shortcuts for quick access to commonly used commands.

Microsoft Office 2010 uses an interface introduced in Office 2007 that makes it easier for users to find and use all the features of an application. This new design introduces ribbons, tabs, galleries, and more. (See Figure 3-2.)

Figure 3-1 Microsoft Office Word 2003 interface

- **Ribbons** replace menus and toolbars by organizing commonly used commands into a set of tabs. These tabs display command buttons that are the most relevant to the tasks being performed by the user.
- **Tabs** are used to divide the ribbon into major activity areas. Each tab is then organized into **groups** that contain related items. Some tabs, called **contextual tabs,** only appear when they are needed and anticipate the next operations to be preformed by the user.
- **Galleries** simplify the process of making a selection from a list of alternatives. This is accomplished by displaying small graphic representations of the alternatives.

This new interface is the first major change in over a decade and promises to greatly improve user functionality and efficiency.

Some applications support **speech recognition,** the ability to accept voice input to select menu options and dictate text. See Making IT Work for You: Speech Recognition on pages 68 and 69. To learn more about how speech recognition works, visit our Web site at www.computing2011.com and enter the keyword **speech.**

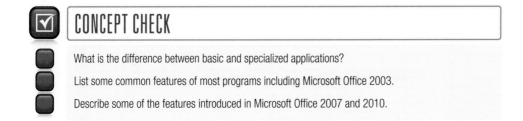

CONCEPT CHECK

What is the difference between basic and specialized applications?

List some common features of most programs including Microsoft Office 2003.

Describe some of the features introduced in Microsoft Office 2007 and 2010.

Making IT work for you

SPEECH RECOGNITION

Tired of using your keyboard to type term papers? Have you ever thought about using your voice to control application software? Perhaps speech recognition is just what you are looking for.

Training the Software The first step is to set up your microphone and train your software to recognize your voice. Using the Microsoft Windows Vista operating system:

1
- Click *Start/Control Panel/Ease of Access/Speech Recognition Options.*
- Click *Start Speech Recognition.*

2
- Complete the Microphone Setup Wizard to adjust your microphone for Speech Recognition.

3
- Click *Start/Control Panel/Ease of Access/Speech Recognition.*
- Click *Train your computer to better understand you.*
- Read the text presented to teach the software your unique speech patterns.

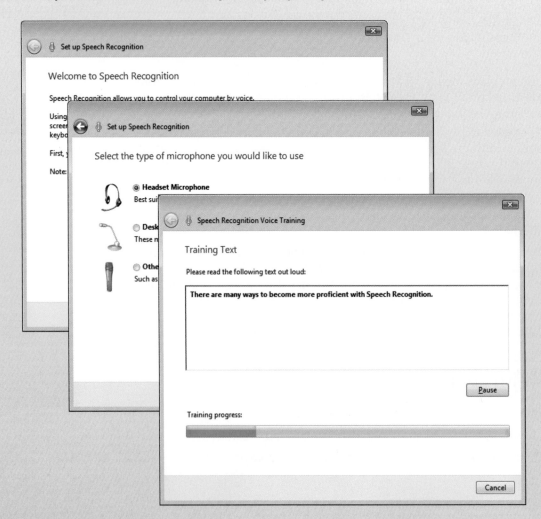

Controlling a Program   Once the software is trained, you can control many computer operations with just your voice. The Speech Reference Card is a handy guide to the commands your computer will understand. To open the Speech Reference Card:

 ● Click *Start/Control Panel/ Ease of Access/ Speech Recognition.*

● Click *Open the Speech Reference Card.*

● Click *Show All* to display a complete list of speech shortcuts, or click the print icon to print the list.

To do this	Say this
Click any item by its name	*File; Start; View*
Click *item*	Click *Recycle Bin;* Click *Computer;* Click *File*
Double-click *item*	Double-click *Recycle Bin;* Double-click *Computer;* Double-click *File*
Switch to an open program	Switch to *Paint;* Switch to *WordPad;* Switch to *program name;* Switch *application*

Dictating a Document   You can also dictate text using the Language bar. For example, to insert text into a Microsoft Word document:

● Say, "Open Word," to open a new Microsoft Word document.

● Dictate the text you want to appear in the document.

"Winding through these flatlands ..."

Although speech recognition technology continues to improve, speech recognition is not yet ready for completely hands-free operation. You will get the best results if you use a combination of your voice and the mouse or keyboard.

The Web is continually changing, and some of the specifics presented in the Making IT Work for You section may have changed.

To learn about other ways to make information technology work for you, visit our Web site at www.computing2011.com and enter the keyword miw.

Figure 3-2 **Microsoft Office Word 2007 interface**

Word Processors

Word processors create text-based **documents** and are one of the most flexible and widely used software tools. All types of people and organizations use word processors to create memos, letters, and faxes. Organizations create newsletters, manuals, and brochures to provide information to their customers. Students and researchers use word processors to create reports. Word processors can even be used to create personalized Web pages.

Microsoft Word is the most widely used word processor. Other popular word processors include Corel WordPerfect and Apple Pages.

Features

Word processors provide a variety of features to make entering, editing, and formatting documents easy. One of the most basic features for entering text is **word wrap.** This feature automatically moves the insertion point to the next line once the current line is full. As you type, the words wrap around to the next line.

There are numerous features designed to support **editing** or modifying a document. One of these is a **thesaurus** that provides synonyms, antonyms, and related words for a selected word or phrase. You can quickly locate and replace selected words using the **find and replace** feature. **Spelling** and **grammar checkers** look for misspelled words and problems with capitalization, punctuation, and sentence structure. Other features are designed to improve the **format** or appearance of a document. One of the most basic is the **font** or design of the characters. (See Figure 3-3.) The height of a character is its **font size.** The appearance of characters can be enhanced using such **character effects** as **bold,** *italic,* and **colors.** Rather than individually selecting specific fonts, sizes, and formats, the **styles** feature, found in most word processors, enables users to quickly apply a predefined set of formatting characteristics to text in one easy step. **Bulleted** and **numbered lists** can make a sequence of topics easy to read.

Font	Sample
Calabri	A B C a b c
Impact	**A B C a b c**
Cambria	A B C a b c
Broadway	**A B C a b c**

Figure 3-3 Sample fonts

Case

Assume that you have accepted a job as an advertising coordinator for Adventure Travel Tours, a travel agency specializing in active adventure vacations. Your primary responsibilities are to create and coordinate the company's promotional materials, including flyers and travel reports. To see how you could use Microsoft Word as the advertising coordinator for the Adventure Travel Tours, see Figures 3-4 and 3-5.

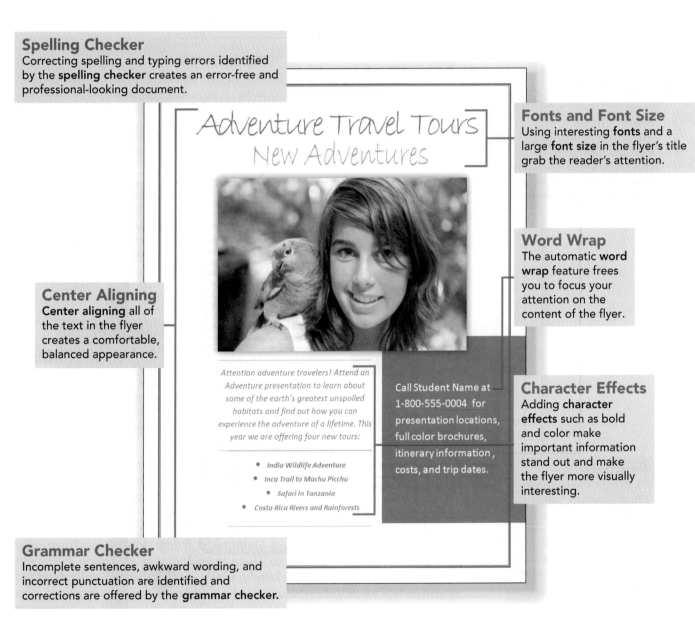

Spelling Checker
Correcting spelling and typing errors identified by the **spelling checker** creates an error-free and professional-looking document.

Fonts and Font Size
Using interesting **fonts** and a large **font size** in the flyer's title grab the reader's attention.

Center Aligning
Center aligning all of the text in the flyer creates a comfortable, balanced appearance.

Word Wrap
The automatic **word wrap** feature frees you to focus your attention on the content of the flyer.

Character Effects
Adding **character effects** such as bold and color make important information stand out and make the flyer more visually interesting.

Grammar Checker
Incomplete sentences, awkward wording, and incorrect punctuation are identified and corrections are offered by the **grammar checker.**

Figure 3-4 Flyer

A cell can contain text or numeric entries. **Text entries** or **labels** provide structure to a worksheet by describing the contents of rows and columns. For example, in Figure 3-6, cell B8 contains the label Food. The cell D8 contains a number identified as the food expense.

A **numeric entry** can be a number or a formula. A **formula** is an instruction to calculate or process. For example, the cell F15 contains the formula = E5–E13. This formula will calculate a value and display that value in cell F15. The value is calculated by taking the value in cell E5 and subtracting the value in cell E13. **Functions** are prewritten formulas provided by the spreadsheet program that perform calculations such as adding a series of cells. For example, the cell E13 contains the function SUM(D8:D12), which adds the values in the range from D8 to D12. A **range** is a series of continuous cells. In this case, the range includes D8, D9, D10, D11, and D12. The sum of the values in this range is displayed in cell E13. Spreadsheet programs typically provide a variety of different types of functions, including financial, mathematical, statistical, and logical functions. Some of these functions are presented in Figure 3-7.

Analytical graphs or **charts** are visual representations of data in a spreadsheet. You can readily create graphs in a spreadsheet program by selecting the cells containing the data to be charted and then selecting the type of chart to display. If you change one or more numbers in your spreadsheet, all related formulas will automatically recalculate and charts will be recreated.

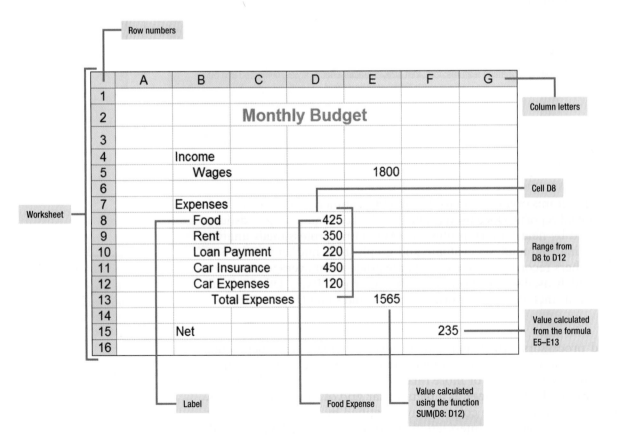

Figure 3-6 Worksheet

Type	Function	Calculates
Financial	PMT	Size of loan payments
	PV	Present value for an investment
Mathematical	SUM	Sum of the numbers in a range of cells
	ABS	Absolute value of a number
Statistical	AVERAGE	Average or mean of the numbers in a range of cells
	MAX	Largest number in a range of cells
Logical	IF	Whether a condition is true; if true, a specified value is displayed; if not true, then a different specified value is displayed
	AND	Whether two conditions are true; if both are true, then a specified value is displayed; if either one or both are not true, then a different specified value is displayed

Figure 3-7 Selected spreadsheet functions

This is called **recalculation.** The process of observing the effect of changing one or more cells is often referred to as **what-if analysis.** For example, to analyze the effect of a rent increase in the Monthly Budget worksheet in Figure 3-6, all you would need to do is replace the contents in cell D9. The entire spreadsheet, including any charts that had been created, would be recalculated automatically.

CONCEPT CHECK

What are spreadsheets used for? What is a workbook file? What is a worksheet?

Define rows, columns, cells, ranges, text, and numeric entries.

Describe the following spreadsheet features: formulas, functions, charts, recalculation, and what-if analysis.

Case

Assume that you have just accepted a job as manager of the Downtown Internet Café. This cafe provides a variety of flavored coffees as well as Internet access. One of your responsibilities is to create a financial plan for the next year. To see how you could use Microsoft Excel, the most widely used spreadsheet program, as the manager for the Downtown Internet Café, see Figures 3-8 through 3-10.

creating a sales forecast

Your first project is to develop a first-quarter sales forecast for the cafe. You begin by studying sales data and talking with several managers. After obtaining sales and expense estimates, you are ready to create the first-quarter forecast. You start structuring the *worksheet* by inserting descriptive *text entries* for the row and column headings. Next, you insert *numeric entries,* including *formulas* and *functions* to perform calculations. To test the accuracy of the worksheet, you change the values in some cells and compare the recalculated spreadsheet results with hand calculations. See Figure 3-8. ●

Worksheets

Worksheets are used for a wide range of different applications. One of the most common uses is to create, analyze, and forecast budgets.

Text Entries

Text entries provide meaning to the values in the worksheet. The rows are labeled to identify the various sales and expense items. The columns are labeled to specify the months.

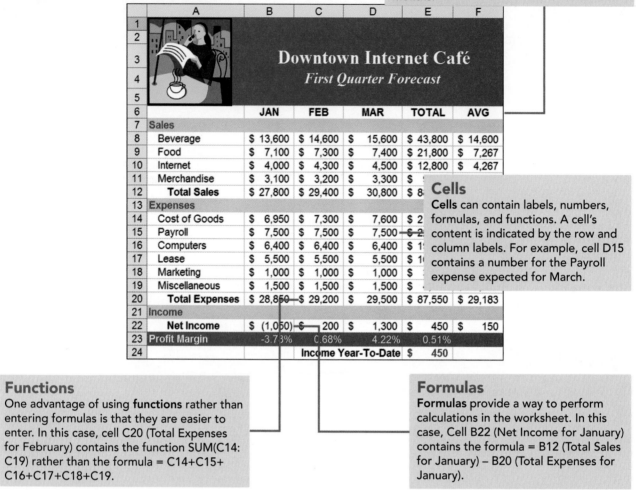

Cells

Cells can contain labels, numbers, formulas, and functions. A cell's content is indicated by the row and column labels. For example, cell D15 contains a number for the Payroll expense expected for March.

Functions

One advantage of using **functions** rather than entering formulas is that they are easier to enter. In this case, cell C20 (Total Expenses for February) contains the function SUM(C14: C19) rather than the formula = C14+C15+ C16+C17+C18+C19.

Formulas

Formulas provide a way to perform calculations in the worksheet. In this case, Cell B22 (Net Income for January) contains the formula = B12 (Total Sales for January) – B20 (Total Expenses for January).

Figure 3-8 Worksheet

creating a chart

After completing the First-Quarter Forecast for the Downtown Internet Café, you decide to *chart* the sales data to better visualize the projected growth in sales. You select the 3D column *chart type* to show each month's projected sales category. Using a variety of chart options, you enter descriptive *titles* for the chart, the x-axis, and the y-axis. Then you use *data labels* to focus attention on the growing Internet sales. Finally, you insert a *legend* to define the chart's different columns. See Figure 3-9. ●

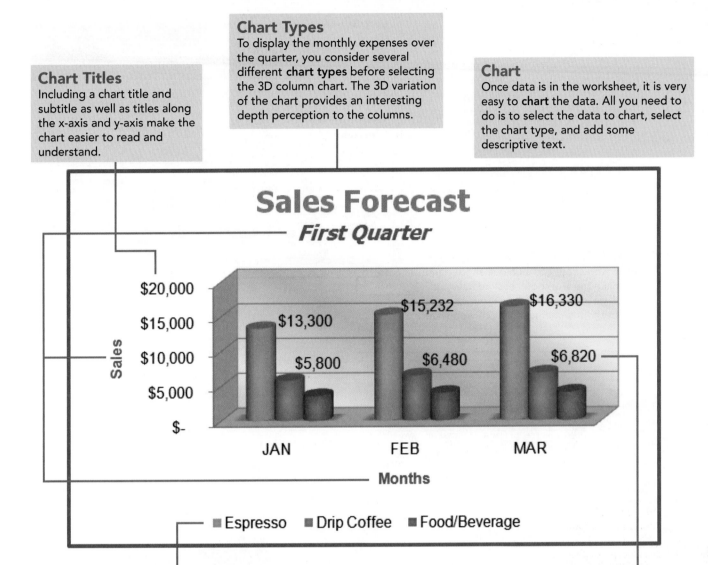

Chart Titles
Including a chart title and subtitle as well as titles along the x-axis and y-axis make the chart easier to read and understand.

Chart Types
To display the monthly expenses over the quarter, you consider several different **chart types** before selecting the 3D column chart. The 3D variation of the chart provides an interesting depth perception to the columns.

Chart
Once data is in the worksheet, it is very easy to **chart** the data. All you need to do is to select the data to chart, select the chart type, and add some descriptive text.

Legend
The **legend** defines each sales expense by a color. Legends are essential to charts that depict more than one set of data.

Data Labels
Data labels draw the viewer's attention to selected pieces of information in the chart.

Figure 3-9 **Chart**

analyzing your data

After presenting the First-Quarter Forecast to the owner, you revise the format and expand the *workbook* to include worksheets for each quarter and an annual forecast summary. You give each worksheet a descriptive *sheet name*. At the request of the owner, you perform a *what-if analysis* to test the effect of different estimates for payroll, and you use *Goal Seek* to determine how much Total Internet Sales would have to increase to produce a profit margin of 15 percent for the first quarter. See Figure 3-10.

Workbook

The first worksheet in a **workbook** is often a summary of the following worksheets. In this case, the first worksheet presents the entire year's forecast. The subsequent worksheets provide the details.

Sheet Name

Each worksheet has a unique **sheet name**. To make the workbook easy to navigate, it is a good practice to always use simple yet descriptive names for each worksheet.

What-If Analysis

What-if analysis is a very powerful and simple tool to test the effects of different assumptions in a spreadsheet.

Goal Seek

A common goal in many financial workbooks is to achieve a certain level of profit. **Goal seek** allows you to set a goal and then will analyze other parts of the workbook that would need to be adjusted to meet that goal.

Figure 3-10 Workbook

Database Management Systems

A **database** is a collection of related data. It is the electronic equivalent of a file cabinet. A **database management system (DBMS)** or **database manager** is a program that sets up, or structures, a database. It also provides tools to enter, edit, and retrieve data from the database. All kinds of individuals use databases, from teachers recording grades to police officers checking criminal histories. Colleges and universities use databases to keep records on their students, instructors, and courses. Organizations of all types maintain employee databases.

Three of the most widely used database management systems designed for microcomputers are Microsoft Access, Corel Paradox, and Lotus Approach.

Features

The **relational database** is the most widely used database structure. Data is organized into related **tables.** Each table is made up of rows called **records** and columns called **fields.** Each record contains fields of data about some specific person, place, or thing.

A DBMS provides a variety of tools to create and use databases. A **sort** tool will quickly rearrange a table's records according to a selected field. A **filter** tool will quickly display only those records meeting the conditions you specify.

The greatest power of a DBMS, however, comes from its ability to quickly find and bring together information stored in separate tables using queries, forms, and reports. A **query** is a question or a request for spe-

cific data contained in a database. Database **forms** look similar to traditional printed forms. These electronic forms are displayed on the computer monitor and typically reflect the contents for one record in a table. They are primarily used to enter new records and to make changes to existing records. Data from tables and queries can be printed in a variety of different types of **reports** from a simple listing of an entire field in a table to a list of selected fields based on a query involving several tables.

tips

Are you overwhelmed by your collection of music, videos, and books? **Would you like some help getting your life in order? Fortunately, Microsoft provides a variety of Access templates that might be just right for you. Here's how to find them:**

1 Connect to office.microsoft.com.

2 Click the *Templates* tab to display the Templates Web page. Type Access in the Templates search box and click the Search button.

3 Look through the templates and select the ones that might be valuable to you.

To see more tips, visit our Web site at www.computing2011.com and enter the keyword tips.

CONCEPT CHECK

What is a database? What is a DBMS? A relational database?

What are tables, records, and fields?

Describe the following DBMS features: sort, filter, query, form, and report.

Case

Assume that you have accepted a job as an employment administrator for the Lifestyle Fitness Club. One of your responsibilities is to create a database management system to replace the club's manual system for recording employee information. To see how you could use Microsoft Access, one of the most widely used relational DBMS programs, as the employment administrator for the Lifestyle Fitness Club, see Figures 3-11 and 3-12.

The first step in creating the database management system is to plan. You study the existing manual system focusing on how and what data is collected and how it is used. Next, you design the basic structure or organization of the new database system to have two related *tables,* which will make entering data and using the database more efficient. Focusing on the first table, Employees, you create the table structure by specifying the *fields,* and *primary key* field. To make the process faster and more accurate, you create a *form* and enter the data for each employee as a *record* in the table. See Figure 3-11. ●

Primary Key
The **primary key** is the unique employee identification number. You considered using the last name field as the primary key but realized that more than one employee could have the same last name. Primary keys are often used to link tables.

Fields
Fields are given field names that are displayed at the top of each table. You select the field names to describe their contents.

Table
Tables make up the basic structure of a relational database with columns containing field data and rows containing record information. This table records basic information about each employee, including name, address, and telephone number.

Record
Each **record** contains information about one employee. A record often includes a combination of numeric, text, and object data types.

Employee ID	Last Name	First Name	Address	City	State	ZIP	Home Phone	Gender	Birth Date	
12920	Larson					40	(941) 555-7717	F	6/21/1983	🖉(0)
13416	Lembi					41	(941) 555-4747	M	9/12/1979	🖉(0)
11747	Lettow					40	(507) 555-2805	M	11/15/1981	🖉(0)
22085	Lindau					41	(941) 555-6363	F	2/24/1977	🖉(0)
03406	Lopez					40	(507) 555-5050	F	2/25/1977	🖉(0)
04731	Marchant					41	(507) 555-6707	F	5/13/1980	🖉(2)
13543	Martinez	Julie	1920 First Ave.	Maldin	CA	92121-3740	(941) 555-1044	F	12/10/1982	🖉(0)
13635	Martinez	Juan	7115 E Roosevelt Dr.	Maldin	CA	92121-3740	(507) 555-2935	M	12/10/1983	🖉(0)
22407	Mazeau	Rebecca	7383 Oak Dr.	Landis	CA	92120-3741	(941) 555-1093	F	9/23/1979	🖉(0)
03225	Morgan	Dan	564 S. Lemon Dr.	Maldin	CA	92121	(507) 555-5567	M	3/5/1975	🖉(0)
99999	Name	Student	1234 N. Fifth St.	Chesterfield	CA	92121-1268	(507) 555-1234	F	4/1/1982	🖉(0)
00617	Nichols	Cathy	75 Brooklea Dr.	Landis	CA	92120-3741	(507) 555-0001	F	5/19/1965	🖉(0)
00907	Pennington	Mark	23 Mill Ave.	Landis	CA	92120-3741	(507) 555-3333	M	7/7/1969	🖉(0)
12194	Polonsky	Mitch	8701 E. Sheridan	Maldin	CA	92121-3740	(507) 555-1018	M	3/13/1980	🖉(0)
12247	Rath	Kathy	87 E. Aurora Ave.	Chesterfield	CA	92122-1268	(507) 555-9797	F	5/30/1978	🖉(0)
12594	Reddie	Mark	900 W. Campus Dr.	Maldin	CA	92121	(507) 555-1139	M	11/5/1983	🖉(0)
12230	Reddie	Suzanne	932 E. Parkway Dr.	Landis	CA	92120-3741	(507) 555-1191	F	7/14/1978	🖉(0)
13005	Reilly	Emily	125 N. Marigold St.	Maldin	CA	92121-3740	(941) 555-6532	F	5/21/1985	🖉(0)
12612	Richards	Melissa	5522 W. Marin Lane	River Mist	CA	92123	(507) 555-7789	F	9/30/1978	🖉(0)
06000	Robertson	Kirk	832 S. William Ave.	Maldin	CA	92121	(507) 555-3730	M	4/5/1974	🖉(0)
22297	Rogondino	Patricia	7583 Turquoise	Chesterfield	CA	92122-1268	(941) 555-7539	F	8/30/1977	🖉(0)
07287	Roman	Anita	2348 S. Bala Dr.	Maldin	CA	92121-3740	(507) 555-9870	F	3/15/1981	🖉(0)
12918	Ruiz	Carlos	10101 First St.	Maldin	CA	92121-3740	(507) 555-5125	M	7/27/1980	🖉(1)
08391	Ruiz	Enrique	35 Palm St.	Chesterfield	CA	92122-1268	(507) 555-0091	M	12/10/1973	🖉(0)
04321	Sabin	Greg	90 E. Rawhide Ave							
00212	Schiff	Chad	235 N. Cactus Dr.							
22114	Schneider	Paul	1731 Jackson Ave							
01421	Spehr	Timothy	90 Royal Dr.							
12366	Stacey	David	737 S. College Rd							
13497	Steele	Jeff	1011 E. Holly Ln.							
12668	Stueland	Valerie	34 University Dr.							
12583	Sullivan	Marie	78 Omega Drive							
12867	Talic	Elvis	21 Oasis St.							
03890	Thi	Erona	7867 Forest Ave.							
22304	Torcivia	Peter	904 S. Dorsey Dr.							

Form
Like printed paper forms, electronic **forms** should be designed to be easy to read and use. This form makes it easy to enter and view all employees' data, including their photographs.

Employee Records

Employee ID	12918
First Name	Carlos
Last Name	Ruiz
Address	10101 First St.
City	Maldin
State	CA
ZIP Code	92121-3740
Home Phone	(507) 555-5125
Gender	M
Birth Date	7/27/1980

Photo/Resume

Record: ◀ ◀ 41 of 55 ▶ ▶ No Filter   Search

Figure 3-11 Table and form

Query

Your **query** requests the names, addresses, and telephone numbers of all employees living in Maldin or Chesterfield who work in Landis.

Joined

Since the query involves two tables, they must be linked or **joined** by common fields. You chose to link the tables by the key field Employee ID.

Criteria

The query **criteria** to produce the car pool list requires that both the Employee Records table and the jobs table be consulted. The criteria identifies all employees who work at Landis and live either in Maldin or Chesterfield.

Report

From a variety of different **report** formats, you selected this format to display the names, addresses, and telephone numbers of all employees who might commute from either Maldin or Chesterfield to Landis.

Sorted

To make the report easier for employees to locate employees who live in the same city, you **sorted** the query results alphabetically by city.

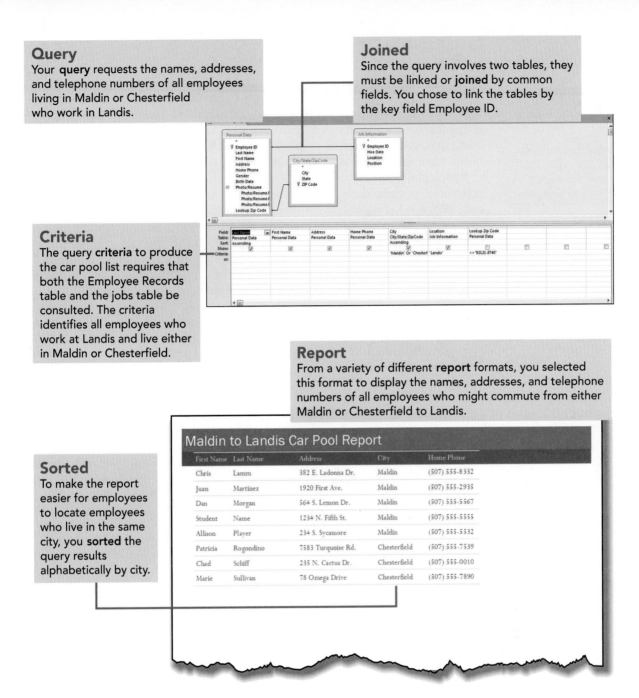

Maldin to Landis Car Pool Report

First Name	Last Name	Address	City	Home Phone
Chris	Lamm	382 E. Ladonna Dr.	Maldin	(507) 555-8332
Juan	Martinez	1920 First Ave.	Maldin	(507) 555-2935
Dan	Morgan	564 S. Lemon Dr.	Maldin	(507) 555-5567
Student	Name	1234 N. Fifth St.	Maldin	(507) 555-5555
Allison	Player	234 S. Sycamore	Maldin	(507) 555-5532
Patricia	Rogondino	7583 Turquoise Rd.	Chesterfield	(507) 555-7539
Chad	Schiff	235 N. Cactus Dr.	Chesterfield	(507) 555-0010
Marie	Sullivan	78 Omega Drive	Chesterfield	(507) 555-7890

Figure 3-12 Query and report

creating a query

You have continued to build the database by creating a second table named Job containing information about each employee's work location and job title. This table is linked or *joined* with the Employee Records table by the common field, Employee ID. After you completed this second table, you received a request to create car pool information for those employees who live in either Maldin or Chesterfield and work in Landis. You created a *query* using the appropriate *criteria* to create the car pool list. Then *sorting* alphabetically according to city, you created a *report* to distribute to interested employees. See Figure 3-12. ●

Presentation Graphics

On the Web Explorations

Lotus is one of the leaders in developing presentation graphics.

To learn more about the company, visit our Web site at www.computing2011 .com and enter the keyword lotus.

Research shows that people learn better when information is presented visually. A picture is indeed worth a thousand words or numbers. **Presentation graphics** are programs that combine a variety of visual objects to create attractive, visually interesting presentations. They are excellent tools to communicate a message and to persuade people.

People in a variety of settings and situations use presentation graphics programs to make their presentations more interesting and professional. For example, marketing managers use presentation graphics to present proposed marketing strategies to their superiors. Salespeople use these programs to demonstrate products and encourage customers to make purchases. Students use presentation graphics programs to create high-quality class presentations.

Three of the most widely used presentation graphics programs are Microsoft PowerPoint, Corel Presentations, and Apple Keynote.

Features

An electronic presentation consists of a series of **slides** or **pages.** Presentation programs include a variety of features to help you create effective dynamic presentations. Most include design and content templates that help you quickly create a professional-looking presentation. **Design templates** provide professionally selected combinations of color schemes, slide layouts, and special effects. **Content templates** include suggested content for each slide. Other features include tools to select alternative color schemes and slide layouts, to create animated graphics and charts, and to help you rehearse the presentation.

More advanced features include the capability to use **animations,** special effects that add action to text and graphics on a slide. Additionally, **transitions** can be used to animate how the presentation moves from one slide to the next. Other features allow you to print slides, create speaker notes, and provide handouts for your audience.

 CONCEPT CHECK

 What are presentation graphics programs? What are they used for?

 What are slides? What are design and content templates? What are they used for?

 What are animations and transitions? What are they used for?

Case

Assume that you have volunteered for the Animal Rescue Foundation, a local animal rescue agency. You have been asked to create a powerful and persuasive presentation to encourage other members from your community to volunteer. To see how you could use Microsoft PowerPoint, one of the most widely used presentation graphics programs, as a volunteer for the Animal Rescue Foundation, see Figures 3-13 and 3-14.

creating a presentation

You start creating the presentation using the Presentation on Product or Service *template*. The template consists of a sample presentation containing suggested content in each slide and uses a consistent design style throughout. After replacing the sample content, you are on your way to the director's office to show what you have. See Figure 3-13.

Customize the Template

You customize the presentation by replacing the sample text and modifying the design as needed. This includes inserting and deleting slides as needed, rearranging slide order, and inserting graphics and pictures.

How Does The Foundation Help?

- Provide temporary homes
- Provide obedience training
- Provide veterinary care
- Find loving permanent homes

Who Is An Animal Angel?

- Believes unwanted pets deserve a home
- Believes you can teach an old dog new
- Believes you can retrain animals to be

Join Animal Angels

Animal Rescue Foundation

Templates

Templates provide an excellent way to quickly create a presentation by providing predesigned styles and layouts as well as suggested content based on the type of template you select.

Figure 3-13 Presentation

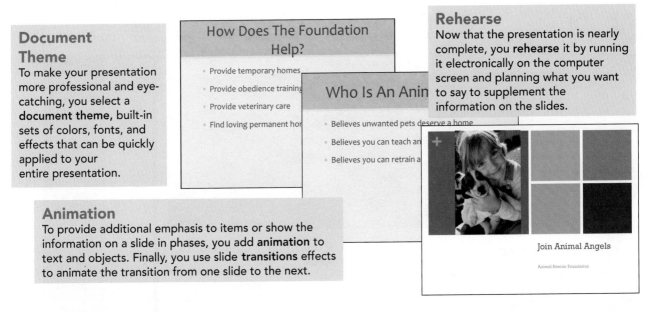

Document Theme

To make your presentation more professional and eye-catching, you select a **document theme**, built-in sets of colors, fonts, and effects that can be quickly applied to your entire presentation.

How Does The Foundation Help?

- Provide temporary homes
- Provide obedience training
- Provide veterinary care
- Find loving permanent hor

Who Is An Anin

- Believes unwanted pets deserve a home
- Believes you can teach an
- Believes you can retrain a

Rehearse

Now that the presentation is nearly complete, you **rehearse** it by running it electronically on the computer screen and planning what you want to say to supplement the information on the slides.

Join Animal Angels

Animal Rescue Foundation

Animation

To provide additional emphasis to items or show the information on a slide in phases, you add **animation** to text and objects. Finally, you use slide **transitions** effects to animate the transition from one slide to the next.

Figure 3-14 Revised presentation

updating a presentation

After discussing the presentation with the director, you have some ideas to enhance the effectiveness of the message. First, you select a different document theme to change the colors, fonts, and effects used throughout the presentation. Then to add interest to the presentation as it is running, you add animation and transition effects. Then you add animations to selected objects and add slide transition effects. Finally, you practice or rehearse the presentation, create speaker notes, and print out audience handouts. You're ready to give a professionally designed, dynamic presentation. See Figure 3-14. ●

Integrated Packages

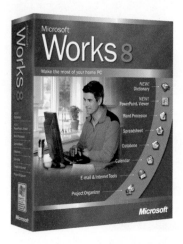

Figure 3-15 Microsoft Works

An **integrated package** is a single program that provides the *functionality* of a word processor, spreadsheet, database manager, and more. The primary disadvantage of an integrated package is that the capabilities of each function (such as word processing) are not as extensive as in the individual programs (such as Microsoft Word). The primary advantages are cost and simplicity. The cost of an integrated package is much less than the cost of the individual powerful, professional-grade application programs discussed thus far in this chapter.

Integrated packages are popular with many home users and are sometimes classified as **personal** or **home software.** The most widely used integrated package is Microsoft Works. See Figure 3-15. AppleWorks is also widely used. Both products, however, have been recently discontinued.

Case

Assume that you publish a gardening newsletter that you distribute to members of the Desert Gardening Club. Using the word processing function, you entered text, formatted titles and subtitles, and inserted several photographs. (See Figure 3-16.) Using the spreadsheet function, you analyzed daily rainfall

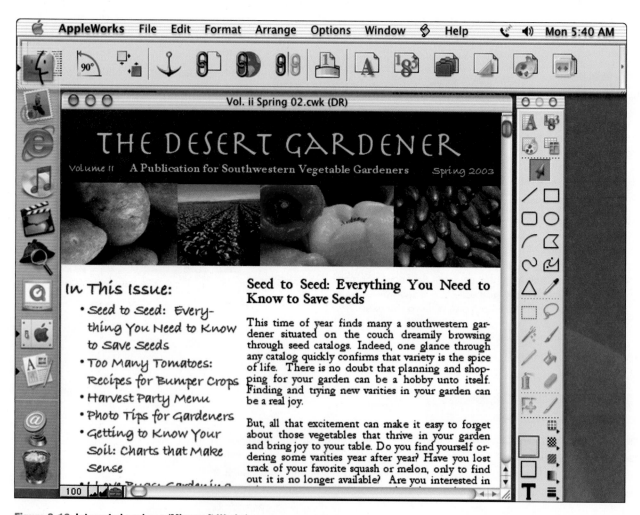

Figure 3-16 Integrated package (Microsoft Works)

for the feature article and included a chart. After completing the newsletter, you will use the database function and the membership database to print mailing labels.

CONCEPT CHECK

What is an integrated package?

Describe the advantages and disadvantages of an integrated package.

Figure 3-17 Microsoft Office

Software Suites

A **software suite** is a collection of separate application programs bundled together and made available as a group. While the applications function exactly the same whether purchased in a suite or separately, it is significantly less expensive to buy a suite of applications than to buy each application separately. There are four basic categories of software suites:

- **Productivity suite.** Productivity suites, also known as **office software suites** or simply **office suites** contain professional-grade application programs that are typically used in a business situation. Productivity suites commonly include a word processor, spreadsheet, database manager, and a presentation application. The best known is Microsoft Office. (See Figure 3-17.) Other well-known productivity suites are Apple iWork, Sun StarOffice, Corel WordPerfect Office Suite, and Lotus SmartSuite.

- **Alternative office suites.** Traditionally, when you purchase an office suite you are licensed to use the application and a copy of the software is stored on your computer. Recently, several alternative office suites are available for free as downloadable software or as online applications. The **downloadable office suites** are stored on your desktop computer just like the traditional office suites. The **online office suites** are stored online and are available anywhere you can access the Internet. Documents created using online applications can also be stored online, making it easy to share and collaborate on documents with others. However, the downside to online applications is that you are dependent upon the server providing the application to be available whenever you need it. For this reason, when using online applications, it is important to have backup copies of your documents on your computer and to have a desktop office application available to use. Documents created using these applications are compatible with Microsoft Office. Popular downloadable office suites include StarOffice, IBM Lotus Symphony, and OpenOffice. Popular online office suites are Google Docs, Zoho, and ThinkSmart. (See Figure 3-18.) To learn more about one of the most widely used online office suites, see Making IT Work for You: Google Docs on pages 86 and 87.

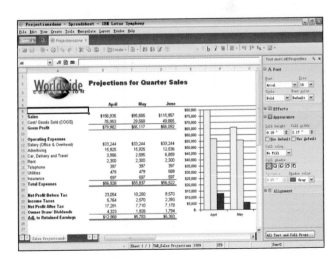

Figure 3-18 IBM Lotus Symphony

GOOGLE DOCS

Do you need to collaborate with others on a document, presentation, or spreadsheet? Do you need access to a document from both home and school? Would you like to try a free alternative to traditional office software suites? If so, an online office suite might be for you. Online office suites, such as Google Docs, allow you to create and edit documents directly though a Web page with no additional software to install on your computer.

Creating a Document   To create a new online document:

1
●   **Visit http://docs.google.com. Follow the on-screen instructions to create a free Google account if you do not already have one.**

●   **Click the *New* button.**

●   **Select the type of document you want to create, such as a word processing document, presentation, or spreadsheet.**

The new document is dispayed and can be edited directly through the Web page.

Sharing a Document To give others access to view and edit your document:

1 ● Click the *Share* button.

● Select *Invite people*. . .

2 ● Enter the e-mail addresses of people to invite.

● Optionally enter a brief message to the people you are inviting.

● Click the *Send* button.

The people you invited will receive an e-mail with instructions for accessing your document. You will be able to see any changes others make to the document, and they will see yours.

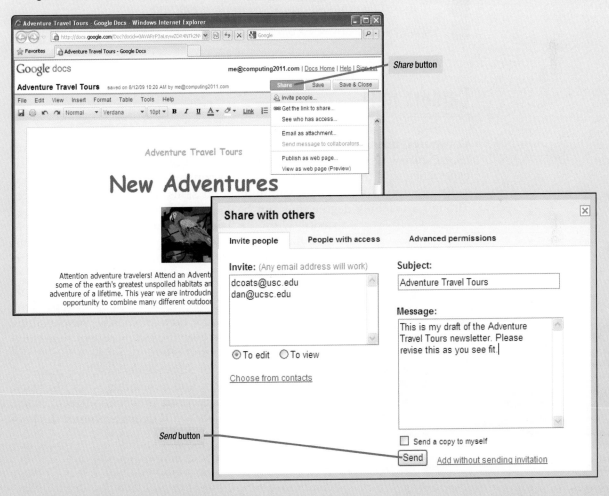

The Web is continually changing, and some of the specifics presented in Making IT Work for You may have changed.

To learn about other ways to make information technology work for you, visit our Web site at www.computing2011.com and enter the keyword miw.

- **Specialized suite.** Specialized suites focus on specific applications. These include graphics suites, financial planning suites, and many others. (Graphics suites will be discussed in Chapter 4.)
- **Utility suite.** These suites include a variety of programs designed to make computing easier and safer. Two of the best known are Norton System-Works and Norton Internet Security Suite. (Utility suites will be discussed in detail in Chapter 5.)

Many times it is convenient to share data between applications. For example, when writing a report, it may be useful to include a chart from a spreadsheet or data from a database. Data created by one application can be shared with another application in a variety of different ways, including copying and pasting, object linking, and object embedding. To learn more about sharing data between applications, visit us on the Web at www.computing2011.com and enter the keyword **sharing**.

CONCEPT CHECK

What is a software suite? What are the advantages of purchasing a suite?

List and describe four categories of software suites?

What is the difference between a productivity suite and a utility suite?

What is the difference between a downloadable and an online office suite?

Careers in IT

Computer trainers instruct new users on the latest software or hardware. (See Figure 3.19.) Many computer training positions are offered to those with experience with the most popular business software.

Employers look for good communication skills and teaching experience. Though a teaching degree may not be required, it may be preferred. Experience with the latest software and/or hardware is essential, but this varies depending on the position. Employers often seek detail-oriented individuals with IT experience.

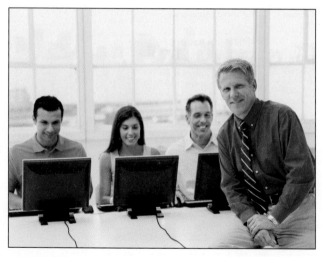

Computer trainers can expect to earn an annual salary of $25,000 to $50,500. However, salary is dependent on experience and may vary drastically. Responsibilities typically include preparation of course materials, grading coursework, and continuing education in the field. Opportunities for advancement include management of other trainers and consulting work. To learn more about other careers in information technology, visit us at www.computing2011.com and enter the keyword **careers**.

Figure 3-19 Computer trainer

A LOOK TO THE FUTURE

Agents Will Help Write Papers, Pay Bills, and Shop on the Internet

Wouldn't it be great to have your own personal assistant? Your assistant could research topics for a term paper, collect relevant information, and even suggest famous quotes that apply to your topic. Your assistant could monitor your personal budget using a spreadsheet and even evaluate the impact of a rental income. Or your assistant could punch up a classroom presentation by suggesting and locating relevant photos and videos. All this is likely with special programs called *agents.*

An agent is an intelligent program that can understand your needs and act to fulfill those needs. Today, primitive agents already exist in

many help tools to interpret user questions and to formulate appropriate responses. Computer scientists at the University of Maryland are working on the next-generation agents that may provide the most efficient way to locate information on the Web. These agents promise to understand words and the context in which they are used. They will locate Web sites that not only have the *words* you are looking for but also the *meaning.* This future is not far off, but as agent technology improves, it is only a matter of time until agents act in more autonomous ways and can help you use basic applications to do complex tasks, like prepare an essay, a budget, or a presentation.

What do you think? Should we all have our own personal agent to help us write papers, pay bills, and shop on the Internet?

VISUAL SUMMARY Basic Application Software

APPLICATION SOFTWARE

Button

Dialog box

Menu bar

Toolbar

Portabella's Garden Café

There are two basic types of software. **System software** focuses on handling technical details. **Application software** focuses on completing specific tasks or applications. Two categories are **basic applications** and **specialized applications**.

Common Features

You control and interact with a program using a **user interface**. A **graphical user interface (GUI)** uses **icons** selected by a mouse-controlled **pointer**. A **window** contains a document, program, or message. Most software programs, including Microsoft Office 2003, also have

- **Menus**—present commands listed on the **menu bar.**
- **Dialog box**—provides additional information or requests user input.
- **Toolbars**—contain **buttons** for quick access to commonly used commands.

Microsoft Office 2010 uses and interface introduced with Microsoft Office 2007 which includes

- **Ribbons** replace menus and toolbars.
- **Tabs** divide ribbons into major activity areas organized into **groups. Contextual tabs** automatically appear when needed.
- **Galleries** display graphic representations of alternatives.

Some applications support **speech recognition** by allowing voice input.

WORD PROCESSORS

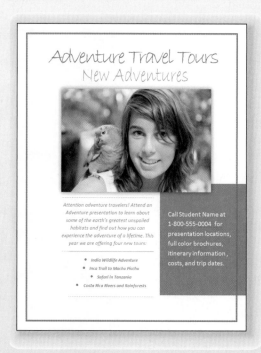

Word processors allow you to create, edit, save, and print text-based **documents**, including flyers, reports, newsletters, and Web pages.

Features

Word wrap is a basic feature that automatically moves the insertion point to the next line. **Editing** features include

- **Thesaurus,** which provides synonyms, antonyms, and related words.
- **Find and replace,** which locates (finds), removes, and inserts (replaces) another word(s).
- **Spelling** and **grammar checkers,** which automatically locate misspelled words and grammatical problems.

Formatting features include

- **Font**—design of characters. **Font size** is the height of characters.
- **Character effects**—include **bold,** *italic,* and **colors.**
- **Styles**—feature that quickly applies predefined formats.
- **Bulleted** and **numbered lists**—used to present sequences of topics or steps.

To be a competent end user, you need to understand the capabilities of basic application software, which includes word processors, spreadsheets, database management systems, and presentation programs. You need to know how to use these applications and how data can be shared between them.

SPREADSHEETS

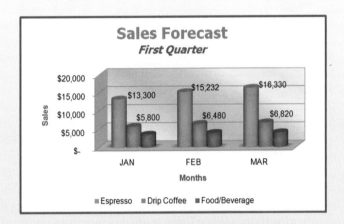

Sales Forecast
First Quarter

Spreadsheet programs are used to organize, analyze, and graph numeric data.

Features

Principal spreadsheet features include the following

- **Workbook files** consist of one or more related worksheets.
- **Worksheets,** also known as **spreadsheets** or **sheets,** are rectangular grids of **rows** and **columns.** Rows are identified by numbers, columns by letters.
- **Cells** are formed by the intersection of a row and column; used to hold text and numeric entries.
- **Text entries (labels)** provide structure and **numeric entries** can be numbers or formulas.
- **Formulas** are instructions for calculations. **Functions** are prewritten formulas.
- **Range** is a series of cells.
- **Analytical graphs (charts)** represent data visually.
- **Recalculation** occurs whenever a value changes in one cell that affects another cell(s).
- **What-if analysis** is the process of observing the effect of changing one or more values.

DATABASE MANAGEMENT SYSTEMS

A **database** is a collection of related data. A **database management system (DBMS),** also known as a **database manager,** structures a database and provides tools for manipulating data.

Features

Principal database management system features include the following

- **Relational database** organizes data into related tables.
- **Tables** have rows (**records**) and columns (**fields**).
- **Sort** is a tool to rearrange records.
- **Filter** is a tool to display only those records meeting specified conditions.
- **Query** is a question or request for specific data contained in a database.
- **Forms** are used to enter and edit records.
- **Reports** are printed output in a variety of forms.

PRESENTATION GRAPHICS

Join Animal Angels

Animal Rescue Foundation

Presentation graphics combine a variety of visual objects to create attractive, visually interesting presentations. They are excellent tools to communicate a message and to persuade people.

Features

Principal presentation graphics features include the following:

- **Slides**—individual **pages** or screens of a presentation.
- **Design templates**—professionally selected combination of color schemes, slide layouts, and special effects.
- **Content templates**—provide suggested content for each slide.
- **Animation**—adds action to text and graphics. **Transitions** animate moving from one slide to the next.

INTEGRATED PACKAGES

An **integrated package,** also known as **personal** or **home software,** is a single program that provides the functionality of several application packages. Some important characteristics include

- Functions that typically include word processing, spreadsheet, database manager, and more. Each function is not as extensive or powerful as a single-function application program.
- Less expensive than purchasing several individual application programs and simple to use.
- Popular with home users who are willing to sacrifice some advanced features for cost and simplicity.

SOFTWARE SUITES

A **software suite** is a collection of individual application packages sold together.

- **Productivity suites (office software suites** or **office suites)** contain professional-grade application programs.
- **Alternative office suites** include **downloadable office suites** (stored on your computer) or **online office suites** (stored online).
- **Specialized suites** focus on specific applications such as graphics.
- **Utility suites** include a variety of programs designed to make computing easier and safer.

CAREERS IN IT

Computer trainers instruct new users on the latest software or hardware. Teaching degree is preferred and experience with latest software and/or hardware is essential. Salary range $25,000 to $50,500.

KEY TERMS

analytical graph   (74)
animation   (82)
application software   (66)
basic application   (66)
bulleted list   (71)
button   (66)
cell   (73)
character effect   (71)
chart   (73)
column   (73)
computer trainer   (88)
content template   (82)
contextual tab   (67)
database   (78)
database management system
   (DBMS)   (78)
database manager   (78)
design template   (82)
dialog box   (66)
document   (70)
downloadable office suite   (85)
editing   (70)
field   (79)
find and replace   (70)
filter   (79)
font   (71)
font size   (71)
form   (79)
format   (70)
formula   (74)
function   (74)
gallery   (67)
grammar checker   (70)
graphical user interface (GUI)   (66)
group   (67)
home software   (84)
icons   (66)
integrated package   (84)
label   (74)
menu   (66)
menu bar   (66)
numbered list   (71)

numeric entry   (74)
office software suite   (85)
office suite   (85)
online office suite   (85)
page   (82)
personal software   (84)
pointer   (66)
presentation graphics   (82)
productivity suite   (85)
query   (79)
range   (74)
recalculation   (75)
record   (79)
relational database   (79)
report   (79)
ribbon   (67)
row   (73)
sheet   (73)
slide   (82)
software suite   (85)
sort   (79)
specialized application   (66)
specialized suite   (88)
speech recognition   (67)
spelling checker   (70)
spreadsheet   (73)
styles   (71)
system software   (66)
tab   (67)
table   (79)
text entry   (74)
thesaurus   (70)
toolbar   (66)
transition   (82)
user interface   (66)
utility suite   (88)
what-if analysis   (75)
window   (66)
word processor   (70)
word wrap   (70)
workbook file   (73)
worksheet   (73)

To test your knowledge of these key terms with animated flash cards, visit our Web site at www.computing2011.com and enter the keyword terms3.

MULTIPLE CHOICE

Circle the letter or fill in the correct answer.

1. This type of software works with end users, application software, and computer hardware to handle the majority of technical details.
   - **a.** application software
   - **b.** communications software
   - **c.** system software
   - **d.** Web software

2. _____ are narrowly focused on specific disciplines and occupations.
   - **a.** Basic applications
   - **b.** Business suites
   - **c.** Specialized applications
   - **d.** Utility programs

3. The primary purpose of this type of software is to create text-based documents.
   - **a.** spreadsheet
   - **b.** presentation
   - **c.** word processing
   - **d.** Web development

4. Organizations create newsletters, manuals, and brochures with this type of software.
   - **a.** graphics
   - **b.** presentation
   - **c.** spreadsheet
   - **d.** word processing

5. Letters, memos, term papers, reports, and contracts are all examples of
   - **a.** models
   - **b.** spreadsheets
   - **c.** documents
   - **d.** menus

6. Numbers and formulas entered in a cell are called
   - **a.** labels
   - **b.** numeric entries
   - **c.** intersection
   - **d.** text

7. The acronym DBMS stands for what?
   - **a.** double-blind management setup
   - **b.** document binder management system
   - **c.** data binding and marketing structure
   - **d.** database management system

8. Database _____ are primarily used to enter new records and to make changes to existing records.
   - **a.** reports
   - **b.** tables
   - **c.** forms
   - **d.** queries

9. A file that includes predefined settings that can be used to create many common types of presentations is called a
   - **a.** pattern
   - **b.** model
   - **c.** template
   - **d.** blueprint

10. A(n) _____ is a single program that provides the functionality of a word processor, spreadsheet, database manager, and more.
    - **a.** specialized application
    - **b.** integrated package
    - **c.** basic application
    - **d.** software suite

For an interactive multiple-choice practice test, visit our Web site at www.computing-2011.com and enter the keyword multiple3.

MATCHING

Match each numbered item with the most closely related lettered item. Write your answers in the spaces provided.

a. analytical
b. cell
c. integrated package
d. range
e. relational database
f. software suite
g. sort
h. spelling checker
i. what-if analysis
j. window

1. Area that contains a document, program, or message. _____
2. Type of graph or chart. _____
3. Includes the functionality of a word processor, spreadsheet, database manager, and more. _____
4. Identifies incorrectly spelled words and suggests alternatives. _____
5. The intersection of a row and column in a spreadsheet. _____
6. A collection of two or more cells in a spreadsheet. _____
7. Spreadsheet feature in which changing one or more numbers results in the automatic recalculation of all related fields. _____
8. Database structure that organizes data into related tables. _____
9. Arranging objects numerically or alphabetically. _____
10. Collection of individual applications that are bundled together. _____

For an interactive matching practice test, visit our Web site at www.computing 2011.com and enter the keyword matching3.

OPEN-ENDED

On a separate sheet of paper, respond to each question or statement.

1. Explain the difference between general-purpose and special-purpose applications.
2. Discuss the common features of most software programs. Describe the new interface introduced with Microsoft Office 2007 and used with Microsoft 2010.
3. What is the difference between a function and a formula? How is a formula related to what-if analysis?
4. What are presentation graphics programs? How are they used?
5. What is the difference between an integrated package and a software suite? What are the advantages and disadvantages of each?

APPLYING TECHNOLOGY

The following questions are designed to demonstrate ways that you can effectively use technology today. The first question relates directly to this chapter's Making IT Work for You feature.

1 SPEECH RECOGNITION

Tired of using your keyboard? Have you ever thought about speaking to your computer? Perhaps speech recognition is for you. To learn more about speech recognition, review Making IT Work for You: Speech Recognition on pages 68 and 69. Then answer the following questions: (a) What menu item is selected to begin training the software? (b) What are the verbal commands to start the Microsoft Word application? (c) Have you ever used speech recognition? If you have, describe how you used it and discuss how effective it was for you. If you have not, discuss how you might use it in the future. Be specific.

2 PRESENTATION GRAPHICS

For presentations, having the right software can help grab your audience's attention. Connect to our Web site at www.computing2011.com and enter the keyword presentation to link to a presentation graphics software package. Once connected, review the product's features and answer the following questions: (a) What computer hardware and software are required to use the presentation graphics product? (b) List and describe three features that could help you organize or present your ideas. (c) What types of files can be embedded with a presentation using this software?

3 OFFICE SUITES

Microsoft is the leader in the office suite market, but several competing suites are also available. Visit our site at www.computing2011.com and enter the keyword office to connect to a maker of office suites. Review the site, and then answer the following questions: (a) What applications are provided in the suite? (b) What are the similarities and differences between the Microsoft and the competing office suite? (c) Which suite would you choose? Why?

EXPANDING YOUR KNOWLEDGE

The following questions are designed to add depth and detail to your understanding of specific topics presented within this chapter. The questions direct you to sources other than the textbook to obtain this knowledge.

1 HOW SPEECH RECOGNITION WORKS

Speech recognition is an emerging technology. To learn how speech recognition works, visit our Web site at www.computing2011.com and enter the keyword speech. Then answer the following: (a) Create a drawing similar to the one on our Web site that would represent dictating a mailing address for an address label. (b) What hardware is required to use voice recognition software? (c) Describe how speech recognition could enhance your use of each of the following types of applications: word processing, spreadsheet, and presentation. (d) Describe a profession that could benefit from speech recognition software. Be specific.

2 SHARING DATA BETWEEN APPLICATIONS

Sharing data between applications can be very convenient and can greatly increase your productivity. The three most common ways to share information are copy and paste, object linking, and object embedding. To learn more about sharing data between applications, visit out Web site at www.computing2011.com and enter the keyword sharing. Then respond to the following: (a) Discuss how copy and paste works. Provide a specific example. (b) What is the difference between object linking and object embedding? Provide specific examples. (c) Describe a specific situation in which you might use all three types of sharing data between applications.

3 SHAREWARE

One way to acquire new application software is by downloading shareware. Conduct a Web search for shareware programs. Connect to and explore a shareware site offering a program that might interest you. Then respond to the following: (a) What is shareware? Who creates it? (b) What does shareware cost to use? What about support if you have a problem using it? (c) What are the risks of using shareware? Be thorough. (d) Would you use shareware? Why or why not?

WRITING ABOUT TECHNOLOGY

The ability to think critically and to write effectively is essential to nearly every profession. The following questions are designed to help you develop these skills by posing thought-provoking questions about computer privacy, security, and/or ethics.

1 ACQUIRING SOFTWARE

There are three common ways to obtain new software: use public domain software, use shareware, buy commercial software. In addition to these three ways, two others are to copy programs from a friend or to purchase unauthorized copies of programs. Investigate each of these five options, and then answer the following in a one-page paper: (a) Define and discuss each option. Be sure to discuss both the advantages and disadvantages of each. (b) Which seems like the best method to you? Why? (c) Do you think there is anything wrong with obtaining and using unauthorized software? Identify and explore the key issues.

2 SOFTWARE STANDARDS

Most of the products you encounter every day, such as cars, electronics, and food, are required by law to meet certain conditions to ensure your safety and a minimum level of quality. Software, however, can be written by anyone with few of these constraints. Fortunately, some standards of certification do exist. Research a certification program for software vendors. Write a one-page paper to answer the following: (a) Describe the certification program you selected. What type of software is it intended for? (b) What requirements must software meet to receive certification? (c) Who performs the software tests to ensure compliance? (d) As a consumer of software, what additional certification requirements would you like to see? Explain your answer.

NOTES

Specialized Application Software

Competencies

After you have read this chapter, you should be able to:

1 Describe graphics software, including desktop publishing, image editors, illustration programs, image galleries, and graphics suites.

2 Discuss audio and video editing software.

3 Describe multimedia, including links, buttons, and multimedia authoring programs.

4 Explain Web authoring, Web site design, and Web authoring programs.

5 Describe artificial intelligence and virtual reality.

6 Discuss knowledge-based (expert) systems.

7 Describe robotics including perception systems, industrial robots, mobile robots, and household robots.

Only a few years ago, to produce an album you would need an expensive recording studio, professional musicians, and experts to run the equipment. Today's specialized application software makes it possible to record music without these expenses. Now to write, produce, record, and play an album digitally, you need a basic computer and readily available hardware and software.

Some experts suggest that someday you might even be able to create virtual digital personalities to tour and perform your music. Imagine a world where you could watch your virtual band perform your newest album from the comfort of your living room, using only your personal computer.

chapter 4

Introduction

Expect surprises—exciting and positive opportunities. The latest technological developments offer you new opportunities to extend your range of computer competency. As we show in this chapter, software that for years was available only for larger computers has become available for microcomputers. This new generation of specialized application makes it possible to perform advanced tasks at home.

For example, it is now possible, and quite common, for people to create their own Web sites. Home users also have access to software that helps manipulate and create graphic images. Many musicians and artists work from home to create complex and beautiful work using specialized applications.

Some of these same technological advances have allowed researchers and computer scientists to make advances in the field of artificial intelligence that previously were envisioned only in science fiction. Robots now provide security and assistance in homes. Virtual reality is providing opportunities in the fields of medicine and science but also commonly appears in video games.

Competent end users need to be aware of specialized applications. They need to know who uses them, what they are used for, and how they are used. These advanced applications include graphics programs, audio and video editing software, multimedia, Web authoring, and artificial intelligence, including virtual reality, knowledge-based systems, and robotics.

Specialized Applications

In the previous chapter, we discussed basic applications that are widely used in nearly every profession. This chapter focuses on specialized applications that are widely used within specific professions. (See Figure 4-1.) Specifically, we will examine

- Graphics programs for creating professional-looking published documents, for creating and editing images, and for locating and inserting graphics.
- Audio and video software to create, edit, and play music and videos.
- Multimedia programs to create dynamic interactive presentations.
- Web authoring programs to create, edit, and design Web sites.
- Artificial intelligence, including virtual reality, knowledge-based systems, and robotics.

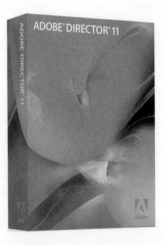

Figure 4-1 Specialized applications

Graphics

In Chapter 3, we discussed analytical and presentation graphics, which are widely used to analyze data and to create professional-looking presentations. Here we focus on more specialized graphics programs used by professionals in the graphic arts profession.

Desktop Publishing

Desktop publishing programs, or **page layout programs,** allow you to mix text and graphics to create publications of professional quality. While word processors focus on creating text and have the ability to combine text and graphics, desktop publishers focus on page design and layout and provide greater flexibility. Professional graphic artists use desktop publishing programs to create documents such as brochures, newsletters, newspapers, and textbooks.

Popular desktop publishing programs include Adobe InDesign, Microsoft Publisher, and QuarkXPress. While these programs provide the capability to create text and graphics, typically graphic artists import these elements from other sources, including word processors, digital cameras, scanners, image editors, illustration programs, and image galleries.

Image Editors

One of the most common types of graphic files is bitmap. **Bitmap images,** also known as **raster images,** use thousands of dots or **pixels** to represent images. Each dot has a specific location, color, and shade. One limitation of bitmap images, however, is that when they are expanded, the images can become pixilated, or jagged on the edges. For example, when the letter A in Figure 4-2 is expanded, the borders of the letter appear jagged, as indicated by the expanded view.

Image editors, also known as **photo editors,** are specialized graphics programs for editing or modifying digital photographs. Popular image editors include Adobe Photoshop, Corel Paint Shop Pro, and Paint.NET. (See Figure 4-3.)

Letter A

Expanded view

Figure 4-2 Bitmap image

Paint Tools

Filter

Brush

Pen

Figure 4-3 Adobe Photoshop

Figure 4-4 Vector image

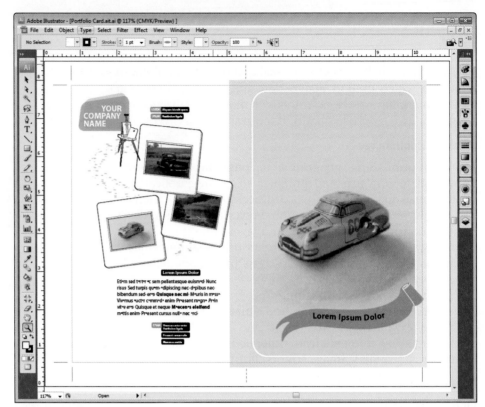

Figure 4-5 Adobe Illustrator

On the Web Explorations

Graphics programs have made desktop publishing affordable and available to the average user.

To learn more about a leading developer of powerful graphics programs, visit our Web site at www.computing2011.com and enter the keyword graphics.

Illustration Programs

Vector is another common type of graphic file. While bitmap images use pixels to represent images, **vector images,** also known as **vector illustrations,** use geometric shapes or objects. (See Figure 4-4.) These objects are created by connecting lines and curves. Because these objects can be defined by mathematical equations, they can be rapidly and easily resized, colored, textured, and manipulated. An image is a combination of several objects. **Illustration programs,** also known as **drawing programs,** are used to create and edit vector images.

Popular illustration programs include Adobe Illustrator, CorelDRAW, and Inkscape. (See Figure 4-5.)

Image Galleries

Image galleries are libraries of electronic images. These images are used for a wide variety of applications from illustrating textbooks to providing visual interest to presentations. There are two basic types of electronic images in these galleries:

- **Stock photographs**—photographs on a variety of subject material from people to landscapes.
- **Clip art**—graphic illustrations representing a wide range of topics. Most applications provide access to a limited selection of free clip art. For example, in Microsoft Word, you can gain access to several pieces of clip art by issuing the command Insert>Clip Art.

There are numerous Web image galleries. (See Figure 4-6.) Some of these sites offer free images and clip art while others charge a fee.

Organization	Site
Classroom Clipart	www.classroomclipart.com
ClipArt.com	www.clipart.com
Graphics Factory	www.graphicsfactory.com
MS Office clip art	office.microsoft.com/clipart
iStockphoto	istockphoto.com
Flickr Creative Commons	www.flickr.com/creativecommons/

Figure 4-6 Selected Web image galleries

Graphics Suites

Some companies have combined or bundled their separate graphics programs in groups called **graphics suites.** The advantage of the graphics suites is that you can buy a larger variety of graphics programs at a lower cost than if purchased separately.

Two popular suites are CorelDRAW Graphics Suite and Adobe Creative Suite. CorelDRAW Graphics Suite includes five individual graphics programs plus a large library of clip art, media clips, and fonts. (See Figure 4-7.)

 CONCEPT CHECK

What is desktop publishing?

What is the difference between an image editor and an illustration program?

Describe image galleries. What are graphics suites?

Figure 4-7 CorelDRAW Graphics Suite

Audio and Video

In the past, professional-quality editing of home audio and video was a job for professional photo labs or studios. For example, if you wanted to assemble footage from all your Fourth of July picnics, you sent all the tapes to a lab and waited for a compilation tape. Now, using audio and video editing software, you can create your own compilation movies.

- **Video editing software** allows you to reorganize, add effects, and more to your digital video footage. Two commonly used video editing software programs are Apple iMovie and Windows Movie Maker. (See Figure 4-8.) These programs are designed to allow you to assemble and edit new home videos and movies from raw digital video footage. To see how digital video editors work, visit our Web site at www.computing2011.com and enter the keyword **video.** To learn how to use a digital video editor, see Making IT Work for You: Digital Video Editing on pages 106 and 107.

Figure 4-8 Apple iMovie

Making IT work for you

DIGITAL VIDEO EDITING

Do you want to make your own movie? Would you like to edit some home movies and distribute them to family and friends on DVDs? It's easy with the right equipment and software.

Capturing Video   You can capture video to your computer from a device such as a digital camcorder. Once captured, the video can be edited using digital video editing software. Follow the steps below to capture video from a digital camcorder using Windows Vista.

1 ● Connect the digital camcorder to your computer and turn it on.

● Select *Import Video*.

● Enter a name and select a location to save the imported video.

2 ● Select the portion of the video to import. You can import the entire video or only a particular section.

3 ● Preview the video as it is captured from your camera to the file you specified.

Editing a Movie Windows Movie Maker divides your captured video into clips, or scenes that make up your movie. Follow the steps below to create a movie by arranging clips and adding special effects.

1 ● Drag movie clips from the Contents Pane and arrange them in the Storyboard.

● Use the options in the Tasks Pane to add sounds, transitions, title screens, and effects to your movie.

● Use the Preview Monitor to preview your movie.

Tasks Pane

Contents Pane

Storyboard   Preview Monitor

Creating a DVD Once you have edited your movies, you can create a DVD to share with friends and family. You will need a DVD writer and a blank writable DVD. Follow the steps below to design a menu, add movies, and create your DVD.

1 ● Launch Windows DVD Maker, and click the *Choose Photos and Videos* button.

● Select the video file you created with Windows Movie Maker in the previous step.

● Click *Next* button.

2 ● Select a menu style that will be displayed when your DVD is played.

● Insert a writable DVD in your DVD drive and click the *Burn* button to create your DVD.

The Web is continually changing, and some of the specifics presented in this Making IT Work for You may have changed.

To learn about other ways to make information technology work for you, visit our Web site at www.computing2011.com and enter the keyword miw.

Figure 4-9 Apple GarageBand

- **Audio editing software** allows you to create and edit audio clips. Most audio editing software also has features that allow you to add audio effects, like filters, to your tracks. For example, you can use this type of software to filter out pops or scratches in an old recording. You can even use this software to create your own MP3s. Some commonly used audio editing software programs are Apple GarageBand and Sony ACID. (See Figure 4-9.)

Multimedia

Multimedia is the integration of all sorts of media into one presentation. For example, a multimedia presentation may include video, music, voice, graphics, and text. You may have seen multimedia applied in video games, Web presentations, or even a word processing document. Many of the basic application software programs you learned about in Chapter 3 include features that make the incorporation of multimedia in documents easy. Although these applications include multimedia features, they create documents that are generally accessed in a linear fashion and provide very limited user interaction.

Effective multimedia presentations incorporate user participation or interactivity. **Interactivity** allows the user to choose the information to view, to control the pace and flow of information, and to respond to items and receive feedback. When experiencing an interactive multimedia presentation, users customize the presentation to their needs. For example, Figure 4-10 presents an opening page of a multimedia presentation. Users are able to select the language to be used and decide whether to include sound.

Once used almost exclusively for computer games, interactive multimedia is now widely used in business, education, and the home. Business uses include high-quality interactive presentations, product demonstrations, and Web page design. In education, interactive multimedia is used for in-class presentations and demonstrations, distance education, and online testing. In the home, multimedia is frequently used for entertainment.

Figure 4-10 Opening page of a multimedia presentation

Figure 4-11 Links and buttons are used to navigate the multimedia presentation

Links and Buttons

An interactive multimedia presentation is typically organized as a series of related pages. Each page presents information and provides **links,** or connections, to related information. These links can be to video, sound, graphics, and text files, and to other pages and resources. By clicking special areas called **buttons** on a page, you can make appropriate links and navigate through a presentation to locate and discover information. Typically, there are several buttons on a page. You can select one, several, or none of them. You are in control. You direct the flow and content of the presentation. (See Figure 4-11.)

Multimedia Authoring Programs

Multimedia authoring programs are special programs used to create multimedia presentations. They bring together all the video, audio, graphics, and text elements into an interactive framework. Widely used authoring programs include Adobe Director and Toolbook.

☑ CONCEPT CHECK

What is video editing software? What is audio editing software?

What are multimedia, interactivity, links, and buttons?

What are multimedia authoring programs?

Web Authoring

There are over a billion Web sites on the Internet, and more are being added every day. Corporations use the Web to reach new customers and to promote their products. (See Figure 4-12.) Individuals create their own personal sites, called **blogs.** Creating a site is called **Web authoring.** It begins with site design followed by creation of a document file that displays the Web site's content.

Web Site Design

A Web site is an interactive multimedia form of communication. Designing a Web site begins with determining the site's overall content. The content is then broken down into a series of related pieces of information. The overall site design is commonly represented in a **graphical map.** (See Figure 4-13.)

Notice that in the graphical map shown in Figure 4-13 each block in the map represents a Web page. Lines joining the blocks represent links to related pages of information that make up the Web site. The first page, or home page, typically serves as an introduction and supplies a table of contents. The following pages present the specific pieces or blocks of information.

Multimedia elements are added to individual pages to enhance interest and interactivity. One multimedia element found on many Web sites is moving graphics called **animations.** These animations can be simple moving text or complicated interactive features. There are many specialized programs available to aid in the creation of animation. One type of interactive animation is produced using software called Adobe Flash. **Flash** movies can be inserted as a part of the page or encompass the entire screen.

Web Authoring Programs

As we mentioned in Chapter 2, Web pages are typically HTML documents. With knowledge of HTML and a simple text editor, you can create Web pages. Even without knowledge of HTML, you can create simple Web pages using a word processing package like Microsoft Word.

More specialized and powerful programs, called **Web authoring programs,** are typically used to create sophisticated commercial sites. Also known as **Web page editors** and **HTML editors,** these programs provide support for Web site design and HTML coding. Some Web authoring programs are **WYSIWYG** (**what you see is what you get**) **editors,** which means you can build a page without interacting directly with HTML code. WYSIWYG editors preview the page described by HTML code. Widely used Web authoring programs include Adobe Dreamweaver, NetObjects Fusion, and Microsoft Expression. The Web site depicted in Figure 4-12 was created using Adobe Dreamweaver. (See Figure 4-14.)

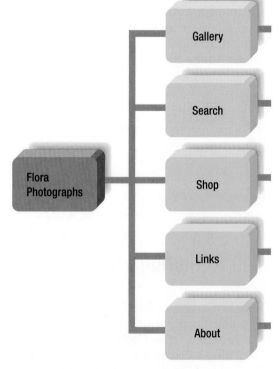

Figure 4-13 Partial graphical map for the Flora Photographs Web site

Figure 4-12 Flora Photographs Web site

WYSIWYG Editing

Dreamweaver provides tools to help you lay out pages with common elements such as text, images, and links.

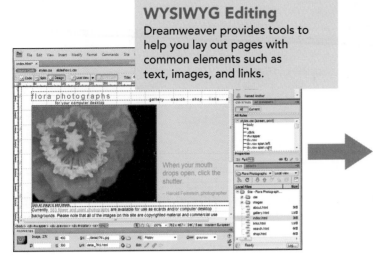

HTML Coding

Using descriptions of each Web page, Adobe Dreamweaver creates HTML code for the entire site.

Web Page

Using a browser, the completed HTML document can be displayed. This is the first page of the Flora Photographs site.

Figure 4-14 Adobe Dreamweaver and the Flora Photographs Web site

Are you thinking about creating your own Web site? Perhaps you already have one and would like to spruce it up a bit? Here are a few suggestions that might help.

1 Use a common design and theme. Consistency in the use of colors, fonts, background designs, and navigation features gives a Web site a unified feeling and makes it easier to use.

2 Use graphics and animations to add interest. Graphics and animations add interest and focus the user's attention. However, they take time to download and the wait frustrates users. Be selective and limit the size of graphics. Also reuse graphics from one page to another.

3 Make navigating your Web site easy. Create a simple method of navigating that allows users to get to their desired information as quickly as possible. None of your content should be more than three clicks from the home page.

4 Design your site for a standard display. To maximize the impact of your site for the largest number of users, design it to be viewed on a monitor with a standard 1024 × 768 resolution.

To see additional tips, visit us at www.computing2011.com and enter the keyword tips.

CONCEPT CHECK

Describe Web authoring.

What are graphical maps, animation, and Flash?

What are Web authoring programs? What are WYSIWYG editors?

Artificial Intelligence

The field of computer science known as **artificial intelligence (AI)** attempts to develop computer systems that can mimic or simulate human senses, thought processes, and actions. These include reasoning, learning from past actions, and using senses such as vision and touch. Artificial intelligence that corresponds to human intelligence is still a long way off. However, several tools that emulate human senses, problem solving, and information processing have been developed.

These modern applications of artificial intelligence are designed to help people and organizations become more productive. Many of these tools have practical applications for business, medicine, law, and so on. In the past, computers used calculating power to solve structured problems, which can be broken down into a series of well-defined steps. People—using intuition, reasoning, and memory—were better at solving unstructured problems, whether building a product or approving a loan. Organizations have long been able to computerize the tasks once performed by clerks. Now knowledge-intensive work and unstructured problems, such as activities performed by many managers, are being automated. Let us now consider three areas in which human talents and abilities have been enhanced with "computerized intelligence": virtual reality, knowledge-based systems, and robotics.

On the Web Explorations

Many people believe that the next big leap forward in computing will involve artificial intelligence.

To learn about a leading developer of artificial intelligence software, visit our Web site at www.computing2011.com and enter the keyword ai.

Virtual Reality

Suppose you could create and virtually experience any new form of reality you wished. You could see the world through the eyes of a child, a robot—or even a lobster. You could explore faraway resorts, the moon, or inside a nuclear waste dump without leaving your chair. This simulated experience is possible with virtual reality.

Virtual reality is an artificial, or simulated, reality generated in 3-D by a computer. Virtual reality is also commonly known as **VR, artificial reality,** or **virtual environments.** In some cases, to navigate in a virtual space, you use virtual reality hardware including headgear and gloves. The headgear has earphones and three-dimensional stereoscopic screens (one type is called Eyephones). The gloves have sensors that collect data about your hand movements (one type is called DataGlove). Coupled with software, this interactive sensory equipment lets you immerse yourself in a computer-generated world. See Figure 4-15.

Creating virtual reality programs once required very-high-end software costing several thousands of dollars. Recently, several lower-cost yet powerful authoring programs have been introduced. One of the best known is

Figure 4-15 Virtual reality

Second Life from Linden Labs, which allows users to create animated characters to represent themselves and to develop their own environment.

There are any number of possible applications for virtual reality. The ultimate recreational use might be something resembling a giant virtual amusement park. More serious applications can simulate important experiences or training environments such as in aviation, surgical operations, spaceship repair, or nuclear disaster cleanup. Some virtual reality strives to be an **immersive experience,** allowing a user to walk into a virtual reality room or view simulations on a **virtual reality wall.** (See Figure 4-16.)

Figure 4-16 **Virtual reality wall**

Knowledge-based (Expert) Systems

People who are expert in a particular area—certain kinds of medicine, accounting, engineering, and so on—are generally well paid for their specialized knowledge. Unfortunately for their clients and customers, these experts are expensive, not always available, and hard to replace when they move on.

What if you were to somehow capture the knowledge of a human expert and make it accessible to everyone through a computer program? This is exactly what is being done with so-called knowledge-based or expert systems. **Knowledge-based systems,** also known as **expert systems,** are a type of artificial intelligence that uses a database to provide assistance to users. These systems use a database or **knowledge base** that contains specific facts, rules to relate these facts, and user input to formulate recommendations and decisions. The sequence of processing is determined by the interaction of the user and the knowledge base. Many expert systems use so-called **fuzzy logic,** which allows users to respond to questions in a very humanlike way. For example, if an expert system asked how your classes were going, you could respond, "great," "OK," "terrible," and so on.

Over the past decade, expert systems have been developed in areas such as medicine, geology, architecture, and nature. There are expert systems with such names as Oil Spill Advisor, Bird Species Identification, and even Midwives Assistant. A system called Grain Marketing Advisor helps farmers select the best way to market their grain.

Robotics

Robotics is the field of study concerned with developing and using robots. **Robots** are computer-controlled machines that mimic the motor activities of living things. For example, Honda's Asimo robot resembles a human and is capable of walking upstairs, dancing, shaking hands, and much more. (See Figure 4-17.) Some robots can even solve unstructured problems using artificial intelligence.

Robots are used in factories, manufacturing, home security, the military, and many other fields of human endeavor. They differ from other assembly-line machines because they can be reprogrammed to do more than one task. Robots often are used to handle dangerous, repetitive tasks. There are four types of robots.

environmental facts

Did you know that robots may someday help clear our oceans of pollution? Investigators are currently exploring the use of robots and special companion ocean vessels for just that purpose. The robots would roam the ocean bottom looking for garbage, oil, and other pollutants. Once located the robots would either clean up the mess on their own or radio other robots for assistance. When full, the robots would resurface and deposit the offensive materials on the companion vessel and then go back for more. The future of robotics promises many opportunities for this kind of robotic clean up.

Figure 4-17 **Asimo**

Figure 4-18 Industrial robot

- **Perception systems: Perception system robots** imitate some of the human senses. For example, robots with television-camera vision systems are particularly useful. They can guide machine tools, inspect products, and secure homes.

- **Industrial robots: Industrial robots** are used to perform a variety of tasks. Examples are machines used in automobile plants to do welding, polishing, and painting. Some types of robots have claws for picking up objects and handling dangerous materials. (See Figure 4-18.)

- **Mobile robots: Mobile robots** act as transports and are widely used for a variety of different tasks. For example, the police and military use them to locate and disarm explosive devices. In the early 2000s, mobile robots entered the world of entertainment with their own television program, called *Battlebots*. You can even build your own mobile robot from a kit.

- **Household robots: Household robots** are now widely available and are designed to vacuum or scrub floors, mow lawns, patrol the house, or simply provide entertainment.

 CONCEPT CHECK

 Define artificial intelligence. What are virtual reality and virtual reality walls?

 Describe knowledge-based systems and fuzzy logic.

 Describe four types of robots.

Careers in IT

Desktop publishers use computers to format and create publication-ready material. (See Figure 4-19.) They may create books, magazines, newsletters, and newspapers on home computers using special application software. A large part of the job is designing page layout, importing text, and manipulating graphics. Most desktop publishers work for companies that handle commercial printing accounts. However, there are also many independent contractors.

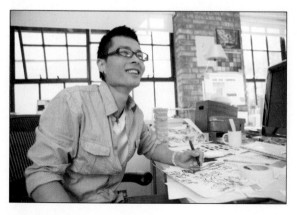

Figure 4-19 Desktop publisher

Desktop publishing positions usually require completion of a program at a vocational school or a university. Internships and part-time work can be a valuable asset to someone pursuing this career. Employers typically look for individuals with good communication skills and artistic ability.

Desktop publishers can expect to earn an annual salary of $26,500 to $44,500. Advancement opportunities include management positions or independent contracting. To learn about other careers in information technology, visit us at www.computing2011.com and enter the keyword **careers.**

A LOOK TO THE FUTURE

Robots Can Look, Act, and Think Like Us

Would you like to talk with your mom through a robot that both resembles you and demonstrates your emotions on their rubber faces? What if you received a companion robot with a set of moral values? Would you trust a robot to trade the stocks in your portfolio? Researchers are currently at work on robots with the artificial intelligence needed to perform these tasks and more.

The Saya robot, with its artificial skin and muscles, is currently under development in Tokyo. Researchers hope that eventually it will be used as a communication device similar to a current Web cam. For example, you could connect to a robot that resembles you at your mother's house and communicate through it with her. You would see your mother through the robot's visual system. Your mother would hear your voice come from the robot and your emotions would be displayed on its face.

Other research is being conducted that will give robots a sense of values. It is hoped that these robots will be able to make decisions independently based on this set of values. Researchers in California are creating robots that act as surveillance instruments, capable of following a target without direction from a human. The robots can predict potential escape routes and pursue a subject through crowded areas.

The Feelix Growing project, a European research project, is developing robots that detect human emotions using simple video cameras and sensors combined with sophisticated software. These robots can then be programmed to respond with similar emotional cues. These robots recognize faces and respond to stimuli like a person would with emotions ranging from surprise to disgust. These robots might be used to help children with developmental disabilities in the near future. Someday, you might interact with a robot that can respond to how you are feeling.

All of these projects are designed to move beyond simple computing and into a decidedly human realm of emotional intelligence. Some experts have even suggested that human intelligence relies on emotional input for all important decision making. Thus, by definition, for a machine to approximate human intelligence, it would have to understand and rely on emotions. If computers could read human emotions, and had emotional intelligence of their own, it could be possible for your computer to act as a stress counselor when you stay up all night working on a project.

Computers with their own emotional intelligence could be the ultimate human companions. Computer scientists have suggested they may read your mood and play music accordingly. Or they could search through audio and video files for media you would find moving, funny, or dramatic. If computers had their own emotional sense, it is possible that they, like the humans they emulate, would require interaction for mental health.

Would you use a robot as a communication device? Do you think we should build robots with a sense of moral values? Some researchers have suggested that robots with artificial intelligence could serve as ideal supervisors and managers. What do you think? Would you like to have an "emotional" robot for a boss?

GRAPHICS

Professionals in graphic arts use specialized graphics programs.

Desktop Publishing

Desktop publishing programs (page layout programs) mix text and graphics to create professional publications.

Image Editors

Image editors (photo editors) create and modify **bitmap (raster) image** files. Images are recorded as dots or **pixels**.

Illustration Programs

Illustration programs, also known as **drawing programs**, modify **vector images (vector illustrations)**. In a vector file, images are recorded as a collection of objects such as lines, rectangles, and ovals.

Image Galleries

Image galleries are libraries of electronic images, widely available from the Web. Two types are **stock photographs** and **clip art**.

Graphics Suites

A **graphics suite** is a collection of individual graphics programs sold as a unit.

AUDIO AND VIDEO

Recent advances in video and audio technology allow individuals to assemble near-professional-quality video and audio footage.

Video Software

Video editing software allows you to reorganize, add effects, and more to digital video.

Audio Software

Audio editing software allows you to create and edit audio clips. You can add audio effects, like filters, to your tracks. You can create MP3s.

To be a competent end user, you need to be aware of specialized applications. You need to know who uses them, what they are used for, and how they are used. Specialized applications include graphics programs, audio and video editing software, multimedia, Web authoring, and the field of artificial intelligence.

MULTIMEDIA

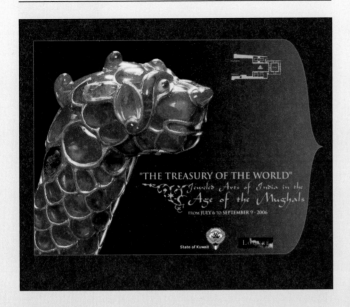

Multimedia integrates all sorts of media into one presentation. An essential feature is user participation or **interactivity**.

Links and Buttons

A multimedia presentation is organized as a series of related pages. Pages are **linked,** or connected, by clicking **buttons.**

Multimedia Authoring Programs

Multimedia authoring programs bring together video, audio, graphics, and text elements in an interactive framework.

WEB AUTHORING

Blogs are personal Web sites. Creating Web sites is called **Web authoring.** It begins with Web site design, followed by creating a document file that displays the Web site content.

Web Site Design

Web sites are an interactive multimedia form of communication.

Graphical maps use linked blocks to represent a Web site's overall content. Typically, blocks represent individual Web pages and links indicate relationships between related pages.

The first Web page (home page) usually introduces the site and supplies a table of contents. Multimedia elements are added to pages. **Animations** are moving graphics. **Flash** is a widely used application for Web animation.

Web Authoring Programs

Web sites can be created using a simple text editor or word processor. **Web authoring programs,** also known as **Web page editors** or **HTML editors,** are specifically designed to create Web sites. They provide support for Web site design and HTML coding. Some offer **WYSIWYG (what you see is what you get) editors.**

Artificial intelligence (AI) attempts to develop computer systems that mimic human senses, thought processes, and actions.

Virtual Reality

Virtual reality (VR, artificial reality, or virtual environments) creates computer-generated simulated environment using sensory equipment, including head gear and gloves.

Applications include recreational and other areas such as aviation, surgical operations, spaceship repair, and nuclear disaster cleanup. Some applications strive for immersive experiences and can be viewed on virtual reality walls.

Knowlege-Based (Expert) Systems

Knowledge-based (expert) systems are programs that duplicate the knowledge that humans use to perform specific tasks. Knowledge bases are databases containing facts and rules. Fuzzy logic allows users to respond to questions in a very humanlike way.

Robotics

Robotics is concerned with developing and using robots. Robots are computer-controlled machines that mimic the motor activities of living things. Four types of robots are

- **Perception systems** imitate human senses such as vision.
- **Industrial robots** perform a variety of tasks such as welding, polishing and painting.
- **Mobile robots** act as transports for such things as locating and disarming explosive devices.
- **Household robots** are designed to vacuum and scrub floors, mow lawns, patrol the house, or provide entertainment.

CAREERS IN IT

Desktop publishers use computers to format and create publication-ready material. Vocational or university degree is preferred plus good communication skills and artistic ability. Salary range $26,500 to $44,500.

KEY TERMS

animation   (110)
artificial intelligence (AI)   (112)
artificial reality   (112)
audio editing software   (108)
bitmap image   (103)
blog   (109)
button   (109)
clip art   (104)
desktop publisher   (114)
desktop publishing program   (103)
drawing program   (104)
expert system   (113)
Flash   (110)
fuzzy logic   (113)
graphical map   (110)
graphics suite   (105)
household robot   (114)
HTML editor   (110)
illustration program   (104)
image editors   (103)
image gallery   (104)
immersive experience   (113)
industrial robot   (114)
interactivity   (108)
knowledge base   (113)

knowledge-based system   (113)
link   (109)
mobile robot   (114)
multimedia   (108)
multimedia authoring program   (109)
page layout program   (103)
perception system robot   (114)
photo editors   (103)
pixel   (103)
raster image   (103)
robot   (113)
robotics   (113)
stock photograph   (104)
vector   (104)
vector illustration   (104)
vector image   (104)
video editing software   (105)
virtual environment   (112)
virtual reality   (112)
virtual reality wall   (113)
VR   (112)
Web authoring   (109)
Web authoring program   (110)
Web page editor   (110)
WYSIWIG editors   (110)

To test your knowledge of these key terms with animated flash cards, visit our Web site at www.computing2011.com and enter the keyword terms4.

APPLYING TECHNOLOGY

The following questions are designed to demonstrate ways that you can effectively use technology today. The first question relates directly to this chapter's Making IT Work for You feature.

① DIGITAL VIDEO EDITING

Have you ever thought of making your own movie? Would you like to edit some home videos and distribute them to family and friends on DVDs? It's easy with the right equipment and software. To learn more about digital video editing, review Making IT Work for You: Digital Video Editing, on pages 106 and 107. Then answer the following questions: (a) Briefly describe the steps necessary to begin transferring video from a camcorder to your computer. (b) Where can you preview your movie in Windows Movie Maker? (c) What is Windows DVD Maker and what is it used for?

② ADOBE FLASH

Web sites aren't all just text and pictures anymore. Many are taking advantage of browser plug-ins that add new functionality and display abilities to Web browsers, as we discussed in Chapter 2. One of the most popular plug-ins is Adobe Flash. Visit our Web site at www.computing2011.com and enter the keyword flash for a link to the Adobe site. Once connected, read about Flash and answer the following questions: (a) What is Flash? What types of content can it display? (b) How is the Flash plug-in obtained? (c) What types of companies are using Flash in their Web page designs? (d) Do you think Flash is a valuable Web page addition or just a flashy distraction? Explain your answer.

③ STREAMING MULTIMEDIA PLAYERS

Streaming multimedia files come in many varieties. There are several formats for streaming audio and video files available, each with is own advantage. To play these files, a user needs software known as a *player,* which must support the type of file the user wishes to play. Visit our Web site at www.computing2011.com and enter the keyword streaming for a link to a popular streaming multimedia player. Read about the player and then answer the following questions: (a) What types of streaming multimedia files can be played with this player? (b) How does the user receive and install the player? (c) As streaming multimedia becomes more widely available on the Internet, how might the role of player software change? Be specific.

EXPANDING YOUR KNOWLEDGE

The following questions are designed to add depth and detail to your understanding of specific topics presented within this chapter. The questions direct you to sources other than the textbook to obtain this knowledge.

1 HOW DIGITAL VIDEO EDITING WORKS

The falling prices of digital camcorders and improvements in computer technology have made digital video editing affordable for individuals. To learn more about digital video editing, visit our Web site at www.computing2011.com and enter the keyword video. Then answer the following questions: (a) What hardware is needed to capture video from a VCR tape? Why is this hardware necessary? (b) How can video editing software be used to improve a video? (c) What are some common ways to share videos?

2 PERSONAL WEB SITE

Would you like a personal Web site but don't want to deal with learning HTML? There are many services available to get you started. To learn more about personal Web sites, visit our Web site at www.computing2011.com and enter the keyword blog. Then answer the following questions: (a) What are Web logs? What are they used for? (b) What is Blogger.com? Describe the following features provided by Blogger.com: templates, upload file, hyperlink, post, publish, and view Web page. (c) Have you ever created a Web log or other types of personal Web site? If you have, describe how you created it and what you used it for. If you have not, discuss why and how you might use one.

3 STREAMING MULTIMEDIA

Many Web sites are now enhanced with streaming multimedia. Some sites offer streaming audio or video to augment text, such as news sites with file footage. For others, the content *is* the streaming multimedia, such as Internet radio or animation sites. Locate several Web sites that offer streaming multimedia and pick one to review. Then answer the following: (a) Define "streaming multimedia." (b) What type of streaming multimedia did the site offer? Who is the intended audience? (c) In what ways was the experience limited? Be specific.

WRITING ABOUT TECHNOLOGY

The ability to think critically and to write effectively is essential to nearly every profession. The following questions are designed to help you develop these skills by posing thought-provoking questions about computer privacy, security, and/or ethics.

1 DIGITAL PHOTO MANIPULATION

Image editing software has made it easy to alter photographs, which in the past were accepted as visual records of real events. In some cases, the purpose of digital editing is humor and exaggeration, while other times subtle changes are used to alter a photo's deeper meaning. Research examples of digital photo editing that resulted in controversy and then answer the following questions in a one-page paper: (a) Do you see any ethical issues related to altering photographs? (b) What do you consider the boundary between acceptable photo editing and deceptive or misleading practices? (c) Do you feel the old saying "seeing is believing" needs to be reconsidered for the digital age? Defend your answers.

2 ONLINE EXPERT SYSTEMS

Expert systems have been integrated into many Web sites for consumers. For example, health-related Web sites help patients "self-diagnose" illnesses before seeing a physician. Research Web sites that make expert systems available and address the following items in a one-page paper: (a) Define "expert system." (b) What benefits do these expert systems offer the user? (c) Are there ways these systems could be harmful? What responsibilities do users of online expert systems have? (d) What responsibilities do providers of online expert systems have?

System Software

Competencies

After you have read this chapter, you should be able to:

1 Describe the differences between system software and application software.

2 Discuss the four types of system software.

3 Discuss the basic functions, features, and categories of operating systems.

4 Describe Windows, Mac OS, UNIX, Linux, and virtualization.

5 Describe the purpose of utilities and utility suites.

6 Identify the five most essential utilities.

7 Discuss Windows utility programs.

8 Describe device drivers, including Windows' Add a Device Wizard and Update.

Just a few years ago, the operating system installed on a computer determined much of its function. The application software you wanted to use may have only worked with one type of operating system. Today more applications are cross platforms, which means that the software runs on more than one operating system. And as more software becomes Web-based, the operating system becomes less central in the lives of daily users.

Some experts predict that in the future people might never really interact with the operating system on their computers at all. And because most software is moving to the Web, the user interface of the future will most likely take a form similar to a browser window. Imagine a world where your computer is like your TV. The inner workings of your TV, and the software that may be running behind the scenes, are unimportant. It's the content the TV connects to that really matters.

chapter 5

Introduction

When most people think about computers, they think about surfing the Web, creating reports, analyzing data, storing information, making presentations, and any number of other valuable applications. We typically think about applications and application software. Computers and computer applications have become a part of the fabric of our everyday lives. Most of us agree that they are great . . . as long as they are working.

We usually do not think about the more mundane and behind-the-scenes computer activities: loading and running programs, coordinating networks that share resources, organizing files, protecting our computers from viruses, performing periodic maintenance to avoid problems, and controlling hardware devices so that they can communicate with one another. Typically, these activities go on behind the scenes without our help.

That is the way it should be, and the way it is, as long as everything is working perfectly. But what if new application programs are not compatible and will not run on our current computer system? What if we get a computer virus? What if our hard disk fails? What if we buy a new digital video camera and can't store and edit the images on our computer system? What if our computer starts to run slower and slower?

These issues may seem mundane, but they are critical. This chapter covers the vital activities that go on behind the scenes. A little knowledge about these activities can go a long way to making your computing life easier. To effectively use computers, competent end users need to understand the functionality of system software, including operating systems, utility programs, and device drivers.

System Software

End users use application software to accomplish specific tasks. For example, we use word processors to create letters, documents, and reports. However, end users also use system software. **System software** works with end users, application software, and computer hardware to handle the majority of technical details. For example, system software controls where a word processing program is stored in memory, how commands are converted so that the system unit can process them, and where a completed document or file is saved. See Figure 5-1.

System software is not a single program. Rather it is a collection or a system of programs that handle hundreds of technical details with little or no user intervention. System software consists of four types of programs:

- **Operating systems** coordinate computer resources, provide an interface between users and the computer, and run applications.
- **Utilities** perform specific tasks related to managing computer resources.
- **Device drivers** are specialized programs that allow particular input or output devices to communicate with the rest of the computer system.
- **Language translators** convert the programming instructions written by programmers into a language that computers understand and process.

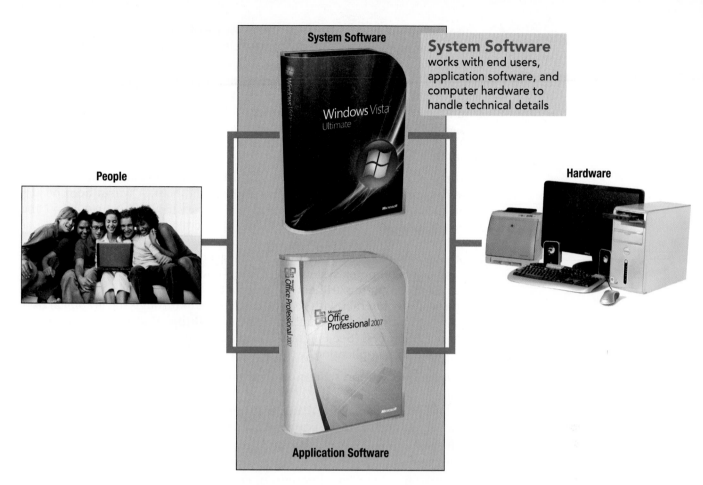

People

System Software

System Software works with end users, application software, and computer hardware to handle technical details

Hardware

Application Software

Figure 5-1 System software handles technical details

Operating Systems

An **operating system** is a collection of programs that handle many of the technical details related to using a computer. In many ways, an operating system is the most important type of computer program. Without a functioning operating system, your computer would be useless.

Functions

Every computer has an operating system and every operating system performs a variety of functions. These functions can be classified into three groups:

- **Managing resources:** Operating systems coordinate all the computer's resources including memory, processing, storage, and devices such as printers and monitors. They also monitor system performance, schedule tasks, provide security, and start up the computer.
- **Providing user interface:** Operating systems allow users to interact with application programs and computer hardware through a **user interface.** Many older operating systems used a character-based interface in which users communicated with the operating system through written commands such as "Copy A: assign.doc C:". Almost all newer operating systems

use a **graphical user interface (GUI).** As we discussed in Chapter 3, a graphical user interface uses graphical elements such as icons and windows.

- **Running applications:** Operating systems load and run applications such as word processors and spreadsheets. Most operating systems support **multitasking,** or the ability to switch between different applications stored in memory. With multitasking, you could have Word and Excel running at the same time and switch easily between the two applications.

Features

Starting or restarting a computer is called **booting** the system. There are two ways to boot a computer: a warm boot and a cold boot. A **warm boot** occurs when the computer is already on and you restart it without turning off the power. A warm boot can be accomplished in several ways. For many computer systems, they can be restarted by simply pressing a sequence of keys. Starting a computer that has been turned off is called a **cold boot.** To learn more about booting your computer system and POST (power on self-test), visit our Web site at www.computing2011.com and enter the keyword **boot.**

You typically interact with the operating system through the graphical user interface. Most provide a place, called the **desktop,** that provides access to computer resources. (See Figure 5-2.) Operating systems have several features in common with application programs, including

- **Icons**—graphic representations for a program, type of file, or function.
- **Pointer**—controlled by a mouse, trackpad, or touchscreen, the pointer changes shape depending upon its current function. For example, when shaped like an arrow, the pointer can be used to select items such as an icon.
- **Windows**—rectangular areas for displaying information and running programs.
- **Menus**—provide a list of options or commands.
- **Dialog boxes**—provide information or request input.
- **Help**—provides online assistance for operating system functions and procedures.

Most operating systems store data and programs in a system of files and folders. Unlike the traditional filing cabinet, computer files and folders are stored on a storage device such as your hard disk. **Files** are used to store data and programs. Related files are stored within a **folder,** and for organizational purposes, a folder can contain other folders. For example, you might organize

Figure 5-2 Desktop

your electronic files in the *My Documents* folder on your hard disk. This folder could contain other folders, each named to indicate its contents. One might be "Computers" and could contain all the files you have created (or will create) for this course.

Categories

While there are hundreds of different operating systems, there are only three basic categories: embedded, network, or stand-alone.

- **Embedded operating systems** are used for handheld devices such as smart phones, cable and satellite television tuner boxes, video game systems, and other small electronics. (See Figure 5-3.) The entire operating system is stored within or embedded in the device. The operating system programs are permanently stored on ROM, or read-only memory, chips. Popular embedded operating systems include Windows CE and Windows XP Embedded.

Figure 5-3 Handheld devices have embedded operating systems

- **Network operating systems (NOS)** are used to control and coordinate computers that are networked or linked together. Many networks are small and connect only a limited number of microcomputers. Other networks, like those at colleges and universities, are very large and complex. These networks may include other smaller networks and typically connect a variety of different types of computers.

  Network operating systems are typically located on one of the connected computers' hard disks. Called the **network server,** this computer coordinates all communication between the other computers. Popular network operating systems include NetWare, Windows Server, and UNIX.

- **Stand-alone operating systems,** also called **desktop operating systems,** control a single desktop or notebook computer. (See Figure 5-4.)

Figure 5-4 Stand-alone operating system

These operating systems are located on the computer's hard disk. Often desktop computers and notebooks are part of a network. In these cases, the desktop operating system works with the network's NOS to share and coordinate resources. In these situations, the desktop operating system is referred to as the *client operating system*. Popular desktop operating systems include Windows, Mac OS, and various versions of UNIX and Linux.

The operating system is often referred to as the **software environment** or **platform.** Almost all application programs are designed to run with a specific platform. For example, Apple's iMovie software is designed to run with the Mac OS environment. Many applications, however, have different versions, each designed to operate with a particular platform. For example, one version of Microsoft Office is designed to operate with Windows. Another version is designed to operate with Mac OS.

 ## CONCEPT CHECK

What is system software? What are the four kinds of system software programs?

What is an operating system? Discuss operating system functions and features.

Describe each of the three categories of operating systems.

Windows

Microsoft's **Windows** is by far the most popular microcomputer operating system today with nearly 90 percent of the market. Because its market share is so large, more application programs are developed to run under Windows than any other operating system. Windows comes in a variety of different versions and is designed to run with Intel and Intel-compatible microprocessors such as the Core 2 Quad and Atom series. For a summary of Microsoft's desktop operating systems, see Figure 5-5.

There are many versions of Windows. The latest, **Windows 7,** was released in 2009. (See Figure 5-6.) Compared to the previous system, **Windows Vista,** Windows 7 provides several improvements including:

- Improved handwriting recognition for tablet computers.
- A taskbar that features previews, large icons, and personalization features.
- Advanced searching capabilities for finding files and content on your computer.

Name	Description
Windows 98	Stand-alone operating system
Windows 2000 Professional	Upgrade to Windows NT Workstation
Windows ME	Upgrade to Windows 98 specifically designed for home users
Windows XP	Upgrade to Windows 2000 with improved interface, stability, and reliability
Windows Vista	Upgrade to Windows XP with improved security, three-dimensional workspace, and filtering capabilities.
Windows 7	Microsoft's latest operating system with improved user experience, speed, and stability

Figure 5-5 Microsoft desktop operating systems

Figure 5-6 Windows 7

Mac OS

Apple introduced its Macintosh microcomputer and operating system in 1984. It provided one of the first GUIs, making it easy even for novice computer users to move and delete files. Designed to run with Apple computers, **Mac OS** is not nearly as widely used as the Windows operating system. As a result, fewer application programs have been written for it. Nonetheless, Mac OS is considered to be one of the most innovative operating systems. It is a powerful, easy-to-use operating system that is popular with professional graphic designers, desktop publishers, and many home users.

One of the latest versions of the Macintosh operating system is **Mac OS X.** (See Figure 5-7.) This operating system provides a wide array of powerful features including Spotlight and Dashboard Widgets. **Spotlight** is an advanced search tool that can rapidly locate files, folders, e-mail messages, addresses, and much more. **Dashboard Widgets** are a collection of specialized programs that will constantly update and display information. Some versions of Mac OS X also include **Boot Camp,** which allows Macintosh computers to run both the Mac OS and the Windows operating system.

Unix and Linux

The **UNIX** operating system was originally designed to run on minicomputers in network environments. Now, it is also used by powerful microcomputers and by servers on the Web. There are a large number of different versions of UNIX. One receiving a great deal of attention today is **Linux.**

Have you ever thought about updating your current operating system? Keeping your computer updated with the latest security features and corrections is essential to avoiding viruses and other security problems. You can keep Windows 7 up to date automatically by following these steps:

1 Click *Start*, point to *All Programs*, and then click *Windows Update.*

2 In the left pane, click *Change settings.*

3 Select *Install updates automatically (recommended).*

4 Under *Recommended updates*, select the check box labeled *Give me recommended updates the same way I receive important updates*, and then click *OK.*

To see additional tips, visit our Web site at www.computing2011.com and enter the keyword tips.

Figure 5-7 Mac OS X

Linux was originally developed by a graduate student at the University of Helsinki, Linus Torvalds, in 1991. He allowed free distribution of the operating system code and encouraged others to modify and further develop the code. Linux is a popular and powerful alternative to the Windows operating system. (See Figure 5-8.)

Virtualization

As we have discussed, application programs are designed to run with particular operating systems. What if you wanted to run two or more applications each requiring a different operating system? One solution would be to install each of the operating systems on a different computer. There is, however, a way in which a single physical computer can support multiple operating systems that operate independently. This approach is called **virtualization.**

With **virtualization software,** the physical machine can be logically separated into separate and independent virtual computers known as **virtual machines.** Each virtual machine appears to the user as a separate independent computer with its own operating system. The operating system of the physical machine is known as the **host operating system.** The operating system for each virtual machine is known as the **guest operating system.** Users can readily switch between virtual computers and programs running on them. (See Figure 5-9.)

CONCEPT CHECK

What is Windows? What is Windows Vista? What is Windows 7?

What is Mac OS? Spotlight? Dashboard Widgets? Boot Camp?

What is UNIX? What is Linux?

What are virtualization and virtualization software? What are host and guest operating systems?

Figure 5-8 Linux

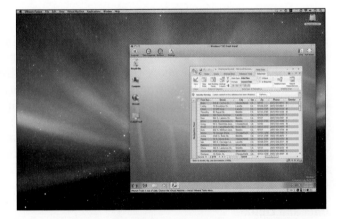

Figure 5-9 Windows 7 running within a window on the Mac OS X operating system

Utilities

Ideally, microcomputers would continuously run without problems. However, that simply is not the case. All kinds of things can happen—internal hard disks can crash, computers can freeze up, operations can slow down, and so on. These events can make computing very frustrating. That's where utilities come in. **Utilities** are specialized programs designed to make computing easier. There are hundreds of different utility programs. The most essential are

- **Troubleshooting** or **diagnostic programs** that recognize and correct problems, ideally before they become serious.
- **Antivirus programs** that guard your computer system against viruses or other damaging programs that can invade your computer system.
- **Uninstall programs** that allow you to safely and completely remove unneeded programs and related files from your hard disk.

> **Did you know** you can search the content of e-mail messages, files, notes and contacts all at once using a simple utility in Windows Vista? Here's how:
>
> **1** Click *Start* and begin typing the term you want to search for into the *Search Programs and Files* blank.
>
> **2** As you type, a list of files and other items containing your search term is displayed.
>
> **3** Continue typing to further narrow the list, or click an item in the list to view it instantly.
>
> To see additional tips, visit our Web site at www.computing2011.com and enter the keyword tips.

- **Backup programs** that make copies of files to be used in case the originals are lost or damaged.
- **File compression programs** that reduce the size of files so they require less storage space and can be sent more efficiently over the Internet.

Most operating systems provide some utility programs. Even more powerful utility programs can be purchased separately or in utility suites.

Windows Utilities

The Windows operating systems are accompanied by several utility programs, including Backup and Restore, Disk Cleanup, and Disk Defragmenter.

Backup and Restore is a utility program included with the many versions of Windows that makes a copy of all files or selected files that have been saved onto a disk. It helps to protect you from the effects of a disk failure. For example, you can select *Backup and Restore* from the Windows 7 Maintenance menu to create a backup for your hard disk as shown in Figure 5-10.

When you surf the Web, a variety of programs and files are saved on your hard disk. Many of these and other files are not essential. **Disk Cleanup** is a troubleshooting utility that identifies and eliminates nonessential files. This frees up valuable disk space and improves system performance.

For example, by selecting Disk Cleanup from the Windows 7 System Tools menu, you can eliminate unneeded files on your hard disk as shown in Figure 5-11.

As we will discuss in detail in Chapter 8, files are stored and organized on a disk according to tracks and sectors. A **track** is a concentric ring. Each track is divided into wedge-shaped sections called **sectors.** (See Figure 5-12.) The operating system tries to save a file on a single track across contiguous sectors. Often, however, this is not possible and the file has to be broken up, or **fragmented,** into small parts that are stored wherever space is available. Whenever a file is retrieved, it is reconstructed from the fragments. After a period of time, a hard disk becomes highly fragmented, slowing operations.

1. ● Click *Start*, and then select *Maintenance* from the *All Programs* menu.

   ● Select *Backup and Restore*, and then click *Set up backup*.

   ● Choose the destination for the backup.

2. ● Choose the files you want to back up.

3. ● Set up Backup Wizard to back up the selected files.

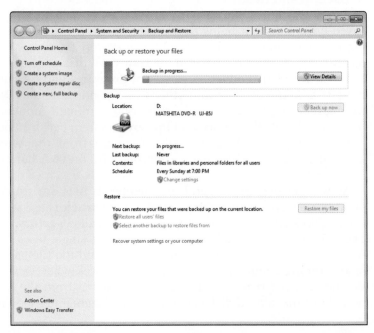

Figure 5-10 Backup and Restore utility

1 ● Click *Start*, and then select *Accessories* from the *All Programs* menu.

● Select *Disk Cleanup* from the *System Tools* menu.

● Review the files suggested for cleanup, and then click *OK*.

2 ● The utility cleans the selected files.

Figure 5-11 **Disk Cleanup utility**

1 sector

1 track

Figure 5-12 Tracks and sectors

Disk Defragmenter is a utility program that locates and eliminates unnecessary fragments and rearranges files and unused disk space to optimize operations. For example, by selecting Disk Defragmenter from the Windows 7 System Tools menu, you can defrag your hard disk as shown in Figure 5-13.

Utility Suites

Like application software suites, **utility suites** combine several programs into one package. Buying the package is less expensive than buying the programs separately. The three best-known utility suites are McAfee Office, Norton SystemWorks, and V Communications System-Suite. (See Figure 5-14.) These suites provide a variety of utilities, including programs that will protect your system from dangerous programs called computer **viruses.** You can "catch" a computer virus many ways, including by opening attachments to e-mail messages and downloading software from the Internet. (We will discuss computer viruses in detail in Chapter 10.)

1 ● Click *Start.*

● Select *Accessories* from the *All Programs* menu.

● Select *Disk Defragmenter* from the *System Tools* menu. If necessary, click *Continue.*

2 ● Click the *Defragment disk* button to begin defragging.

● If necessary, choose the drive you want to defragment.

● When defragmentation is complete for the selected drive, view the report or close the window.

Figure 5-13 Disk Defragmenter utility

Figure 5-14 Norton SystemWorks

To learn more about virus protection, visit our Web site at www.computing 2011.com and enter the keyword **virus.** Also see Making IT Work for You: Virus Protection and Internet Security on pages 140 and 141.

CONCEPT CHECK

Discuss the five most essential utilities.

Describe Windows Backup and Restore, Disk Cleanup, and Disk Defragmenter.

What is the difference between a utility and a utility suite?

Device Drivers

Every device, such as a mouse or printer, that is connected to a computer system has a special program associated with it. This program, called a **device driver** or simply a **driver,** works with the operating system to allow communication between the device and the rest of the computer system. Each time the computer system is started, the operating system loads all of the device drivers into memory.

Whenever a new device is added to a computer system, a new device driver must be installed before the device can be used. Windows supplies hundreds of different device drivers with its system software. For many devices, the appropriate drivers are automatically selected and installed when the device is first connected to the computer system. For others, the device driver must be manually installed. Fortunately, Windows provides wizards to assist in this process. For example, Windows' **Add a Device Wizard** provides step-by-step guidance for selecting the appropriate hardware driver and installing that driver. If a particular device driver is not included with the Windows system software, the product's manufacturer will supply one. Many times these drivers are available directly from the manufacturer's Web site.

You probably never think about the device drivers in your computer. However, when your computer behaves unpredictably, you may find reinstalling or updating

Making IT work for you

VIRUS PROTECTION AND INTERNET SECURITY

Are you worried that a computer virus will erase your personal files? Did you know that others could be intercepting your private e-mail? It is even possible for others to gain access to and control over your computer system. Fortunately, Internet security suites are available to help ensure your safety while you are on the Internet.

Getting Started   The first step is to install an Internet security suite. Once installed, the software will continually work to ensure security and privacy. For example, to install McAfee Security Center follow the instructions below.

1 ● Connect to www.mcafee.com and follow the instructions to subscribe to this Internet security suite.

2 ● Follow the instructions at the Web site to download and install the security suite on your computer.

SecurityCenter McAfee SecurityCenter runs a number of programs continually to monitor your computer. Some of Security Center's most powerful features include VirusScan, PersonalFirewall, and SiteAdvisor. You can modify the way these programs run with the McAfee SecurityCenter.

VirusScan is a program that controls how frequently the computer system is searched for computer viruses. When a file is checked, it is compared to the profile of known viruses. Once a virus is detected, the infected file is quarantined or deleted.

PersonalFirewall is a program that monitors all inbound and outbound traffic to a computer system. It limits access to authorized users and applications.

SiteAdvisor is a program that helps protect your privacy online. It installs in your Web browser, and warns you of potentially harmful Web sites as you surf.

The Web is continually changing, and some of the specifics presented in this Making IT Work for You may have changed.

To learn about other ways to make information technology work for you, visit our Web site at www.computing2011.com and enter the keyword miw.

your device drivers solves your problems. Windows makes it easy to update the drivers on your computer using **Windows Update,** as shown in Figure 5-15.

☑ CONCEPT CHECK

What are device drivers and what do they do?

What is Windows' Add a Device Wizard and what does it do?

What is Windows Update? What does it do?

1 Access *Windows Update* from the *All Programs* list of the *Start* menu.

Click *Check for updates.*

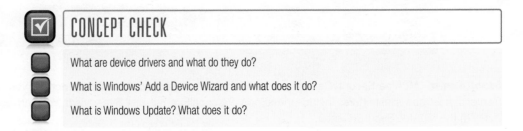

2 Review the list of recommended updates.

3 Click *Install updates* to download updates to your computer.

Figure 5-15 Using Windows Update

Careers in IT

Computer support specialists provide technical support to customers and other users. (See Figure 5.16.) They also may be called technical support specialists or help-desk technicians. Computer support specialists manage the everyday technical problems faced by computer users. They resolve common networking problems and may use troubleshooting programs to diagnose problems. Most computer support specialists are hired to work within a company and provide technical support for other employees and divisions. However, it is increasingly common for companies to provide technical support as an outsourced service.

Employers generally look for individuals with a bachelor's degree to fill computer support specialist positions. Degrees in computer science or information systems may be preferred. However, because demand for qualified applicants is so high, those with practical experience and certification from a training program increasingly fill these positions. Employers seek individuals with good analytical and communication skills. Those with good people skills and customer service experience have an advantage in this field.

Computer support specialists can expect to earn an annual salary of $32,000 to $53,500. Opportunities for advancement are very good and may involve design and implementation of new systems. To learn about other careers in information systems, visit us at www.computing2011.com and enter the keyword **careers**.

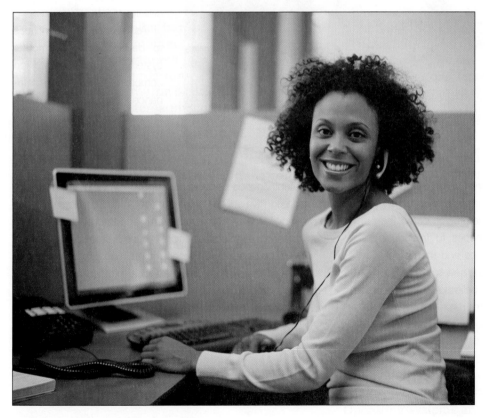

Figure 5-16 Computer support specialist

To effectively use computers, competent end users need to understand the functionality of system software, including operating systems, utility programs, and device drivers.

OPERATING SYSTEMS

Windows

Windows, the most widely used operating system, is designed to run with Intel and Intel-compatible microprocessors. There are numerous versions of Windows. **Windows 7** is the most recent version of Windows. It provides improved handwriting recognition; taskbar with previews, large icons, and personalization features; and advanced search capabilities.

Mac OS

Mac OS, an innovative, powerful, easy-to-use operating system, runs on Macintosh computers. Recent versions provide **Spotlight,** an advanced search tool, and **Dashboard Widgets,** a collection of specialized programs. Some versions of MAC OS X come with **Boot Camp,** which allows Macintosh computers to run both Mac OS and Windows operating systems.

UNIX and Linux

UNIX was originally designed to run on minicomputers in network environments. Now, it is used by powerful microcomputers and servers on the Web. There are many different versions of UNIX. One version, **Linux,** is a popular and powerful alternative to the Windows operating system.

Virtualization

Virtualization is a process that allows a single physical computer to support multiple operating systems that operate independently. **Virtualization software** creates **virtual machines. Host operating systems** run on the physical machine. **Guest operating systems** operate on virtual machines.

UTILITIES

Utilities make computing easier. The most essential are **troubleshooting (diagnostic), antivirus, uninstall, backup,** and **file compression.**

Windows Utilities

Windows operating systems are accompanied by several utility programs, including **Backup and Restore, Disk Cleanup**, and **Disk Defragmenter** (eliminates unnecessary **fragments; tracks** are concentric rings; **sectors** are wedge-shaped).

Utility Suites

Utility **suites** combine several programs into one package. Computer **viruses** are dangerous programs.

DEVICE DRIVERS

Device drivers (drivers) allow communication between hardware devices. **Add a Device Wizard** gives step-by-step guidance to install printer drivers. **Windows Update** automates the process of updating device drivers.

CAREERS IN IT

Computer support specialists provide technical support to customers and other users. Degrees in computer science or information systems are preferred plus good analytical and communication skills. Salary range $32,000 to $53,500.

KEY TERMS

Add a Device Wizard   (139)
antivirus program   (135)
Backup and Restore   (135)
backup program   (135)
Boot Camp   (133)
booting   (130)
cold boot   (130)
computer support specialist   (143)
Dashboard Widgets   (133)
desktop   (130)
desktop operating system   (131)
device driver (128, 139)
diagnostic program   (135)
dialog box   (130)
Disk Cleanup   (135)
Disk Defragmenter   (138)
driver   (139)
embedded operating systems   (131)
file   (130)
file compression program   (135)
folder   (130)
fragmented   (135)
graphical user interface (GUI)   (130)
guest operating system   (134)
Help   (130)
host operating system   (134)
icon   (130)
language translator   (128)
Linux   (133)
Mac OS   (133)

Mac OS X   (133)
menu   (130)
multitasking   (130)
network operating systems (NOS)   (131)
network server   (131)
operating system (128, 129)
platform   (132)
pointer   (130)
sector   (135)
software environment   (132)
Spotlight   (133)
stand-alone operating system   (131)
system software   (128)
track   (135)
troubleshooting program   (135)
uninstall program   (135)
UNIX   (133)
user interface   (129)
utility (128, 135)
utility suite   (138)
virtualization   (134)
virtualization software   (134)
virtual machine   (134)
virus   (138)
warm boot   (130)
window   (130)
Windows   (132)
Windows 7   (132)
Windows Update   (142)
Windows Vista   (132)

To test your knowledge of these key terms with animated flash cards, visit our Web site at www.computing2011.com and enter the keyword terms5.

WRITING ABOUT TECHNOLOGY

The ability to think critically and to write effectively is essential to nearly every profession. The following questions are designed to help you develop these skills by posing thought-provoking questions about computer privacy, security, and/or ethics.

① OPEN SOURCE

The Linux operating system is one of the most famous examples of open source software. In an open source model, the underlying code for an application is freely available for other computer programmers to improve and redistribute it. This is much different from traditional models of development in which software companies hold the copyright to software and prevent others from imitating it. Research the concept of open source software and write a one-page paper responding to the following questions: (a) What is the basic licensing model for open source projects? (b) What are some examples of corporations that have supported or contributed to open source projects? (c) What might be some of the benefits of open source development? What are some of the drawbacks? Explain your answer.

② ONLINE BACKUP

One of the best ways to safeguard important personal or corporate data is to use an online backup service. Research three or four online backup services and then answer the following questions in a one-page paper: (a) What are the general features of online backup services? (b) What types of emergencies do online backups help with that other backup methods do not? (c) How are backups scheduled? (d) Is this service a replacement for making backups locally? Why or why not?

NOTES

The System Unit

Competencies

After you have read this chapter, you should be able to:

1 Describe the six basic types of system units.

2 Discuss how a computer can represent numbers and encode characters electronically.

3 Describe each of the major system unit components.

4 Discuss microprocessors, including microprocessor chips and specialty processors.

5 Discuss memory including RAM, ROM, and flash memory.

6 Discuss expansion slots and cards.

7 Describe five principal types of expansion buses.

8 Compare standard, specialized, and legacy ports.

9 Discuss power supply for desktop and notebook computers.

The first computer ever built was too big to fit into a modern home, but today's computer chips are smaller than our fingertips. These tiny circuits are the brains inside your computer. They run the video game you are playing *and* keep track of the tiny movements of your mouse as you play.

Introduction

Why are some microcomputers more powerful than others? The answer lies in three words: speed, capacity, and flexibility. After reading this chapter, you will be able to judge how fast, powerful, and versatile a particular microcomputer is. As you might expect, this knowledge is valuable if you are planning to buy a new microcomputer system or to upgrade an existing system. (The Buyer's Guide and the Upgrader's Guide at the end of this book provide additional information.) It also will help you to evaluate whether or not an existing microcomputer system is powerful enough for today's new and exciting applications. For example, with the right hardware, you can use your computer to watch TV while you work and to capture video clips for class presentations.

Sometime you may get the chance to watch when a technician opens up a microcomputer. You will see that it is basically a collection of electronic circuitry. While there is no need to understand how all these components work, it is important to understand the principles. Once you do, you will be able to determine how powerful a particular microcomputer is. This will help you judge whether it can run particular kinds of programs and can meet your needs as a user.

Competent end users need to understand the functionality of the basic components in the system unit, including the system board, microprocessor, memory, expansion slots and cards, bus lines, ports, cables, and power supply units.

System Unit

The **system unit,** also known as the **system chassis,** is a container that houses most of the electronic components that make up a computer system. There are a variety of different categories or types of system units.

Categories

All computer systems have a system unit. For microcomputers, there are six basic types (see Figure 6-1):

- **Desktop system units** typically contain the system's electronic components and selected secondary storage devices. Input and output devices, such as a mouse, keyboard, and monitor, are located outside the system unit. This type of system unit is designed to be placed either horizontally or vertically.
- **Media center system units** blur the line between desktop computers and dedicated entertainment devices. Media center system units use powerful desktop system hardware with specialized graphics cards for interfacing with televisions and other home entertainment devices. A special operating system like Microsoft Windows Media Center provides on-demand TV programs, movies, music, and games.
- **Notebook system units** are portable and much smaller. These system units contain the electronic components, selected secondary storage devices, and input devices (keyboard and pointing device). Located outside the system unit, the monitor is attached by hinges. Notebook system units are often called **laptops.**
- **Netbook system units** are similar to notebook system units. They are, however, smaller, less powerful, and less expensive. **Netbooks** are designed to support on-the-go Web browsing and e-mail access. They reduce space and weight by leaving out components such as optical drives.
- **Tablet PC system units** are similar to notebook system units. **Tablet PCs** are highly portable devices that support the use of a stylus or pen to input

Desktop

Media Center

Notebook

Netbook

Tablet PC

Handheld

Figure 6-1 Basic types of system units

commands and data. There are two basic types. One type is effectively a notebook computer that accepts stylus input and has a monitor that swivels and folds onto its keyboard. The other type has a removable keyboard. With the keyboard attached, this second type can be used like a traditional notebook computer. With the keyboard detached, the unit is more portable and all input is typically with a stylus.

• **Handheld computer system units** are the smallest and are designed to fit into the palm of one hand. These systems contain an entire computer system, including the electronic components, secondary storage, and input and output devices. **Personal digital assistants (PDAs)** and **smartphones** are the most widely used handheld computers.

Figure 6-2 **System unit components**

Components

While the actual size may vary, each type of system unit has the same basic system components including system board, microprocessor, and memory. (See Figure 6-2.) Before considering these components, however, a more basic issue must be addressed. How do we as human beings communicate with and control all this electronic circuitry?

CONCEPT CHECK

What is the system unit?

Describe the six basic types of microcomputer system units.

What is a tablet PC? Describe the two basic types.

Electronic Data and Instructions

Have you ever wondered why it is said that we live in a digital world? It's because computers cannot recognize information the same way you and I can. People follow instructions and process data using letters, numbers, and special characters. For example, if we wanted someone to add the numbers 3 and 5 together and record the answer, we might say "please add 3 and 5." The system unit, however, is electronic circuitry and cannot directly process such a request.

Our voices create **analog,** or continuous, signals that vary to represent different tones, pitches, and volume. Computers, however, can recognize only **digital** electronic signals. Before any processing can occur within the system unit, a conversion must occur from what we understand to what the system unit can electronically process.

Numeric Representation

What is the most fundamental statement you can make about electricity? It is simply this: It can be either on or off. Indeed, there are many forms of technology that can make use of this two-state on/off, yes/no, present/absent arrangement. For instance, a light switch may be on or off, or an electric circuit open or closed. A specific location on a tape or disk may have a positive charge or a negative charge. This is the reason, then, that a two-state or binary system is used to represent data and instructions.

The decimal system that we are all familiar with has 10 digits (0, 1, 2, 3, 4, 5, 6, 7, 8, 9). The **binary system,** however, consists of only two digits—0 and 1. Each 0 or 1 is called a **bit**—short for binary digit. In the system unit, the 1 can be represented by a positive charge and the 0 by no electrical charge. In order to represent numbers, letters, and special characters, bits are combined into groups of eight called **bytes.** Whenever you enter a number into a computer system, that number must be converted into a binary number before it can be processed. To learn more about binary systems and binary arithmetic, visit our Web site at www.computing2011.com and enter the keyword binary.

Any number can be expressed as a binary number. Binary numbers, however, are difficult for humans to work with because they require so many digits. Instead, binary numbers are often represented in a format more readable by humans. The **hexadecimal system,** or **hex,** uses 16 digits (0, 1, 2, 3, 4, 5, 6, 7, 8, 9, A, B, C, D, E, F) to represent binary numbers. Each hex digit represents four binary digits, and two hex digits are commonly used together to represent 1 byte (8 binary digits). (See Figure 6-3.) You may have already seen hex when selecting a color in a Web site design or drawing application, or when entering the password for access to a wireless network.

Decimal	Binary	Hex
0	00000000	00
1	00000001	01
2	00000010	02
3	00000011	03
4	00000100	04
5	00000101	05
6	00000110	06
7	00000111	07
8	00001000	08
9	00001001	09
10	00001010	0A
11	00001011	0B
12	00001100	0C
13	00001101	0D
14	00001110	0E
15	00001111	0F

Figure 6-3 Numeric representations

Character Encoding

As we've seen, computers must represent all numbers with the binary system internally. What about text? How can a computer provide representations of the nonnumeric characters we use to communicate, such as the sentence you are reading now? The answer is character encoding schemes or standards.

Character encoding standards assign a unique sequence of bits to each character. Historically, microcomputers used the **ASCII (American Standard Code for Information Interchange)** to represent characters while mainframe computers used **EBCDIC (Extended Binary Coded Decimal Interchange Code).** These schemes were quite effective; however, they are limited. ASCII, for example, only uses 7 bits to represent each character, which means that only 128 total characters could be represented. This was fine for most characters in the English language but was not large enough to support other languages such as Chinese and Japanese. These languages have too many characters to be represented by the 7-bit ASCII code.

The explosion of the Internet and subsequent globalization of computing has led to a new character encoding called **Unicode.** The Unicode standard is the most widely used character encoding standard and is recognized by virtually every computer system. The first 128 characters are assigned the same sequence of bits as ASCII to maintain compatibility with older ASCII-formatted information. However, Unicode uses a variable number of bits to represent each character, which allows non-English characters and special characters to be represented.

CONCEPT CHECK

What is the difference between an analog and a digital electronic signal?

What are decimal and binary systems? How are they different?

Compare EBCDIC, ASCII, and Unicode.

System Board

On the Web Explorations

Improvements in system unit components are being made every day.

To learn more about a company on the forefront of these technologies, visit our Web site at www.computing2011.com and enter the keyword component.

The **system board** is also known as the **motherboard.** The system board controls communications for the entire computer system. Every component of the system unit connects to the system board. It acts as a data path and traffic monitor, allowing the various components to communicate efficiently with one another. External devices such as the keyboard, mouse, and monitor could not communicate with the system unit without the system board.

On a desktop computer, the system board is typically located at the bottom of the system unit or along one side. It is a large flat circuit board covered with a variety of different electronic components including sockets, slots, and bus lines. (See Figure 6-4.)

Figure 6-4 System board

Figure 6-5 Chip

Figure 6-6 Chip mounted onto a carrier package

- **Sockets** provide a connection point for small specialized electronic parts called chips. **Chips** consist of tiny circuit boards etched onto squares of sandlike material called silicon. These circuit boards can be smaller than the tip of your finger. (See Figure 6-5.) A chip is also called a **silicon chip, semiconductor,** or **integrated circuit.** Chips are mounted on **carrier packages.** (See Figure 6-6.) These packages either plug directly into sockets on the system board or onto cards that are then plugged into slots on the system board. Sockets are used to connect the system board to a variety of different types of chips, including microprocessor and memory chips.

- **Slots** provide a connection point for specialized cards or circuit boards. These cards provide expansion capability for a computer system. For example, a modem card plugs into a slot on the system board to provide a connection to the Internet.

- Connecting lines called **bus lines** provide pathways that support communication among the various electronic components that are either located on the system board or attached to the system board. (See Figure 6-7.)

Figure 6-7 Bus lines

Notebook, tablet PC, and handheld system boards are smaller than desktop system boards. However, they perform the same functions as desktop system boards.

☑ CONCEPT CHECK

What is the system board and what does it do?

Define and describe sockets, slots, and bus lines.

What are chips? How are chips attached to the system board?

Microprocessor

In a microcomputer system, the **central processing unit (CPU)** or **processor** is contained on a single chip called the **microprocessor.** The microprocessor is the "brains" of the computer system. It has two basic components: the control unit and the arithmetic-logic unit.

Unit	Speed
Microsecond	Millionth of a second
Nanosecond	Billionth of a second
Picosecond	Trillionth of a second

Figure 6-8 Processing speeds

- **Control unit:** The **control unit** tells the rest of the computer system how to carry out a program's instructions. It directs the movement of electronic signals between memory, which temporarily holds data, instructions, and processed information, and the arithmetic-logic unit. It also directs these control signals between the CPU and input and output devices.

- **Arithmetic-logic unit:** The **arithmetic-logic unit,** usually called the **ALU,** performs two types of operations: arithmetic and logical. **Arithmetic operations** are, as you might expect, the fundamental math operations: addition, subtraction, multiplication, and division. **Logical operations** consist of comparisons. That is, two pieces of data are compared to see whether one is equal to (=), less than (<), or greater than (>) the other.

Microprocessor Chips

Chip processing capacities are often expressed in word sizes. A **word** is the number of bits (such as 16, 32, or 64) that can be accessed at one time by the CPU. The more bits in a word, the more data a computer can process at one time. As mentioned previously, eight bits group together to form a byte. A 32-bit-word computer can access 4 bytes at a time. A 64-bit-word computer can access 8 bytes at a time. Therefore, the computer designed to process 64-bit words is faster. Other factors affect a computer's processing capability including how fast it can process data and instructions.

The processing speed of a microprocessor is typically represented by its **clock speed,** which is related to number of times the CPU can fetch and process data or instructions in a second. Older microcomputers typically process data and instructions in millionths of a second, or microseconds. Newer microcomputers are much faster and process data and instructions in billionths of a second, or nanoseconds. Supercomputers, by contrast, operate at speeds measured in picoseconds—1,000 times as fast as microcomputers. (See Figure 6-8.) Logically, the higher a microprocessor's clock speed, the faster the microprocessor. However, some processors can handle multiple instructions per cycle or tick of the clock; this means that clock speed comparisons can only be made between processors that work the same way.

The two most significant recent developments in microprocessors are the 64-bit processor and the multicore chip. Until recently, 64-bit processors were only used in large mainframe and supercomputers. All of that is changing as 64-bit processors have become standard for most of today's desktop and laptop computers.

The other recent development is the multicore chip. As mentioned previously, a traditional microcomputer's CPU is typically contained on a single microprocessor chip. A new type of chip, the **multicore chip,** can provide two or more separate and independent CPUs. These chips allow a single computer to run two or more operations at the same time. For example, a dual-core process could have one core computing a complex Excel spreadsheet while the other is running a multimedia presentation. More significantly, however, is the potential for microcomputers to run very large, complex programs that previously required expensive and specialized hardware.

For multicore processors to be used effectively, computers must understand how to divide tasks into parts that can be distributed across each core—an operation called **parallel processing.** Operating systems such as Windows Vista and Mac OS X support parallel processing. Software developers use this technology for a wide range of applications from scientific programs to sophisticated computer games.

On the Web Explorations

The most powerful microprocessors are capable of multicore and 64-bit processing.

To learn more about one of the manufacturers of these chips, visit our Web site at www.computing2011.com and enter the keyword multi.

See Figure 6-9 for a table of popular microprocessors.

Specialty Processors

In addition to microprocessor chips, a variety of more specialized processing chips have been developed.

- **Coprocessors** are specialty chips designed to improve specific computing operations. One of the most widely used is the **graphics coprocessor,** also called a **GPU (graphics processing unit).** These processors are designed to handle a variety of specialized tasks such as displaying 3-D images and encrypting data.
- **Smart cards** are plastic cards the size of a regular credit card that have an embedded specialty chip. Many colleges and universities provide smart cards to their students for identfication.
- Many cars have as many as 70 separate specialty processors to control nearly everything from fuel efficiency to satellite entertainment and tracking systems.
- **RFID tags** are specialty chips embedded in merchandise to track their location. The International Civil Aviation Organization has proposed inserting RFID chips in over a billion passports to track visitors as they enter or leave the United States.

Processor	Manufacturer	Description
Atom	Intel	32- and 64-bit, single- and dual-core
Core 2 Duo	Intel	64-bit, dual-core
Core 2 Quad	Intel	64-bit, quad-core
Xeon	Intel	64-bit, dual- and quad-core
Athlon 64 X2	AMD	64-bit, dual-core
Nano	Via	64-bit, low power
Cell	Sony/Toshiba/IBM	64-bit, eight-core

Figure 6-9 Popular microprocessors

CONCEPT CHECK

Name and describe the two components of a microprocessor.

Define word, clock speed, multicore chip, and parallel processing.

What are specialty processors? Describe coprocessors, smart cards, and RFID tags.

Memory

Memory is a holding area for data, instructions, and information. Like microprocessors, **memory** is contained on chips connected to the system board. There are three well-known types of memory chips: random-access memory (RAM), read-only memory (ROM), and flash memory.

RAM

Random-access memory (RAM) chips hold the program (sequence of instructions) and data that the CPU is presently processing. (See Figure 6-10.) RAM is called temporary or volatile storage because everything in most types of RAM is lost as soon as the microcomputer is turned off. It is also lost if there is a power

Figure 6-10 RAM chips mounted on circuit board

Unit	Capacity
Megabyte (MB)	1 million bytes
Gigabyte (GB)	1 billion bytes
Terabyte (TB)	1 trillion bytes

Figure 6-11 Memory capacity

failure or other disruption of the electric current going to the microcomputer. Secondary storage, which we shall describe in Chapter 8, does not lose its contents. It is permanent or nonvolatile storage, such as the data stored on a hard disk. For this reason, as we mentioned earlier, it is a good idea to frequently save your work in progress to a secondary storage device. That is, if you are working on a document or a spreadsheet, every few minutes you should save, or store, the material.

Cache (pronounced "cash") **memory** improves processing by acting as a temporary high-speed holding area between the memory and the CPU. The computer detects which information in RAM is most frequently used and then copies that information into the cache. When needed, the CPU can quickly access the information from the cache.

Having enough RAM is important! For example, to use Microsoft Office 2007 effectively, you need a minimum of 256 MB of RAM to hold the program and another 512 MB–1024 MB of RAM for the operating system.

Some applications, such as photo editing software, may require even more. Fortunately, additional RAM can be added to a computer system by inserting an expansion module called a **DIMM (dual in-line memory module)** into the system board. The capacity or amount of RAM is expressed in bytes. There are three commonly used units of measurement to describe memory capacity. (See Figure 6-11.)

Other types of RAM include DRAM, SDRAM, DDR, and Direct RDRAM. To learn more about these other types of RAM, visit our Web site at www.computing 2011.com and enter the keyword **ram.**

Even if your computer does not have enough RAM to hold a program, it might be able to run the program using **virtual memory.** Most of today's operating systems support virtual memory. With virtual memory, large programs are divided into parts and the parts are stored on a secondary device, usually a hard disk. Each part is then read into RAM only when needed. In this way, computer systems are able to run very large programs. To learn more about how virtual memory works, visit our Web site at www.computing2011.com and enter the keyword **memory.**

ROM

Read-only memory (ROM) chips have information stored in them by the manufacturer. Unlike RAM chips, ROM chips are not volatile and cannot be changed by the user. "Read only" means that the CPU can read, or retrieve, data and programs written on the ROM chip. However, the computer cannot write—encode or change—the information or instructions in ROM.

ROM chips typically contain special instructions for detailed computer operations. For example, ROM instructions are needed to start a computer, to access memory, and to handle basic keyboard input.

Flash Memory

Flash memory offers a combination of the features of RAM and ROM. Like RAM, it can be updated to store new information. Like ROM, it does not lose that information when power to the computer system is turned off.

Flash memory is used for a wide range of applications. For example, it is used to store the startup instructions for a computer. This information would include the specifics concerning the amount of RAM and the type of keyboard, mouse, and secondary storage devices connected to the

tips

Does your computer seem to be getting slower and slower? Perhaps it's so slow you are thinking about buying a new one. Before doing that, consider the following suggestions that might add a little zip to your current system.

1 Uninstall programs you no longer need. Explore the contents of your hard disk and identify programs that you no longer need. If you have Windows XP, use Start/Control Panel/Add/Remove Programs (for Windows 2000 use Start/Settings/Control Panel/Add/Remove Programs) to access the Uninstall feature.

2 Empty the Recycle Bin. If you have either Windows 2000 or Windows XP, files are not removed from your hard disk when you delete them. Rather, they are moved to the Recycle Bin. To empty or remove files from the Recycle Bin, open the Recycle Bin and use File/Empty Recycle Bin.

3 Upgrade your hardware. See the Upgrader's Guide on page 348 to help determine which components to consider upgrading.

To see more tips, visit our Web site at www.computing2011.com and enter the keyword tips.

system unit. If changes are made to the computer system, these changes are reflected in flash memory.

See Figure 6-12 for a summary of the three types of memory.

Type	Use
RAM	Programs and data
ROM	Fixed start-up instructions
Flash	Flexible start-up instructions

Figure 6-12 Memory

☑ CONCEPT CHECK

What is memory? Name and describe three types.

What are cache memory, DIMM, and virtual memory?

Define ROM and flash memory.

Expansion Slots and Cards

Most microcomputers allow users to expand their systems by providing **expansion slots** on the system board. Users can insert optional devices known as **expansion cards** into these slots. (See Figure 6-13.) Ports on the cards allow cables to be connected from the expansion cards to devices outside the system unit. (See Figure 6-14.) There are a wide range of different types of expansion cards. Some of the most commonly used expansion cards are

- **Advanced graphics cards** provide high-quality 3D graphics and animation for games and simulations.
- **Sound cards** accept audio input from a microphone and convert it into a form that can be processed by the computer. Also, these cards convert internal electronic signals to audio signals so they can be heard from external speakers or home theater systems.
- **Modem cards** allow distant computers to communicate with one another by converting electronic signals from within the system unit into electronic signals that can travel over telephone lines and other types of connections.
- **Network interface cards (NIC),** also known as **network adapter cards,** are used to connect a computer to a network. (See Figure 6-15.) The network allows connected computers to share data, programs, and hardware. The network adapter card typically connects the system unit to a cable that connects to the network, or it provides a wireless connection.

Slot

Figure 6-13 Expansion cards fit into slots on the system board

Ports

Figure 6-14 Expansion card with three ports

- Now you can watch television, capture video, and surf the Internet at the same time. **TV tuner cards** contain a TV tuner and a video converter that changes a traditional TV signal into one that can be displayed on your monitor. To see how TV tuner cards work, visit our Web site at www.computing2011.com and enter the keyword **tv.** To learn about using TV tuner cards, see Making IT Work for You: TV Tuner Cards and Video Clips on pages 168 and 169.

Plug and Play was originally a set of specific hardware and software standards developed by Intel, Microsoft, and others. As hardware and software have evolved, however, Plug and Play has become a generic term that is associated with the ability to plug any device into a computer and have it play or work immediately. Some devices, however, are not plug and play and require that new device drivers be installed, as discussed in Chapter 5.

To meet the size constraints of notebook and handheld computers, small credit card–sized expansion cards have been developed. These cards plug into PCM-CIA (called **PC Cards**) or, most recently, **ExpressCard** slots. (See Figure 6-16.)

 CONCEPT CHECK

What are expansion slots and cards? Name five expansion cards.

Discuss Plug and Play.

What are PC card and ExpressCard slots?

 tips

Having problems or want to upgrade your system and would like professional help? Here are a few suggestions:

1 **Select a reputable computer store.** Consider local as well as national chain stores. Check them out with the Better Business Bureau.

2 **Visit the store with your computer.** Ideally, have a knowledgeable friend accompany you. Describe the problem and get a written estimate. Ask about the company's warranty.

3 **Tag your system.** If you leave the system, attach a tag with your name, address, and telephone number.

4 **Pay by credit card.** If a dispute occurs, many credit card companies will intervene on your side.

To see additional tips, visit our Web site at www.computing2011.com and enter the keyword tips.

Figure 6-15 Network interface card

Figure 6-16 PC card

Bus Lines

A **bus line**—also known simply as a **bus**—connects the parts of the CPU to each other. Buses also link the CPU to various other components on the system board. (See Figure 6-17.) A bus is a pathway for bits representing data and instructions. The number of bits that can travel simultaneously down a bus is known as the **bus width.**

A bus is similar to a multilane highway that moves bits rather than cars from one location to another. The number of traffic lanes determines the bus width. A highway (bus line) with more traffic lanes (bus width) can move traffic (data and instructions) more efficiently. For example, a 64-bit bus can move twice as much information at a time as a 32-bit bus. Why should you even care about what a bus line is? Because as microprocessor chips have changed, so have bus lines. Bus design or bus architecture is an important factor relating to the speed and power for a particular computer. Additionally, many devices, such as expansion boards, will work with only one type of bus.

Expansion Buses

Every computer system has two basic categories of buses. One category, called **system buses,** connects the CPU to memory on the system board. The other category, called **expansion buses,** connects the CPU to other components on the system board, including expansion slots.

Computer systems typically have a combination of different types of expansion buses. The principal types are PCI, USB, Firewire, SATA, and PCIe.

Figure 6-17 Bus is a pathway for bits

- **Peripheral component interconnect (PCI)** was originally developed to meet the video demands of graphical user interfaces. When first introduced, it had a 32-bit bus width and was over 20 times faster than the older buses that it replaced. Almost all PCI buses are now 64-bit and are very common on older computers.

- **Universal serial bus (USB)** is widely used today. It combines with a PCI bus on the system board to support several external devices without using expansion cards or slots. External USB devices are connected from one to another or to a common point or hub and then onto the USB bus. The USB bus then connects to the PCI bus on the system board. The current USB standard, USB 2.0, is soon to replaced by the recently announced USB 3.0.

- **FireWire buses** are similar to USB buses. Although reports differ, FireWire buses are generally considered slightly faster than the USB 2.0 bus. Both are used to support a variety of specialized applications such as digital camcorders and video editing devices.

- **Serial Advanced Technology Attachment (SATA)** buses are one of the newest buses. It is much faster than USB 2.0 and FireWire buses and is now widely used to connect high-speed storage devices to the system board.

- **PCI Express (PCIe)** is another recently developed bus. It is widely used in many of today's most powerful computers. Unlike the PCI bus and most other buses that share a single bus line or path with several devices, the PCIe bus provides a single dedicated path for each connected device. PCIe buses are much faster and are replacing the PCI bus.

Making IT work for you

TV TUNER CARDS AND VIDEO CLIPS

Want to watch your favorite television program while you work? Perhaps you would like to include a video clip from television in a class presentation. It's easy using a TV tuner card.

Viewing Once a TV tuner card has been installed, you can view your favorite TV shows, even while running other applications such as PowerPoint. For example, you could use a Hauppauge TV tuner product and Hauppauge software as shown below.

1 ● **Launch the WinTV application.**

● **Size and move the television application window.**

● **Select a channel to view.**

Channel selector

Television application window

Capturing You can capture the video playing in the TV window into a digital file by following the steps shown below.

1 • Click the *Record* button to begin recording.

   • Click the *Stop* button to stop recording.

   • Select a location and name to save your captured video file.

Record/Stop button

Using Once captured in a file, a video can be used in any number of ways. It can be added to a Web page, attached to an e-mail, or added to a class presentation. For example, you could include a video clip in a PowerPoint presentation by following the steps below.

1 • Select the *Insert* tab, and then select *Movie* from the Media Clips group.

   • Select the video file you saved in the previous step.

   • Choose whether the video file should start automatically, or only when you click it during your presentation.

   • Drag and resize the inserted movie clip as needed.

Inserted movie clip

TV tuner cards are relatively inexpensive and easy to install. Some factors limiting their performance on your computer are the speed of your processor, the amount of memory, and secondary storage capacity.

TV tuner cards are continually changing, and some of the specifics presented in this Making IT Work for You may have changed.

To learn about other ways to make information technology work for you, visit our Web site at www.computing2011.com and enter the keyword miw.

CONCEPT CHECK

What is a bus and what is bus width?

What is the difference between a system and an expansion bus?

Discuss the five principal types of buses.

Ports

A **port** is a socket for external devices to connect to the system unit. (See Figure 6-18.) Some ports connect directly to the system board while others connect to cards that are inserted into slots on the system board. Some ports are standard features of most computer systems and others are more specialized.

Standard Ports

Most microcomputers come with a standard set of ports for connecting a monitor, keyboard, and other peripheral devices. The most common ports include

- **VGA (Video Graphics Adapter)** and **DVI (Digital Video Interface) ports** provide connections to analog and digital monitors, respectively.

Figure 6-18 Ports

DVI has become the most commonly used standard, but VGA ports are still provided on almost all systems for compatibility with older/lower-cost monitors.

- **Universal serial bus (USB) ports** can be used to connect several devices to the system unit and are widely used to connect keyboards, mice, printers, and storage devices to the system unit. A single USB port can be used to connect many USB devices to the system unit.
- **FireWire ports** provide high-speed connections to specialized FireWire devices such as camcorders and storage devices.
- **Ethernet ports** are a high-speed networking port that has become a standard for many of today's computers. Ethernet allows you to connect multiple computers for sharing files, or to a DSL or cable modem for high-speed Internet access.

Specialized Ports

In addition to standard ports, there are numerous specialty ports including S/PDIF, HDMI, and MIDI.

- **Sony/Philips Digital Interconnect Format (S/PDIF)** ports are also known as **optical audio connections.** These ports are used to integrate computers into high-end audio and home theatre systems.
- **High Definition Multimedia Interface (HDMI)** ports provide high-definition video and audio, making it possible to use a computer as a video jukebox or an HD video recorder.
- **Musical instrument digital interface (MIDI)** ports are a special type of serial port for connecting musical instruments like an electronic keyboard to a sound card. The sound card converts the music into a series of digital instructions. These instructions can be processed immediately to reproduce the music or saved to a file for later processing.

Legacy Ports

In the past, additional ports were common on microcomputer systems to connect specific types of devices. These older ports, known as **legacy ports,** have largely been replaced by faster, more flexible ports such as the universal serial bus (USB).

- **Serial ports** were used for a wide variety of purposes, such as connecting a mouse, keyboard, modem, and many other devices to the system unit. Serial ports sent data one bit at a time and were good for sending information over long distances.
- **Parallel ports** were used to connect external devices that needed to send or receive a lot of data over a short distance. These ports typically sent eight bits of data simultaneously across eight parallel wires. Parallel ports were mostly used to connect printers to the system unit.
- **Keyboard** and **mouse ports** were used to connect keyboards and mice to the system unit. Different types of keyboard ports existed for different types of keyboards, making some keyboards incompatible with some system units.
- **Infrared Data Association (IrDA) ports** were used to provide a wireless mechanism for transferring data between devices. Instead of cables, the

Figure 6-19 Cables

IrDA ports from each device were directly aligned and infrared light waves were used to transmit data. One of the most common applications was to transfer data from either a handheld or notebook computer to a desktop computer.

- **Game ports** were used to connect video game controllers and joysticks.

Cables

Cables are used to connect exterior devices to the system unit via the ports. One end of the cable is attached to the device and the other end has a connector that is attached to a matching connector on the port. (See Figure 6-19.)

Power Supply

Computers require direct current (DC) to power their electronic components and to represent data and instructions. DC power can be provided indirectly by converting alternating current (AC) from standard wall outlets or directly from batteries.

- Desktop computers have a **power supply unit** located within the system unit. (See Figure 6-20.) This unit plugs into a standard wall outlet, converts AC to DC, and provides the power to drive all of the system unit components.
- Notebook computers use **AC adapters** that are typically located outside the system unit. (See Figure 6-21.) AC adapters plug into a standard wall outlet, convert AC to DC, provide power to drive the system unit components, and can recharge the batteries. Notebook computers can be operated either using an AC adapter plugged into a wall outlet or using battery power. Notebook batteries typically provide sufficient power for four to six hours before they need to be recharged.

Figure 6-20 Power supply unit

Figure 6-21 AC adapter

- Like notebook computers, handheld computers use AC adapters located outside the system unit. Unlike notebook computers, however, handheld computers typically operate only using battery power. The AC adapter is used to recharge the batteries.

CONCEPT CHECK

What are ports? What do they do?

Describe four standard, three specialized, and five legacy ports.

What is a power supply unit? What is an AC adaptor?

Careers in IT

Computer technicians repair and install computer components and systems. (See Figure 6-22.) They may work on everything from personal computers and mainframe servers to printers. Some computer technicians are responsible for setting up and maintaining computer networks. Experienced computer technicians may work with computer engineers to diagnose problems and run routine maintenance on complex systems. Job growth is expected in this field as computer equipment becomes more complicated and technology expands.

Employers look for those with certification in computer repair or associate degrees from vocational schools. Employment usually begins with training, but most employers expect applicants to have prior technical experience. Computer technicians also can expect to continue their education to keep up with technological changes. Good communication skills are important in this field.

Computer technicians can expect an hourly wage of $13.50 to $22.50. Opportunities for advancement typically come in the form of work on more advanced computer systems. Some computer technicians move into customer service positions or go into sales. To learn more about other careers in information technology, visit us at www.computing2011.com and enter the keyword **careers**.

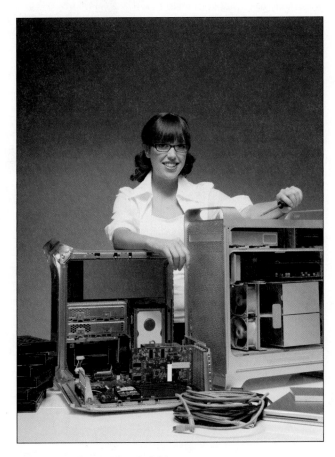

Figure 6-22 Computer technician

A LOOK TO THE FUTURE

As You Walk out the Door, Don't Forget Your Computer

Wouldn't it be nice if you could conveniently access the Internet wirelessly at any time during the day? What if you could send and receive e-mail while jogging without touching a screen, or send a friend live video of what you are looking at? What If a computer on your body could help you remember the names of people at a party? Of course, many people currently use wireless phone technology when they are away from their home or office. What if these users could accomplish these tasks with an even smaller, more portable, and less intrusive system? Will people be wearing computers rather than carrying them?

Wearable computers already exist for specialized military and industrial use. Imagine using your hands to prepare a meal or work on a car with instructions and diagrams instantly available in your line of sight. Some of these systems are composed of a computer that is worn inside a jacket or in a belt and a head-mounted display. The display allows you to see the equivalent of a desktop monitor via a small screen that is worn in front of one eye or projected onto the inside of a regular pair of eyeglasses. Such devices might be used in airports by security personnel. These devices are currently being used by the U.S. Department of Defense for military applications and by the Toronto Blue Jays to end long lines at ticket windows. When coupled with face recognition technology, these products provide security personnel portable and instant communication with the command center. Police and security officers may someday use this technology to check IDs and verify your identity.

Experts say that wearable computers will be used by surgeons in operating rooms to "view" their patients. Will we be wearing computers soon? Some of us already are. And some experts predict the majority of us will employ a wearable computer before the end of the decade. Many computer manufacturers are currently working on wearable computers, and there is even a wearable computer fashion show that showcases the latest designs.

Many people are already wearing their computers, and making use of this mobile technology to read e-mail while waiting in lines or even studying their notes for the next exam. What do you think? Will people someday grab their keys and their computers before they leave the house? Will your computer one day be housed in your jacket? Do you see any potential issues that might come up if wearable computers were widespread?

SYSTEM UNIT

System unit (system chassis) contains electronic components.

Categories
There are six basic categories of system units: **desktop, media center, notebook (laptop), netbook, tablet PC,** and **handheld.**

Components
Each type of system unit has the same basic components including system board, microprocessor, and memory.

ELECTRONIC REPRESENTATION

Human voices create **analog** (continuous) signals; computers only recognize **digital** electronic signals.

Numeric Representation
Data and instructions can be represented electronically with a two-state or **binary system** of numbers (0 and 1). Each 0 or 1 is called a **bit. A byte** consists of eight bits. **Hexadecimal system (hex)** uses 16 digits to represent binary numbers.

Character Encoding
Character encoding standards assign unique sequences of bits to each character. Three standards are **ASCII (American Standard Code for Information Interchange)**, **EBCDIC (Extended Binary Coded Decimal Interchange Code)**, and **Unicode.**

SYSTEM BOARD

The **system board (motherboard)** connects all system components and allows input and output devices to communicate with the system unit. It is a flat circuit board covered with these electronic components:

- **Sockets** provide connection points for **chips (silicon chips, semiconductors, integrated circuits)**. Chips are mounted on **carrier packages.**
- **Slots** provide connection points for specialized cards or circuit boards.
- **Bus lines** provide pathways to support communication.

To be a competent end user, you need to understand how data and programs are represented electronically. Additionally, you need to understand the functionality of the basic components in the system unit: system board, microprocessor, memory, expansion slots and cards, bus lines, and ports and cables.

MICROPROCESSOR

Processor	Manufacturer	Description
Atom	Intel	32- and 64-bit, single- and dual-core
Core 2 Duo	Intel	64-bit, dual-core
Core 2 Quad	Intel	64-bit, quad-core
Xeon	Intel	64-bit, dual- and quad-core
Athlon 64 X2	AMD	64-bit, dual-core
Nano	Via	64-bit, low power
Cell	Sony/Toshiba/IBM	64-bit, eight-core

The **microprocessor** is a single chip that contains the **central processing unit (CPU)** or **microprocessor.** It has two basic components:

- **Control unit** tells the computer system how to carry out program instructions.
- **Arithmetic-logic unit (ALU)** performs **arithmetic** and **logical operations.**

Microprocessor Chips

A **word** is the number of bits that can be accessed by the microprocessor at one time. **Clock speed** represents the number of times the CPU can fetch and process data or instructions in a second. Older microprocessors process data and instructions in microseconds; newer ones process in nanoseconds. Supercomputers process in picoseconds.

The two most significant developments are 64-bit processors and **multicore chips. Parallel processing** requires programs that allow multiple processors to work together to run large complex programs.

Specialty Processors

Specialty processors include **graphics coprocessors** also known as **GPU** or **graphics processing unit** (process graphic images), **smart cards** (plastic cards containing embedded chips), processors in automobiles (monitor fuel efficiency, satellite entertainment, and tracking systems), and **RFID tags** (track merchandise).

MEMORY

Memory holds data, instructions, and information. There are three types of memory chips: RAM, ROM, and **flash memory.**

RAM

RAM (random-access memory) chips are called temporary or volatile storage because their contents are lost if power is disrupted.

- **Cache memory** is a high-speed holding area for frequently used data and information.
- **DIMM (dual in-line memory module)** is used to expand memory.
- **Virtual memory** divides large programs into parts that are read into RAM as needed.

ROM

ROM (read-only memory) chips are nonvolatile storage and control essential system operations.

Flash Memory

Flash memory is a type of memory that does not lose its contents when power is removed. It is used to store information about a computer's configuration.

Unit	Capacity
Megabyte (MB)	1 million bytes
Gigabyte (GB)	1 billion bytes
Terabyte (TB)	1 trillion bytes

EXPANSION SLOTS AND CARDS

Most computers allow users to expand their systems by providing **expansion slots** on their system boards to accept **expansion cards.**

Examples of expansion cards include **advanced graphics cards, sound cards, modem cards, network interface cards (NIC; network adapter cards), and TV tuner cards.**

Plug and Play is the ability for a computer to recognize and configure a device without human interaction.

PC Card and **ExpressCard** slots accept credit card–sized expansion cards in notebook computers.

BUS LINES

Bus lines, also known as **buses,** provide data pathways that connect various system components. **Bus width** is the number of bits that can travel simultaneously.

Expansion Buses

System buses connect CPU and memory. **Expansion buses** connect CPU and slots. Five principal expansion bus types are **PCI (peripheral component interconnect), USB (universal serial bus), FireWire bus, SATA (Serial Advanced Technology Attachment), and PCIe (PCI Express).**

PORTS

Ports are connecting sockets on the outside of the system unit.

Standard Ports

Four standard ports are

- **VGA (Video Graphics Adapter)** and **DVI (Digital Video Interface)**—provide connections to monitors.
- **USB (universal serial bus)**—widely used to connect keyboards, mice, printers, and storage devices; one port can connect several devices to system unit.
- **FireWire**—almost twice as fast as USB 2.0; provide connections for specialized FireWire devices.
- **Ethernet**—high-speed networking port that has become a standard for many of today's computers.

Specialized Ports

Three specialty ports are

- **S/PDIF (Sony/Philips Digital Interface)** for high-end audio and home theatre systems, **HDMI (High Definition Multimedia Interface)** for high-definition digital audio and video, **and MIDI** for digital music.

Legacy Ports

Legacy ports have largely been replaced by faster, more flexible ports such as the universal serial bus (USB). These ports include **serial, parallel, keyboard, mouse,** and **Infrared Data Association (IrDA).**

Cables

Cables are used to connect external devices to the system unit via ports.

POWER SUPPLY

Power supply units convert AC to DC; they are located within the desktop computer's system unit. **AC adapters** power notebook computers and tablet PCs and recharge batteries.

CAREERS IN IT

Computer technicians repair and install computer components and systems. Certification in computer repair or associate degrees from vocational schools required. Hourly wage $13.50 to $22.50.

KEY TERMS

AC adapter (172)
advanced graphics
  card (165)
analog (158)
arithmetic-logic unit
  (ALU) (162)
arithmetic
  operation (162)
ASCII (159)
binary system (159)
bit (159)
bus (167)
bus line (161, 167)
bus width (167)
byte (159)
cable (172)
cache memory (164)
carrier package (161)
central processing unit
  (CPU) (161)
character encoding
  standards (159)
chip (161)
clock speed (162)
computer
  technician (173)
control unit (162)
coprocessor (163)
desktop system
  unit (156)
digital (158)
DIMM (164)
DVI (Digital Video
  Interface) port (171)
EBCDIC (159)
Ethernet ports (171)
expansion bus (167)
expansion card (165)
expansion slot (165)
ExpressCard (166)
FireWire bus (167)
FireWire port (171)
flash memory (164)
game port (172)
GPU (163)

graphics
  coprocessor (163)
handheld computer
  system unit (157)
hexadecimal system
  (hex) (159)
High Definition
  Multimedia Interface
  (HDMI) (171)
Infrared Data Association
  (IrDA) port (171)
integrated circuit (161)
keyboard port (171)
laptop computer (156)
legacy port (171)
logical operation (162)
media center system
  unit (156)
memory (163)
microprocessor (161)
modem card (165)
motherboard (159)
mouse port (171)
multicore chips (162)
musical instrument
  digital interface
  (MIDI) (171)
netbook (156)
netbook system
  unit (156)
network adapter
  card (165)
network interface card
  (NIC) (165)
notebook system
  unit (156)
optical audio
  connections (171)
parallel port (171)
parallel
  processing (162)
PC card (166)
PCI Express
  (PCIe) (167)

peripheral component
  interconnect
  (PCI) (167)
personal digital assistant
  (PDA) (157)
Plug and Play (166)
port (170)
power supply unit (172)
processor (161)
random-access memory
  (RAM) (163)
read-only memory
  (ROM) (164)
RFID tag (163)
semiconductor (161)
Serial Advanced
  Technology Attachment
  (SATA) (167)
serial port (171)
silicon chip (161)
slot (161)
smart card (163)
smartphone (157)
socket (161)
Sony/Philips Digital
  Interconnect Format
  (S/PDIF) (171)
sound card (165)
system board (160)
system bus (167)
system chassis (156)
system unit (156)
tablet PC (156)
tablet PC system
  unit (156)
TV tuner card (166)
Unicode (159)
universal serial
  bus (167)
universal serial bus
  (USB) port (171)
VGA (Video Graphics
  Adapter) port (170)
virtual memory (164)
word (162)

To test your knowledge of these key terms with animated flash cards, visit our Web
site at www.computing2011.com and enter the keyword terms6.

MULTIPLE CHOICE

Circle the letter or fill in the correct answer.

1. The container that houses most of the electronic components that make up a computer system is known as the
   a. arithmetic-logic unit
   b. central processing unit
   c. RFID
   d. system unit

2. The smallest unit in a digital system is a
   a. byte
   b. bit
   c. word
   d. character

3. The _____ controls communications for the entire computer system.
   a. arithmetic-logic unit
   b. semiconductor
   c. motherboard
   d. coprocessor

4. These provide expansion capability for a computer system.
   a. sockets
   b. slots
   c. bytes
   d. bays

5. The _____ tells the rest of the computer how to carry out a program's instructions.
   a. ALU
   b. control unit
   c. system unit
   d. motherboard

6. A 32-bit word computer can access _____ bytes at a time.
   a. 4
   b. 8
   c. 16
   d. 32

7. These chips are specifically designed to handle the processing requirements related to displaying and manipulating 3-D images.
   a. graphics coprocessors
   b. arithmetic-logic unit processors
   c. control unit processors
   d. CISC chips

8. This type of memory improves processing by acting as a temporary high-speed holding area between the memory and the CPU.
   a. RAM
   b. ROM
   c. cache memory
   d. flash memory

9. _____ refers to a computer's ability to configure and use a device without human interaction.
   a. CPU
   b. Plug and Play
   c. Cache
   d. ALU

10. _____ ports connect special types of music instruments to sound cards.
    a. BUS
    b. CPU
    c. USB
    d. MIDI

For an interactive multiple-choice practice test, visit our Web site at www.computing 2011.com and enter the keyword multiple6.

MATCHING

Match each numbered item with the most closely related lettered item. Write your answers in the spaces provided.

a. bus width
b. cables
c. control unit
d. expansion card
e. ExpressCard
f. port
g. RAM
h. smart card
i. system bus
j. system unit

1. Houses most of the electronic components in a computer system. _____
2. The number of bits that can travel down a bus at the same time. _____
3. Tells the computer system how to carry out a program's instructions. _____
4. A credit card–sized piece of plastic with an embedded chip. _____
5. Volatile storage that holds the program and data the CPU is currently processing. _____
6. Connects the CPU to memory. _____
7. Plugs into slots on the system board. _____
8. A type of slot used by notebook computers. _____
9. Connecting socket on the outside of the system unit. _____
10. Connects input and output devices to the system unit via the ports. _____

For an interactive matching practice test, visit our Web site at www.computing2011.com and enter the keyword matching6.

OPEN-ENDED

On a separate sheet of paper, respond to each question or statement.

1. Describe the six basic types of system units.
2. Describe the two basic components of the CPU.
3. What are the differences and similarities between the three types of memory?
4. Identify five expansion cards and describe the function of each.
5. Identify and describe four standard ports, three specialized ports, and five legacy ports.

APPLYING TECHNOLOGY

The following questions are designed to demonstrate ways that you can effectively use technology today. The first question relates directly to this chapter's Making IT Work for You feature.

1 TV TUNER CARDS AND VIDEO CLIPS

Want to watch your favorite television program while you work? Perhaps you would like to include a video clip in a class presentation. It's easy using a video TV card. To learn more about this technology, review Making IT Work for You: TV Tuner Cards and Video Clips on pages 168 and 169. Then visit our Web site at www.computing2011.com and enter the keyword tuner. Play the video and answer the following: (a) Describe the two windows that open when the TV icon is selected. (b) What are the basic functions of the control box? (c) What is the command sequence to insert a video clip into a PowerPoint presentation?

2 DESKTOP AND NOTEBOOK COMPUTERS

Are you thinking about purchasing a new computer? Visit our Web site at www.computing2011.com and enter the keyword computer to link to a site that presents information about the newest desktop and notebook computers. Check out different desktop and notebook models and then answer the following questions: (a) If you were to purchase a desktop computer, which one would you select? Describe how it would fit your needs and print out its specifications. (b) If you were to purchase a notebook computer, which one would you select? Describe how it would fit your needs and print out its specifications. (c) If you had to choose between the desktop and notebook, which one would you choose? Why?

3 CUSTOM SYSTEM UNITS

When it is time for you to purchase your next computer, you might consider shopping online. A big advantage to choosing a computer online instead of in a store is that many computer manufacturers allow you to customize your new computer and build it to order. Visit our Web site at www.computing2011.com and enter the keyword custom to connect to a retailer of customized computers and use their online tools to customize and price a computer that meets your current needs. Then answer the following questions: (a) Which of the three types of system units did you configure? (b) What microprocessor did you choose? (c) How much and what type of memory option did you choose? (d) Would you purchase the computer you customized? Why or why not?

EXPANDING YOUR KNOWLEDGE

The following questions are designed to add depth and detail to your understanding of specific topics presented within this chapter. The questions direct you to sources other than the textbook to obtain this knowledge.

1 HOW TV TUNER CARDS WORK

The advent of digital TV and the success of digital video recorders have made TV tuner cards a popular addition to many computers. TV tuner cards allow you to watch and record TV shows on your computer, even while running other applications. To learn more about how TV tuner cards work, visit our Web site at www.computing2011.com and enter the keyword tv. Then answer the following questions: (a) What are some examples of inputs to a TV tuner card? (b) What is the function of a TV tuner card? (c) Where can the TV tuner card send the video signal once it is converted?

2 HOW VIRTUAL MEMORY WORKS

Typically before a program can be executed, it must be read into RAM. Many programs, however, are too large to fit into many computer systems' RAM. One option is to increase the RAM in the system. Another way is to use virtual memory. To learn more about how virtual memory works, visit our Web site at www.computing2011.com and enter the keyword memory. Then answer the following: (a) What is virtual memory? (b) Define page file, page, and paging. (c) What is thrashing?

3 BINARY NUMBERS

Binary numbers are the most basic unit that computers use to perform tasks. To learn more about how binary numbers work, visit our Web site at www.computing2011.com and enter the keyword binary. Then answer the following questions: (a) What character is represented by the binary number 01000011 in ASCII code? (b) What is the binary result of 1011 + 0010? What is the decimal equivalent to this number? (c) How many numbers can be represented with 1 bit (one binary "place")? How many by 2 bits? How many by 3 bits?

WRITING ABOUT TECHNOLOGY

The ability to think critically and to write effectively is essential to nearly every profession. The following questions are designed to help you develop these skills by posing thought-provoking questions about computer privacy, security, and/or ethics.

1 RFIDS

RFIDs have been touted by the media as an up-and-coming technology for several years. These tiny chips (that can be embedded in virtually everything) can be used to identify groceries, vehicles, and even people! Without knowing where RFID readers are placed and where RFID chips are embedded, it is unclear what information we might be sharing about ourselves and who we might be sharing it with. Write a one-page paper that addresses the following items: (a) What benefits do you see in using RFIDs in daily life? Explain your answers. (b) What privacy issues does an RFID raise for consumers? (c) Describe how RFIDs might be misused.

2 SMART CARDS

There have been numerous proposals in recent years to use smart card technology for personal identification, such as driver's licenses or a national ID card. Advocates claim that this would reduce identity fraud because the cards would contain biometric information such as a fingerprint scan. Research smart card technology on the Web and then answer the following questions in a one-page paper: (a) What are the benefits of using smart cards for identification? List several examples. (b) What privacy concerns exist? Be specific. (c) Would you be in favor of using smart cards for personal identification? Why or why not?

Input and Output

Competencies

After you have read this chapter, you should be able to:

1 Define input.

2 Describe keyboard entry including the different types of keyboards and keyboard features.

3 Discuss pointing devices including mice, touch screens, joysticks, and styluses.

4 Describe scanning devices including optical scanners and card readers.

5 Discuss image capturing devices including digital cameras and digital video cameras.

6 Define output.

7 Discuss monitor features, flat-panel, CRT, e-book readers, data projectors, and HDTVs.

8 Define printing features as well as ink-jet, laser, dot-matrix, thermal, plotter, photo, and portable printers.

9 Discuss audio-output devices.

10 Define combination input and output devices.

In the beginning the only input device was the keyboard. Every task on the computer began with a line of typed text. And most computers did not even have speakers; the only output was through a simple monitor and a dot-matrix printer. Today's input and output devices are much more diverse and sophisticated, allowing users to interact with their computers with their voice or handwriting.

Some experts predict in the future input devices will rely on gesture recognition. Computers will view human movement and interpret those gestures as commands. Output devices are expected to become more powerful as well. Imagine a world where the flick of your wrist controls the lights in your house or even starts your household appliances.

chapter 7

Introduction

How do you send instructions and information to the CPU? How do you get information out? Here we describe one of the most important places where computers interface with people. We input text, music, and even speech, but we probably never think about the relationship between what we enter and what the computer processes. People understand language, which is constructed of letters, numbers, and punctuation marks. However, at a basic level, computers can understand only the binary machine language of 0s and 1s. Input devices are essentially translators. Input devices translate numbers, letters, and actions that people understand into a form that computers can process.

Have you ever wondered how information processed by the system unit is converted into a form that you can use? That is the role of output devices. While input devices convert what we understand into what the system unit can process, output devices convert what the system unit has processed into a form that we can understand. Output devices translate machine language into letters, numbers, sounds, and images that people can understand.

Competent end users need to know about the most commonly used input devices, including keyboards, mice, scanners, digital cameras, voice recognition, and audio-input devices. Additionally, they need to know about the most commonly used output devices, including monitors, printers, and audio output devices. And end users need to be aware of combination input and output devices such as fax machines, multifunctional devices, and Internet telephones.

What Is Input?

Input is any data or instructions that are used by a computer. They can come directly from you or from other sources. You provide input whenever you use system or application programs. For example, when using a word processing program, you enter data in the form of numbers and letters and issue commands such as to save and to print documents. You also can enter data and issue commands by pointing to items, or using your voice. Other sources of input include scanned or photographed images.

Input devices are hardware used to translate words, sounds, images, and actions that people understand into a form that the system unit can process. For example, when using a word processor, you typically use a keyboard to enter text and a mouse to issue commands. In addition to keyboards and mice, there are a wide variety of other input devices. These include pointing, scanning, image capturing, and audio-input devices.

Keyboard Entry

One of the most common ways to input data is by **keyboard.** As mentioned in Chapter 6, keyboards convert numbers, letters, and special characters that people understand into electrical signals. These signals are sent to, and processed by, the system unit. Most keyboards use an arrangement of keys given

Figure 7-1 Ergonomic keyboard

the name QWERTY. This name reflects the keyboard layout by taking the letters of the first six alphabetic characters found on the top row of keys displaying letters.

Keyboards

There are a wide variety of different keyboard designs. They range from the full-sized to miniature and from rigid to flexible. There are even virtual keyboards that project an interactive key layout onto a flat surface. The most common types are

- **Traditional keyboards**—full-sized, rigid, rectangular keyboards that include function, navigational, and numeric keys.
- **Ergonomic keyboards**—similar to traditional keyboards. The keyboard arrangement, however, is not rectangular and a palm rest is provided. They are designed specifically to alleviate wrist strain associated with the repetitive movements of typing. (See Figure 7-1.)
- **Wireless keyboards**—transmit input to the system unit through the air. By eliminating connecting wires to the system unit, these keyboards provide greater flexibility and convenience.
- **PDA keyboards**—miniature keyboards for PDAs and smart phones to send e-mail, create documents, and more. (See Figure 7-2.)
- **Virtual keyboards**—display an image of a keyboard on a touch screen device. The screen functions as the actual input device, which is why the keyboard is considered virtual. Virtual keyboards are common on tablet computers and mobile devices.

Features

A computer keyboard combines a typewriter keyboard with a **numeric keypad,** used to enter numbers and arithmetic symbols. It also has many special-purpose keys. Some keys, such as the CAPS LOCK key, are **toggle keys.** These

On the Web Explorations

People are spending more time at their computers than ever before. Consequently, the need for ergonomic keyboards is increasing.

To learn more about one manufacturer of ergonomic keyboards, visit our Web site at www.computing2011.com and enter the keyword ergonomic.

Figure 7-2 **PDA keyboard**

Escape Key typically cancels a selection or a procedure.

Function Keys shortcut for specific tasks, F1, for example, typically displays on Help.

Numeric Keypad enters numbers and arithmetic symbols and controls cursor or insertion point.

Navigation Keys control the cursor or insertion point on the screen.

Spacebar displays the Start menu.

Figure 7-3 Keyboard features

keys turn a feature on or off. Others, such as the CTRL key, are **combination keys,** which perform an action when held down in combination with another key. To learn more about keyboard features, see Figure 7-3.

CONCEPT CHECK

What is input? What are input devices?

Discuss the five most common types of keyboard.

Define some common keyboard features?

Pointing Devices

Pointing, of course, is one of the most natural of all human gestures. Pointing devices provide a comfortable interface with the system unit by accepting pointing gestures and converting them into machine-readable input. There are a wide variety of different pointing devices, including the mouse, joystick, touch screen, and stylus.

Mice

A **mouse** controls a pointer that is displayed on the monitor. The **mouse pointer** usually appears in the shape of an arrow. It frequently changes shape, however, depending on the application. A mouse can have one, two, or more buttons, which are used to select command options and to control the mouse pointer on the monitor. Some mice have a **wheel button** that can be rotated to scroll through information that is displayed on the monitor.

Figure 7-4 Optical mouse

Figure 7-5 Trackball

Although there are several different mouse types, there are three basic designs:

- **Optical mouse** has no moving parts and is currently the most widely used. It emits and senses light to detect mouse movement. An optical mouse can be used on almost any surface with high precision. (See Figure 7-4.)

- **Mechanical mouse** has a ball on the bottom and is attached with a cord to the system unit. As you move the mouse across a smooth surface, the roller rotates and controls the pointer on the screen.

- **Cordless** or **wireless mouse** is a battery-powered device that typically uses radio waves or infrared light waves to communicate with the system unit. These devices eliminate the mouse cord and free up desk space.

Three devices similar to a mouse are trackballs, touch pads, and pointing sticks. You can use the **trackball,** also known as the **roller ball,** to control the pointer by rotating a ball with your thumb. (See Figure 7-5.) You can use **touch pads** to control the pointer by moving and tapping your finger on the surface of a pad. (See Figure 7-6.) You can use a **pointing stick,** located in the middle of the keyboard, to control the pointer by directing the stick with one finger. (See Figure 7-7.)

Figure 7-6 Touch pad

Figure 7-7 **Pointing stick**

Figure 7-8 **A touch screen**

Touch Screens

A **touch screen** is a particular kind of monitor with a clear plastic outer layer. Behind this layer are crisscrossed invisible beams of infrared light. This arrangement enables someone to select actions or commands by touching the screen with a finger. Touch screens are easy to use, especially when people need information quickly. They are commonly used at restaurants, automated teller machines (ATMs), and information centers. (See Figure 7-8.)

Multi-touch screens can be touched with more than one finger, which allows for interactions such as rotating graphical objects on the screen with your hand or zooming in and out by pinching and stretching your fingers. Multi-touch screens are commonly used on mobile devices such as the Apple iPhone, as well as some notebook computers and desktop monitors. (See Figure 7-9.)

Joysticks

The **joystick** is a popular input device for computer games. You control game actions by varying the pressure, speed, and direction of the joystick. Additional controls, such as buttons and triggers, are used to specify commands or initiate specific actions. (See Figure 7-10.)

Stylus

A **stylus** is a penlike device commonly used with tablet PCs and PDAs. (See Figure 7-11.) A stylus uses pressure to draw images on a screen. Often, a stylus interacts with the computer through handwriting recognition software. **Handwriting recognition software** translates handwritten notes into a form that the system unit can process.

Figure 7-9 **Multi-touch screen**

Figure 7-10 **Joystick**

Stylus

Figure 7-11 **Stylus**

Scanning Devices

Scanners move across text and images. Scanning devices convert scanned text and images into a form that the system unit can process. There are four types of scanning devices: optical scanners, card readers, bar code readers, and character and mark recognition devices.

Optical Scanners

An **optical scanner,** also known simply as a scanner, accepts documents consisting of text and/or images and converts them to machine-readable form. These devices do not recognize individual letters or images. Rather, they recognize light, dark, and colored areas that make up individual letters or images. Typically, scanned documents are saved in files that can be further processed, displayed, printed, or stored for later use. There are three basic types of optical scanners: flatbed, document, and portable. (See Figure 7-12.)

- **Flatbed scanner** is much like a copy machine. The image to be scanned is placed on a glass surface and the scanner records the image from below.

Flatbed scanner

Portable scanner

Document scanner

Figure 7-12 **Three types of scanners**

- **Document scanner** is similar to a flatbed scanner except that it can quickly scan multipage documents. It automatically feeds one page of a document at a time through a scanning surface.
- **Portable scanner** is typically a handheld device that slides across the image, making direct contact.

Optical scanners are powerful tools for a wide variety of end users, including graphics and advertising professionals who scan images and combine them with text. Lawyers and students use portable scanners as a valuable research tool to record information.

Card Readers

Nearly everyone uses a credit card, debit card, access (parking or building) card, and/or some type of identification card. These cards typically have the user's name, some type of identification number, and signature embossed on the card. Additionally, encoded information is often stored on the card as well. Card readers interpret this encoded information. There are two basic types:

- By far the most common is the **magnetic card reader.** The encoded information is stored on a thin magnetic strip located on the back of the card.

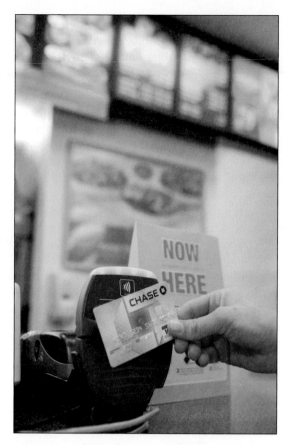

Figure 7-13 **Radio frequency card reader**

Figure 7-14 **Bar code reader**

When the card is swiped through the magnetic card reader, the information is read.

- **Radio frequency card readers** are not as common but more convenient because they do not require the card to actually make contact with the reader. The card has a small **RFID (radio frequency identification)** microchip that contains the user's encoded information. Whenever the card is passed within a few inches of the card reader, the user's information is read. (See Figure 7-13.)

Bar Code Readers

You are probably familiar with **bar code readers** or **scanners** from grocery stores. (See Figure 7-14.) These devices are either handheld **wand readers** or **platform scanners.** They contain photoelectric cells that scan or read **bar codes,** or the vertical zebra-striped marks printed on product containers.

Almost all supermarkets use electronic cash registers and a bar code system called the **Universal Product Code (UPC).** At the checkout counter, electronic cash registers use a bar code reader to scan each product's UPC code. The codes are sent to the supermarket's computer, which has a description, the latest price, and an inventory level for each product. The computer processes this input to update the inventory level and to provide the electronic cash register with the description and price for each product. These devices are so easy to use that many supermarkets are offering customers self-checkout stations.

Character and Mark Recognition Devices

Character and mark recognition devices are scanners that are able to recognize special characters and marks. They are specialty devices that are essential tools for certain applications. Three types are

- **Magnetic-ink character recognition (MICR)**—used by banks to automatically read those unusual numbers on the bottom of checks and deposit slips. A special-purpose machine known as a reader/sorter reads these numbers and provides input that allows banks to efficiently maintain customer account balances.
- **Optical-character recognition (OCR)**—uses special preprinted characters that can be read by a light source and changed into machine-readable code. A common OCR device is the handheld wand reader. (See Figure 7-15.) These are used in department stores to read retail price tags by reflecting light on the printed characters.
- **Optical-mark recognition (OMR)**—senses the presence or absence of a mark, such as a pencil mark. OMR is often used to score standardized multiple-choice tests.

Figure 7-15 Wand reader

 CONCEPT CHECK

How are pointing and scanning devices different?

Describe four types of scanners.

Describe three common character and mark recognition devices.

Image Capturing Devices

Optical scanners, like traditional copy machines, can make a copy from an original. For example, an optical scanner can make a digital copy of a photograph. Image capturing devices, on the other hand, create or capture original images. These devices include digital cameras and digital video cameras.

Digital Cameras

Digital cameras are similar to traditional cameras except that images are recorded digitally on a disk or in the camera's memory rather than on film and then downloaded, or transferred, to your computer. (See Figure 7-16.) You can take a picture, view it immediately, and even place it on your own Web page, within minutes.

To learn more about how digital photography works, visit us on the Web at www.computing2011.com and enter the keyword **photo.** Digital photographs can be shared easily with others over the Internet.

Digital Video Cameras

Unlike traditional video cameras, **digital video cameras** record motion digitally on a disk or in the camera's

Figure 7-16 Digital camera

Built-in WebCam

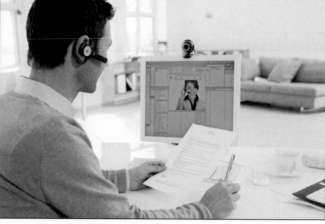

Attached WebCam

Figure 7-17 Two types of WebCams

memory. Most have the capability to take still images as well. **Web-Cams** are specialized digital video cameras that capture images and send them to a computer for broadcast over the Internet. Some Web-Cams are built-in while others are designed to be attached to the computer monitor. (See Figure 7-17.) To learn more about WebCams, visit our Web site at www.computing2011.com and enter the keyword **webcam.** To learn how you can videoconference, see Making IT Work for You: WebCams and Instant Messaging on pages 196 and 197.

tips

Are you having trouble getting the kind of photos you want with a digital camera? Would you like to make the most of digital technology in your photos? Here are some tips to help you get started:

1 **Buttons and Knobs.** Get to know the functions of your camera before you begin. Most cameras have an automatic mode, but be sure you know how to turn on the flash, zoom the lens, and set the image resolution.

2 **Photography Basics.** Many digital cameras have an LCD screen on the back. You can use it to help frame your shots more accurately. Just be aware that using the LCD screen uses more battery power.

3 **Red-Eye Reduction.** Many digital cameras have a red-eye reduction feature. When photographing people in low light, you can use this setting to eliminate glassy red eyes in photos. Consult your owner's manual to learn more about this feature.

4 **Blurry Photos.** Hold the camera still with your arms at your sides while snapping a photo. Many cameras also have built-in image-stabilization features.

To see additional tips, visit our Web site at www.computing2011.com and enter the keyword tips.

Audio-Input Devices

Audio-input devices convert sounds into a form that can be processed by the system unit. By far the most widely used audio-input device is the microphone. Audio input can take many forms, including the human voice and music.

Voice Recognition Systems

Voice recognition systems use a microphone, a sound card, and special software. These systems allow users to operate computers and other devices as well as to create documents using voice commands. Examples include voice-controlled dialing features on mobile phones, navigation on GPS devices, and control of car audio systems such as Microsoft Sync. Specialized portable voice recognition systems are widely used by doctors, lawyers, and others to record dictation. (See Figure 7-18.) These devices are able to record for several hours before connecting to a computer system to edit, store, and print the dictated information. Some systems are even able to translate dictation from one language to another, such as from English to Japanese.

Figure 7-18 Portable voice recognition system

WEBCAMS AND INSTANT MESSAGING

Do you enjoy chatting with your friends? Are you working on a project and need to collaborate with others in your group? What if you could see and hear your group online? Perhaps instant messaging is just what you're looking for. It's easy and free with an Internet connection and the right software.

Sending Messages   In instant messaging applications, your friends are added to a list of contacts that shows you when they are online and available to chat. For example, you could use Windows Live Messenger as follows:

1 • Add contacts by clicking the *Add a Contact* button and following the on-screen instructions.

• Double-click the name of a friend in the *Online* section.

• Enter your message in the window that appears.

• Click the *Send* button.

Your message appears on your friend's screen instantly. Your friend can then continue the conversation by following the steps above.

Transferring Files   While chatting, it is sometimes useful to share a file. For example, you might want to send a copy of a report you have been working on to a classmate to review. To send a file during an online chat:

1 ● Click the *Share files* button and select *Send a file or photo...*

● Browse your computer for the file you want to share and click *Open*.

Your friend is given an option to accept your file. A notification appears in your conversation when your file upload is complete. An additional notification is added when your friend has completed the download of your file. You can continue to chat throughout this process.

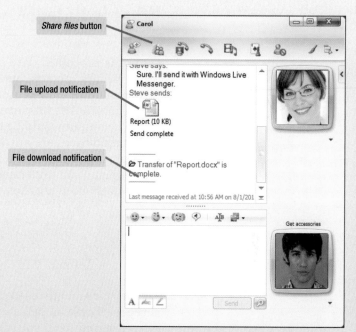

Share files button

File upload notification

File download notification

Using a WebCam   In addition to typing text messages, some instant messaging software allows you to have voice or video conversations over the Internet so you can see and hear the person you are collaborating with. To do this, both users must have a microphone and speakers, as well as Web cameras for video conferencing. You could hold a video conference using Windows Live Messenger by following these steps.

1 ● Start a conversation with a contact as shown on the previous page.

● Click the *Video call* button.

Your friend is given the option to accept the video conference. Once he or she accepts, the video conference begins.

Video call button

Video image of your friend

Video image you are sending

The Web is continually changing, and some of the specifics presented in this Making IT Work for You may have changed.

To learn about other ways to make information technology work for you, visit our Web site at www.computing2011.com and enter the keyword miw.

What Is Output?

Output is processed data or information. Output typically takes the form of text, graphics, photos, audio, and/or video. For example, when you create a presentation using a presentation graphics program, you typically input text and graphics. You also could include photographs and even add voice narration. The output would be the completed presentation.

Output devices are any hardware used to provide or to create output. They translate information that has been processed by the system unit into a form that humans can understand. There are a wide range of output devices. The most widely used are monitors, printers, and audio-output devices.

Monitors

The most frequently used output device is the **monitor.** Also known as **display screens,** monitors present visual images of text and graphics. The output is often referred to as soft copy. Monitors vary in size, shape, and cost. Almost all, however, have some basic distinguishing features.

Features

The most important characteristic of a monitor is its clarity. **Clarity** refers to the quality and sharpness of the displayed images. It is a function of several monitor features, including resolution, dot pitch, refresh rate, size, and aspect ratio.

Pixel

Figure 7-19 Monitor resolution

- **Resolution** is one of the most important features. Images are formed on a monitor by a series of dots or **pixels (picture elements).** (See Figure 7-19.) Resolution is expressed as a matrix of these dots or pixels. For example, many monitors today have a resolution of 1,600 pixel columns by 1,200 pixel rows for a total of 1,920,000 pixels. The higher a monitor's resolution (the more pixels), the clearer the image produced. See Figure 7-20 for the most common monitor resolutions.

- **Dot (pixel) pitch** is the distance between each pixel. Most newer monitors have a dot pitch of .31 mm (31/100th of a millimeter) or less. The lower the dot pitch (the shorter the distance between pixels), the clearer the images produced.

- **Refresh rate** indicates how often a displayed image is updated or refreshed. Most monitors operate at a rate of 75 hertz, which means that the monitor is refreshed 75 times each second. Images displayed on monitors with refresh rates lower than 75 hertz appear to flicker and can cause eye strain. The faster the refresh rate (the more frequently images are redrawn), the better the quality of images displayed.

- Size, or active display area, is measured by the diagonal length of a monitor's viewing area. Common sizes are 15, 17, 19, 21, and 24 inches.
- **Aspect ratio** is determined by the width of a monitor divided by its height. Common aspect ratios for monitors are 4:3 (standard, similar to traditional television pictures) and 16:10 (wide screen).

Flat-Panel Monitors

Flat-panel monitors are the most widely used type of monitor today. Compared to other types, they are thinner, are more portable, and require less power to operate. (See Figure 7-21.)

Many of today's flat-panel monitors are **LCD (liquid crystal display).** There are two basic types: passive-matrix and active-matrix. **Passive-matrix** or **dual-scan monitors** create images by scanning the entire screen. This type requires very little power, but the clarity of the images is not as sharp. **Active-matrix** or **thin film transistor (TFT) monitors** do not scan down the screen; instead, each pixel is independently activated. They can display more colors with better clarity. Active-matrix monitors are more expensive and require more power.

OLED (organic light-emitting diode) is a newer technology and is becoming widely used. Unlike LCD, OLED technology has the benefits of lower power consumption and longer battery life, as well as possibilities for much thinner displays.

Cathode-Ray Tubes

Until recently, the most common type of monitor for the office and the home was the **cathode-ray tube (CRT).** (See Figure 7-22.) These monitors are typically placed directly on the system unit or on the desktop. CRTs are similar in size and technology to televisions. Compared to other types of monitors, their

Standard	Pixels
SVGA	800 × 600
XGA	1,024 × 768
SXGA	1,280 × 1,024
UXGA	1,600 × 1,200
QXGA	2,048 × 1,536
QXSGA	2,560 × 2,048

Figure 7-20 Resolution standards

On the Web Explorations

Flat-panel monitors have become the standard for personal computers.

To learn more about a leading manufacturer in this industry, visit our Web site at www.computing2011.com and enter the keyword flatpanel.

Figure 7-21 Flat-panel monitor

Figure 7-22 CRT monitor

primary advantages are low cost and excellent resolution. Their primary disadvantages are that they are bulky, are less energy efficient, and occupy a considerable amount of space on the desktop.

Other Monitors

There are several other types of monitors. These monitors are used for more specialized applications, such as reading books, making presentations, and watching television. Three of these specialized devices are E-book readers, data projectors, and high-definition television.

- **E-book readers** are handheld, book-sized devices that display text and graphics. To learn more about one of the most widely used e-book readers, see Making IT Work for You: Amazon Kindle on page 201. Using content downloaded from the Web or from special cartridges, these devices are used to read

Figure 7-23 **E-book reader**

newspapers, magazines, and entire books. (See Figure 7-23.) These devices use a special type of screen called **electronic paper** or **e-paper** that requires power only when changing pages, and not the entire time a page is displayed on the screen.

- **Data projectors** are specialized devices similar to slide projectors. These devices, however, connect to microcomputers and project computer output just as it would appear on a monitor. Data projectors are commonly used for presentations almost anywhere from the classroom to the boardroom.

- **High-definition television (HDTV)** delivers a much clearer and more detailed wide-screen picture than regular television. Because the output is digital, users can readily freeze video sequences to create high-quality still images. The video and still images can then be digitized, edited, and stored on disk for later use. This technology is very useful to graphic artists, designers, and publishers.

On the Web Explorations

HDTV is a higher-quality alternative to standard-definition television.

To learn more about HDTV, visit our Web site at www.cmputing2011.com and enter the keyword hdtv.

    ## CONCEPT CHECK

What is output? What are output devices?

Define these monitor features: resolution, dot pitch, refresh rate, size, and aspect ratio.

Describe flat-panel, CRT, and other more specialized monitors.

Making IT work for you

AMAZON KINDLE

E-book readers are a great way to enjoy reading on the go. Did you know they can also help you stay current in your profession? Many e-book readers feature subscriptions to newspapers and magazines, including publications that will keep you up-to-date on topics important to your career. Some devices, such as the Amazon Kindle, can even download subscriptions automatically wherever you are without the need for a computer connection.

Subscribing   To subscribe to a magazine using the Kindle:

1 ● Press the *Menu* button and select *Shop in Kindle Store*

> Turn Wireless Off
>
> Shop in Kindle Store
>
> View Archived Items
>
> Search
>
> Settings
>
> Experimental
>
> Sync & Check for Items

2 ● Select *Magazines* from the *Browse* menu.

> ### Browse:
>
> **Books** - *Over 300,000 titles available*
>
> **Newspapers**
>
> **Magazines**
>
> **Blogs**

3 ● Select a publication of interest and follow the on-screen instructions to complete your subscription.

The Web in continually changing, and some of the specifics presented in Making IT Work for You may have changed.

To learn about other ways to make information technology work for you, visit our Web site at www.computing2011.com and enter the keyword miw.

Figure 7-24 Dpi comparison

300 dpi

1200 dpi

Printers

You probably use a printer with some frequency to print homework assignments, photographs, and Web pages. **Printers** translate information that has been processed by the system unit and present the information on paper. Printer output is often called hard copy.

Features

There are many different types of printers. Almost all, however, have some basic distinguishing features, including resolution, color capability, speed, and memory.

- **Resolution** for a printer is similar to monitor resolution. It is a measure of the clarity of images produced. Printer resolution, however, is measured in **dpi (dots per inch).** (See Figure 7-24.) Most printers designed for personal use average 1,200 dpi. The higher the dpi, the better the quality of images produced.

- Color capability is provided by most printers today. Users typically have the option to print either with just black ink or with color. Because it is more expensive to print in color, most users select black ink for letters, drafts, and homework. Color is used more selectively for final reports containing graphics and for photographs.

- Speed is measured in the number of pages printed per minute. Typically, printers for personal use average 15 to 19 pages per minute for single-color (black) output and 13 to 15 pages per minute for color output.

- Memory within a printer is used to store printing instructions and documents waiting to be printed. The more memory in a printer, the faster it will be able to create large documents.

Ink-Jet Printers

Ink-jet printers spray ink at high speed onto the surface of paper. This process not only produces a letter-quality image but also permits printing to be done in a variety of colors, making them ideal for select special applications. (See Figure 7-25.) Ink-jet printers are the most widely used printers. They are reliable, quiet, and relatively inexpensive. The most costly aspect of ink-jet printers is replacing the ink cartridges. For this reason, most users specify black ink for the majority of print jobs and use the more expensive color printing for select applications. Typical ink-jet printers produce 17 to 19 pages per minute of black-only output and 13 to 15 pages of color output.

Laser Printers

The **laser printer** uses a technology similar to that used in a photocopying machine. Laser printers use a laser light beam to produce images with excellent letter and graphics quality. More expensive than ink-jet printers, laser printers are faster and are used in applications requiring high-quality output. (See Figure 7-26.)

There are two categories of laser printers. **Personal laser printers** are less expensive and are used by many single users. They typically can print 15 to 17 pages a minute. **Shared laser printers** typically support color, are more expensive, and are used (shared) by a group of users. Shared laser printers typically print over 50 pages a minute.

Figure 7-25 A special-application ink-jet printer

Figure 7-26 Laser printer

environmental facts

Did you know that the ingredients in most printer cartridges contain hazardous chemicals? In fact, much of the production of new printer ink and toner has moved to third-world nations as a result of pollution concerns. One approach to minimizing the impact is to recycle printer cartridges. However, some have approached the problem from a completely different direction. What if the ink your printer used was a by-product readily available in your house? At least one manufacturer thinks this is the way of the future. Their new green printer design uses coffee grounds to print your text and images.

Figure 7-27 Photo printer

Other Printers

There are several other types of printers. These printers include dot-matrix printers, thermal printers, plotters, photo printers, and portable printers:

- **Dot-matrix printers** form characters and images using a series of small pins on a print head. Once a widely used microcomputer printer, they are inexpensive and reliable but quite noisy. In general, they are used for tasks where high-quality output is not required.

- **Thermal printers** use heat elements to produce images on heat-sensitive paper. These printers are widely used with ATMs and gasoline pumps to print receipts.

- **Plotters** are special-purpose printers for producing a wide range of specialized output. Using output from graphics tablets and other graphical input devices, plotters create maps, images, and architectural and engineering drawings. Plotters are typically used by graphic artists, engineers, and architects to print out designs, sketches, and drawings.

- **Photo printers** are special-purpose printers designed to print photo-quality images from digital cameras. (See Figure 7-27.) Most photo printers print 3 × 5" or 4 × 6" images on glossy, photo-quality paper.

- **Portable printers** are usually small and lightweight printers designed to work with a notebook computer. Portable printers may be ink-jet or laser printers, print in black and white or color, and connect with USB.

 CONCEPT CHECK

 Discuss these printer features: resolution, color capability, speed, and memory.

 Compare ink-jet printers and laser printers.

 Discuss dot-matrix, thermal, plotter, photo, and portable printers.

Figure 7-28 **Digital music player**

Audio-Output Devices

Audio-output devices translate audio information from the computer into sounds that people can understand. The most widely used audio-output devices are **speakers** and **headphones.** These devices are connected to a sound card in the system unit. The sound card is used to capture as well as play back recorded sounds. Audio-output devices are used to play music, vocalize translations from one language to another, and communicate information from the computer system to users.

Creating voice output is not anywhere near as difficult as recognizing and interpreting voice input. In fact, voice output is quite common. It is used with many soft-drink machines, telephones, and cars. It is used as a reinforcement tool for learning, such as to help students study a foreign language. It also is used in many supermarkets at the checkout counter to confirm purchases. One of its most powerful capabilities is to assist the physically challenged.

Digital music players, also known as **digital media players,** are specialized devices for storing, transferring, and playing audio files. Older players are only able to play music saved in a special compressed audio file format known as MP3. Today, most players are able to use a wide variety of audio files. Many are capable of displaying video files as well. Some of the best-known audio and video players are the Apple iPod, Creative Zen, Microsoft Zune, and iRiver. (See Figure 7-28.)

Combination Input and Output Devices

Many devices combine input and output capabilities. Sometimes this is done to save space. Other times it is done for very specialized applications. Common combination devices include fax machines, multifunctional devices, Internet telephones, and terminals.

Fax Machines

A **fax machine** is a standard tool in nearly every office. At one time, all fax machines were separate stand-alone devices for sending and receiving images over telephone lines. Now, most computer systems have that capability with the simple addition of a fax/modem board. To send a fax, these devices scan the image of a document converting the light and dark areas into a format that can be sent electronically over standard telephone lines. To receive a fax, these devices reverse the process and print the document (or display the document on your monitor) using signals received from the telephone line.

Multifunctional Devices

Multifunctional devices (MFD) typically combine the capabilities of a scanner, printer, fax, and copy machine. These multifunctional devices offer a cost and space advantage. They cost about the same as a good printer or copy machine but require much less space than the single-function devices they replace. Their disadvantage is that the quality and functionality are not quite as good as those of the separate single-purpose devices. Even so, multifunctional devices are widely used in home and small business offices.

Internet Telephones

Internet telephones are specialized input and output devices for receiving and sending voice communication. (See Figure 7-29.)

Voice over IP (VoIP) is the transmission of telephone calls over computer networks. Also known as **telephony, Internet telephony,** and **IP telephony** VoIP uses the Internet rather than traditional communication lines to support voice communication. To place telephone calls using Internet telephony requires a high-speed Internet connection and special software and/or hardware. Skype and Vonage are two examples of popular Internet telephony service providers. The three most popular approaches are

- **Computer-to-computer** communications allow individuals to place free long-distance calls. This application requires that both parties have a computer and that their computers are on and connected to the Internet when a call is placed. The required software is available from a variety of sources for free or at very low cost.
- **Computer-to-traditional telephone** communications allow a user to call almost any traditional telephone from his or her computer. Only the person making the call needs to have a computer connected to the Internet. The calling party subscribes to a special Internet phone service provider that supplies the required software and charges a small monthly and/or per-minute fee. To see how this works, visit our Web site at www. computing2011.com and enter the keyword **phone.**
- **Traditional telephone-to-traditional telephone** communications do not require a computer. The calling party subscribes to a special Internet phone service provider that supplies a special hardware adapter that connects a traditional telephone to the Internet. The cost for this service is similar to the computer-to-traditional telephone approach.

Compared to traditional telephone calls, Internet-supported calls may have a lower sound quality and may have an audio delay. However, most users report that this difference is not significant.

Figure 7-29 Internet telephone

CONCEPT CHECK

What are the two most widely used audio-output devices?

Describe the following combination devices: fax machine, MFD, and Internet telephone.

Describe the three most popular Internet telephony approaches.

Careers in IT

Technical writers prepare instruction manuals, technical reports, and other scientific or technical documents. (See Figure 7-30.) Most technical writers work for computer software firms, government agencies, or research institutions. They translate technical information into easily understandable instructions or summaries. As new technology continues to develop and expand, the need for technical writers who can communicate technical expertise to others is expected to increase.

Technical writing positions typically require a college degree in communications, journalism, or English and a specialization in, or familiarity with, a technical field. However, individuals with strong writing skills sometimes transfer from jobs in the sciences to positions in technical writing.

Technical writers can expect to earn an annual salary in the range of $46,500 to $76,500. Advancement opportunities can be limited within a firm or company, but there are additional opportunities in consulting. To learn about other careers in information technology, visit us at www.computing2011.com and enter the keyword **careers.**

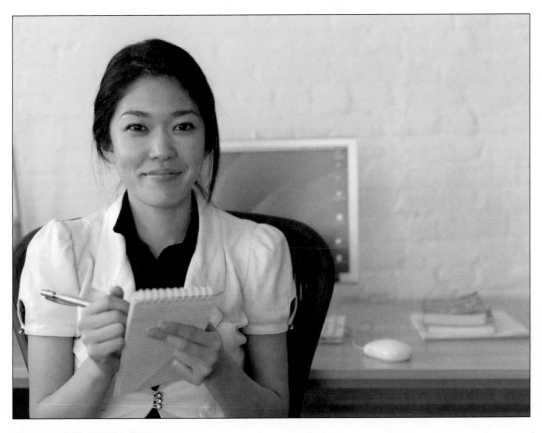

Figure 7-30 Technical writer

Crashing Through the Foreign Language Barrier

Have you ever wished you could speak more than one language fluently? What if you could speak hundreds of languages instantly? Would you like to have your own personal interpreter to accompany you whenever you traveled to a foreign country? What if you could take a picture of a foreign road sign or restaurant menu and have it immediately translated for you? Technology called machine translation (MT) may soon exist to do all of these things. The military and private sector are funding a variety of research projects on electronic interpreters, and the commercial opportunities are enormous. The worldwide translation services market is an over $8 billion a year industry and is expected to grow even more.

Prototype portable handheld electronic interpreters are currently in a testing phase at the U.S. Office of Naval Research. In fact, it is expected that these devices will be widely used in the near future. The company Speech-Gear has developed software called Compadre that takes verbal statements in one language, converts the statements to text, translates that text to another language, and then vocalizes the translated text. And it does all this in two seconds! The military is particularly interested in instant electronic interpreters as they focus on peacekeeping objectives. More than ever before, U.S. soldiers find themselves needing to communicate with non-English-speaking civilians to settle disputes and maintain order.

Despite advances in translation software, several challenges remain. Current translation techniques are labor intensive; they require linguists and programmers to create large lists of words and their corresponding meanings. Unfortunately, computers have a difficult time understanding idioms, such as "It is raining cats and dogs." They may also have difficulty correctly identifying words by their context. For example, the sentences "The stove is hot" and "The latest tech gadget is hot" use the same word, *hot,* but it has a very different meaning in each sentence. Researchers have been working on a solution to these problems. One is the EliMT project. Instead of translating from word to word, EliMT compares books that have been translated in different languages, looking for sentence fragment patterns. By comparing sentence fragments, it is hoped that translation programs will be able to identify word groupings and translate them into another language's comparable word grouping, essentially translating concepts instead of individual words. Other systems are supplementing machine translation with expert human translators for verification of unusual phrases.

What are the uses for such software and devices? Will the average person want or need an electronic translator? What type of professions and professionals will use them? What industries would benefit most from electronic translators? How could you use this technology?

VISUAL SUMMARY | Input and Output

INPUT

Input is any data or instructions used by a computer. Input devices translate words, images, and actions into a form a computer can process.

Keyboards

Keyboards are the most common way to input data. The most common types are

- **Traditional**—full-sized, rigid, rectangular.
- **Ergonomic**—designed to minimize wrist strain.
- **Wireless**—no wire provides greater flexibility.
- **PDA**—miniature keyboards for PDAs and smart phones.
- **Virtual**—an image of a keyboard displayed on a touch screen device.

Features include **numeric keypads, toggle keys,** and **combination keys.**

Pointing Devices

Pointing devices accept pointing gestures and convert them to machine-readable input.

- **Mouse** controls a **mouse pointer. A wheel button** rotates to scroll through information. Three basic mouse designs are **optical, mechanical,** and **cordless (wireless).** Similar devices include t**rackball (roller ball), touch pad,** and **pointing stick.**
- **Touch screens** operations are controlled by finger touching the screen. **Multi-touch screens** can be touched with more than one finger; commonly used on mobile devices such as the Apple iPhone.

INPUT

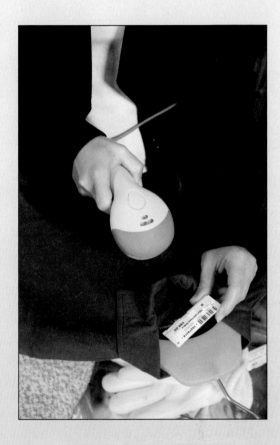

- **Joystick** operations are controlled by varying pressure, speed, and direction.
- **Stylus** is a penlike device used with tablet PCs and PDAs. **Handwriting recognition software** translates handwritten notes.

Scanning Devices

Scanners move across text and graphics. Scanning devices convert scanned text and images into a form that can be processed by the system unit.

- **Optical scanners** record light, dark, and colored areas of scanned text or images. There are three types: **flatbed, document,** and **portable.**
- **Card readers** interpret encoded information. Two types: **magnetic** (reads **magnetic strip)** and **radio frequency** (reads **RFID** microchip) card readers.

To be a competent end user, you need to be aware of the most commonly used input and output devices. These devices are translators for information into and out of the system unit. Input devices translate words, sounds, and actions into symbols the system unit can process. Output devices translate symbols from the system unit into words, images, and sounds that people can understand.

INPUT

- **Bar code readers** are used with electronic cash registers in supermarkets. **Wand readers** or **platform scanners** read **UPC** codes that are used to determine product descriptions and prices and to update inventory levels.
- Character and mark recognition devices recognize special characters and marks. Three types: **MICR** (read by readers/sorters), **OCR,** and **OMR.**

Image Capturing Devices

Image capturing devices create or capture original images. These devices include **digital cameras** (images downloaded to system unit for further processing and/or printing) and **digital video cameras. WebCams** capture and send images over the Internet, one design is built-in and the other is attached.

Audio-Input Devices

Audio-input devices convert sounds into a form that can be processed by the system unit. Audio input takes many forms, including the human voice and music. **Voice recognition systems** use a combination of a microphone, a sound card, and special software.

OUTPUT

Output is data or information processed by a computer. Output devices translate processed text, graphics, audio, and video into a form humans can understand.

Monitors

Monitors **(display screens)** present visual images of text and graphics. Monitor output is described as soft copy.

Clarity is a function of several monitor features including **resolution** (expressed as matrix of **pixels** or **picture elements**), **dot (pixel) pitch, refresh rate,** size, and **aspect ratio.**

- **Flat-panel monitors** have become the standard for computer systems. Many are **LCD (liquid crystal display).** Two basic types are **passive-matrix (dual-scan)** and **active-matrix (thin film transistor, TFT).** OLED (organic light-emitting diode) is newer technology requiring lower power consumption, longer battery life, and potential for thinner displays.

OUTPUT

- **Cathode-ray tubes (CRTs)** use technology similar to a television. Compared to flat-panels, CRTs are bulky, require more electricity to run, and occupy considerable space on the desktop.

Three specialized types of monitors are **e-book readers** (screen known as **electronic paper** or **e-paper**), **data projectors**, and **high-definition television (HDTV)**.

Printers

Printers translate information processed by the system unit and present the information on paper. Output from printers is described as **hard copy**. Some distinguishing features of printers include **resolution** (measured in **dpi** or **dots per inch**), color capability, speed, and memory.

- **Ink-jet printers** spray ink to produce high-quality output. These printers are inexpensive and the most widely used type of printer.
- **Laser printers** use technology similar to photocopying machines. Two categories are **personal** and **shared**.

Other printers include **dot-matrix printers, thermal printers, plotters, photo printers**, and **portable printers**.

Audio-Output Devices

Audio-output devices translate audio information from the computer into sounds that people can understand. **Speakers** and **headphones** are the most widely used audio-output devices.

Digital music players (digital media players) store, transfer, and play audio files. Many players also display video files.

COMBINATION DEVICES

Combination devices combine input and output capabilities. Common types include

Fax Machines

Fax machines send and receive images via standard telephone lines.

Multifunctional Devices

Multifunctional devices (MFD) typically combine the capabilities of a scanner, printer, fax, and copy machine.

Internet Telephones

Internet telephones receive and send voice communication. **Voice over IP (VoIP)**, also known as **telephony, Internet telephony**, and **IP telephony**, use the Internet to transmit telephone calls. Three approaches are computer-to-computer, computer-to-traditional telephone, and traditional telephone-to-traditional telephone.

CAREERS IN IT

Technical writers prepare instruction manuals, technical reports, and other documents. Bachelor's degree in communication, journalism, or English and a specialization in, or familiarity with, a technical field required. Salary range $46,500 to $76,500.

Secondary Storage

Competencies

After you have read this chapter, you should be able to:

1   Distinguish between primary and secondary storage.

2   Discuss the important characteristics of secondary storage including media, capacity, storage devices, and access speed.

3   Describe hard disk platters, tracts, sectors, and head crashes.

4   Compare internal and external hard drives.

5   Discuss performance enhancements including disk caching, RAIDs, file compression, and file decompression.

6   Define solid-state storage including solid-state drives, flash memory, and USB drives.

7   Define optical storage including compact, digital versatile, and high-definition discs.

8   Describe more specialized storage such as online storage services, floppy disk drives, and magnetic tape.

9   Discuss mass storage devices, enterprise storage systems, and storage area networks.

Floppy disks were once the only way to distribute software and the only way to share files between personal computers. These disks were everywhere, and they were essential, but they were also extremely fragile. Today's compact discs and USB flash drives are more reliable and hold more information than hundreds of floppy disks, but many believe there are still advances in this field ahead.

Some experts predict that the future of secondary storage is holographic. Compact discs use two dimensions to record data, but advances in optics now make it possible to record data in three dimensions. This holographic data storage could make it possible to inexpensively store hundreds of today's DVDs on one disc. Imagine buying a disk that holds hundreds of movies, for less than the cost of one of today's DVDs.

chapter 8

Introduction

Secondary storage devices are used to save, to back up, and even to transport files consisting of data or programs from one location or computer to another. Not long ago, almost all files contained only numbers and letters. The demands for saving these files were easily met with low-capacity storage devices.

Data storage has expanded from text and numeric files to include digital music files, photographic files, video files, and much more. These new types of files require secondary storage devices that have much greater capacity.

Secondary storage devices have always been an indispensable element in any computer system. They have similarities to output and input devices. Like output devices, secondary storage devices receive information from the system unit in the form of the machine language of 0s and 1s. Rather than translating the information, however, secondary storage devices save the information in machine language for later use. Like input devices, secondary storage devices send information to the system unit for processing. However, the information, since it is already in machine form, does not need to be translated. It is sent directly to memory (RAM), where it can be accessed and processed by the CPU.

Competent end users need to be aware of the different types of secondary storage. They need to know the capabilities, limitations, and uses of hard disks, solid-state drives, optical discs, and other types of secondary storage. Additionally, they need to be aware of specialty storage devices for portable computers and to be knowledgeable about how large organizations manage their extensive data resources.

Storage

An essential feature of every computer is the ability to save, or store, information. As discussed in Chapter 6, random-access memory (RAM) holds or stores data and programs that the CPU is presently processing. Before data can be processed or a program can be run, it must be in RAM. For this reason, RAM is sometimes referred to as **primary storage.**

Unfortunately, most RAM provides only temporary or volatile storage. That is, it loses all of its contents as soon as the computer is turned off. Its contents also are lost if there is a power failure that disrupts the electric current going into the system unit. This volatility results in a need for more permanent or nonvolatile storage for data and programs. We also need external storage because users need much more storage capacity than is typically available in a computer's primary or RAM memory.

Secondary storage provides permanent or nonvolatile storage. Using **secondary storage devices** such as a hard disk drive, data and programs can be retained after the computer has been shut off. This is accomplished by *writing* files to and *reading* files from secondary storage devices. Writing is the process of saving information *to* the secondary storage device. Reading is the process of accessing information *from* secondary storage. This chapter focuses on secondary storage devices.

Some important characteristics of secondary storage include

- **Media** are the actual physical material that holds the data and programs. (See Figure 8-1.)
- **Capacity** measures how much a particular storage medium can hold.
- **Storage devices** are hardware that reads data and programs from storage media. Most also write to storage media.

Figure 8-1 **Secondary storage media**

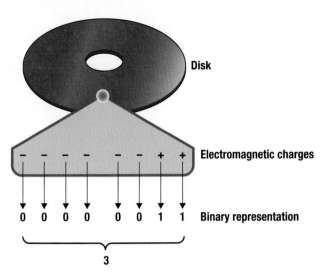

Figure 8-2 **How charges on a disk surface store the number 3**

- **Access speed** measures the amount of time required by the storage device to retrieve data and programs.

Most desktop microcomputer systems have hard and optical disk drives, as well as ports where additional storage devices can be connected.

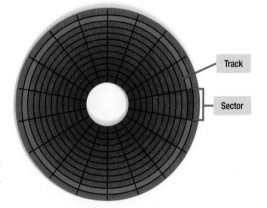

Figure 8-3 **Tracks and sectors**

Hard Disks

Hard disks save files by altering the magnetic charges of the disk's surface to represent 1s and 0s. Hard disks retrieve data and programs by reading these charges from the magnetic disk. Characters are represented by positive (+) and negative (−) charges using the ASCII, EBCDIC, or Unicode binary codes. For example, the number 3 would require a series of 8 charges. (See Figure 8-2.) **Density** refers to how tightly these charges can be packed next to one another on the disk.

Hard disks use rigid metallic **platters** that are stacked one on top of another. Hard disks store and organize files using tracks, sectors, and cylinders. **Tracks** are rings of concentric circles without visible grooves. Each track is divided into invisible wedge-shaped sections called **sectors.** (See Figure 8-3.) A **cylinder** runs through each track of a stack of platters. Cylinders are necessary to differentiate files stored on the same track and sector of different platters. When a hard disk is formatted, tracks, sectors, and cylinders are assigned.

Hard disks are sensitive instruments. Their read/write heads ride on a cushion of air about 0.000001 inch thick. It is so thin that a smoke particle, fingerprint, dust, or human hair could cause what is known as a head crash. (See Figure 8-4.)

A **head crash** occurs when a read/write head makes contact with the hard disk's surface or with particles on its surface. A head crash is a disaster for a

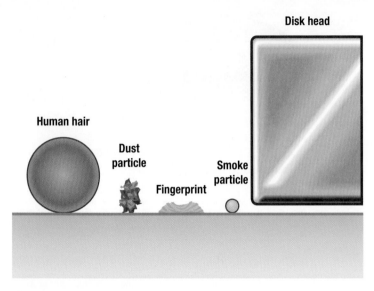

Disk head

Human hair

Dust particle

Fingerprint

Smoke particle

Figure 8-4 Materials that can cause a head crash

hard disk. The disk surface is scratched and some or all of the data is destroyed. At one time, head crashes were commonplace. Now, fortunately, they are rare.

There are two basic types of hard disks: internal and external.

Internal Hard Disk

An **internal hard disk** is located inside the system unit. These hard disks are able to store and retrieve large quantities of information quickly. They are used to store programs and data files. For example, nearly every microcomputer uses its internal hard disk to store its operating system and major applications such as Word and Excel.

To see how a hard disk works, visit our Web site at www.computing2011.com and enter the keyword **disk.**

To ensure adequate performance of your internal hard disk and the safety of your data, you should perform routine maintenance and periodically make backup copies of all important files. For hard-disk maintenance and backup procedures, refer to Chapter 5's coverage of the Windows utilities Backup and Restore, Disk Cleanup, and Disk Defragmenter.

External Hard Drives

While internal hard disks provide fast access, they have a fixed amount of storage and cannot be easily removed from the system cabinet. External hard disks typically connect to a USB or FireWire port on the system unit, are easily removed, and effectively provide an unlimited amount of storage. (See Figure 8-5.)

tips

Does your internal hard disk run a lot and seem slow? The problem could be with fragmented files—files that when saved were broken into pieces (fragments) and stored in different locations on your hard disk, which take longer for the hard disk to access. Defragging rearranges the file parts so they are stored in adjacent locations. To clean up the disk and speed up access times, consider defragmenting. If you are using Windows Vista:

1 **Start Disk Defragmenter.** Type *defrag* into the Start menu search box and press Enter to open the Disk Defragmenter utility. Click *Defragment* now to begin defragmenting your disk.

2 **Keep working.** You can continue running other applications while your disk is being defragmented. Unfortunately, your computer operates more slowly, and Disk Defragmenter takes longer to finish.

3 **Automate.** Windows 7 will defragment your disk for you automatically. Click *Configure schedule* in the Disk Defragmenter utility to set this to a time that is convenient for you.

To see additional tips, visit our Web site at www.computing 2011.com and enter the keyword *tips.*

Figure 8-5 External hard drive

External hard drives use the same basic technology as internal hard disks and are used primarily to complement an internal hard disk. Because they are easily removed, they are particularly useful to protect or secure sensitive information. Other uses for external drives include backing up the contents of the internal hard disk and providing additional hard-disk capacity.

Performance Enhancements

Three ways to improve the performance of hard disks are disk caching, redundant arrays of inexpensive disks, and file compression/decompression.

Disk caching improves hard-disk performance by anticipating data needs. It performs a function similar to cache memory discussed in Chapter 6. While cache memory improves processing by acting as a temporary high-speed holding area between memory and the CPU, disk caching improves processing by acting as a temporary high-speed holding area between a secondary storage device and the CPU. Disk caching requires a combination of hardware and software. During idle processing time, frequently used data is read from the hard disk into memory (cache). When needed, the data is then accessed directly from memory. The transfer rate from memory is much faster than from the hard disk. As a result, overall system performance is often increased by as much as 30 percent.

Figure 8-6 RAID storage device

Redundant arrays of inexpensive disks (RAID) improve performance by expanding external storage, improving access speed, and providing reliable storage. Several inexpensive hard-disk drives are connected to one another. These connections can be by a network or within specialized RAID devices. (See Figure 8-6.) The connected hard-disk drives are related or grouped together, and the computer system interacts with the RAID system as though it were a single large-capacity hard-disk drive. The result is expanded storage capability, fast access speed, and high reliability. For these reasons, RAID is often used by Internet servers and large organizations.

File compression and **file decompression** increase storage capacity by reducing the amount of space required to store data and programs. File compression is not limited to hard-disk systems. It is frequently used to compress files on DVDs, CDs, and flash drives as well. File compression also helps to speed up transmission of files from one computer system to another. Sending and receiving compressed files across the Internet is a common activity.

File compression programs scan files for ways to reduce the amount of required storage. One way is to search for repeating patterns. The repeating patterns are replaced with a token, leaving enough tokens so that the original can be rebuilt or decompressed. These programs often shrink files to a quarter of their original size. To learn more about file compression, visit our Web site at www.computing2011.com and enter the keyword **compression**.

You can compress and decompress files using specialized utilities such as WinZip. Or, if a specialized utility is not available, you can use utility programs in Windows. For a summary of performance enhancement techniques, see Figure 8-7.

On the Web Explorations

A computer can be a library, a jukebox, even a home entertainment system, but to do any of these tasks requires large amounts of hard-disk space.

To learn more about the leaders in high-capacity hard disks, visit our Web site at www.computing2011.com and enter the keyword capacity.

Technique	Description
Disk caching	Uses cache and anticipates data needs
RAID	Linked, inexpensive hard-disk drives
File compression	Reduces file size
File decompression	Expands compressed files

Figure 8-7 Performance enhancement techniques

environmental facts

Did you know that hard disk storage requires more energy than solid state storage? Unlike solid state storage which has no moving parts, hard disks have to be rotating in order to save or to retrieve data. Almost all large data centers have thousands of hard drives running 24 hours a day, 7 days a week, 365 days a year. This means that hard drives are tremendous energy consumers. Solid state storage requires only a fraction of the energy requirements to provide comparable storage capacity and access. For this reason, many data centers are switching from traditional hard disk to solid state storage.

Solid-State Storage

Unlike hard disks, which rotate and have read/write heads that move in and out, **solid-state storage** devices have no moving parts. Data and information are stored and retrieved electronically directly from these devices much as they would be from conventional computer memory.

Solid-State Drives

Solid-state drives (SSDs) are designed to be connected inside a microcomputer system the same way an internal hard disk would be but contain solid-state memory instead of magnetic disks to store data. (See Figure 8-8.) SSDs are faster and more durable than hard disks. SSDs also require less power, which can lead to increased battery life for laptops and mobile devices. SSDs are more expensive and generally have a lower capacity than hard disks, but this is changing as the popularity of SSDs continues to increase.

Flash Memory

Flash memory cards are small solid-state storage devices widely used in portable devices such as mobile phones and GPS navigation systems. (See Figure 8-9.) Flash memory also is used in a variety of specialized input devices to capture and transfer data to desktop computers.

Figure 8-8 Solid-state drive

Figure 8-9 Flash memory card

For example, flash memory is used to store images captured from digital cameras and then to transfer the images to desktop and other computers. Flash memory is used in digital media players like the iPod to store and play music and video files. To learn more about digital video players, see Making IT Work for You: iPods and Video from the Internet on page 226.

USB Drives

USB drives, or **flash drives,** are so compact that they can be transported on a key ring. (See Figure 8-10.) These drives conveniently connect directly to a computer's USB port to transfer files and can have capacities ranging from 1 GB to 256 GB, with a broad price range to match. Due to their convenient size and large capacities, USB drives have become a very popular option for transporting data and information between computers, specialty devices, and the Internet. To learn more about using flash drives to transport data, see Making IT Work for You: Flash Camcorders and YouTube on pages 228 and 229.

CONCEPT CHECK

  What is solid-state storage?

  Compare solid-state technology to that used in hard disks.

  What are SSDs? What is flash memory? What are USB drives?

Optical Discs

Today's **optical discs** can hold over 50 gigabytes of data. (See Figure 8-11.) That is the equivalent of millions of typewritten pages or a medium-sized library all on a single disc. Optical discs are having a great impact on storage today, but we are probably only beginning to see their effects.

In optical-disc technology, a laser beam alters the surface of a plastic or metallic disc to represent data. Unlike hard disks, which use magnetic charges to represent 1s and 0s, optical discs use reflected light. The 1s and 0s are represented

Figure 8-10 USB drive

Figure 8-11 Optical disc

IPODS AND VIDEO FROM THE INTERNET

Did you know you can use the Internet to locate and play movies and television shows? You can even transfer video to a digital media player. All you need is the right software, hardware, and a connection to the Internet.

Finding videos   There are many services on the Internet for finding movies. The first step is to download software that connects with a video service. You can use this software to search for programs and play them. For example, to find television shows using Apple iTunes:

1 ● Visit www.apple.com and follow the on-screen instructions to download and install the iTunes software.

2 ● Start the iTunes application.

● Select *iTunes Store* and browse to find movies or television shows you want to download.

iTunes Store

Purchased movies and shows are automatically downloaded and listed in the *Movies* and *TV Shows* categories of the library. To watch a downloaded video:

3 ● Select *Movies* or *TV Shows* from the Library.

● Double-click the video you want to watch.

Uploading to a Digital Media Player   Another popular way to take your favorite videos with you is to upload them to a digital media player. For example, you could transfer video to an iPod using iTunes software by following the steps below:

1 ● Connect your iPod to your computer. iTunes starts automatically.

● Select your iPod from the *Devices* list.

● Select the *TV Shows* tab and select which programs you would like to transfer to your iPod.

● Click the *Sync* button to transfer your videos.

The Web is continually changing, and some of the specifics presented in this Making IT Work for You may have changed.

To learn about other ways to make information technology work for you, visit our Web site at www.computing2011.com and enter the keyword miw.

by flat areas called **lands** and bumpy areas called **pits** on the disc surface. The disc is read by an **optical disc drive** using a laser that projects a tiny beam of light on these areas. The amount of reflected light determines whether the area represents a 1 or a 0. To see how an optical disc drive works, visit our Web site at www.computing2011.com and enter the keyword optical.

Like hard disks, optical discs use tracks and sectors to organize and store files. Unlike the concentric tracks and wedge-shaped sectors used for hard disks, however, optical discs typically use a single track that spirals toward the center of the disc. This single track is divided into equally sized sectors.

Figure 8-12 DVD disc drive

Compact Disc

Compact disc, or as it is better known, **CD,** is one of the most widely used optical formats. CD drives are standard on many microcomputer systems. Typically, CD drives can store from 650 MB (megabytes) to 1 GB (gigabyte) of data on one side of a CD.

There are three basic types of CDs: read only, write once, and rewritable:

- **Read only—CD-ROM,** which stands for **compact disc–read-only memory,** is similar to a commercial music CD. *Read only* means it cannot be written on or erased by the user. Thus, you as a user have access only to the data imprinted by the publisher. CD-ROMs are used to distribute large databases and references. They also are used to distribute large software application packages.

- **Write once—CD-R,** which stands for **CD-recordable,** can be written to once. After that they can be read many times without deterioration but cannot be written on or erased. CD-R drives often are used to archive data and to record music downloaded from the Internet.

- **Rewriteable—CD-RW** stands for **compact disc rewritable.** Also known as **erasable optical discs,** these discs are very similar to CD-Rs except that the disc surface is not permanently altered when data is recorded. Because they can be changed, CD-RWs are often used to create and edit multimedia presentations.

Digital Versatile Disc

DVD stands for **digital versatile disc** or **digital video disc.** This is a newer format that has replaced CDs as the standard optical disc. DVDs are very similar to CDs except that more data can be packed into the same amount of space. (See Figure 8-12.) DVD discs can store 4.7 GB to 17 GB on a single DVD disc—17 times the capacity of CDs. There are three basic types of DVDs, similar to CDs: read only, write once, and rewriteable.

- **Read only—DVD-ROM** stands for **digital versatile disc–read-only memory.** DVD-ROM drives are also known as **DVD players.** DVD-ROMs are having a major impact on the video market. While CD-ROMs are effective for

Are you concerned about damaging your optical discs? Actually, they are quite durable, and taking care of them boils down to just a few basic rules.

1 **Don't stack.** Don't stack or bend discs.

2 **Don't touch.** Don't touch the recording surfaces. Hold only by their edges.

3 **Don't remove.** Never attempt to remove a disc when it is rotating and in use.

4 **Avoid extreme conditions.** Keep discs from extreme heat and direct sunlight.

5 **Use storage boxes.** Store discs in plastic storage boxes.

Of course, the best protection is to make a backup or duplicate copy of your disc.

To see additional tips, visit our Web site at www.computing 2011.com and enter the keyword tips.

FLASH CAMCORDERS AND YouTube

Would you like to make short videos to share with family and friends? Traditional camcorders can be expensive, and often require a special connection to transfer video to your computer. Recently, flash memory–based camcorders have made creating digital video simpler and more affordable, and connect to your computer as easily as other flash memory secondary storage devices.

Capture   To capture video using a Pure Digital Flip camcorder:

1 • **Press the record button to record what you see on the view screen.**

• **Press the record button again to stop recording.**

View screen

Record button

Connect   Connecting the camcorder to your computer is as simple as connecting other secondary storage devices such as USB flash drives:

1 • **Slide the switch on the side of the camcorder to extend the built-in USB connector.**

• **Plug the camcorder directly into a USB port on your computer.**

USB connector

Slide to extend USB connector

Share The FlipShare software included with the camcorder allows you to save your video to your computer, e-mail videos to friends, or upload videos directly to Internet sites such as YouTube and MySpace.

The Web is continuously changing, and some of the specifics presented in this Making IT Work for You may have changed.

To learn about other ways to make information technology work for you, visit our Web site at www.computing2011.com and enter the keyword miw.

distributing music, they can only contain just over an hour of fair-quality video. DVD-ROMs can provide over two hours of high-quality video and sound comparable to that found in motion picture theaters. The motion picture industry has rapidly shifted video distribution from video cassettes to DVD-ROMs.

- **Write once—DVD+R** and **DVD−R** are two competing write-once formats. Both stand for **DVD recordable.** Each has a slightly different way in which it formats its discs. Fortunately, most new DVD players can use either format. These drives are typically used to create permanent archives for large amounts of data and to record videos. DVD recordable drives are rapidly replacing CD-R drives due to their massive capacity.
- **Rewriteable—DVD+RW, DVD−RW,** and **DVD-RAM** are the three most widely used formats. DVD+RW and DVD−RW stand for **DVD rewriteable. DVD-RAM** stands for **DVD random-access memory.** Each format has a unique way of storing data. Unfortunately, older DVD players typically can read only one type of format. Newer DVD players, however, are able to read and use any of the formats. Rewriteable DVD disc drives have rapidly replaced CD rewriteable drives. Applications range from recording video from camcorders to developing multimedia presentations that include extensive graphics and video.

High-Definition Discs

While CDs and DVDs are the most widely used optical discs today, the future belongs to discs of even greater capacity. While DVD discs have sufficient capacity to record standard-definition movies and music, they are insufficient for recording high-definition video, which requires about four times as much storage. This next generation of optical disc is called **hi def (high definition),** with a far greater capacity than DVDs. The hi def standard is **Blu-ray Disc (BD).** The name comes from the blue-colored laser that is used to read the disc.

Blu-ray Discs have a capacity of 25 to 50 gigabytes, more than 10 times the capacity of a standard single-layer DVD. Although Blu-ray media are the same size as other optical media, the discs require special drives. Most of these drives are capable of reading standard DVDs and CDs in addition to Blu-ray.

Like CDs and DVDs, Blu-ray has three basic types: read only, write once, and rewriteable. As with any optical disc, a device with recording capabilities is required for writing data.

For a summary of the different types of optical discs, see Figure 8-13.

☑ **CONCEPT CHECK**

How is data represented on optical discs?

Compare CD and DVD formats. Why did DVDs replace CDs?

What is hi def? What is Blu-ray? Compare Blu-ray to standard DVD.

Format	Typical Capacity	Description
CD	650 MB to 1 GB	Once the standard optical disc
DVD	4.7 GB to 17 GB	Current standard
Blu-ray	25 GB to 50 GB	Hi-def format, large capacity

Figure 8-13 Types of optical discs

Other Types of Secondary Storage

For the typical microcomputer user, the three basic storage options—hard disk, optical disc, and solid-state storage—are complementary, not competing. Almost all microcomputers have one hard-disk drive and one optical drive, with USB ports that can support portable solid-state drives. For many users, these secondary storage devices are further complemented with more specialized storage such as online storage services, floppy disk drives, and magnetic tape.

Online Storage Services

Online storage services provide users with storage space that can be accessed from a Web site. (See Figure 8-14.) This type of storage has several advantages compared to other types of secondary storage including low cost and the flexibility to access information from any location using the Internet. Because all information must travel across the Internet, however, access speed is slower. Another consideration is that users are dependent on the availability and security procedures of the service site. Because of these limitations, online storage services are typically used as a specialized secondary storage device and not for storing highly personalized or sensitive information.

Typically, service sites focus on supplying their services either to businesses or to individuals. The business-oriented sites provide faster access and greater security for a fee. The individual-focused sites provide limited storage for much lower cost and some sites are free. (See Figure 8-15.)

Figure 8-14 An online storage service

Floppy Disks

Floppy disks are portable or removable storage media that were once commonly used to transport relatively small word processing, spreadsheet, and other types of files. (See Figure 8-16.) They use flexible flat circular pieces of Mylar plastic that have been coated with a magnetic material. Like hard disks, **floppy disk drives (FDD)** store data and programs by altering the electromagnetic charges on the disk's surface. As with hard disks, files are stored and organized according to tracks and sectors.

There are two kinds of floppy disks: traditional and high-capacity. The **traditional floppy disk**

Focus	Company	Location
Individual	iBackup	www.ibackup.com
Individual	Apple	www.me.com
Individual	xDrive	www.xdrive.com
Business	Amerivault	www.amerivault.com
Business	Mozy	www.mozy.com

Figure 8-15 Online storage services

Figure 8-16 Floppy disk

Figure 8-17 Magnetic tape cartridge

is the 1.44 MB 2HD 3½-inch disk; 2HD means two-sided, high-density. These disks have a capacity of 1.44 megabytes—the equivalent of over 350 typewritten pages. Like the traditional floppy, the **high-capacity floppy disks** are 3½ inches in diameter. However, they are able to store more information, are thicker, and require special disk drives. These disks typically have a 100 MB, 250 MB, or 750 MB capacity—over 500 times as much as a standard floppy disk.

Magnetic Tape

On a traditional audiotape, you may have to fast-forward or rewind through several feet of tape to find a particular song. Finding a song on an audio compact disc, in contrast, can be much faster. You select the track, and the disc player moves directly to it. That, in brief, represents the two different approaches to external storage. The two approaches are called **sequential access** and **direct access.**

Disks provide fast direct access. Tapes provide slower sequential access. With tape, information is stored in sequence, such as alphabetically. For example, all the grades of students at your school could be recorded on tape arranged alphabetically by their last names. To find the grades for one student, say Chris Reed, the search would begin at the start of the tape and search alphabetically past all the last names beginning with A to Q before ultimately reaching Reed. This may involve searching several inches or feet, which takes time.

Like floppy and hard disks, **magnetic tape** stores data and programs by altering the electromagnetic charges on a recording surface. Although slower to access specific information, magnetic tape is an effective and commonly used tool for backing up data. At one time, mainframe computers used **magnetic tape reels** exclusively. This type of tape is typically ½ inch wide and 1½ miles long and provides massive storage capacity. Now, most mainframes as well as microcomputers use **tape cartridges** or **magnetic tape streamers** to back up data. (See Figure 8-17.)

 CONCEPT CHECK

 What are online storage services? What are they used for?

 What is the traditional floppy disk? What is a high-capacity floppy disk?

 Discuss magnetic tape reels and tape cartridges.

Mass Storage Devices

It is natural to think of secondary storage media and devices as they relate to us as individuals. It may not be as obvious how important these matters are to organizations. **Mass storage** refers to the tremendous amount of secondary storage required by large organizations. **Mass storage devices** are specialized high-capacity secondary storage devices designed to meet organizational demands for data.

Enterprise Storage System

Most large organizations have established a strategy called an **enterprise storage system** to promote efficient and safe use of data across the networks within their organizations. (See Figure 8-18.) Some of the mass storage devices that support this strategy are

- **File servers**—dedicated computers with very large storage capacities that provide users access to fast storage and retrieval of data.
- **Network attached storage (NAS)**—similar to a file server except simpler and less expensive; widely used for home and small business storage needs.
- **RAID systems**—larger versions of the specialized devices discussed earlier in this chapter that enhance organizational security by constantly making backup copies of files moving across the organization's networks.
- **Tape library**—device that provides automatic access to data archived on a large collection or library of tapes.
- **Organizational online storage**—high-speed Internet connection to a dedicated remote organizational online storage site.

Figure 8-18 Enterprise storage system

Storage Area Network

A recent mass storage development is **storage area network (SAN)** systems. SAN is an architecture to link remote computer storage devices, such as enterprise storage systems, to computers such that the devices are as available as locally attached drives. In a SAN system, the user's computer provides the file system for storing data, but the SAN provides the disk space for data.

The key to a SAN is a high-speed network, connecting individual computers to mass storage devices. Special file systems prevent simultaneous users from interfering with each other. SANs provide the ability to house data in remote locations and still allow efficient and secure access.

CONCEPT CHECK

Define mass storage and list five mass storage devices.

What is an enterprise storage system?

What is a storage area network system?

Careers in IT

Software engineers analyze users' needs and create application software. (See Figure 8-19.) Software engineers typically have experience in programming but focus on the design and development of programs using the principles of mathematics and engineering. They rarely write code themselves.

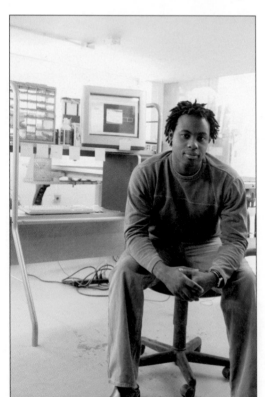

A bachelor's degree in computer science or information systems and an extensive knowledge of computers and technology are required by most employers. Internships may provide students with the kinds of experience employers look for in a software engineer. Those with specific experience with networking, the Internet, and Web applications may have an advantage over other applicants. Employers typically look for software engineers with good communication and analytical skills.

Software engineers can expect to earn an annual salary in the range of $63,000 to $98,500. Advancement opportunities are usually tied to experience. Experienced software engineers may be promoted to project manager or have opportunities in systems design. To learn about other careers in information technology, visit us at www.computing2011.com and enter the keyword **careers**.

Figure 8-19 Software engineer

A LOOK TO THE FUTURE

Will Cloud Computing Rain on Secondary Storage?

Recently, many applications that would have required installation on your computer to run have moved to the Web. Numerous Web sites now exist to provide application services. This is known as *cloud computing,* where the Internet acts as a "cloud" of servers that supply applications as a *service* rather than a *product.* Many examples already exist. For example, you may have created a word processing document or spreadsheet online using Google Apps, managed your financial information using Mint .com, or stored files and folders using Amazon S3.

With cloud computing, data is typically stored on the application provider's server. The processing power of the service provider's server is used to run applications, with the local computer responsible only for displaying the results. The applications and data can be accessed from any Internet-ready device. This means that even devices with little storage, memory, or processing power, such as mobile phones, can run the same powerful applications as a desktop computer.

The benefits to this arrangement are numerous. Imagine how much easier it would be to deploy or upgrade a customer relationship management software application in a large company. In the past, an IT professional would need to visit every computer the company owned to install the software from disk and manage licensing for the number of computers the software was purchased for. With software delivered as a service, the company can simply purchase the appropriate number of accounts from the service provider and direct employees to use the provider's Web site.

As wireless access to the Internet becomes available in more locations, devices used to store or transport information might use the network instead. For example, if you could instantly access music and video across the network from anywhere, would you still use CDs, DVDs, or portable music devices? Would you need a CD or USB storage to transport files from your home computer to school if they were centrally located on the Web?

Could cloud computing spell the end for secondary storage? With faster connections to the Internet and newer Internet-ready devices, will it be necessary to store data or install software on one's personal computer? What issues do you see with storing sensitive personal data on a provider's system rather than your own? What might happen, for example, if a provider were to go out of business or raise the price for using the application? Can you think of any applications that would not work well as a service?

STORAGE

RAM is **primary storage.** Most RAM is volatile, meaning that it loses its contents whenever power is disrupted. **Secondary storage** provides nonvolatile storage. Secondary storage retains data and information after the computer system is turned off.

Writing is the process of saving information to **secondary storage devices.** Reading is the process of accessing information from secondary storage devices.

Important characteristics of secondary storage include

- **Media**—actual physical material that retains data and programs.
- **Capacity**—how much a particular storage medium can hold.
- **Storage devices**—hardware that reads and writes to storage media.
- **Access speed**—time required to retrieve data from a secondary storage device.

HARD DISKS

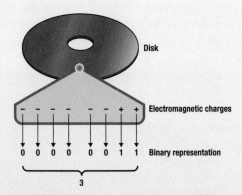

Hard disks use rigid metallic **platters** that provide a large amount of capacity. They store data and programs by altering the electromagnetic charges on the platter's surface. Files are organized according to **tracks, sectors,** and **cylinders. Density** refers to how tightly electromagnetic charges can be packed next to one another on the disk.

A **head crash** occurs when the hard disk makes contact with the drive's read/write heads.

Two types of hard disks are internal and external hard disks.

Internal Hard Disk

Internal hard disks are located within the system unit. Used to store programs and data files.

External Hard Drives

Unlike internal hard disks, **external hard drives** are removable. External drives use the same basic technology as internal disks.

To be a competent end user, you need to be aware of the different types of secondary storage. You need to know their capabilities, limitations, and uses. There are three widely used storage media: hard disk, solid-state storage, and, optical disc.

HARD DISKS

Performance Enhancements
Three ways to improve hard disk performance are disk caching, RAID, and file compression and decompression.

- **Disk caching**—provides a temporary high-speed holding area between a secondary storage device and the CPU; improves performance by anticipating data needs and reducing time to access data from secondary storage.
- **RAID (redundant array of inexpensive disks)**—several inexpensive hard-disk drives are connected together; improves performance by providing expanded storage, fast access, and high reliability.
- **File compression** and **decompression**—files compressed before storing and then decompressed before being used again; improves performance through efficient storage.

SOLID-STATE STORAGE

Solid-state storage devices have no moving parts and are more reliable and require less power than hard disks.

Solid-State Drives
Solid-state drives are similar to internal hard disk drives except they use solid-state memory; are faster, more durable, and more expensive; and generally provide less capacity.

Flash Memory
Flash memory cards are small solid state storage devices that are widely used with notebook computers. They are used with a variety of specialized input devices including digital cameras to store and transfer images and digital media players like the iPod to store and transfer music and video files.

USB Drives
USB drives (flash drives) are so small that they fit onto a key ring. These drives connect to a computer's USB port and are widely used to transfer data and information between computers, specialty devices, and the Internet.

OPTICAL DISCS

Optical discs use laser technology. 1s and 0s are represented by **pits** and **lands**. **Optical disc drives** project light and measure the reflected light.

Compact Disc

Compact discs (CDs) have typical capacity of 650 MB to 1 GB. Three types are **CD-ROM (compact disc–read-only memory)**, **CD-R (CD-recordable (CD-R drives are also known as CD burners))**, and **CD-RW (compact disc rewritable, erasable optical discs)**.

Digital Versatile Disc

DVDs (digital versatile discs, digital video discs) have far greater capacity than CDs (4.7 GB to 17 GB). Three types are **DVD-ROM (digital versatile disc–read-only memory; DVD players** are drives), write once (**DVD+R, DVD−R**), and rewriteable (**DVD+RW, DVD−RW, DVD−RAM**).

High-Definition Discs

Hi-def (high-definition) Blu-ray Discs are the next standard optical disc. **Blu-ray Discs (BDs)** have a capacity of 25 GB to 50 GB. Same size as other optical media, but much greater capacity and requires special drives. Three basic types: read only, write once, and rewriteable.

OTHER TYPES

The three basic storage options (hard, solid-state, and optical) are complementary and not necessarily competitive. Many users complement with more specialized devices including

- **Online storage services**—Web-based, low-cost storage. Accessible from any Internet connection, these drives are often slow and security is an issue.
- **Traditional** and **high-capacity floppy disks**—portable, removable storage media that were once widely used. Like a hard disk, they store data and programs by charging the disk surface.
- **Magnetic tape**—**sequential access** (disks provide **direct access**) used primarily for backing up data. **Magnetic tape reels** were widely used with mainframes. Now **tape cartridges (magnetic tape streamers)** are most widely used for mainframes and microcomputers.

MASS STORAGE

Mass storage refers to the tremendous amount of secondary storage required by large organizations. **Mass storage devices** are specialized high-capacity secondary storage devices.

Most large organizations have established a strategy called an **enterprise storage system** to promote efficient and safe use of data across the networks within their organizations.

Mass storage devices that support this strategy are **file servers, network attached storage (NAS), RAID systems, tape libraries,** and **organizational online storage**. A **storage area network (SAN)** is a method of using enterprise-level remote storage systems as if they were local to your computer.

CAREERS IN IT

Software engineers analyze users' needs and create application software. Bachelor's degree in computer science or information systems and extensive knowledge of computers and technology required. Salary range $63,000 to $98,500.

KEY TERMS

access speed   (221)
Blu-ray Disc (BD)   (230)
capacity   (220)
CD (compact disc)   (227)
CD-R (CD-recordable)   (227)
CD-ROM (compact disc–read-only memory)   (227)
CD-RW (compact disc rewriteable)   (227)
cylinder   (221)
density   (221)
direct access   (232)
disk caching   (223)
DVD (digital versatile disc or digital video disc)   (227)
DVD player   (227)
DVD−R (DVD recordable)   (230)
DVD+R (DVD recordable)   (230)
DVD-RAM (DVD random-access memory)   (230)
DVD-ROM (DVD–read-only memory)   (227)
DVD−RW (DVD rewriteable)   (230)
DVD+RW (DVD rewriteable)   (230)
enterprise storage system   (233)
erasable optical disc   (227)
external hard drive   (223)
file compression   (223)
file decompression   (223)
file server   (233)
flash drive   (225)
flash memory card   (224)
floppy disk   (231)
floppy disk drive (FDD)   (231)
hard disk   (221)
head crash   (221)

hi def (high definition)   (230)
high-capacity floppy disk   (232)
internal hard disk   (222)
land   (227)
magnetic tape   (232)
magnetic tape reel   (232)
magnetic tape streamer   (232)
mass storage   (232)
mass storage devices   (233)
media   (220)
network attached storage (NAS)   (233)
online storage service   (231)
optical disc   (225)
optical disc drive   (227)
organizational online storage   (233)
pit   (227)
platter   (221)
primary storage   (220)
RAID system   (233)
redundant array of inexpensive disks (RAID)   (223)
secondary storage   (220)
secondary storage device   (220)
sector   (221)
sequential access   (232)
software engineer   (234)
solid-state drive (SSD)   (224)
solid-state storage   (224)
storage area network (SAN)   (234)
storage device   (220)
tape cartridge   (232)
tape library   (233)
track   (221)
traditional floppy disk   (231)
USB drive   (225)

To test your knowledge of these key terms with animated flash cards, visit our Web site at www.computing2011.com and enter the keyword terms8.

MULTIPLE CHOICE

Circle the letter or fill in the correct answer.

1. RAM is referred to as _____ storage.
   a. direct
   b. nonvolatile
   c. secondary
   d. sequential

2. The amount of time required by a storage device to retrieve data and programs is its
   a. access speed
   b. capacity
   c. memory
   d. storage

3. How tightly the bits can be packed next to one another on a disk is referred to as
   a. tracks
   b. sectors
   c. density
   d. configuration

4. Thick, rigid metal platters that are capable of storing and retrieving information at a high rate of speed are known as
   a. hard disks
   b. soft disks
   c. flash memory
   d. SAN

5. This type of storage device has no moving parts.
   a. hard disks
   b. floppy disks
   c. optical discs
   d. solid state

6. The data on an optical disc is represented by flat areas called _____ on the disc surface.
   a. surfaces
   b. flats
   c. lands
   d. pits

7. DVD stands for
   a. digital video data
   b. direct video disc
   c. digital versatile disc
   d. direct versatile disc

8. _____ is the hi-def standard.
   a. Blu-ray
   b. CD-ROM
   c. DVD+R
   d. Max RL

9. Tape is described as using this type of access.
   a. magneto-optical
   b. DVD
   c. direct
   d. sequential

10. Specialized high-capacity secondary storage device designed to meet organizational demands for data.
    a. Blue-ray Disc
    b. hi def
    c. mass storage
    d. floppy disk

For an interactive multiple-choice practice test, visit our Web site at www.computing 2011.com and enter the keyword multiple8.

MATCHING

Match each numbered item with the most closely related lettered item. Write your answers in the spaces provided.

a. access speed
b. file compression
c. flash memory card
d. hi def
e. online storage service
f. RAID
g. RAM
h. solid-state storage
i. track
j. USB drive

1. A type of storage that is volatile. _____
2. Time required to retrieve data and programs. _____
3. A solid-state storage device small enough to fit onto a key ring. _____
4. Closed concentric ring on a disk on which data is recorded. _____
5. Several connected inexpensive hard-disk drives. _____
6. Increases storage capacity by reducing the amount of space required to store data and programs. _____
7. Stores data electronically and has no moving parts. _____
8. A credit card–sized solid-state storage device used in portable computers. _____
9. Provides free or low-cost storage available at special Web sites. _____
10. The next generation of optical discs. _____

For an interactive matching practice test, visit our Web site at www.computing 2011.com and enter the keyword matching8.

OPEN-ENDED

On a separate sheet of paper, respond to each question or statement.

1. What are the two types of hard disks? Describe three ways to improve hard disk performance.
2. Compare solid-state and hard disk storage.
3. What are the three most common optical disc formats? What is Blu-ray?
4. Discuss online storage services, floppy disks, and magnetic tape. What are the advantages and disadvantages of each?
5. Discuss mass storage systems including enterprise storage systems and storage area networks.

APPLYING TECHNOLOGY

The following questions are designed to demonstrate ways that you can effectively use technology today. The first question relates directly to this chapter's Making IT Work for You feature.

1 IPODS AND VIDEO FROM THE INTERNET

Did you know that you could use the Internet to locate movies and television shows, download them to your computer, and transfer them to a portable media player to watch on the go? All it takes is the right software, hardware, and a connection to the Internet. To learn more about using portable media players, review Making IT Work for You: iPods and Video from the Internet on page 226. Then answer the following questions: (a) What item is clicked in the iTunes application to locate movies and television shows? (b) Which television show was selected for purchase in the Making IT Work feature? (c) Describe the procedure to transfer video from the iTunes application to an iPod.

2 IPOD

Apple's iPod is a personal portable music player that stores a large number of digital music files. Connect to our Web site at www.computing2011.com and enter the keyword ipod to link to the iPod Web site. Once connected, read about the features and capabilities of iPod, and then answer the following questions: (a) How are music files transferred to iPod? (b) What type of secondary storage does iPod use? (c) What is iPod's storage capacity?

3 USB STORAGE DEVICES

Do you need to carry more data than will fit on a single floppy disk or CD? A USB storage device might be for you. These devices store large amounts of data in a package small enough to travel with your car keys. Connect to our Web site at www.computing2011.com and enter the keyword keychain to link to a site that features USB storage devices. Explore the site and then answer the following questions: (a) What type of secondary storage do USB storage devices use? (b) How is data transferred to and from computer systems? (c) What system software are the USB storage devices compatible with? (d) What are typical capacities of the USB storage devices?

EXPANDING YOUR KNOWLEDGE

The following questions are designed to add depth and detail to your understanding of specific topics presented within this chapter. The questions direct you to sources other than the textbook to obtain this knowledge.

1 HOW MUSIC IS DOWNLOADED FROM THE INTERNET

One of the most popular activities on the Internet is to locate and download music files. Using a CD-R drive, the files are saved onto an optical disc. These discs can then be played in a variety of different types of devices. To learn more about how music is downloaded, visit our Web site at www.computing2011.com and enter the keyword music. Then answer the following questions: (a) Go to the Web and find a Web site where you can download music from the Internet. What Web site did you find? How much do they charge to download music? (b) When you download music from the Internet, where is it stored on your computer? (c) Name three ways you can play music from the Internet.

2 FILE COMPRESSION

A common problem for computer users is that they run out of hard disk space. File compression software can open up space on a full hard drive, improve system performance, and make files easier to find and organize. To learn more about file compression, visit our Web site at www.computing2011.com and enter the keyword compression. Then answer the following questions: (a) What are the two types of file compression? How do they differ? (b) What type of file compression is used for home movies? Why? (c) What type of file compression is used for a resume? Why? (d) Research a compression/decompression utility on the Web. What types of files does your utility create? Is this a lossy or lossyless file compression?

3 ONLINE STORAGE SERVICES

Online storage services offer remote file storage or backup. Research an online storage service on the Web and then answer the following questions: (a) What online storage service did you research? (b) What is the cost for using the service, and what features do you get for that price? (c) How are files accessed from and uploaded to the service? (d) What assurances does the service provider offer concerning availability of your data? What about security?

WRITING ABOUT TECHNOLOGY

The ability to think critically and to write effectively is essential to nearly every profession. The following questions are designed to help you develop these skills by posing thought-provoking questions about computer privacy, security, and/or ethics.

① CD-R AND MUSIC FILES

Creating a custom CD of your favorite music is a popular use of secondary storage. Many sites on the Web offer free music that you can download. However, not all music files that are available on the Internet are freely distributable. Consider the following questions and write a one-page paper addressing them: (a) Is it fair to make a copy on your computer of a CD you have purchased? (b) Would it be fair to give a burned copy of a CD to a friend? What if the friend would not have otherwise purchased that CD? (c) People have been making illegal copies of music cassette tapes for some time. Why is using the Internet to make and distribute copies of music receiving so much attention?

② ARCHIVING ELECTRONIC RECORDS

At one time in the recent past, floppy disks were the standard for storing and exchanging files. However, they do not have the capacity to store most of today's video, image, and music files. As a result, floppy disk drives are no longer a standard feature on many computers, which instead offer optical drives for CDs and DVDs. Consider the following questions and address the following items in a one-page paper: (a) Do you currently back up or save documents that you want to keep for the future, including digital photos, e-mail messages, and school projects? If so, which media do you use? (b) Are there electronic files you feel you may want to access far into the future? (c) What does the demise of floppy disks suggest about the challenges of archiving important documents for future generations? Explain your answer.

NOTES

Communications and Networks

Competencies

After you have read this chapter, you should be able to:

1 Discuss connectivity, the wireless revolution, and communication systems.

2 Describe physical and wireless communications channels.

3 Discuss connection devices and services including dial-up, DSL, cable, satellite/air, and cellular.

4 Describe data transmission factors, including bandwidths and protocols.

5 Discuss networks and key network terminology including network interface cards and network operating systems.

6 Describe different types of networks, including local, home, wireless, personal, metropolitan, and wide area networks.

7 Describe network architectures, including topologies and strategies.

8 Discuss the organization issues related to Internet technologies and network security.

The first truly global communications network was the telegraph, which made it possible to send a message across the globe. Letters could take weeks to travel between cities, but the telegraph cut the transmission to minutes. E-mail cuts the transmission to seconds.

Some predict that humans will eventually be connected with a neural network, making the cables of any kind unnecessary. Imagine a world where you can send your thoughts and ideas directly to another person's mind, without typing or talking.

chapter 9

Introduction

We live in a truly connected society. We can communicate almost instantaneously with others worldwide; changing events from the smallest of countries and places are immediately broadcast to the world; our e-mail messages are delivered to handheld devices; cars access the Internet to provide driving instructions and solve mechanical problems. Even household appliances can connect to the Internet and be remotely controlled. The communications and information options we have at our fingertips have changed how we react and relate to the world around us.

As the power and flexibility of our communication systems have expanded, the sophistication of the networks that support these systems has become increasingly critical and complex. The network technologies that handle our cellular, business, and Internet communications come in many different forms. Satellites, broadcast towers, telephone lines, even buried cables and fiber optics carry our telephone messages, e-mail, and text messages. These different networks must be able to efficiently and effectively integrate with one another.

Competent end users need to understand the concept of connectivity, wireless networking, and the elements that make up network and communications systems. Additionally, they need to understand the basics of communications channels, connection devices, data transmission, network types, network architectures and organizational networks.

Communications

Computer communications is the process of sharing data, programs, and information between two or more computers. We have discussed numerous applications that depend on communication systems, including

- **E-mail**—provides a fast, efficient alternative to traditional mail by sending and receiving electronic documents.
- **Instant messaging**—supports direct, "live" electronic communication between two or more friends or buddies.
- **Internet telephone**—provides a very low-cost alternative to long-distance telephone calls using electronic voice and video delivery.
- **Electronic commerce**—buying and selling goods electronically.

In this chapter, we will focus on the communication systems that support these and many other applications. Connectivity, the wireless revolution, and communication systems are key concepts and technologies for the 21st century.

Connectivity

Connectivity is a concept related to using computer networks to link people and resources. For example, connectivity means that you can connect your microcomputer to other computers and information sources almost anywhere. With this connection, you are linked to the world of larger computers and the Internet. This includes hundreds of thousands of Web servers and their extensive information resources. Thus, becoming computer competent and knowledgeable becomes a matter of knowing not only about connectivity through networks to microcomputers, but also about larger computer systems and their information resources.

The Wireless Revolution

The single most dramatic change in connectivity and communications in the past few years has been the widespread use of mobile telephones with wireless Internet connectivity. Students, parents, teachers, businesspeople, and others routinely talk and communicate with these devices. It is estimated that over 3 billion mobile telephones are in use worldwide. This wireless technology allows individuals to stay connected with one another from almost anywhere at any time.

So what's the revolution? While wireless technology was originally used primarily for voice communications, many of today's cell phones support e-mail, Web access, and a variety of Internet applications. In addition, wireless technology allows a wide variety of nearby devices to communicate with one another without any physical connection. You can share a high-speed printer, share data files, and collaborate on working documents with a nearby co-worker without having your computers connected by cables or telephone—wireless communication. Highspeed Internet wireless technology allows individuals to connect to the Internet and share information from almost anywhere in the world. (See Figure 9-1.) But is it a revolution? Most experts say yes and that the revolution is just beginning.

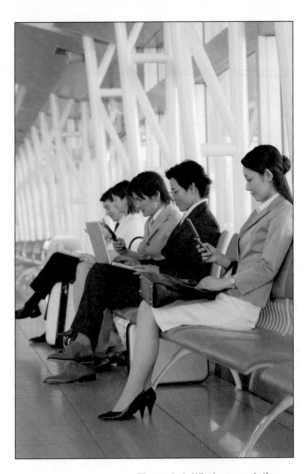

Figure 9-1 Wireless revolution

Communication Systems

Communication systems are electronic systems that transmit data from one location to another. Whether wired or wireless, every communication system has four basic elements. (See Figure 9-2.)

- **Sending and receiving devices.** These are often a computer or specialized communication device. They originate (send) as well as accept (receive) messages in the form of data, information, and/or instructions.
- **Communication channel.** This is the actual connecting or transmission medium that carries the message. This medium can be a physical wire or cable, or it can be wireless.
- **Connection devices.** These devices act as an interface between the sending and receiving devices and the communication channel. They convert

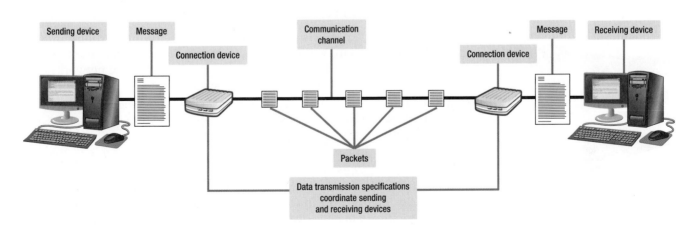

Figure 9-2 Basic elements of a communication system

outgoing messages into packets that can travel across the communication channel. They also reverse the process for incoming messages.

- **Data transmission specifications.** These are rules and procedures that coordinate the sending and receiving devices by precisely defining how the message will be sent across the communication channel.

For example, if you wanted to send an e-mail to a friend, you could create and send the message using your computer, the *sending device.* Your modem, a *connection device,* would modify and format the message so that it could travel efficiently across *communication channels,* such as telephone lines. The specifics describing how the message is modified, reformatted, and sent would be described in the *data transmission specifications.* After your message traveled across the channel, the receiver's modem, a connection device, would reform it so that it could be displayed on your friend's computer, the *receiving device.* (Note: This example presents the basic communication system elements involved in sending e-mail. It does not and is not intended to demonstrate all the specific steps and equipment involved in an e-mail delivery system.)

 CONCEPT CHECK

Define computer communications and connectivity.

What is the wireless revolution?

Describe the four elements of every communication system.

Communication Channels

Communication channels are an essential element of every communication system. These channels actually carry the data from one computer to another. There are two categories of communication channels. One category connects sending and receiving devices by providing a physical connection, such as a wire or cable. The other category is wireless.

Physical Connections

Physical connections use a solid medium to connect sending and receiving devices. These connections include telephone lines (twisted pair), coaxial cable, and fiber-optic cable.

Figure 9-3 Twisted-pair cable

- **Twisted-pair cable** consists of pairs of copper wire that are twisted together. Both standard **telephone lines** and **Ethernet cables** use twisted-pair. (See Figure 9-3.) Ethernet cables are commonly used in networks and to connect a variety of components to the system unit.

Figure 9-4 Coaxial cable

- **Coaxial cable,** a high-frequency transmission cable, replaces the multiple wires of telephone lines with a single solid-copper core. (See Figure 9-4.) In terms of the number of telephone connections, a coaxial cable has over 80 times the transmission capacity of twisted pair. Coaxial cable is used to deliver television signals as well as to connect computers in a network.

Figure 9-5 Fiber-optic cable

- **Fiber-optic cable** transmits data as pulses of light through tiny tubes of glass. (See Figure 9-5.) In terms of the number of telephone connections, fiber-optic cable has over 26,000 times the transmission capacity of twisted-pair cable. Compared to coaxial cable, they are lighter and more

Standard	Maximum speed
802.11b	11 Mbps
802.11a	54 Mbps
802.11g	54 Mbps
802.11n	600 Mbps

Figure 9-6 Wi-Fi standards

reliable at transmitting data. They transmit information using beams of light at light speeds instead of pulses of electricity, making them far faster than copper cable. Fiber-optic cable is rapidly replacing twisted-pair cable telephone lines.

Wireless Connections

Wireless connections do not use a solid substance to connect sending and receiving devices. Rather, they use the air itself. Primary technologies used for wireless connections are radio frequency, microwave, satellite, and infrared.

Figure 9-7 Microwave dish

- **Radio frequency (RF)** uses radio signals to communicate between wireless devices. For example, cellular telephones and many Internet-enabled devices use RF to place telephone calls and/or to connect to the Internet. Some end users connect their notebook or handheld computers to a cellular telephone to access the Web from remote locations. Most home or business wireless networks are based on a technology called **Wi-Fi (wireless fidelity).** A number of standards for Wi-Fi exist, and each can send and receive data at a different speed. (See Figure 9-6.) **Bluetooth** is a short-range radio communication standard that transmits data over short distances of up to approximately 33 feet. Bluetooth is widely used for wireless headsets, printer connections, and handheld devices.

- **Microwave** communication uses high-frequency radio waves. Like infrared, microwave communication provides line-of-sight communication because microwaves travel in a straight line. Because the waves cannot bend with the curvature of the earth, they can be transmitted only over relatively short distances. Thus, microwave is a good medium for sending data between buildings in a city or on a large college campus. For longer distances, the waves must be relayed by means of microwave stations with microwave dishes or antennas. (See Figure 9-7.)

- **Satellite** communication uses satellites orbiting about 22,000 miles above the earth as microwave relay stations. Many of these are offered by Intelsat, the International Telecommunications Satellite Consortium, which is owned by 114 governments and forms a worldwide communication system. Satellites rotate at a precise point and speed above the earth. They can amplify and relay microwave signals from one transmitter on the ground to another. Satellites can be used to send and receive large volumes of data. Uplink is a term relating to sending data to a satellite. Downlink refers to receiving data from a satellite. The major drawback to satellite communication is that bad weather can sometimes interrupt the flow of data.

One of the most interesting applications of satellite communications is for global positioning. A network of 24 satellites owned and managed by the Defense Department continuously sends location information to earth. **Global positioning system (GPS)** devices (See Figure 9-8.) use that information to uniquely

Figure 9-8 GPS navigation

Channel	Description
Twisted pair	Twisted copper wire, used for standard telephone lines and Ethernet cables
Coaxial cable	Solid copper core, more than 80 times the capacity of twisted pair
Fiber-optic cable	Light carries data, more than 26,000 times the capacity of twisted pair
Radio frequency	Radio waves connect wireless devices including cell phones and computer components
Microwave	High-frequency radio waves, travels in straight line through the air
Satellite	Microwave relay station in the sky, used by GPS devices
Infrared	Infrared light travels in a straight line

Figure 9-9 Communication channels

determine the geographical location of the device. Available in many automobiles to provide navigational support, these systems are often mounted into the dash with a monitor to display maps and speakers to provide spoken directions. Many of today's cell phones, including the Apple iPhone, use GPS technology for handheld navigation.

- **Infrared** uses infrared light waves to communicate over short distances. It is sometimes referred to as line-of-sight communication because the light waves can only travel in a straight line. This requires that sending and receiving devices must be in clear view of one another without any obstructions blocking that view. One of the most common applications is to transfer data and information from a portable device such as a notebook computer or PDA to a desktop computer.

For a summary of communication channels, see Figure 9-9.

CONCEPT CHECK

What are communication channels?

List and discuss three physical connections.

List and discuss four wireless connections.

What is Wi-Fi? Bluetooth? GPS?

Connection Devices

A great deal of computer communication takes place over telephone lines. However, because the telephone was originally designed for voice transmission, telephones typically send and receive **analog signals,** which are continuous electronic waves. Computers, in contrast, send and receive **digital signals.** (See Figure 9-10.) These represent the presence or absence of an electronic pulse—the on/off binary signals we mentioned in Chapter 6. To convert the digital signals to analog signals and vice versa, you need a modem.

Analog

Digital

Figure 9-10 Analog and digital signals

Modems

The word **modem** is short for *modulator-demodulator*. **Modulation** is the name of the process of converting from digital to analog. **Demodulation** is the process of converting from analog to digital. The modem enables digital microcomputers to communicate across different mediums, including telephone wires, cable lines, and radio waves.

The speed with which modems transmit data varies. This speed, called **transfer rate,** is typically measured in **thousands of bits (kilobits) per second (Kbps).** (See Figure 9-11.) The higher the speed, the faster you can send and receive information. For example, transferring an image like Figure 9-10 might take 75 seconds with a 33.6 Kbps modem and only 45 seconds with a 56 Kbps modem. To learn more about transfer rates, visit our Web site at www.computing2011.com and enter the keyword **rate.**

There are four commonly used types of modems: telephone, DSL, cable, and wireless. (See Figure 9-12.)

- A **telephone modem** is used to connect a computer directly to a telephone line. These modems can be either internal or external. Internal modems are on an expansion card that plugs into a slot on the system board. An external modem is typically connected to the system unit through a serial or USB port.

- A **DSL (digital subscriber line)** modem uses standard phone lines to create a high-speed connection directly to your phone company's offices. These devices are usually external and connect to the system unit using either USB or Ethernet ports.

- A **cable modem** uses the same coaxial cable as your television. Like a DSL modem, a cable modem creates high-speed connections using the system unit's USB or Ethernet port.

Unit	Speed
Kbps	thousand bits per second
Mbps	million bits per second
Gbps	billion bits per second

Figure 9-11 Typical transfer rates

Telephone

DSL

Cable

Wireless

Figure 9-12 Basic types of modems

- A **wireless modem** is also known as a **WWAN (wireless wide area network) modem.** It is usually a small plug-in USB or ExpressCard device that provides very portable high-speed connectivity from virtually anywhere.

Connection Service

For years, large corporations have been leasing special high-speed lines from telephone companies. Originally, these were copper lines, known as **T1** lines, that could be combined to form higher-capacity options known as **T3** or **DS3** lines. These lines have largely been replaced by **optical carrier (OC)** lines, which are substantially must faster.

While the special high-speed lines are too costly for most individuals, Internet service providers (as discussed in Chapter 2) do provide affordable connections. These include dial-up, DSL, cable, satellite/air, and cellular services.

- **Dial-up service** uses existing telephones and telephone modems to connect to the Internet. For years this had been the most widely used service; however, it is very slow and is being replaced by other higher-speed connection services.
- **Digital subscriber line (DSL) service** is provided by telephone companies using existing telephone lines to provide high-speed connections. **ADSL (asymmetric digital subscriber line)** is one of the most widely used types of DSL. DSL is much faster than dial-up.
- **Cable service** is provided by cable television companies using their existing television cables. These connections are faster than DSL.
- **Satellite/air connection services** use satellites to provide wireless connections. While slower than DSL and cable modem, satellite/air connections are available almost anywhere that a satellite-receiving disk can be aimed at the southern skies.
- **Cellular services** use **3G cellular networks** to provide wireless connectivity to the Internet. Although not as fast as the other services, cellular services are rapidly growing in popularity for mobile devices such as cell phones and laptop computers.

For a comparison of typical user connection costs and speeds, see Figure 9-13.

CONCEPT CHECK

What is the function of a modem?

Compare four types of modems.

What is a connection service?

Compare five affordable connection services.

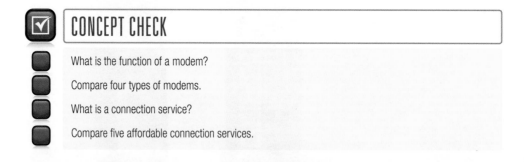

Type	Monthly Fee	Speed	Seconds to Receive Image
Dial-up	$10	56 Kbps	45.0 seconds
DSL	30	1.5 Mbps	1.5 seconds
Cable	40	8 Mbps	0.32 second
Satellite/air	75	900 Kbps	2.8 seconds
Cellular	55	768 Kbps	3.2 seconds

Figure 9-13 Typical user connection costs and speeds

Data Transmission

Several factors affect how data is transmitted. These factors include bandwidth and protocols.

Bandwidth

Bandwidth is a measurement of the width or capacity of the communication channel. Effectively, it means how much information can move across the communication channel in a given amount of time. For example, to transmit text documents, a slow bandwidth would be acceptable. However, to effectively transmit video and audio, a wider bandwidth is required. There are four categories of bandwidth.

- **Voiceband,** also known as **low bandwidth,** is used for standard telephone communication. Microcomputers with telephone modems and dial-up service use this bandwidth. While effective for transmitting text documents, it is too slow for many types of transmission, including high-quality audio and video.
- **Medium band** is used in special leased lines to connect minicomputers and mainframes as well as to transmit data over long distances. This bandwidth is capable of very high-speed data transfer.
- **Broadband** is widely used for DSL, cable, and satellite connections to the Internet. Several users can simultaneously use a single broadband connection for high-speed data transfer.
- **Baseband** is widely used to connect individual computers that are located close to one another. Like broadband, it is able to support high-speed transmission. Unlike broadband, however, baseband can only carry a single signal at one time.

Protocols

For data transmission to be successful, sending and receiving devices must follow a set of communication rules for the exchange of information. These rules for exchanging data between computers are known as **protocols.**

The standard protocol for the Internet is **TCP/IP (transmission control protocol/Internet protocol).** The essential features of this protocol involve (1) identifying sending and receiving devices and (2) breaking information into small parts for transmission across the Internet.

- **Identification:** Every computer on the Internet has a unique numeric address called an **IP address (Internet protocol address).** Similar to the way a postal service uses addresses to deliver mail, the Internet uses IP addresses to deliver e-mail and to locate Web sites. Because these numeric addresses are difficult for people to remember and use, a system was developed to automatically convert text-based addresses to numeric IP addresses. This system uses a **domain name server (DNS)** that converts text-based addresses to IP addresses. For example, whenever you enter a URL, say www.computing2011.com, a DNS converts this to an IP address before a connection can be made. (See Figure 9-14.)
- **Packetization:** Information sent or transmitted across the Internet usually travels through numerous interconnected networks. Before the message is sent, it is reformatted or broken down into small parts called **packets.** Each packet is then sent separately over the Internet, possibly traveling different routes to one common destination. At the receiving end, the packets are reassembled into the correct order.

DNS

URL

www.computing2011.com

IP Address

65.39.69.50

Figure 9-14 **DNS converts text-based addresses to numeric IP addresses**

CONCEPT CHECK

What is bandwidth? Describe the four categories.

What are protocols? What is the standard protocol for the Internet?

Define TCP/IP, IP address, and packets.

Networks

A **computer network** is a communication system that connects two or more computers so that they can exchange information and share resources. Networks can be set up in different arrangements to suit users' needs. (See Figure 9-15.)

Terms

There are a number of specialized terms that describe computer networks. These terms include

- **Node**—any device that is connected to a network. It could be a computer, printer, or data storage device.
- **Client**—a node that requests and uses resources available from other nodes. Typically, a client is a user's microcomputer.
- **Server**—a node that shares resources with other nodes. Dedicated servers specialize in performing specific tasks. Depending on the specific task, they may be called an application server, communication server, database server, file server, printer server, or Web server.
- **Directory server**—a specialized server that manages resources, such as user accounts, for an entire network.
- **Host**—any computer system that can be accessed over a network.
- **Switch**—central node that coordinates the flow of data by sending messages directly between sender and receiver nodes. A **hub** previously filled this purpose by sending a received message to all connected nodes, rather than just the intended node.

Directory server

Switch

Printer

Nodes

Servers

Clients   **Clients**

Figure 9-15 Computer network

- **Network interface cards (NIC)**—as discussed in Chapter 6, these are expansion cards located within the system unit that connect the computer to a network. Sometimes referred to as a LAN adapter.
- **Network operating systems (NOS)**—control and coordinate the activities of all computers and other devices on a network. These activities include electronic communication and the sharing of information and resources.
- **Network administrator**—a computer specialist responsible for efficient network operations and implementation of new networks.

A network may consist only of microcomputers, or it may integrate microcomputers or other devices with larger computers. Networks can be controlled by all nodes working together equally or by specialized nodes coordinating and supplying all resources. Networks may be simple or complex, self-contained or dispersed over a large geographical area.

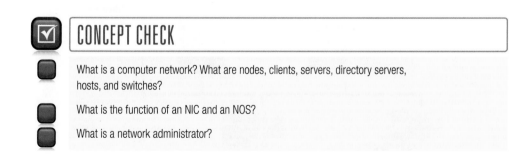

CONCEPT CHECK

What is a computer network? What are nodes, clients, servers, directory servers, hosts, and switches?

What is the function of an NIC and an NOS?

What is a network administrator?

Network Types

Clearly, different types of channels—cable or air—allow different kinds of networks to be formed. Telephone lines, for instance, may connect communications equipment within the same building or within a home. Networks also may be citywide and even international, using both cable and air connections. Local area, metropolitan area, and wide area networks are distinguished by the geographical area they serve.

Local Area Networks

Networks with nodes that are in close physical proximity—within the same building, for instance—are called **local area networks (LANs).** Typically, LANs span distances less than a mile and are owned and operated by individual organizations. LANs are widely used by colleges, universities, and other types of organizations to link microcomputers and to share printers and other resources. For a simple LAN, see Figure 9-16.

The LAN represented in Figure 9-16 is a typical arrangement and provides two benefits: economy and flexibility. People can share costly equipment. For instance, the four microcomputers share the laser printer and the file server, which are expensive pieces of hardware. Other equipment or nodes also may be added to the LAN—for instance, more microcomputers, a mainframe computer, or optical-disc storage devices. Additionally, the **network gateway** is a device that allows one LAN to be linked to other LANs or to larger networks. For example, the LAN of one office group may be connected to the LAN of another office group.

There are a variety of different standards or ways in which nodes can be connected to one another and ways in which their communications are controlled in a LAN. The most common standard is known as **Ethernet.** LANs using this standard are sometimes referred to as Ethernet LANs.

Home Networks

While LANs have been widely used within organizations for years, they are now being commonly used by individuals in their homes and apartments. These LANs, called **home networks,** allow different computers to share resources, including a common Internet connection. Computers can be connected in a variety of ways, including electrical wiring, telephone wiring, and special cables. One of the simplest ways, however, is without cables, or wireless.

On the Web Explorations

Wireless home networks are becoming fast, cheap, and popular.

To learn more about a company helping to "unwire" our homes, visit our Web site at www.computing2011.com and enter the keyword wireless.

Figure 9-16 Local area network

Wireless LAN

A wireless local area network is typically referred to as a **wireless LAN (WLAN).** It uses radio frequencies to connect computers and other devices. All communications pass through the network's centrally located **wireless access point** or **base station.** This access point interprets incoming radio frequencies and routes communications to the appropriate devices. To see how home networks work, visit our Web site at www.computing2011.com and enter the keyword **network.**

To learn more about how to set up and use a wireless home network, see Making IT Work for You: Home Networking on pages 262 and 263.

Personal Area Network

A **personal area network (PAN)** is a type of wireless network that works within a very small area—your immediate surroundings. PANs connect cell phones to headsets, PDAs to other PDAs, keyboards to cell phones, and so on. These tiny, self-configuring networks make it possible for all of our gadgets to interact wirelessly with each other. The most popular PAN technology is Bluetooth, with a maximum range of around 30 feet. Virtually all wireless peripheral devices available today use Bluetooth, including the controllers on popular game systems like the PlayStation and Wii.

Metropolitan Area Networks

The next step up from the LAN is the **MAN**—the **metropolitan area network.** MANs span distances up to 100 miles. These networks are frequently used as links between office buildings that are located throughout a city.

Do you use your laptop to connect to wireless networks at school or in public places such as coffee shops, airports, or hotels? If so, it is important to use caution to protect your computer and your privacy. Here are a few suggestions:

1 **Use a firewall.** A personal firewall is essential when connecting your computer directly to public networks. Some firewalls, such as the one built into Windows Vista, can be set to use more restrictive rules for public networks.

2 **Turn off file sharing.** Turning off file-sharing features in your operating system will ensure that no one can read or delete your files, or add infected files to your computer.

3 **Avoid typing sensitive information.** When possible, avoid sites that require personal information such as passwords or credit card numbers for home.

4 **Turn it off.** Turn off your laptop's wireless connection when you are not using it. This prevents automatic connections to wireless networks you do not authorize and limits your exposure to public networks.

To see additional tips, visit our Web site at www.computing2011.com and enter the keyword tips.

Unlike a LAN, a MAN is typically not owned by a single organization. Rather, it is either owned by a group of organizations who jointly own and operate the network or by a single network service provider who provides network services for a fee.

Wide Area Networks

Wide area networks (WANs) are countrywide and worldwide networks. These networks provide access to regional service (MAN) providers and typically span distances greater than 100 miles. They use microwave relays and satellites to reach users over long distances—for example, from Los Angeles to Paris. Of course, the widest of all WANs is the Internet, which spans the entire globe.

The primary difference between a LAN, MAN, and WAN is the geographical range. Each may have various combinations of hardware, such as microcomputers, minicomputers, mainframes, and various peripheral devices.

For a summary of network types, see Figure 9-17.

 ## CONCEPT CHECK

 Describe LANs, home networks, wireless LAN, and PAN.

What is a MAN? What is a WAN?

Type	Description
LAN	Local area network; located within close proximity
Home	Local area network for home and apartment use; typically wireless
WLAN	Wireless local area network; all communication passes through access point
PAN	Personal area network; connects digital devices, such as PDAs
MAN	Metropolitan area network; typically spans cities with coverage up to 100 miles
WAN	Wide area network for countrywide or worldwide coverage; the Internet is the largest WAN

Figure 9-17 **Types of networks**

Network Architecture

Network architecture describes how a network is arranged and how resources are coordinated and shared. It encompasses a variety of different network specifics, including network topologies and strategies. Network topology describes the physical arrangement of the network. Network strategies define how information and resources are shared.

Topologies

A network can be arranged or configured in several different ways. This arrangement is called the network's **topology.** While many different topologies can be used for networks, six basic categories represent the past and present.

The past is represented by two network topologies that can still be found today but have been replaced in large part by newer, more efficient topologies. These older or legacy networks are

Figure 9-18 **Ring network**

- **Bus network**—each device is connected to a common cable called a **bus** or backbone and all communications travel along this bus.

- **Ring network**—each device is connected to two other devices, forming a ring. (See Figure 9-18.) When a message is sent, it is passed around the ring until it reaches the intended destination.

Both of these legacy topologies pass messages device-to-device in sequence, which causes several disadvantages. A single incorrectly configured or malfunctioning device could cause errors or even bring the whole network down. Since all messages must pass through all nodes between the source and destination, bandwidth usage is high, making this type of topology slow and less efficient. Finally, security is a greater challenge since intermediate devices receive messages that are not intended for them.

The present is represented by four network topologies that are widely used today. These current network topologies are

Figure 9-19 Star network

- **Star network**—each device is connected directly to a central network switch. (See Figure 9-19.) Whenever a node sends a message, it is routed to the switch, which then passes the message along to the intended recipient. The star network is the most widely used network topology today. It is applied to a broad range of applications from small networks in the home to very large networks in major corporations.

- **Tree network**—each device is connected to a central node, either directly or through one or more other devices. The central node is connected to two or more subordinate nodes that in turn are connected to other subordinate nodes, and so forth, forming a treelike structure. (See Figure 9-20.) This

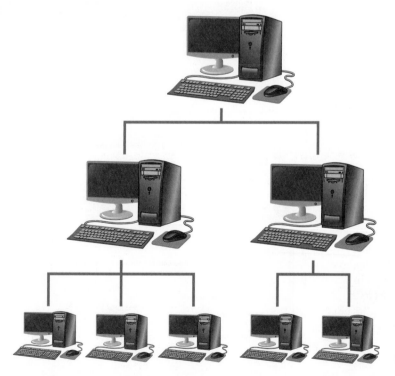

Figure 9-20 Tree network

Making IT work for you

HOME NETWORKING

Computer networks are not just for corporations and schools anymore. If you have more than one computer, you can use a home network to share files and printers, to allow multiple users access to the Internet at the same time, and to play multiplayer computer games.

Installing the Access Point A wireless access point is a device that broadcasts wireless signals for the network and is the gateway to the Internet for the wireless network. To set up a wireless access point using Windows Vista:

1 ● Click *Start/ControlPanel/Network and Internet/ Network and Sharing Center.*

● Click *Set up a connection or network.*

● Choose *Set up a wireless router or access point.*

2 ● Follow the on-screen instructions, which might include opening a special Web page to configure your access point.

Connecting Computers Each computer on a wireless network requires a wireless network card. Many laptops and some desktops come equipped with a wireless network card built-in. Add-on cards can also be purchased. Once a computer is equipped with a wireless network card, it is simple to connect it to the wireless network. For example, to connect to a wireless network using Windows Vista:

1 ● Click *Start/Connect To.*

● Select the name of the network you configured in the previous step.

● Enter the password you chose in the previous step to connect to the wireless network.

262

Using the Network Now your wireless devices are ready to share their resources. Some common uses are file and printer sharing, online gaming, Internet phone, and streaming music and video.

Online Games Some video game systems can connect to your home network and let you play with others over the Internet.

Internet Phone Special phones can connect to your home network and allow you to talk over the Internet.

Streaming Media Special devices can connect your television or stereo to your home network and allow you to stream content from other devices on your network or from the Internet.

File and Printer Sharing Computers on your home network can exchange files and print to shared printers.

Wireless Access Point The wireless access point is the central component of your home network. It connects your wireless devices together and shares your home's Internet connection.

Home networks are continually changing, and some of the specifics presented in this Making IT Work for You may have changed.

To learn about other ways to make information technology work for you, visit our Web site at www.computing2011.com and enter the keyword miw.

Figure 9-21 Mesh network

network, also known as a **hierarchical network,** is often used to share corporatewide data.

- **Hybrid network**—is a combination of different topologies. For example, large organizations today typically have a complex network of smaller networks. These smaller networks have been created over time and use a variety of different topologies. Connected together, these smaller networks form a hybrid network.

- **Mesh network**—this topology is the newest type and does not use a specific physical layout (such as a star or a tree). Rather, the mesh network requires that each node have more than one connection to the other nodes. The resulting pattern forms the appearance of a mesh. (See Figure 9-21.) If a path between two nodes is somehow disrupted, data can be automatically rerouted around the failure using another path. Wireless technologies are frequently used to build mesh networks.

For a summary of the network topologies, see Figure 9-22.

Topology	Description
Bus	Past; all devices connected to a bus
Ring	Past; each device connected to two other devices
Star	Present; each device connected to central switch
Tree	Present; each device connected directly or indirectly to central node; hierarchical topology
Hybrid	Present; combination of different topologies
Mesh	Present each device connected to more than one other device

Figure 9-22 Network topologies

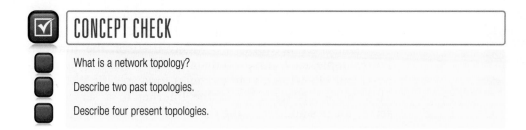
Strategies

Every network has a **strategy,** or way of coordinating the sharing of information and resources. The most common network strategies are terminal, client/server, peer-to-peer, and distributed.

In a **terminal server network,** processing power is centralized in one large computer, with the capacity to handle a large number of connections. The nodes connected to this host computer are either terminals with little or no processing capabilities or microcomputers running special terminal emulation software such as Windows Remote Desktop. (See Figure 9-23.)

Many airline reservation systems are terminal server networks. A large central computer maintains all the airline schedules, rates, seat availability, and so on. Travel agents use terminals to connect to the central computer and to schedule reservations. Although the tickets may be printed along with travel itineraries at the agent's desk, nearly all processing is done at the central computer.

One advantage of terminal server networks is the centralized location and control of technical personnel, software, and data. One disadvantage is the lack of control and flexibility for the end user. Another disadvantage is that terminal server networks do not use the full processing power available with microcomputers.

Client/server networks use central computers to coordinate and supply services to other nodes on the network. The server provides access to resources such as Web pages, databases, application software, and hardware. (See Figure 9-24.) This strategy is based on specialization. Server nodes coordinate and supply specialized services, and client nodes request the services.

Figure 9-23 Terminal server network

Figure 9-24 Client/server network

Commonly used server operating systems are Windows Server, Mac OS X Server, Linux, and Solaris.

Client/server networks are widely used on the Internet. For example, each time you open a Web browser, your computer (the client) sends out a request for a specific Web page. This request is routed over the Internet to a server. This server locates and sends the requested material back to your computer.

One advantage of the client/server network strategy is the ability to handle very large networks efficiently. Another advantage is the availability of powerful network management software to monitor and control network activities. The major disadvantages are the cost of installation and maintenance.

In a **peer-to-peer (P2P) network,** nodes have equal authority and can act as both clients and servers. (See Figure 9-25.) The most common way to share games, movies, and music over the Internet is to use a P2P network. For example, special file-sharing software such as eDonkey or BitTorrent can be used to obtain files located on another microcomputer and also can provide files to other microcomputers.

P2P networks are rapidly growing in popularity as people continue to share information with others around the world. The primary advantage is that they are easy and inexpensive (often free) to set up and use. One disadvantage of P2P networks is the lack of security controls or other common management functions. For this reason, few businesses use this type of network to communicate sensitive information.

Figure 9-25 Peer-to-peer network

Strategy	Description
Terminal	Centralized processing power, location, and control; underutilized processing power of microcomputers
Client/server	Clients request services; servers provide services and coordination; efficient network management software; expensive
Peer-to-peer	All nodes act as clients and servers; easy and inexpensive; lacks security controls
Distributed	Nodes share resources from different locations; used in decentralized organizations

Figure 9-26 Network strategies

In a **distributed processing network,** processing capability is located and shared at different nodes or locations. This type of strategy is common for decentralized organizations where divisional offices have their own computer systems. The computer systems in the divisional offices are networked to the organizations's main or centralized computer.

For a summary of network strategies, see Figure 9-26.

CONCEPT CHECK

What is a network strategy?

Discuss the four most common network strategies.

Organizational Networks

Computer networks in organizations have evolved over time. Most large organizations have a complex and wide range of different network configurations, operating systems, and strategies. These organizations face the challenge of making these networks work together effectively and securely.

Internet Technologies

Many organizations today employ Internet technologies to support effective communication within and between organizations using intranets and extranets.

- An **intranet** is a *private* network within an organization that resembles the Internet. Like the *public* Internet, intranets use browsers, Web sites, and Web pages. Typical applications include electronic telephone directories, e-mail addresses, employee benefit information, internal job openings, and much more. Employees find surfing their organizational intranets to be as easy and as intuitive as surfing the Internet.

- An **extranet** is a *private* network that connects *more than one* organization. Many organizations use Internet technologies to allow suppliers and others limited access to their networks. The purpose is to increase efficiency and reduce costs. For example, an automobile manufacturer has hundreds of suppliers for the parts that go into making a car. By having access to the car production schedules, suppliers can schedule and deliver parts as they are needed at the assembly plants. In this way, operational efficiency is maintained by both the manufacturer and the suppliers.

Network Security

Large organizations face the challenge of ensuring that only authorized users have access to network resources, sometimes from multiple geographic locations or across the Internet. Securing large computer networks requires specialized technology. Three technologies commonly used to ensure network security are firewalls, intrusion detection systems, and virtual private networks.

- A **firewall** consists of hardware and software that control access to a company's intranet and other internal networks. Most use a special computer or software called a **proxy server.** All communications between the company's internal networks and the outside world pass through this server. By evaluating the source and the content of each communication, the proxy server decides whether it is safe to let a particular message or file pass into or out of the organizations' network. (See Figure 9-27.)

- **Intrusion detection systems (NIDS)** work with firewalls to protect an organization's network. These systems use sophisticated statistical techniques to analyze all incoming and outgoing network traffic. Using advanced pattern matching and heuristics, a NIDS system can recognize signs of a network attack and disable access before an intruder can do damage.

- **Virtual private networks (VPN)** create a secure private connection between a remote user and an organization's internal network. Special VPN protocols create the equivalent of a dedicated line between a user's home or laptop computer and a company server. The connection is heavily encrypted and, from the perspective of the user, it appears that their workstation is actually located on the corporate network.

Like organizations, end users have security challenges and concerns. We need to be concerned about the privacy of our personal information. In the

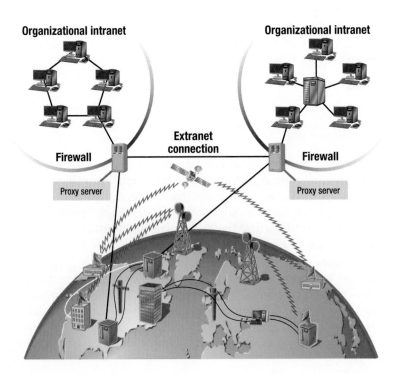

Figure 9-27 Intranets, extranets, firewalls, and proxy servers

next chapter, we will discuss personal firewalls and other ways to protect personal privacy and security.

CONCEPT CHECK

What are Internet technologies? Compare intranets and extranets.

What is a firewall? What is a proxy server?

What are intrusion detection systems?

What are virtual private networks?

On the Web Explorations

A popular and free NIDS system is Snort.

To learn more about Snort and try it on your own computer, visit our Web site at www.computing2011.com and enter the keyword snort.

Careers in IT

Network administrators manage a company's LAN and WAN networks. (See Figure 9-28.) They may be responsible for design, implementation, and maintenance of networks. Responsibilities usually include maintenance of both hardware and software related to a company's intranet and Internet networks. Network administrators are typically responsible for diagnosing and repairing problems with these networks. Some network administrators are responsible for planning and implementations of network security as well.

Employers typically look for candidates with a bachelor's degree in computer science or information systems and practical networking experience. Experience with network security and maintenance is preferred. Technical certification also may be helpful in obtaining this position. Because network administrators are involved directly with people in many departments, good communication skills are essential.

Network administrators can expect to earn an annual salary of $48,500 to $79,000. Opportunities for advancement typically include upper management positions. This position is expected to be among the fastest-growing jobs in the near future. To learn about other careers in information technology, visit us at www.computing2011.com and enter the keyword **careers.**

Figure 9-28 Network administrator

A LOOK TO THE FUTURE

Telepresence Lets You Be There without Actually Being There

How would you like to speak with distant friends or family as though they were in the same room at the touch of a button? Can you imagine receiving a physical examination from a doctor thousands of miles away? All this and more could be possible in the future thanks to the emerging technology known as *telepresence*.

Telepresence seeks to create the illusion that you are actually at a remote location, seeing, hearing, and someday maybe even feeling as though you were really there. Today's early telepresence implementations mainly focus on an extension of video-conferencing, allowing rooms of people in different locations to conduct meetings as though they are sitting across a table from one another, an illusion created with very high definition video, acoustically tuned audio systems, and high-speed networks. However, telepresence could someday go beyond

simple voice and video conferencing available today, and the applications seem endless.

Telepresense might be used to allow people to work in hazardous areas from a safe remote location. Doctors and medical specialists might be able to perform surgeries on people unable to travel. You might use telepresense as a vacation. Imagine touring remote cities or going on a deep sea diving expedition without hassle or risk.

Cisco is already marketing one video-based telepresence solution, known as Cisco Tele-Presence. At schools like MIT, developments are being made in the areas of holography, which is technology that creates 3-dimensional images called holograms, and sophisticated sensors that might pave the way to advanced telepresence. In the coming decade, you might be able to virtually interact with others with no video screen at all.

How would you use telepresence? What benefits do you see from this technology? How might telepresense impact travel in the future? Do you see any disadvantages?

COMMUNICATIONS

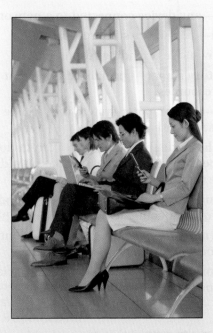

Communications is the process of sharing data, programs, and information between two or more computers. Applications include e-mail, instant messaging, Internet telephones, and electronic commerce.

Connectivity

Connectivity is a concept related to using computer networks to link people and resources. You can link or connect to large computers and the Internet, providing access to extensive information resources.

The Wireless Revolution

Mobile or wireless telephones have brought dramatic changes in connectivity and communications. These wireless devices are becoming widely used for computer communication.

Communication Systems

Communication systems transmit data from one location to another. Four basic elements are

- Sending and receiving devices
- Communication channel (transmission medium)
- Connection (communication) devices
- Data transmission specifications

COMMUNICATION CHANNELS

Communication channels carry data from one computer to another.

Physical Connections

Physical connections use a solid medium to connect sending and receiving devices. These connections include **twisted pair (telephone lines and Ethernet cables), coaxial cable,** and **fiber-optic cable.**

Wireless Connections

Wireless connections use air rather than solid substance to connect devices.

- **Radio frequency (RF)**—uses radio signals; **Wi-Fi (wireless fidelity)** is widely used standard; **Bluetooth** is a short-range RF-based wireless standard.
- **Microwave**—uses high-frequency radio waves; line-of-sight communication; uses microwave stations and dishes.
- **Satellite**—microwave relay station in the sky to uplink and downlink data; **GPS (global positioning system)** tracks geographical locations.
- **Infrared**—uses light waves over a short distance; line-of-sight communication.

KEY TERMS

3G cellular network (254)
analog signal (252)
asymmetric digital
    subscriber line
    (ADSL) (254)
bandwidth (255)
baseband (255)
base station (259)
Bluetooth (251)
broadband (255)
bus (260)
bus network (260)
cable modem (253)
cable service (254)
cellular service (254)
client (256)
client/server
    network (265)
coaxial cable (250)
communication
    channel (249)
communication
    system (249)
computer network (256)
connectivity (248)
demodulation (253)
dial-up service (254)
digital signal (252)
digital subscriber line
    (DSL) (253)
digital subscriber line
    (DSL) service (254)
directory server (256)
distributed processing
    network (267)
domain name server
    (DNS) (255)
DS3 (254)
Ethernet (258)
Ethernet cable (250)
extranet (267)
fiber-optic cable (250)

firewall (268)
global positioning system
    (GPS) (251)
hierarchical
    network (264)
home network (258)
host (256)
hub (256)
hybrid network (264)
infrared (252)
intranet (267)
intrusion detection
    system (NIDS) (268)
IP address (Internet
    protocol address) (255)
kilobits per second
    (Kbps) (253)
local area network
    (LAN) (258)
low bandwidth (255)
medium band (255)
mesh network (264)
metropolitan area
    network (MAN) (259)
microwave (251)
modem (253)
modulation (253)
network
    administrator (257, 268)
network
    architecture (260)
network gateway (258)
network interface card
    (NIC) (257)
network operating system
    (NOS) (257)
node (256)
optical carrier (OC) (254)
packet (255)
peer-to-peer (P2P)
    network (266)

personal area network
    (PAN) (259)
protocol (255)
proxy server (268)
radio frequency
    (RF) (251)
ring network (260)
satellite (251)
satellite/air connection
    service (254)
server (256)
star network (261)
strategy (265)
switch (256)
T1 (254)
T3 (254)
telephone line (250)
telephone modem (253)
terminal server
    network (265)
topology (260)
transfer rate (253)
transmission control
    protocol/Internet
    protocol (TCP/IP) (255)
tree network (261)
twisted pair cable (250)
virtual private network
    (VPN) (268)
voiceband (255)
wide area network
    (WAN) (259)
Wi-Fi (wireless
    fidelity) (251)
wireless access
    point (259)
wireless LAN
    (WLAN) (259)
wireless modem (254)
wireless wide area network
    (WWAN) modem (254)

To test your knowledge of these key terms with animated flash cards, visit our Web
site at www.computing2011.com and enter the keyword terms9.

MULTIPLE CHOICE

Circle the letter or fill in the correct answer.

1. Connectivity is a concept related to
   a. transmitting information, either by computer or by phone
   b. the interconnections within a computer
   c. using computer networks to link people and resources
   d. being in an active session with your computer

2. The transmission medium that carries the data is referred to as the
   a. send and receive device
   b. communication channel
   c. protocol
   d. gateways

3. Bluetooth is a type of radio wave information transmission system that is good for about
   a. 30 feet
   b. 30 yards
   c. 30 miles
   d. 300 miles

4. Special high-speed lines used by large corporations to support digital communications are known as
   a. satellite/air connection service lines
   b. cable modems
   c. ExpressCards
   d. T1 and T3 lines

5. The rules for exchanging data between computers are called
   a. interconnections
   b. synchronous packages
   c. protocols
   d. data transmission synchronization

6. Two or more computers connected so that they can communicate with each other and share information are called a
   a. satellite
   b. protocol
   c. broadcast
   d. network

7. A node that shares resources with other nodes is called a
   a. client
   b. server
   c. host
   d. NOS

8. The arrangement of the computers in a network is called the
   a. NOS
   b. topology
   c. node layout
   d. protocol

9. How a network is arranged and how it shares information and resources is called a network _____.
   a. topology
   b. strategy
   c. protocol
   d. architecture

10. A(n) _____ protects an organization's network from outside attack.
    a. fortress
    b. extranet
    c. DNS
    d. firewall

For an interactive multiple-choice practice test, visit our Web site at www.computing 2011.com and enter the keyword multiple9.

MATCHING

Match each numbered item with the most closely related lettered item. Write your answers in the spaces provided.

a. bandwidth
b. Bluetooth
c. client
d. peer-to-peer
e. DNS
f. firewall
g. infrared
h. packets
i. TCP/IP
j. topology

1. Wireless connection that uses light waves over short distances. _____
2. Uses RF to transmit data over short distances up to 33 feet. _____
3. Measurement of the capacity of a communication channel. _____
4. Standard protocol for the Internet. _____
5. Broken-down parts of a message sent over the Internet. _____
6. Converts text-based addresses to and from IP addresses. _____
7. A node that requests resources from other nodes. _____
8. The configuration of a network. _____
9. Network strategy in which each node has equal authority. _____
10. Protects network from external threats. _____

For an interactive matching practice test, visit our Web site at www.computing2011.com and enter the keyword matching9.

OPEN-ENDED

On a separate sheet of paper, respond to each question or statement.

1. Define and discuss connectivity, the wireless revolution, and communications.
2. Identify and describe the various physical and wireless communication channels.
3. Identify the standard Internet protocol and discuss its essential features.
4. Discuss past and present network topologies.
5. Define and discuss four common network strategies.

APPLYING TECHNOLOGY

The following questions are designed to demonstrate ways that you can effectively use technology today. The first question relates directly to this chapter's Making IT Work for You feature.

1 HOME NETWORKING

Computer networks are not just for corporations and schools anymore. If you have more than one computer, you can use a home network to share files and printers, to allow multiple users access to the Internet at the same time, and to play multiplayer computer games. To learn more about this technology, review Making IT Work for You: Home Networking on pages 262 and 263. Then answer the following: (a) Describe the window shown for the setup of the wireless access point. What brand of access point is demonstrated? (b) What name is used for the wireless home network? (c) What are four common uses for a wireless home network?

2 DISTRIBUTED COMPUTING

When networked computers are not in use, their processing power can be combined with other networked computers to perform a common task. In some cases, the problems that can be solved by many individual computers are far too large to be solved by any single computer. Connect to our site at www.computing2011.com and enter the keyword distributed for a link to a site that features distributed computing. Explore the site and answer the following questions: (a) What type of problem does this site solve with distributed computing? (b) How do users donate unused computer time to this project? (c) Would you donate your extra computer time to a distributed computing project? Why or why not?

3 WIRELESS MOBILE DEVICES

Recent advances in technology allow mobile devices to communicate on the go faster than ever before. Visit our Web site at www.computing2011.com and enter the keyword moblie to link to

a Web site featuring connected mobile devices. Once connected, review the latest products and then answer the following questions: (a) What support for Internet connection is available? How fast is the connection? (b) Are the connection options you researched in part (a) available where you live? Is there any place they are not available? (c) What is required to connect a mobile device to the Internet? (d) What type of Internet information is accessible? Is there any type that is not accessible?

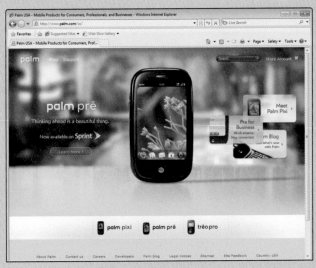

EXPANDING YOUR KNOWLEDGE

The following questions are designed to add depth and detail to your understanding of specific topics presented within this chapter. The questions direct you to sources other than the textbook to obtain this knowledge.

1 HOW WIRELESS HOME NETWORKS WORK

Wireless home networks are becoming very popular. These LANs are easy to set up and use. They allow different computers to share resources including a common Internet connection and printer. To learn how home networks work, visit our Web site at www.computing2011.com and enter the keyword network. Then answer the following questions. (a) What is a node? (b) What is a base station (access point) and what is its function? (c) What is a wireless card and what is its function? (d) If one or more requests to print a document are made at exactly the same time, what node determines which document is printed first? (e) Can the nodes TIM, LINDA, and STEVE access and use the Internet at the same time? If yes, how can this be done with a single Internet connection?

2 BITTORRENT

BitTorrent is a file-sharing protocol used to distribute large files across the Internet. Connect to our Web site at www.computing2011.com and enter the keyword torrent to learn more about how BitTorrent works, and then answer the following: (a) What is a "torrent"? How is a torrent created and published? (b) What network strategy does BitTorrent use? Review the network strategies presented on pages 265 through 267 and justify your answer. (c) What are the advantages to downloading files using BitTorrent rather than traditional client-server methods? How does BitTorrent reduce bandwidth usage for content providers?

3 HOTSPOTS

Hotspots are areas set up to provide public access to wireless Internet service. Find them in coffee shops, airports, or hotels. Connect to our Web site at www.computing 2011.com and enter the keyword hotspots to link to a directory of hotspots. Locate one near you. Where is the hotspot? What equipment is necessary to use the hotspot? What does it cost to use the hotspot?

WRITING ABOUT TECHNOLOGY

The ability to think critically and to write effectively is essential to nearly every profession. The following questions are designed to help you develop these skills by posing thought-provoking questions about computer privacy, security, and/or ethics.

1 ELECTRONIC MONITORING

Programs known as "sniffers" are sometimes used to monitor communications on corporate networks. Recently, the FBI unveiled a technology known as Carnivore that can monitor an individual's Internet activity and eavesdrop on e-mail messages. Write a one-page paper that answers the following questions: (a) Is it a violation of an employee's privacy for an organization or corporation to use sniffer programs to monitor communications on their network? (b) Is it a violation of privacy for a government agency such as the FBI to use programs like Carnivore to monitor communications on the Internet? (c) Under what conditions are the types of monitoring discussed in parts (a) and (b) acceptable and ethical? (d) How can these conditions be enforced?

2 DIGITAL RIGHTS MANAGEMENT

In response to the issue of sharing copyrighted material over computer networks discussed in this chapter, many different forms of digital rights management, or DRM, have been proposed. However, DRM is controversial and hotly debated by industry groups and consumer advocates. Use the Web to research DRM, and then write a one-page paper titled "Digital Rights Management" that addresses the following topics: (a) Define "digital rights management." (b) What systems have been proposed for DRM? (c) Why are some consumers opposed to these systems? (d) Do you think DRM is a fair solution to online piracy? Justify your answer.

Privacy and Security

Competencies

After you have read this chapter, you should be able to:

1 Identify the most significant concerns for effective implementation of computer technology.

2 Discuss the primary privacy issues of accuracy, property, and access.

3 Describe the impact of large databases, private networks, the Internet, and the Web on privacy.

4 Discuss online identity and the major laws on privacy.

5 Describe the security threats posed by computer criminals including employees, hackers, crackers, organized crime, and terrorists.

6 Discuss computer crimes including creation of viruses and worms and implementation of denial of service attacks and Internet scams.

7 Detail ways to protect computer security.

8 Discuss computer ethics including copyright law and plagiarism.

9 Describe ways to protect copyrights and to identify plagiarism, including digital rights management and Turnitin.

In the past, protecting your privacy may have required a paper shredder and an unlisted phone number. Today it is possible to learn the complete life history of a stranger with a few clicks of the mouse.

Some experts believe that in the future details about your entire life may be available online and could be collected and analyzed by the businesses you frequent. Imagine a world where the grocery store where you regularly shop knows what you browse for online and suggests recipes or changes to your diet accordingly.

chapter 10

Introduction

The tools and products of the information age do not exist in a world by themselves. As we said in Chapter 1, a computer system consists not only of software, hardware, data, and procedures, but also of people. Because of people, computer systems may be used for both good and bad purposes.

There are more than 300 million microcomputers in use today. What are the consequences of the widespread presence of this technology? Does technology make it easy for others to invade our personal privacy? When we apply for a loan or for a driver's license, or when we check out at the supermarket, is that information about us being distributed and used without our permission? When we use the Web, is information about us being collected and shared with others?

Does technology make it easy for others to invade the security of business organizations like our banks or our employers? What about health risks to people who use computers? What about the environment? Do computers pose a threat to our ecology?

This technology prompts lots of questions—very important questions. Perhaps these are some of the most important questions for the 21st century. Competent end users need to be aware of the potential impact of technology on people and how to protect themselves on the Web. They need to be sensitive to and knowledgeable about personal privacy, organizational security, ergonomics, and the environmental impact of technology.

People

As we have discussed, information systems consist of people, procedures, software, hardware, and data. This chapter focuses on people. (See Figure 10-1.) While most everyone agrees that technology has had a very positive impact on people, it is important to recognize the negative, or potentially negative, impacts as well.

Effective implementation of computer technology involves maximizing its positive effects while minimizing its negative effects. The most significant concerns are

- **Privacy:** What are the threats to personal privacy and how can we protect ourselves?

Figure 10-1 People are part of an information system

- **Security:** How can access to sensitive information be controlled and how can we secure hardware and software?
- **Ethics:** How do the actions of individual users and companies affect society?

Let us begin by examining privacy.

Privacy

As you have seen, computing technology makes it possible to collect and use data of all kinds, including information about people. The Web sites you visit, the stores where you shop, and the television shows you watch are all examples of information about you. How would you feel if you learned such information was being collected or shared? Would it matter who was collecting it, or how it was being used, or whether it was even correct?

Privacy concerns the collection and use of data about individuals. There are three primary privacy issues:

- **Accuracy** relates to the responsibility of those who collect data to ensure that the data is correct.
- **Property** relates to who owns data and rights to software.
- **Access** relates to the responsibility of those who have data to control and who is able to use that data.

Large Databases

Large organizations are constantly compiling information about us. The federal government alone has over 2,000 databases. Every day, data is gathered about us and stored in large databases. For example, telephone companies compile lists of the calls we make, the numbers called, and so on. A special telephone directory (called a **reverse directory**) lists telephone numbers sequentially. (See Figure 10-2.) Using it, government authorities and others can easily get the names, addresses, and other details about the persons we call.

Credit card companies keep similar records. Supermarket scanners in grocery checkout counters record what we buy, when we buy it, how much we buy, and the price. Financial institutions, including banks and credit unions, record how much money we have, what we use it for, and how much we owe. Publishers of magazines, newspapers, and mail-order catalogues have our names, addresses, phone numbers, and what we order.

A vast industry of data gatherers known as **information resellers** or **information brokers** now exists that collects and sells such personal data. Using publicly available databases and in many cases nonpublic databases, information resellers create **electronic profiles** or highly detailed and personalized descriptions of individuals. Very likely, you have an electronic profile that includes your name, address, telephone number, Social Security number, driver's license number, bank account numbers, credit card numbers, telephone records, and shopping and purchasing patterns. Information resellers sell these electronic profiles to direct marketers, fundraisers, and others. Many provide these services on the Web for free or for a nominal cost. (See Figure 10-3.)

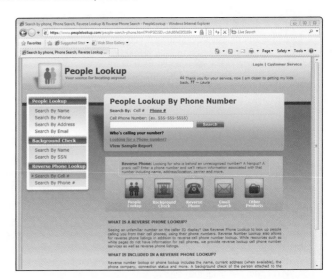

Figure 10-2 Reverse directory Web site

Figure 10-3 Information reseller's Web site

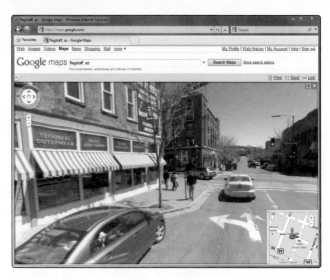

Figure 10-4 Google Street View

Your personal information, including preferences, habits, and financial data, has become a marketable commodity. This raises many issues, including

- **Collecting public, but personally identifying information:** What if people anywhere in the world could view detailed images of you, your home, or your car? Using detailed images captured with a specially equipped van, Google's Street View project allows just that. Street View makes it possible to take a virtual tour of many cities and neighborhoods from any computer with a connection to the Internet. (See Figure 10-4.) Although the images available on Street View are all taken in public locations, some have objected to the project as being an intrusion on their privacy.

- As digital cameras and Webcams become cheaper and software becomes more sophisticated, it is likely that many more issues involving personal privacy in public spaces will need to be addressed. Such a combination of computing technologies could, for example, make real-time tracking of individuals in public places possible.

- **Spreading information without personal consent:** How would you feel if an employer were using your medical records to make decisions about hiring, placement, promotion, and firing? A survey of Fortune 500 companies found that over one-third were using medical records for just these purposes.

How would you feel if someone obtained a driver's license and credit cards in your name? What if that person then assumed your identity to buy clothes, cars, and a house? It happens every day. Every year, nearly 10 million people are victimized in this way. It is called **identity theft.** Identity theft is the illegal assumption of someone's identity for the purposes of economic gain. It is one of the fastest-growing crimes in the country. To learn more about identity theft and how to minimize your risk, visit our Web site at www.computing2011.com and enter the keyword **theft.**

tips

Identity theft is a growing problem, and can be financially devastating if you are a victim. Here are some steps to help protect your identity.

1 Never give personal information on the Internet or in response to e-mail. One common scam known as *phishing* involves e-mail that has been forged to appear to come from your bank or school.

2 Only do business on the Internet with companies you know to be legitimate, or large companies with a solid reputation.

3 When selling a computer, be sure to completely remove all personal information from the hard drive. Many programs are available to ensure data is completely removed.

4 Check your credit reports from the three major credit bureaus for unusual activity or inaccuracy at least once a year.

To see more tips, visit our Web site at www.computing 2011.com and enter the keyword tips.

- **Spreading inaccurate information:** How would you like to be turned down for a home loan because of an error in your credit history? This is much more common than you might expect. What if you could not find a job or were fired from a job because of an error giving you a serious criminal history? This can and has happened due to simple clerical errors. In one case, an arresting officer while completing an arrest warrant incorrectly recorded the Social Security number of a criminal. From that time forward, this arrest and the subsequent conviction became part of another person's electronic profile. This is an example of **mistaken identity** in which the electronic profile of one person is switched with another.

It's important to know that you have some recourse. The law allows you to gain access to those records about you that are held by credit bureaus. Under the **Freedom of Information Act,** you are also entitled to look at your records held by government agencies. (Portions may be deleted for national security reasons.)

CONCEPT CHECK

What are the three primary privacy issues?

What are information resellers, electronic profiles, identity theft, and mistaken identity?

What is the Freedom of Information Act?

Private Networks

Suppose you use your company's electronic mail system to send a co-worker an unflattering message about your supervisor or to send a highly personal message to a friend. Later you find the boss has been spying on your exchange. This is legal and a recent survey revealed that nearly 75 percent of all businesses search employees' electronic mail and computer files using so-called **snoopware.** (See Figure 10-5.) These programs record virtually everything you do on your computer. One proposed law would not prohibit this type of electronic monitoring but would require employers to provide prior written notice. Employers also would have to alert employees during the monitoring with some sort of audible or visual signal.

The Internet and the Web

When you send e-mail on the Internet or browse the Web, do you have any concerns about privacy? Most people do not. They think that as long as they are using their own computer and are selective about disclosing their names or other personal information, then little can be done to invade their personal privacy. Experts call this the **illusion of anonymity** that the Internet brings.

As we discussed in Chapter 9, every computer on the Internet is identified by a unique number known as an IP address. IP addresses can be used to trace Internet activities to their origin, allowing computer security experts and law enforcement officers to investigate computer crimes such as unauthorized access to networks or sharing of copyrighted files without permission.

Figure 10-5 Snoopware

1 ● Select the *Tools* menu.

● Choose *Explorer Bars*.

2 ● Select *History*.

Figure 10-6 Viewing history files

When you browse the Web, your browser stores critical information onto your hard disk, typically without your explicit permission or knowledge. For example, your browser creates a **history file** that includes the locations of sites visited by your computer system. This history file can be displayed by your browser. To view the history file using Internet Explorer version 8.0, follow the steps in Figure 10-6.

Another way your Web activity can be monitored is with **cookies,** or small pieces of information that are deposited on your hard disk from Web sites you have visited. Typically, cookies are deposited without your explicit knowledge or consent. While cookies are harmless in and of themselves, what makes them potentially dangerous is that they can store information about you without your knowledge. Using them, a record of what sites you visit, what you do at the sites, and other information you provide can be created. To view the cookies on a hard drive using Internet Explorer version 8.0, follow the steps in Figure 10-7.

There are two basic types of cookies: traditional and ad network. Most cookies can be displayed by your browser.

- **Traditional cookies** provide information to a single site. When you first visit a site, a cookie is deposited with information that identifies you

1 • Select *Tools* from the menu bar.

• Choose *Internet Options*.

2 • Select *Settings* in the *Browsing history* section of the *General* tab.

• Click *View files*.

Figure 10-7 Viewing cookies

specifically (such as information you provided on a form). Any further pages you visit on the site will have access to the cookie and be able to read its contents. When you leave the site, the cookie is usually saved. When you revisit, the cookie is reactivated and the information accessed. Most cookies are intended to provide customized service. For example, when you revisit an electronic commerce site, you can be greeted by name, presented with customized advertising banners, and directed to Web pages promoting items you have previously purchased.

• **Ad network** or **adware cookies** record your activities across different sites. Once deposited onto your hard drive, they can be activated and accessed from many of the Web sites that you visit. These cookies are deposited on your hard disk by organizations that compile and market the information. Two such organizations are DoubleClick and Avenue A.

Most browsers are able to control many types of cookies. For example, Internet Explorer version 8.0 provides settings to selectively block cookies from being deposited onto a system's hard disk. (See Figure 10-8.)

The term **spyware** is used to describe a wide range of programs that are designed to secretly record and report an individual's activities on the Internet. Ad network cookies are just one type of spyware. Two other types are Web bugs and computer monitoring software.

• **Web bugs** are small images or HTML code hidden within an e-mail message. When a user opens an e-mail containing a Web bug, information is

1 • Select *Tools* from the menu bar.

• Choose *Internet Options.*

2 • Select the *Privacy* tab.

• Move the slide to desired level of protection.

• Click *Apply;* click *OK.*

Figure 10-8 Blocking cookies

sent back to the source of the bug. One of the most common Web bugs is used by companies that sell active mailing lists to spammers. This bug is simply an invisible graphic embedded into an e-mail message. When the e-mail is opened, a request is sent to display the graphic without the reader's knowledge. The request is sent to a remote server that then knows that this e-mail address is active. Although this Web bug does no serious harm, others are more dangerous. To see how Web bugs can work, visit our Web site at www.computing2011.com and enter the keyword **bugs.**

• **Computer monitoring software** is the most invasive and dangerous type of spyware. These programs record every activity and keystroke made on your computer system, including credit card numbers, bank account numbers, and e-mail messages. Also known as **keystroke loggers,** computer monitoring software can be deposited onto your hard drive without your knowledge either from the Web or by someone installing the programs directly onto your computer. The previously mentioned snoopware is a type of computer monitoring software used by businesses to monitor their employees. Computer monitoring software also has been used by the FBI and the CIA to collect incriminating evidence on suspected terrorists and organized crime members. These programs are also widely used by private investigators, criminals, and spouses.

Unfortunately, it is more difficult to remove Web bugs and computer monitoring software than ad network cookies because they are more difficult to detect. There are over 90,000 active spyware programs, and chances are you have one or more of them on your computer. A recent study reported finding an average of 28 active spyware programs on microcomputers it had evaluated.

A category of programs known as **antispyware** or **spy removal programs,** which are designed to detect and remove cookies, Web bugs, and monitoring software, has evolved to battle the threat. (See Figure 10-9.) For a list of some of these programs, see Figure 10-10. To learn more about protecting yourself from spyware, see Making IT Work for You: Spyware Removal on pages 290 and 291.

Figure 10-9 **Protect your privacy**

Online Identity

Another aspect of Internet privacy comes from **online identity,** the information that people voluntarily post about themselves online. With the popularity of social networking, blogging, and photo- and video-sharing sites, many people post intimate details of their lives without considering the consequences. Although it is easy to think of online identity as something shared between friends, the archiving and search features of the Web make it available indefinitely to anyone who cares to look. How would you feel if information you posted about yourself on the Web kept you from getting a job?

Program	Web Site
Windows Defender	www.microsoft.com
Ad-Aware	www.lavasoft.com
CounterSpy	www.counterspy.com
Spy Doctor	www.spydoctor.com
Spy Sweeper	www.spysweeper.com

Figure 10-10 **Antispyware programs**

Major Laws on Privacy

Some federal laws governing privacy matters have been created. For example, the **Gramm-Leach-Bliley Act** protects personal financial information, the **Health Insurance Portability and Accountability Act (HIPAA)** protects medical records, and the **Family Educational Rights and Privacy Act (FERPA)** restricts disclosure of educational records. To learn more about existing privacy laws, visit our Web site at www.computing2011.com and enter the keyword **law.**

Most of the information collected by private organizations is not covered by existing laws. However, as more and more individuals become concerned about controlling who has the right to personal information and how that information is used, companies and law makers will respond.

tips

What can you do to protect your privacy while on the Web? Here are a few suggestions.

1 **Encrypt sensitive e-mail.** Encrypt or code sensitive e-mail using special encryption programs.

2 **Shield your identity.** Use an anonymous remailer or special Web site that forwards your e-mail without disclosing your identity.

3 **Block cookies.** Use your browser or a cookie-cutter program to block unwanted cookies.

4 **Check for Web bugs and computer monitoring software.** Use spy removal programs to check for Web bugs and computer monitoring software.

5 **Notify providers.** Instruct your service provider or whomever you use to link to the Internet not to sell your name or any other personal information.

6 **Be careful.** Never disclose your telephone number, passwords, or other private information to strangers.

To see more tips, visit our Web site at www.computing2011.com and enter the keyword tips.

Making IT work for you

SPYWARE REMOVAL

Have you installed any free software from the Internet? Did you know seemingly harmless software might actually be spying on you, even sending personal information to advertisers or worse? Fortunately, spyware removal software is available to help keep your personal information private.

Finding and Removing Spyware Once spyware removal software is installed on your system, you can scan your system for known spyware and remove it. Follow the steps below to find and remove spyware using Ad-Aware.

1 ● Connect to www.lavasoft.com and follow the on-screen instructions to download and install the Ad-Aware software.

2 ● Launch the Ad-Aware application.

● Click the *Scan Now* button.

● Click the *Scan* button to begin scanning for spyware.

● Review the results of the scan, and place a checkmark next to any detected items you would like to remove.

● Click the *Remove* button to remove the detected spyware from your system.

Automating Spyware Removal To protect your system from spyware, it is recommended that you run your spyware removal software automatically. If you purchase the Plus or Pro version of Ad-Aware, you can follow the steps below to set Ad-Aware to run automatically on a regular schedule.

1
- Click the *Scan* button.
- Click the *Schedule* button.

2
- Choose how frequently you would like your system scanned for spyware.
- Click the *Add* button to add your selection to the scheduler.

Ad-Aware will now run automatically on the days and times you selected.

Staying Up to Date Now that your system is protected from spyware, you'll want to keep it that way. Spyware removal programs keep a profile of known spyware, which must be updated from time to time. Follow the steps below to update the spyware profile in Ad-Aware.

1
- Click the *Web Update* button.

2
- Click the *Update* button.

Ad-Aware connects to the Internet and updates its spyware profile. The newest Ad-Aware reference file is installed automatically. You can now follow the steps in the "Finding and Removing Spyware" section to rid your system of the latest known spyware.

The Web is continually changing, and some of the specifics presented in this Making IT Work for You may have changed.

To learn about other ways to make information technology work for you, visit our Web site at www.computing2011.com and enter the keyword miw.

CONCEPT CHECK

What is snoopware? Describe the illusion of anonymity.

What is a history file? Compare traditional and ad network cookies.

What are spyware, Web bugs, keystroke loggers, antispyware programs, and online identity?

Describe three federal laws to protect privacy.

Security

We are all concerned with having a safe and secure environment to live in. We are careful to lock our car doors and our homes. We are careful about where we walk at night and whom we talk to. This is personal security. What about computer security? What if someone gains unauthorized access to our computer or other computers that contain information about us? What if someone steals our computer or other computers that contain information about us? What are the major threats to computer security, and how can we be protected?

Computer Criminals

A **computer crime** is an illegal action in which the perpetrator uses special knowledge of computer technology. Typically, computer criminals are either employees, outside users, hackers, crackers, organized crime members, or terrorists.

- **Employees:** The largest category of computer criminals consists of those with the easiest access to computers—namely, employees. Sometimes the employee is simply trying to steal something from the employer— equipment, software, electronic funds, proprietary information, or computer time. Sometimes the employee is acting out of resentment and is trying to get back at the company.

- **Outside users:** Not only employees but also some suppliers or clients may have access to a company's computer system. Examples are bank customers who use an automated teller machine. Like employees, these authorized users may be able to obtain confidential passwords or find other ways of committing computer crimes.

- **Hackers and crackers:** Some people think of these two groups as being the same, but they are not. **Hackers** are people who create or improve programs and share those programs with fellow hackers. Typically, they are not criminals. **Crackers,** on the other hand, create and share programs designed to gain unauthorized access to computer systems or disrupt networks. Their motives are malicious and can be very destructive and costly. Typically, they are criminals.

- **Organized crime:** Members of organized crime groups have discovered that they can use computers just as people in legitimate businesses do, but for illegal purposes. For example, computers are useful for keeping track of stolen goods or illegal gambling debts. In addition, counterfeiters and forgers use microcomputers and printers to produce sophisticated-looking documents such as checks and driver's licenses.

- **Terrorists:** Knowledgeable terrorist groups and hostile governments could potentially crash satellites and wage economic warfare by disrupting navigation and communication systems. The Department of Defense reports that its computer systems are probed approximately 250,000 times a year by unknown sources.

Computer Crime

The FBI estimates that businesses lose trillions of dollars a year from computer crimes. The number of these crimes has tripled in the past two years. Computer crime can take various forms including the creation of malicious programs, denial of service attacks, Internet scams, theft, and data manipulation.

Malicious Programs Hackers and crackers are notorious for creating and distributing malicious programs. These programs are called **malware,** which is short for **mal**icious soft**ware.** They are specifically designed to damage or disrupt a computer system. The three most common types of malware are viruses, worms, and Trojan horses.

- **Viruses** are programs that migrate through networks and operating systems, and most attach themselves to different programs and databases. While some viruses are relatively harmless, many can be quite destructive. Once activated, these destructive viruses can alter and/or delete files. Some delete all files on the hard disk and can damage system components. Creating and knowingly spreading a virus is a very serious crime and a federal offense punishable under the **Computer Fraud and Abuse Act.**

  Unfortunately, new computer viruses are appearing all the time. The best way to stay current is through services that keep track of viruses on a daily basis. For example, the Virus Radar On-line project tracks the most serious virus threats. See Figure 10-11.
- **Worms** are a special type of virus that does not attach itself to programs and databases. Rather it fills a computer system with self-replicating information, clogging the system so that its operations are slowed or stopped. A recent worm traveled across the world within hours, stopping tens of thousands of computers along its way. Internet worms also can be carriers of more traditional viruses. Once the traditional virus has been deposited by a worm onto an unsuspecting computer system, the virus will either activate immediately or lie dormant until some future time.

Viruses and worms typically find their way into microcomputers through e-mail attachments and programs downloaded from the Internet. Because viruses can be so damaging, computer users are advised to never open an e-mail attachment from an unknown source and to exercise great care in accepting new programs and data from any source.

As we discussed in Chapter 5, antivirus programs alert users when certain kinds of viruses and worms enter their system. Some of the most widely used are Dr. Solomon's Anti-Virus, McAfee VirusScan, eSafe, and Norton AntiVirus. Unfortunately, new viruses are being developed all the time, and not all viruses can be detected. (See Making IT Work for You: Virus Protection and Internet Security on pages 140 and 141 in Chapter 5.)

- **Trojan horses** are programs that come into a computer system disguised as something else. Trojan horses are not viruses. Like worms, however,

Figure 10-11 Tracking viruses

they can be carriers of viruses. The most common types of Trojan horses appear as free computer games and free screen saver programs that can be downloaded from the Internet. Once the Trojan horse is downloaded onto a computer system, the viruses are deposited and ready to activate. One of the most dangerous types of Trojan horse claims to provide free antivirus programs. They begin by locating and disabling any existing virus protection programs before depositing a virus.

Zombies are computers infected by a virus, worm, or Trojan horse that allows them to be remotely controlled for malicious purposes. A collection of zombie computers is known as a **botnet,** or **robot network.** Botnets harness the combined power of many zombies for malicious activities like password cracking or sending junk e-mail. Because they are formed by many computers distributed across the Internet, botnets are hard to shut down even after they are detected. Unfortunately for individual computer owners, it can also be difficult to detect when a personal computer has been compromised.

Denial of Service A **denial of service (DoS) attack** attempts to slow down or stop a computer system or network by flooding a computer or network with requests for information and data. The targets of these attacks are usually Internet service providers (ISP) and specific Web sites. Once under attack, the servers at the ISP or the Web site become overwhelmed with these requests for service and are unable to respond to legitimate users. As a result, the ISP or Web site is effectively shut down.

Internet Scams A **scam** is a fraudulent or deceptive act or operation designed to trick individuals into providing personal information or spending their time and money for little or no return. An **Internet scam** is simply a scam using the Internet. Internet scams are becoming a serious problem and have created financial and legal problems for thousands of people. Almost all of the scams are initiated by a mass mailing to unsuspecting individuals.

A technique often employed by scammers is **phishing** (pronounced "fishing"). Phishing attempts to trick Internet users into thinking a fake but official-looking Web site or e-mail is legitimate. Phishing has grown in sophistication, replicating entire Web sites like PayPal to try to lure users into divulging their financial information.

See Figure 10-12 for a list of common types of Internet scams.

tips Are you concerned about catching a virus? Here are a few suggestions that might help:

1. **Use an antivirus program.** Install antivirus programs on all computer systems you use and run them frequently.

2. **Check disks.** Before using any floppy or CD, check for viruses.

3. **Check all downloads.** Check all files downloaded from the Internet.

4. **Update your antivirus program.** New viruses are being developed daily, and the virus programs are continually being revised. Update your antivirus program frequently.

To see more tips, visit our Web site at www.computing 2011.com and enter the keyword tips.

Theft Theft can take many forms—of hardware, of software, of data, of computer time. Thieves steal equipment and programs, of course, but there are also white-collar crimes. These crimes include the theft of data in the form of confidential information such as preferred-client lists. Another common crime is the use (theft) of a company's computer time by an employee to run another business.

Data Manipulation Finding entry into someone's computer network and leaving a prankster's message may seem like fun, which is why hackers do it. It is still against the law. Moreover, even if the manipulation seems harmless, it may cause a great deal of anxiety and wasted time among network users.

The **Computer Fraud and Abuse Act** makes it a crime for unauthorized persons even to view—let alone

Type	Description
Identity theft	Individual(s) pose as ISPs, bank representatives, or government agencies requesting personal information. Once obtained, criminal(s) assume a person's identity for a variety of financial transactions.
Chain letter	Classic chain letter instructing recipient to send a nominal amount of money to each of five people on a list. The recipient removes the first name on the list, adds his or her name at the bottom and mails the chain letter to five friends. This is also known as a pyramid scheme. Almost all chain letters are fraudulent and illegal.
Auction fraud	Merchandise is selected and payment is sent. Merchandise is never delivered.
Vacation prize	"Free" vacation has been awarded. Upon arrival at vacation destination, the accommodations are dreadful but can be upgraded for a fee.
Advance fee loans	Guaranteed low-rate loans available to almost anyone. After applicant provides personal loan-related information, the loan is granted subject to payment of an "insurance fee."

Figure 10-12 Common Internet scams

copy or damage—data using any computer across state lines. It also prohibits unauthorized use of any government computer or a computer used by any federally insured financial institution. Offenders can be sentenced to up to 20 years in prison and fined up to $100,000.

For a summary of computer crimes, see Figure 10-13. For a brief history of computer crimes, visit our Web site at www.computing2011.com and enter the keyword **crime.**

Other Hazards

There are plenty of other hazards to computer systems and data besides criminals. They include the following:

- **Natural hazards:** Natural forces include fires, floods, wind, hurricanes, tornadoes, and earthquakes. Even home computer users should store backup disks of programs and data in safe locations in case of fire or storm damage.
- **Civil strife and terrorism:** Wars, riots, and terrorist activities are real risks in all parts of the world. Even people in developed countries must be mindful of these acts.
- **Technological failures:** Hardware and software don't always do what they are supposed to do. For instance, too little electricity, caused by a brownout or blackout, may cause the loss of data in primary storage. Too much

Computer Crime	Description
Malicious programs	Include viruses, worms, and Trojan horses
DoS	Causes computer systems to slow down or stop
Internet scams	Are scams over the Internet usually initiated by e-mail and involving phishing
Theft	Includes hardware, software, and computer time
Data manipulation	Involves changing data or leaving prank messages

Figure 10-13 Computer crimes

Figure 10-14 Crashes can result in lost data

electricity, as when lightning or some other electrical disturbance affects a power line, may cause a **voltage surge,** or **spike.** This excess of electricity may destroy chips or other electronic components of a computer.

Microcomputer users should use a **surge protector,** a device that separates the computer from the power source of the wall outlet. When a voltage surge occurs, it activates a circuit breaker in the surge protector, protecting the computer system.

Another technological catastrophe occurs when a hard-disk drive suddenly crashes, or fails (as discussed in Chapter 8), perhaps because it has been bumped inadvertently. If the user has forgotten to make backup copies of data on the hard disk, data may be lost. (See Figure 10-14.)

- **Human errors:** Human mistakes are inevitable. Data-entry errors are probably the most commonplace and, as we have discussed, can lead to mistaken identity. Programmer errors also occur frequently. Some mistakes may result from faulty design, as when a software manufacturer makes a deletion command closely resembling another command. Some errors may be the result of sloppy procedures. One such example occurs when office workers save important documents under file names that are not descriptive and not recognizable by others.

 CONCEPT CHECK

 Describe malware, including viruses, worms, Trojan horses, zombies, and botnets?

 Compare a worm to a denial of service attack. What are zombies, botnets, and DoS?

 Describe the five most common types of Internet scams.

Measures to Protect Computer Security

Security is concerned with protecting information, hardware, and software from unauthorized use as well as from damage from intrusions, sabotage, and natural disasters. Considering the numerous ways in which computer systems and data can be compromised, we can see why security is a growing field. Some of the principal measures to protect computer security are restricting access, encrypting messages, anticipating disasters, and preventing data loss.

Restricting Access Security experts are constantly devising ways to protect computer systems from access by unauthorized persons. Sometimes security is a matter of putting guards on company computer rooms and checking the identification of everyone admitted. Other times it is using **biometric scanning** devices such as fingerprint and iris (eye) scanners. (See Figure 10-15.)

Oftentimes it is a matter of being careful about assigning passwords to people and of changing the passwords when people leave a company. **Passwords** are secret words or phrases (including numbers) that must be keyed into a computer system to gain access. For many applications on the Web, users assign their own passwords.

Iris scanner

Fingerprint scanner

Figure 10-15 Biometric scanning devices

The strength of a password depends on how easily it can be guessed. A **dictionary attack** uses software to try thousands of common words sequentially in an attempt to gain unauthorized access to a user's account. For this reason, words, names, and simple numeric patterns make poor passwords. It is also important not to reuse passwords for different accounts. If one account is compromised, that password might be tried for access to other systems as well. For example, if a low-security account such as an online Web forum is compromised, that password could also be tried on higher-security accounts such as banking Web sites.

As mentioned in previous chapters, most major corporations today use special hardware and software called firewalls to control access to their internal computer networks. **Firewalls** act as a security buffer between the corporation's private network and all external networks, including the Internet. All electronic communications coming into and leaving the corporation must be evaluated by the firewall. Security is maintained by denying access to unauthorized communications. To learn how to use Windows Vista's built-in firewall, visit our Web site at www.computing 2011.com and enter the keyword **firewall**.

Encrypting Data Whenever information is sent over a network or stored on a computer system, the possibility of unauthorized access exists. The solution is **encryption,** the process of coding information to make it unreadable except to those who have a special piece of information known as an **encryption key,** or, simply, **key.** Some common uses for encryption include

- **E-mail encryption:** Protects e-mail messages as they move across the Internet. One of the most widely used personal e-mail encryption programs is Pretty Good Privacy. (See Figure 10-16.)
- **File encryption:** Protects sensitive files by encrypting them before they are stored on a hard drive.

On the Web Explorations

Encryption is the only thing between criminals and private information on the Internet, such as bank accounts, passwords, and even tax returns.

To learn more about how encryption works, visit our Web site at www.computing2011.com and enter the keyword encryption.

Figure 10-16 Encrypted e-mail

Figure 10-17 File encryption

Files can be encrypted individually, or specialized software can be used to encrypt all files automatically each time they are saved to a certain hard drive location. (See Figure 10-17.)

- **Web site encryption:** Secures Web transactions, especially financial transactions. Web pages that accept passwords or confidential information like a credit card number are often encrypted.
- **Virtual Private Networks: Virtual private networks (VPNs)** encrypt connections between company networks and remote users such as workers connecting from home. This connection creates a secure virtual connection to a company LAN across the Internet.
- **Wireless network encryption:** Restricts access to authorized users on wireless networks.

Anticipating Disasters Companies (and even individuals) should prepare themselves for disasters. **Physical security** is concerned with protecting hardware from possible human and natural disasters. **Data security** is concerned with protecting software and data from unauthorized tampering or damage. Most large organizations have a **disaster recovery plan** describing ways to continue operating until normal computer operations can be restored.

Preventing Data Loss Equipment can always be replaced. A company's *data*, however, may be irreplaceable. Most companies have ways of trying to keep software and data from being tampered with in the first place. They include careful screening of job applicants, guarding of passwords, and auditing of data and programs from time to time. Some systems use redundant storage to prevent loss of data even when a hard drive fails. We discussed RAID in Chapter 6, which is a commonly used type of redundant storage. Backup batteries protect against data loss due to file corruption during unexpected power outages.

Making frequent backups of data is essential to prevent data loss. Backups are often stored at an off-site location to protect data in case of theft, fires, floods, or other disasters. Incremental backups store multiple versions of data at different points in time to prevent data loss due to unwanted changes or accidental deletion.

See Figure 10-18 for a summary of the different measures to protect computer security.

On the Web Explorations

How strong is your password?

To test password strength, visit our Web site a www.computing2011.com and enter the keyword password**.**

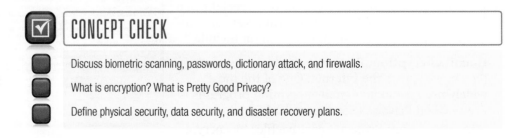

CONCEPT CHECK

Discuss biometric scanning, passwords, dictionary attack, and firewalls.

What is encryption? What is Pretty Good Privacy?

Define physical security, data security, and disaster recovery plans.

Measure	Description
Restricting	Limit access to authorized persons using such measures as passwords and firewalls
Encrypting	Code all messages sent over a network
Anticipating	Prepare for disasters by ensuring physical security and data security through a disaster recovery plan
Preventing	Routinely copy data and store it at a remote location

Figure 10-18 Measures to protect computer security

Ethics

What do you suppose controls how computers can be used? You probably think first of laws. Of course, that is right, but technology is moving so fast that it is very difficult for our legal system to keep up. The essential element that controls how computers are used today is *ethics*.

Ethics, as you may know, are standards of moral conduct. **Computer ethics** are guidelines for the morally acceptable use of computers in our society. We are all entitled to ethical treatment. This includes the right to keep personal information, such as credit ratings and medical histories, from getting into unauthorized hands. These issues, largely under the control of corporations and government agencies, were covered earlier in this chapter. Now we'll examine two important issues in computer ethics where average users have a role to play.

Copyright and Digital Rights Management

Copyright is a legal concept that gives content creators the right to control use and distribution of their work. Materials that can be copyrighted include paintings, books, music, films, and even video games. Some users choose to make unauthorized copies of digital media, which violates copyright. For example, making an unauthorized copy of a digital music file for a friend might be a copyright violation.

Software piracy is the unauthorized copying and distribution of software. According to a recent study, software piracy costs the software industry over $30 billion annually. The **Digital Millennium Copyright Act** establishes the right of a program owner to make a backup copy of any program. The act also establishes that none of these copies may be legally resold or given away. This may come as a surprise to those who copy software from a friend, but that's the law. It is also illegal to download copyright-protected music and videos from the Internet.

To prevent copyright violations, corporations often use **digital rights management (DRM).** DRM encompasses various technologies that control access to electronic media and files. Typically, DRM is used to (1) control the number of devices that can access a given file as well as (2) limit the kinds of devices that can access a file. Although some companies see DRM as a necessity to protect their rights, some users feel they should have the right to use the media they buy—including movies, music, software, and video games—as they choose.

Today, there are many legal sources for digital media. Television programs can be watched online, often for free, on television-network-sponsored sites. Sites like Pandora allow listeners to enjoy music at no cost. There are several online stores for purchasing music and video content. A pioneer in this area is Apple's iTunes Music Store. (See Figure 10-19.)

Plagiarism

Another ethical issue is **plagiarism,** which means representing some other person's work and ideas as your own without giving credit to the original source. Although plagiarism has been a problem long before the invention of computers, computer technology has make plagiarism easier. For example, simply cutting and pasting content from a Web page into a report or paper may seem tempting to an overworked student or employee.

Correspondingly, computer technology has made it easier than ever to recognize and catch **plagiarists.** For example, services such as Turnitin are dedicated to preventing Internet plagiarism. This service will examine the content of a paper and compare it to a wide range of known public electronic documents including Web page content. In this way, Turnitin can identify an undocumented paper or even parts of an undocumented paper. (See Figure 10-20.)

Figure 10-19 iTunes Music Store Web Site

Figure 10-20 Turnitin Web Site

CONCEPT CHECK

What is the distinction between ethics and computer ethics?

Define copyright, software privacy, the Digital Millennium Copyright Act, and digital rights management.

What is plagiarism? What is Turnitin and what does it do?

Careers in IT

Cryptography is the science of disguising and revealing encrypted information; in terms of information technology, cryptography usually refers to keeping any intercepted information private. For example, such information may be financial data, like banking and credit card information used in online shopping, or private e-mail and correspondence. **Cryptographers** design systems, break systems, and do research on encryption. (See Figure 10-21.) Responsibilities typically do not include building and maintaining the computer networks that use cryptography; these are the duties of security engineers and network administrators. In general, cryptographers are mathematicians who specialize in making and breaking codes.

Many cryptographers work as consultants or professors of cryptography, yet there are full-time positions available at some large corporations or for the government. A PhD in cryptography is usually an essential prerequisite for a position as a cryptographer. However, all cryptographers must have broad experience in both mathematics and computer science or information systems.

Cryptographers can expect to earn an annual salary of $60,000 to over $100,000. Opportunities for advancement typically depend on experience; the most competitive field will be research positions in the military and at universities. Those with experience in computer science and information technology should be among the most employable mathematicians and increasingly in demand. To learn more about becoming a cryptographer, visit us at www.computing2011.com and enter the keyword **careers.**

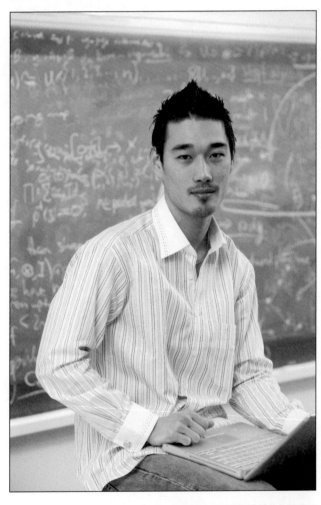

Figure 10-21 Cryptographer

A LOOK TO THE FUTURE

A Webcam on Every Corner

Wireless Internet connections are becoming widely available in public places. At the same time, digital video and still camera technology is becoming more sophisticated and cheaper. As a result, images of public places are more accessible than ever before. Mobile phones are now equipped with cameras and Internet connectivity, and such devices are likely to improve in quality and speed in the future.

In 2007, Google launched Google Street View, a Web site that collected digital photographs from a car that drove around the streets of major cities and associated them with physical addresses. Since that time, many more cities have been added. This allowed users to take "virtual site-seeing tours" from the comfort of their homes. A person could explore the streets of Manhattan or San Francisco, for example, or catch a glimpse of a destination before booking a hotel. However, this service stirred controversy when some of the images captured inadvertently showed people in embarrassing situations or engaged in illegal activities. The U.S. Department of Defense even banned this service from displaying images of military bases.

In the future, you might be able to see live video of a vacation spot, or even check in on your house while you are traveling. Public webcams continue to grow in popularity, and new technology will enhance the images produced so very fine details can be observed. However, others might be able to observe your activities with a simple Web search. What do you think about public webcams? Can you think of some benefits of seeing the world live on your computer? What concerns do you have about your privacy?

PRIVACY

Effective implementation of computer technology involves maximizing positive effects while minimizing negative effects. The most significant concerns are **privacy, security,** and **ethics.**

Large Databases

Large organizations are constantly compiling information about us. **Reverse directories** list telephone numbers followed by subscriber names. **Information resellers (information brokers)** collect and sell personal data. **Electronic profiles** are compiled from databases to provide highly detailed and personalized descriptions of individuals.

Identity theft is the illegal assumption of someone's identity for the purposes of economic gain. **Mistaken identity** occurs when an electronic profile of one person is switched with another. The **Freedom of Information Act** entitles individuals access to governmental records relating to them.

Private Networks

Many organizations monitor employee e-mail and computer files using special software called **snoopware.**

The Internet and the Web

Many people believe that, while using the Web, little can be done to invade their privacy. This is called the **illusion of anonymity.**

PRIVACY

History files record locations of visited sites. **Cookies** store and track information. Two basic types are **traditional cookies** and **ad network cookies (adware cookies).**

Spyware are programs designed to secretly record and report Internet activities. Ad network cookies are one type of spyware. Another type—**computer monitoring (keystroke loggers)**—watches what you do, while **Web bugs** provide information back to spammers about activity on your e-mail account. **Antispyware (spy removal programs)** detects Web bugs and monitoring software.

Online Identity

With the popularity of social networking, blogging, photo- and video-sharing sites, many people post personal information and sometimes intimate details of their lives without considering the consequences. This creates an **online identity.** With the archiving and search features of the Web, this identity is indefinitely available to anyone who cares to look for it.

Major Laws on Privacy

The **Gramm-Leach-Bliley Act** protects personal financial information; the **Health Insurance Portability and Accountability Act (HIPAA)** protects medical records; and the **Family Educational Rights and Privacy Act (FERPA)** restricts disclosure of educational records.

To be a competent end user, you need to be aware of the potential impact of technology on people. You need to be sensitive to and knowledgeable about personal privacy, organizational security, and ethics.

SECURITY

Computer Criminals

Computer criminals include employees, outside users, hackers and crackers, organized crime, and terrorists.

- **Hackers**—create or improve programs and share those programs with fellow hackers. Typically are not criminals.
- **Crackers**—share programs designed to gain unauthorized access to computer systems or disrupt networks. Typically are criminals.

Computer Crime

Computer crime is an illegal action involving special knowledge of computer technology.

- Malicious programs, or **malware**, include **viruses** (the **Computer Fraud and Abuse Act** makes spreading a virus a federal offense), **worms** (self-replicate across a network), and **Trojan horses** (enter a computer system disguised as something else). Antivirus programs alert users when certain viruses and worms enter their systems.
- **Zombies** are remotely controlled infected computers used for malicious purposes. A collection of zombie computers is known as a **botnet,** or **robot network.**
- **Denial of service attack (DoS)** is an attempt to shut down or stop a computer system or network. It floods a computer or network with requests for information and data. Servers

SECURITY

under attack are unable to respond to legitimate users.

- **Scams** are fraudulent or deceptive acts or operations designed to trick individuals into spending their time and money with little or no return. Common **Internet scams** include identity theft, chain letters, auction fraud, vacation prizes, and advance fee loans. These are frequently coupled with **phishing** Web sites or e-mails.
- **Theft** takes many forms including stealing hardware, software, data, and computer time.
- Data manipulation involves changing data or leaving prank messages. The **Computer Fraud and Abuse Act** helps protect against data manipulation.
- Other hazards include natural disasters, civil strife, terrorism, technological failures (**surge protectors** protect against **voltage surges** or **spikes**), and human error.

Measures to Protect Computer Security

Security is concerned with keeping hardware, software, data, and programs safe from unauthorized personnel and unforeseen events. Some measures are restricting access by using **biometric scanning** devices, **passwords**, and **firewalls**; encrypting data using **encryption keys** for e-mail, Web site, **VPN**, and wireless network **encryption**; anticipating disasters (**physical** and **data security, disaster recovery plans**); and preventing data loss.

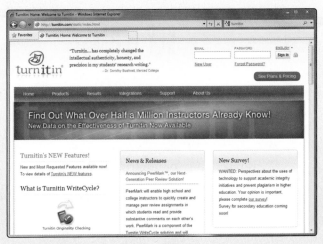

What do you suppose controls how computers can be used? You probably think first of laws. Of course, that is right, but technology is moving so fast that it is very difficult for our legal system to keep up. The essential element that controls how computers are used today is *ethics*.

Ethics are standards of moral conduct. **Computer ethics** are guidelines for the morally acceptable use of computers in our society. We are all entitled to ethical treatment. This includes the right to keep personal information, such as credit ratings and medical histories, from getting into unauthorized hands.

Copyright and Digital Rights Management

Copyright is a legal concept that gives content creators the right to control use and distribution of their work. Materials that can be copyrighted include paintings, books, music, films, and even video games.

Software piracy is the unauthorized copying and distribution of software. The software industry loses over $30 billion annually to software privacy. Two related topics are the Digital Millennium Copyright Act and digital rights management.

- **Digital Millennium Copyright Act** establishes the right of a program owner to make a backup copy of any program and disallows the creation of copies to be sold or given away. It is also illegal to download copyright-protected music and videos from the Internet.
- **Digital rights management (DRM)** is a collection of technologies designed to prevent

copyright violations. Typically, DRM is used to (1) control the number of devices that can access a given file as well as (2) limit the kinds of devices that can access a file.

Today, many legal sources for digital media exist, including

- Television programs that can be watched online, often for free, on television-network-sponsored sites.
- Sites like Pandora that allow listeners to enjoy music at no cost.
- Online stores that legally sell music and video content. A pioneer in this area is Apple's iTunes Music Store.

Plagiarism

Plagiarism is the illegal and unethical representation of some other person's work and ideas as your own without giving credit to the original source. Examples of plagiarism include cutting and pasting Web content into a report or paper.

Recognizing and catching **plagiarists** is relatively easy. For example, services such as **Turnitin** are dedicated to preventing Internet plagiarism. This service examines a paper's content and compares it to a wide range of known public electronic documents including Web page content. Exact duplication or paraphrasing is readily identified.

CAREERS IN IT

Cryptographers design encryption algorithms, break codes, and provide support to national security efforts. PhD in mathematics and broad experience in computer science are required. Salary range $60,000 to over $100,000.

KEY TERMS

access   (283)
accuracy   (283)
ad network cookie   (287)
adware cookie   (287)
antispyware   (289)
biometric scanning   (296)
botnet   (294)
computer crime   (292)
computer ethics   (299)
Computer Fraud and Abuse
   Act   (293, 294)
computer monitoring software   (288)
cookies   (286)
copyright   (299)
cracker   (292)
cryptographer   (301)
cryptography   (301)
data security   (297)
denial of service (DoS) attack   (294)
dictionary attack   (297)
Digital Millennium Copyright
   Act   (300)
digital rights management
   (DRM)   (300)
disaster recovery plan   (298)
electronic profile   (283)
encryption   (297)
encryption key   (297)
ethics   (299)
Family Educational Rights and Privacy
   Act (FERPA)   (289)
firewall   (297)
Freedom of Information Act   (285)
Gramm-Leach-Bliley Act   (289)
hacker   (292)
Health Insurance Portability and
   Accountability Act (HIPAA)   (289)

history file   (286)
identity theft   (284)
illusion of anonymity   (285)
information broker   (283)
information reseller   (283)
Internet scam   (294)
key   (297)
keystroke logger   (288)
malware   (293)
mistaken identity   (285)
online identity   (289)
password   (296)
phishing   (294)
physical security   (298)
plagiarism   (300)
plagiarist   (300)
privacy   (283)
property   (283)
reverse directory   (283)
robot network   (294)
scam   (294)
security   (283)
snoopware   (285)
software piracy   (300)
spike   (296)
spy removal program   (289)
spyware   (287)
surge protector   (296)
traditional cookies   (286)
Trojan horse   (293)
virtual private network (VPN)   (297)
virus   (293)
voltage surge   (296)
Web bug   (287)
worm   (293)
zombie   (294)

To test your knowledge of these key terms with animated flash cards, visit us at www.computing2011.com and enter the keyword terms10.

MULTIPLE CHOICE

Circle the letter or fill in the correct answer.

1. Reverse _____ list telephone numbers followed by subscriber names.
    - a. directories
    - b. order
    - c. databases
    - d. listings

2. The privacy issue that relates to the responsibility of controlling who is able to use data is
    - a. access
    - b. property
    - c. accuracy
    - d. encryption

3. Two basic types of cookies are _____.
    - a. advanced and remedial
    - b. traditional and natural
    - c. natural and ad network
    - d. ad network and traditional

4. A small image or other HTML code that is hidden within in an e-mail message is called a _____.
    - a. virus
    - b. worm
    - c. denial-of-service attack
    - d. Web bug

5. People who create or improve programs and share those programs are _____.
    - a. employees
    - b. hackers
    - c. crackers
    - d. members of organized crime

6. An attempt to slow down or stop a computer system or network by flooding the system with requests for information is called a
    - a. virus
    - b. worm
    - c. denial-of-service attack
    - d. Trojan horse

7. Secret words or phrases used to gain access to a computer system are called
    - a. encryption
    - b. codes
    - c. crackers
    - d. passwords

8. Computer _____ are guidelines for the morally acceptable use of computers in our society.
    - a. business demands
    - b. ethics
    - c. laws
    - d. security requirements

9. Copyright is a(n) _____ concept that gives content creators the right to control use and distribution of their work.
    - a. economic
    - b. ethical
    - c. legal
    - d. moral

10. _____ is a collection of technologies designed to prevent copyright violations.
    - a. DBMS
    - b. DoS
    - c. DRM
    - d. RSS

For an interactive multiple-choice practice test, visit us at www.computing 2011.com and enter the keyword multiple10.

MATCHING

Match each numbered item with the most closely related lettered item. Write your answers in the spaces provided.

a. ad network
b. computer crime
c. cracker
d. DoS
e. firewall
f. illusion of anonymity
g. property
h. snoopware
i. virus checkers
j. worm

1. Relates to who owns data and rights to software. _____
2. Programs that record virtually every activity on a computer system. _____
3. Belief that there is little threat to personal privacy via the Internet. _____
4. A type of cookie that records activities across different sites. _____
5. Illegal action involving special knowledge of computer technology. _____
6. Gains unauthorized access to a system for malicious purposes. _____
7. Replicates itself over a network—spreading to other systems automatically. _____
8. An attack that overwhelms Web sites with data, making them inaccessible. _____
9. Programs that alert users when certain viruses enter a system. _____
10. Security hardware and software that controls access to internal computer networks. _____

For an interactive matching practice test, visit our Web site at www.computing 2011.com and enter the keyword matching10.

OPEN-ENDED

On a separate sheet of paper, respond to each question or statement.

1. Discuss the impact of large databases, private networks, the Internet, and the Web on privacy.
2. Discuss the various kinds of computer criminals.
3. What are the principal measures used to protect computer security? What is encryption? How is it used by corporations and individuals?
4. What is a copyright? Discuss software piracy, the Digital Millennium Copyright Act, and digital rights management.
5. What is plagiarism? Discuss how computers make plagiarism easy and tempting to busy people and how a plagiarist can be easily identified.

APPLYING TECHNOLOGY

The following questions are designed to demonstrate ways that you can effectively use technology today. The first question relates directly to this chapter's Making IT Work for You feature.

1 SPYWARE

Have you installed any free software from the Internet? Did you know that seemingly harmless software might actually be spying on you, even sending personal information to advertisers or worse? Fortunately, spyware removal programs can help. After reviewing Making IT Work for You: Spyware Removal on pages 290 and 291, answer the following: (a) Define spyware and discuss how it works. (b) Describe the process for downloading and installing Lavasoft's Ad-Aware. (c) Describe the capabilities of Ad-Aware. (d) Do you think that spyware might be on your computer? If yes, how do you suppose the spyware was deposited onto your system? If no, why are you so confident?

2 PERSONAL FIREWALLS

At one time, firewalls were used only for large servers. Today firewalls are available for almost any device that connects to the Internet and are essential to ensure security. Connect to our Web site at www.computing2011.com and enter the keyword security to link to a personal firewall product for home users. Once connected, read about the firewall and then answer the following: (a) Is this firewall a hardware or software solution? (b) Describe the procedure for installing the firewall. (c) What types of security risks does this firewall protect against? (d) Are there any security risks the firewall does not cover? If so, how can those risks be reduced?

3 PERSONAL BACKUPS

Do you make backups of your files? If your computer crashed or was lost or stolen today, would you be able to recover all your important data? Backup systems used to be just for large companies and organizations, but today personal backup software makes it simple to keep your information safe. Visit our Web site at www.computing2011.com and enter the keyword backup to link to a site about personal backup software. Once connected, explore the site, and briefly answer the following: (a) Where does the backup software store the backups it makes? (b) Describe the steps necessary to back up a computer using the software. (c) Describe the steps necessary to restore files to a computer from a previous backup using the software.

EXPANDING YOUR KNOWLEDGE

The following questions are designed to add depth and detail to your understanding of specific topics presented within this chapter. The questions direct you to sources other than the textbook to obtain this knowledge.

1 HOW WEB BUGS WORK

The Internet is popular because it is fast, cheap, and open to everyone. These qualities also make it an ideal tool for criminals. Unscrupulous people can use programs called Web bugs to spy on you when you use the Internet. To learn more about how Web bugs work, visit our Web site at www.computing2011.com and enter the keyword bugs. Then answer the following questions: (a) How can a Web bug infect your computer? (b) When a Web bug is delivered by e-mail, it typically sends a copy of that e-mail back to the server. What is the significance or purpose of this activity? (c) Do you think Web bugs are really a privacy concern? Do you think your computer may have one? How could you find out?

2 MISTAKEN IDENTITY

A simple typo can result in mistaken identity. Such mistakes can have a tremendous impact on a person's career, family, and future. To learn more about mistaken identity, visit our Web site at www.computing2011.com and enter the keyword id. Then answer the following questions: (a) Have you been a victim of mistaken identity? If so, please discuss. (b) If your response was "yes," how would you verify that mistaken identity has occurred? (c) Perhaps you have been a victim without knowing it. List the questions that should be considered.

3 AIR TRAVEL DATABASE

To curb possible terrorist threats, the government has implemented a controversial database, known as the Computer Assisted Passenger Pre-screening System (CAPPS). This database determines a "possible threat score" for each individual to determine whether he or she can fly. Research CAPPS on the Internet and then answer the following questions: (a) How does CAPPS determine who is a security risk? (b) What personal information is gathered by CAPPS? (c) How might CAPPS infringe on personal privacy?

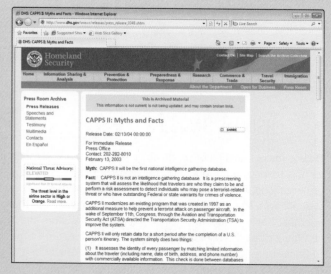

WRITING ABOUT TECHNOLOGY

The ability to think critically and to write effectively is essential to nearly every profession. The following questions are designed to help you develop these skills by posing thought-provoking questions about computer privacy, security, and/or ethics.

1 FACIAL RECOGNITION

As new technologies emerge that promise to enhance our security, our privacy may be at stake. A recent example is the introduction of facial recognition systems in public places for use by police officers. Such systems have recently caught the attention of privacy advocates, as well as the ACLU. Research facial recognition systems on the Web and then write a one-page paper titled "Facial Recognition" that addresses the following topics: (a) Describe how facial recognition technology works. (b) How can facial recognition technology enhance security? (c) In what ways might facial recognition technology compromise privacy? (Hint: Consider security cameras in department or grocery stores.) (d) Do you approve of facial recognition technology? Explain your answer.

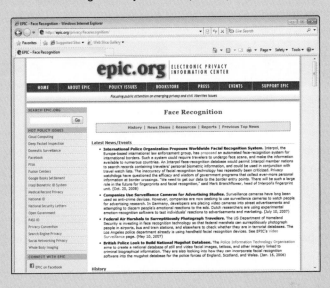

2 PLAGIARISM

Suspicious of cheating, a professor at the University of Virginia developed a program to compare the term papers of his current and past students. Alarmingly, he found that 122 students' work suggested plagiarizing. Consider the implications of this case and then write a one-page paper titled "Plagiarism" that addresses the following questions: (a) With more and more academic submissions being stored in an electronic format and available online, how is it easier to copy another's work? (b) For the same reason, how is detecting an unoriginal work easier? (c) Have you ever copied and pasted text from a Web site or other electronic document and passed it off as your own? (d) How does "borrowing" work in this way affect other students? What about the original author? Explain.

Your Future and Information Technology

Competencies

After you have read this chapter, you should be able to:

1 Explain why it's important to have an individual strategy to be a "winner" in the information age.

2 Describe how technology is changing the nature of competition.

3 Discuss four ways people may react to new technology.

4 Describe how you can stay current with your career.

5 Describe different careers in information technology.

In the past, to maximize your business contacts it may have been necessary to carry business cards with your contact information and frequently attend conferences in your field. Today social networking sites are available for business contacts, allowing users to meet potential business partners around the world or across the street without leaving the office.

Some experts predict that social networking in the business world will soon feature the use of moblie devices. Presence technology and social networking data may combine to make it possible to turn your daily commute into a potential business meeting. Imagine viewing the portfolios of people waiting on the subway next to you or striking up a conversation with a potential business partner based on a mutual friend. It may even be possible to interview for a job on the fly after someone views your resume on their mobile device.

chapter 11

Introduction

Throughout this book, we have emphasized practical subjects that are useful to you now or will be very soon. Accordingly, this final chapter is not about the far future, say, 10 years from now. Rather, it is about today and the near future—about developments whose outlines we can already see. It is about how organizations adapt to technological change. It is also about what you as an individual can do to keep your computer competency up to date.

Are the times changing any faster now than they ever have? It's hard to say. People who were alive when radios, cars, and airplanes were being introduced certainly lived through some dramatic changes. Has technology made our own times even more dynamic? Whatever the answer, it is clear we live in a fast-paced age. The challenge for you as an individual is to devise ways to stay current and to use technology to your advantage. For example, you can use the Web to locate job opportunities.

To stay competent, end users need to recognize the impact of technological change on organizations and people. They need to know how to use change to their advantage and how to be winners. Although end users do not need to be specialists in information technology, they should be aware of career opportunities in the area.

Changing Times

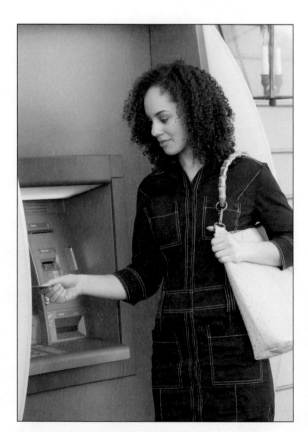

Figure 11-1 Automated teller machines are examples of technology used in business strategy

Almost all businesses have become aware that they must adapt to changing technology or be left behind. Most organizations are now making formal plans to keep track of technology and implement it in their competitive strategies. For example, banks have found that automated teller machines (ATMs) are vital to retail banking. (See Figure 11-1.) Not only do they require fewer human tellers, but also they are available 24 hours a day. More and more banks also are trying to go electronic, doing away with paper transactions wherever possible. ATM cards are used to buy almost anything from gas to groceries.

What's next for the banking industry? Almost all banks also are trying to popularize home banking so that customers can use microcomputers for certain financial tasks. Some banks, known as Internet banks, have even done away with physical bank buildings and conduct all business over the Web. (See Figure 11-2.) In addition, banks are exploring the use of some very sophisticated application programs. These programs will accept cursive writing (the handwriting on checks) directly as input, verify check signatures, and process the check without human intervention.

Clearly, such changes do away with some jobs—those of many bank tellers and cashiers, for example. However, they create opportunities for other people. New technology requires people who are truly capable of working with it. These are not the people who think every piece of equipment is so simple they can just turn it on and use it. Nor are they those who think each new machine is a potential disaster. In other words, new technology needs people who are not afraid to learn about it and are able to manage it. The real issue, then, is not how to make technology better. Rather, it is how to integrate the technology with people.

You are in a very favorable position compared with many other people in industry today. After reading the previous chapters, you have learned more than just the basics of hardware, software, connectivity, and the Internet. You have learned about the most current technology. You are therefore able to use these tools to your advantage—to be a winner.

How do you become and stay a winner? In brief, the answer is: You must form your own individual strategy for dealing with change. First let us look at how businesses are handling technological change. Then let's look at how people are reacting to these changes. Finally, we will offer a few suggestions that will enable you to keep up with and profit from the information revolution.

Figure 11-2 Internet banks conduct business over the Web

Cite examples of ways computers are changing the business world.

What are the human requirements of new technology?

Technology and Organizations

Technology can introduce new ways for businesses to compete with each other. Some of the principal changes are as follows.

New Products

Technology creates products that operate faster, are priced cheaper, are often of better quality, or are wholly new. Indeed, new products can be individually tailored to a particular customer's needs. For example, financial services companies such as Merrill Lynch have taken advantage of technology to launch cash management accounts. (See Figure 11-3.) These accounts combine information on a person's checking, savings, credit card, and securities accounts into a single monthly statement. It automatically sets aside "idle" funds into interest-bearing money market funds. Customers can access their accounts on the Web and get a complete picture of their financial condition at any time. However, even if they don't pay much attention to their statements, their surplus funds are invested automatically.

New Enterprises

Information technology can build entirely new businesses. Two examples are Internet service providers and Web site development companies.

* Just a few years ago, the only computer connectivity options available to individuals were through online service providers like America Online and

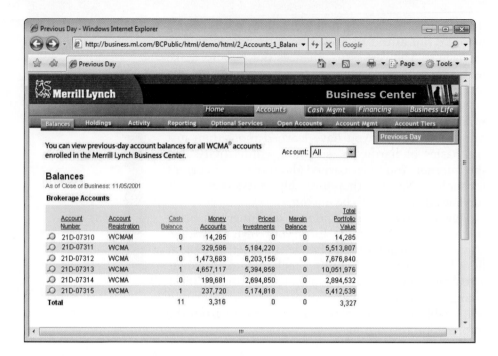

Figure 11-3 Merrill Lynch's cash management account

through colleges and universities. Now, hundreds of national service providers and thousands of local service providers are available.

- Thousands of small companies specializing in Web site development have sprung up in the past few years. These companies help small- to medium-sized organizations by providing assistance in evaluating, creating, and maintaining Web sites.

New Customer and Supplier Relationships

Businesses that make their information systems easily available may make their customers less likely to take their business elsewhere. For instance, Federal Express, the overnight package delivery service, does everything possible to make its customers dependent on it. Upon request, customers receive airbills with their name, address, and account number preprinted on them, making shipping and billing easier. Package numbers are scanned into the company's information system so that they can be tracked from pickup point to destination. (See Figure 11-4.) Thus, apprehensive customers can be informed very quickly of the exact location of their package as it travels toward its destination.

Figure 11-4 New technology helps FedEx maintain customer loyalty

CONCEPT CHECK

- What is the role of technology in creating new products?

- Describe two new enterprises built by information technology.

- Discuss how technology can create new customers and affect supplier relationships.

Technology and People

Clearly, recent technological changes, and those sure to come in the near future, will produce significant changes and opportunities in the years ahead. How should we be prepared for them?

People have different coping styles when it comes to technology. It has been suggested, for instance, that people react to changing technology in one of four ways: cynicism, naivete, frustration, and proactivity.

Cynicism

The **cynic** feels that, for a manager at least, the idea of using a microcomputer is overrated. (See Figure 11-5.) Learning and using it take too much time, time that could be delegated to someone else. Doing spreadsheets and word processing, according to the cynic, are tasks that managers should understand. However, the cynic feels that such tasks take time away from a manager's real job of developing plans and setting goals for the people being supervised.

Cynics may express their doubts openly, especially if they are top managers. Or they may only pretend to be interested in microcomputers, when actually they are not interested at all.

Naivete

Many **naive** people are unfamiliar with computers. They may think computers are magic boxes capable of solving all kinds of problems that computers really can't handle. On the other hand, some naive persons are actually quite familiar with computers but underestimate the difficulty of changing computer systems or of generating certain information.

Frustration

The **frustrated** person may already be quite busy and may hate having to take time to learn about microcomputers. Such a person feels it is an imposition to have to learn something new or is too impatient to try to understand the manuals explaining what hardware and software are supposed to do. The result is continual frustration. (See Figure 11-6.) Some people are frustrated because they try to do too much. Or they're frustrated because they find manuals difficult to understand. In some cases poorly written manuals are at fault.

Proactivity

Webster's Collegiate Dictionary defines **proactive,** in part, as "acting in anticipation of future problems, needs, or changes." A proactive person looks at technology in a positive realistic way. (See Figure 11-7.) They are not cynics, underestimating the likely impact of technology on their

Figure 11-5 **The cynic: "These gadgets are overrated."**

Figure 11-6 The frustrated person: "This stuff doesn't make sense half the time."

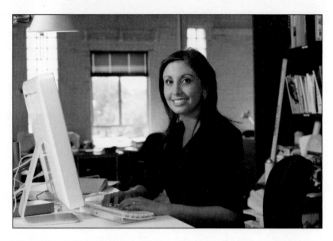

Figure 11-7 The proactive person: "How can I use this new tool?"

lives. They are not naive, overestimating the ability of technology to solve the world's or their problems. They do not become frustrated easily and give up using technology. Proactive people are positive in their outlook and look at new technology as providing new tools that, when correctly applied, can positively impact their lives.

Most of us fall into one of the four categories. Cynicism, naivete, frustration, and proactivity are common human responses to change. Do you see yourself or others around you responding to technology in any of these ways? For those who respond negatively, just being aware of their reaction can help them become more positive and proactive to tomorrow's exciting new changes in technology.

 CONCEPT CHECK

 Describe three negative ways people cope with technological changes in the workplace.

 Describe one positive way people cope with technological change in the workplace.

 Define proactive.

How You Can Be a Winner

So far we have described how progressive organizations are using technology in the information age. Now let's concentrate on you as an individual. (See Making IT Work for You: Locating Job Opportunities Online on pages 320 and 321.) How can you stay ahead? Here are some ideas.

Stay Current

Whatever their particular line of work, successful professionals keep up both with their own fields and with the times. We don't mean you should try to become a computer expert and read a lot of technical magazines. Rather, you should concentrate on your profession and learn how computer technology is being used within it.

Every field has trade journals, whether the field is interior design, personnel management, or advertising. Most such journals regularly present articles about the uses of computers. It's important that you also belong to a trade or industry association and go to its meetings. Many associations sponsor seminars and conferences that describe the latest information and techniques.

Another way to stay current is by participating electronically with special-interest newsgroups on the Internet.

Maintain Your Computer Competency

Actually, you should try to stay ahead of the technology. Books, journals, and trade associations are the best sources of information about new technology that applies to your field. The general business press—*BusinessWeek, Fortune, Inc., The Wall Street Journal,* and the business section of your local newspaper—also carries computer-related articles.

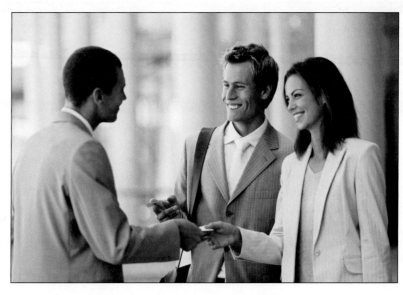

Figure 11-8 **Professional organizations and contacts help you keep up in your field**

However, if you wish, you can subscribe to a magazine that covers microcomputers and information more specifically. Examples are *InfoWorld, PC World,* and *MacWorld.* You also may find it useful to look at newspapers and magazines that cover the computer industry as a whole. An example of such a periodical is *ComputerWorld.* Most of these magazines also have online versions available on the Web.

Develop Professional Contacts

Besides being members of professional associations, successful people make it a point to maintain contact with others in their field. They stay in touch by telephone, e-mail, and newsgroups and go to lunch with others in their line of work. Doing this lets them learn what other people are doing in their jobs. It tells them what other firms are doing and what tasks are being automated. Developing professional contacts can keep you abreast not only of new information but also of new job possibilities. (See Figure 11-8.) It also offers social benefits. An example of a professional organization found in many areas is the local association of Realtors.

Develop Specialties

Develop specific as well as general skills. You want to be well-rounded *within* your field, but certainly not a "jack of all trades, master of none." Master a trade or two within your profession. At the same time, don't become identified with a specific technological skill that might very well become obsolete.

The best advice is to specialize to some extent. However, don't make your specialty so tied to technology that you'll be in trouble if the technology shifts. For example, if your career is in marketing or graphics design, it makes sense to learn about desktop publishing and Web page design. (See Figure 11-9.) In this way, you can learn to make high-quality, inexpensive graphics layouts. It would not make as much sense for you to become an expert on, say, the various types of monitors used to display the graphics layouts because such monitors are continually changing.

Expect to take classes during your working life to keep up with developments in your field. Some professions require more keeping up than others—a

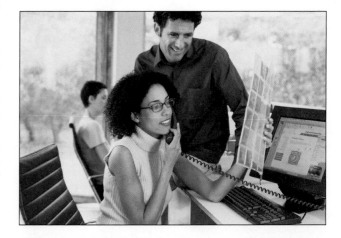

Figure 11-9 **Desktop publishing: A good specialty to develop for certain careers**

LOCATING JOB OPPORTUNITIES ONLINE

Did you know that you can use the Internet to find a job? You can locate and browse through job listings. You can even electronically post your resume for prospective employers to review.

Browsing Job Listings   Three well-known job search sites on the Web are Yahoo! HotJobs (hotjobs.yahoo.com), Monster (monster.com), and CareerBuilder (careerbuilder.com). You can connect to these sites and browse through job opportunities. For example, after connecting to careerbuilder.com, you can search for a job by following steps similar to those shown below.

1 ● **Visit www.careerbuilder.com.**

● **Click** *Find Jobs.*

● **Enter location to search.**

● **Select job categories to search.**

● **Enter optional keywords to refine your search.**

● **Click the** *Find Jobs* **button.**

2 ● **Select a job title from the table of results to learn more about that job posting.**

Posting Your Resume   To make your qualifications known to prospective employers, you can post your resume at the job search site.

1 ● **Click** *Post Resumes.*

● **If you do not have a resume to upload, select** *Resume Builder* **to create one.**

2 ● **Follow the step-by-step instructions on the screen and fill in blanks to create a professional resume.**

Your resume is posted and searchable by potential employers.

Post Resumes

Upload resume

Resume Builder

Automated Alerts   To help you find a job faster, you can set up automatic searches. When new jobs are posted that match your search, you can be alerted instantly by e-mail or mobile phone.

1 ● **Click** *Job Alerts.*

● **Fill in the search form similar to the** *Browse Job Listings* **section on the previous page.**

● **Provide your e-mail address and/or mobile phone number to receive alerts as new matching jobs are posted.**

Job Alerts

Your agent will search new job listings and alert you to new opportunities by e-mail.

The Web is continually changing, and some of the specifics presented in this Making IT Work for You may have changed.

To learn about other ways to make information technology work for you, visit our Web site at www.computing2011.com and enter the keyword miw.

computer specialist, for example, compared to a human resources manager. Whatever the training required, always look for ways to adapt and improve your skills to become more productive and marketable. There may be times when you are tempted to start all over again and learn completely new skills. However, a better course of action may be to use emerging technology to improve your present base of skills. This way you can build on your current strong points and then branch out to other fields from a position of strength.

Be Alert for Organizational Change

Every organization has formal lines of communication—for example, supervisor to middle manager to top manager. However, there is also the *grapevine*—informal lines of communication. (See Figure 11-10.) Some service departments will serve many layers of management and be abreast of the news on all levels. For instance, the art director for advertising may be aware of several aspects of a companywide marketing campaign. Secretaries and administrative assistants know what is going on in more than one area.

Being part of the office grapevine can alert you to important changes—for instance, new job openings—that can benefit you. However, you always have to assess the validity of what you hear on the grapevine. Moreover, it's not advisable to be a contributor to office gossip. Behind-the-back criticisms of other people have a way of getting back to the person criticized.

Be especially alert for new trends within the organization—future hiring, layoffs, automation, mergers with other companies, and the like. Notice which areas are receiving the greatest attention from top management. One tip-off is to see what kind of outside consultants are being brought in. Independent consultants are usually invited in because a company believes it needs advice in an area with which it has insufficient experience.

Look for Innovative Opportunities

You may understand your job better than anyone—even if you've only been there a few months. Look for ways to make it more efficient. How can present procedures be automated? How can new technology make your tasks easier? Discuss your ideas with your supervisor, the training director, or the head of the information systems department. Or discuss them with someone else who

Figure 11-10 Informal communication can alert you to important organizational changes

can see that you get the recognition you deserve. (Co-workers may or may not be receptive and may or may not try to take credit themselves.)

A good approach is to present your ideas in terms of saving money rather than "improving information." Managers are generally more impressed with ideas that can save dollars than with ideas that seem like potential breakthroughs in the quality of decisions.

In general, it's best to concentrate on the business and organizational problems that need solving. Then look for a technological way of solving them. That is, avoid becoming too enthusiastic about a particular technology and then trying to make it fit the work situation.

☑ CONCEPT CHECK

Outline the strategies you can use to stay ahead and be successful in your career.

Discuss the advantages and disadvantages of specialization.

Describe how you would stay alert for organizational changes.

Careers in IT

Being a winner does not necessarily mean having a career in information systems. There are, however, several jobs within information technology that you might like to consider. We have discussed many of these careers in the preceding chapters. (See Figure 11-11.)

To learn more about these careers, visit our Web site at www.computing 2011.com and enter the keyword **careers**.

Career	Responsibilities
Computer support specialist	Provides technical support to customers and other users
Computer technician	Repairs and installs computer components and systems
Computer trainer	Instructs users on the latest software or hardware
Cryptographer	Designs, tests, and researches encryption procedures
Data entry worker	Inputs customer information, lists, and other types of data
Database administrator	Uses database management software to determine the most efficient ways to organize and access data
Desktop publisher	Creates and formats publication-ready material
Information systems manager	Oversees the work of programmers, computer specialists, systems analysts, and other computer professionals
Network administrator	Creates and maintains networks
Programmer	Creates, tests, and troubleshoots computer programs
Software engineer	Analyzes users' needs and creates application software
Systems analyst	Plans and designs information systems
Technical writer	Prepares instruction manuals, technical reports, and other scientific or technical documents
Webmaster	Develops and maintains Web sites and Web resources

Figure 11-11 Careers in information systems

To stay competent, you need to recognize the impact of technological change on organizations and people. You need to know how to use change to your advantage and how to become a winner. Although you do not need to be a specialist in information technology, you should be aware of career opportunities in the area.

TECHNOLOGY AND PEOPLE

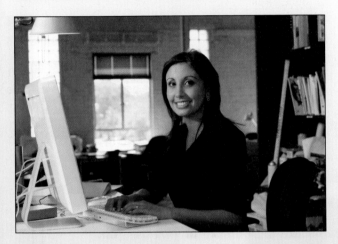

People have different coping styles when it comes to technology. Four common reactions to new technology are cynicism, naivete, frustration, and proactivity.

Cynicism

The **cynics** feel that new technology is over-rated and too troublesome to learn. Some cynics openly express their doubts. Others pretend to be interested.

Naivete

Naive people may be unfamiliar or quite familiar with computers. People who are unfamiliar tend to think of computers as magic boxes. Even those familiar with technology often underestimate the time and difficulty of using technology to generate information.

Frustration

Frustrated users are impatient and irritated about taking time to learn new technology. Often these people have too much to do, find manuals difficult to understand, and/or feel stupid.

Proactivity

A **proactive** person looks at technology in a positive and realistic way. He or she is not cynical, naive, or frustrated regarding new technology. Proactive people are positive and look at new technology as providing new tools that can positively impact their lives.

HOW YOU CAN BE A WINNER

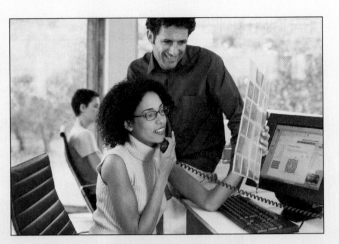

There are six ongoing activities that can help you be successful.

Stay Current

Read trade journals and the general business press, join professional associations, and participate in interest groups on the Internet.

Maintain Your Computer Competency

Stay current by reading computer-related articles in the general press and trade journals.

Develop Professional Contacts

Stay active in your profession and meet people in your field. This provides information about other people, firms, job opportunities, and social contacts.

Develop Specialties

Develop specific as well as general skills. Expect to take classes periodically to stay current with your field and technology.

Be Alert for Organizational Change

Use formal and informal lines of communication. Be alert for new trends within the organization.

Look for Innovative Opportunities

Look for ways to increase efficiency. Present ideas in terms of saving money rather than "improving information."

Computer Support Specialist

Computer support specialists provide technical support to customers and other users.

Computer Technician

Computer technicians repair and install computer components and systems.

Computer Trainer

Computer trainers instruct users on the latest software or hardware.

Cryptographer

Cryptographers design, test, and research encryption procedures.

Data Entry Worker

Data entry workers input customer information, lists, and other types of data.

Database Administrator

Database administrators use database management software to determine the most efficient ways to organize and access data.

Desktop Publisher

Desktop publishers create and format publication-ready material.

Information Systems Manager

Information systems managers oversee the work of programmers, computer specialists, systems analysts, and other computer professionals.

Network Administrator

Network administrators create and maintain networks.

Programmer

Programmers create, test, and troubleshoot computer programs.

Software Engineer

Software engineers analyze users' needs and create application software.

Systems Analyst

Systems analysts plan and design information systems.

Technical Writer

Technical writers prepare instruction manuals, technical reports, and other scientific or technical documents.

Webmaster

Webmasters develop and maintain Web sites and Web resources.

KEY TERMS

To test your knowledge of these key terms with animated flash cards, visit our Web site at www.computing2011.com and enter the keyword terms11.

MULTIPLE CHOICE

Circle the letter or fill in the correct answer.

1. Changes in technology require people who
   a. are not afraid to learn and manage new technology
   b. know just the basics about the technology
   c. think each new machine is a potential disaster
   d. think every piece of equipment is so simple they can just turn it on and use it

2. One of the advantages of the changes in information technology is
   a. data can be lost and/or stolen
   b. new businesses are created
   c. new skills are constantly in demand
   d. people are put out of work

3. The _____ user believes that learning and using computers take time away from his or her real job.
   a. cynical
   b. frustrated
   c. naive
   d. proactive

4. Generally, a proactive person
   a. feels that the idea of using a microcomputer is overrated
   b. is unfamiliar with computers
   c. hates to take time to learn about microcomputers
   d. looks at technology in a positive, realistic way

5. To maintain your computer competence, you should try to stay ahead of technology by
   a. learning a new trade
   b. quitting your current job and going back to school
   c. reading books, journals, newspapers, and magazines
   d. reviewing the systems life cycle

6. Successful people make it a point to
   a. avoid contact with others
   b. develop nonspecific skills
   c. get their education and relax
   d. maintain contact with others in their field

7. These individuals design, test, and research encryption procedures.
   a. database administrators
   b. computer trainers
   c. cryptographers
   d. technical writers

8. _____ oversee the work of programmers, computer specialists, and other computer professionals.
   a. Database administrators
   b. Information systems managers
   c. Network managers
   d. Systems analysts

9. These individuals are responsible for creating, testing, and troubleshooting computer programs.
   a. database administrators
   b. network managers
   c. programmers
   d. systems analysts

10. _____ develop and maintain Web sites and Web resources.
    a. Network managers
    b. Programmers
    c. Systems analysts
    d. Webmasters

For an interactive multiple-choice practice test, visit our Web site at www.computing 2011.com and enter the keyword multiple11.

MATCHING

Match each numbered item with the most closely related lettered item. Write your answers in the spaces provided.

a. computer technician
b. computer trainer
c. cynic
d. database administrator
e. network administrator
f. programmer
g. software engineer
h. systems analyst
i. technical writer
j. Webmaster

1. Computer user who feels the idea of using micro-computers is overrated. _____
2. A computer specialist employed to evaluate, create, and maintain Web sites. _____
3. Computer professional who creates, tests, and troubleshoots computer programs. _____
4. Computer specialist who uses database management software to determine the most efficient ways to organize and access data. _____
5. Computer professional who analyzes users' needs and creates application software. _____
6. Computer professional who plans and designs information systems. _____
7. Computer professional who repairs and installs computer components and systems. _____
8. Computer professional who creates and maintains networks. _____
9. Computer professional who instructs users on the latest software or hardware. _____
10. Computer professional who prepares instruction manuals, technical reports, and other scientific or technical documents. _____

For an interactive matching practice test, visit our Web site at www.computing2011.com and enter the keyword matching11.

OPEN-ENDED

On a separate sheet of paper, respond to each question or statement.

1. Why is strategy important to individual success in the information age? What is your strategy?
2. Describe how technology changes the nature of competition.
3. How can your computer competencies and knowledge help you get ahead in today's market?
4. What does proactive mean? What is a proactive computer user? What advantages does this type of user have over the other types?
5. Discuss several different careers in information technology. Which are of interest to you?

APPLYING TECHNOLOGY

The following questions are designed to demonstrate ways that you can effectively use technology today. The first question relates directly to this chapter's Making IT Work for You feature.

1 JOBS ONLINE

Did you know that you can use the Internet to find a job? You can browse through job listings, post resumes for prospective employers, and even use special agents to continually search for that job that's just right for you. To learn more about online job searches, review Making IT Work for You: Locating Job Opportunities Online on pages 320 and 321. Then visit our Web site at www.computing 2011.com and enter the keyword jobs. Once at that site, play the video and answer the following: (a) What locations and categories were selected for the job search? (b) Describe the process for posting a resume. (c) What search criteria were used to set up the job search agent?

2 MAINTAIN COMPUTER COMPETENCE

There are several sources of information to help keep you up to date on current computing trends. Visit our Web site at www.computing 2011.com and enter the keyword competence to link to a few computing sites. Explore the sites and then answer the following: (a) List the sites you visited and describe the focus of each. (b) Which of these sites was most useful? Why? (c) Which of these sites was least useful? Why? (d) What are other ways you can stay in step with current computing issues?

EXPANDING YOUR KNOWLEDGE

The following questions are designed to add depth and detail to your understanding of specific topics presented within this chapter. The questions direct you to sources other than the textbook to obtain this knowledge.

1 YOUR CAREER

Have you thought about what your career might be? Perhaps it is in marketing, education, or information technology. If you have a career in mind, conduct a Web search to learn more about your chosen career. If you don't have a career in mind, select one of the information systems careers presented in this chapter and conduct a Web search to learn more about that career. After reviewing at least five sites, answer the following: (a) Describe your career of choice. (b) Why did you choose that career? (c) How is information technology used in this career? (d) How will changing technology impact your chosen career?

2 RESUME ADVICE

There are several excellent resources available online to help you write a winning resume. Conduct a Web search using the keywords "resume help" to learn more. Review at least five sites and then compose a sample resume for yourself, applying the information from the sites.

WRITING ABOUT TECHNOLOGY

The ability to think critically and to write effectively is essential to nearly every profession. The following questions are designed to help you develop these skills by posing thought-provoking questions about computer privacy, security, and/or ethics.

1 WRITING ABOUT PRIVACY AND ETHICS

Regardless of your career path, critical thinking, analysis, and writing are essential skills. In each of the preceding chapters, the Writing About Technology feature presented questions about privacy and ethics. These questions are designed to help you develop critical thinking, analysis, and writing skills. Select the five questions you feel are most important to privacy or ethics from the Writing About Technology questions in the preceding chapters. Write a two-page paper that addresses the questions you chose and describe why they are of interest to you.

2 WRITING ABOUT SECURITY

The importance of computer security is often overshadowed by the functions and features of new technology. The Writing About Technology feature presented many questions about security in the preceding chapters. These questions are designed to increase your awareness of important computer security topics and further develop your writing skills. Select the five questions you feel are most important to security from the Writing About Technology questions in the preceding chapters. Write a two-page paper that addresses the questions you chose and describe why they are of interest to you.

The Evolution of the Computer Age

Many of you probably can't remember a world without computers, but for some of us, computers were virtually unknown when we were born and have rapidly come of age during our lifetime.

Although there are many predecessors to what we think of as the modern computer—reaching as far back as the 18th century, when Joseph Marie Jacquard created a loom programmed to weave cloth and Charles Babbage created the first fully modern computer design (which he could never get to work)—the computer age did not really begin until the first computer was made available to the public in 1951.

The modern age of computers thus spans slightly more than 50 years (so far), which is typically broken down into five generations. Each generation has been marked by a significant advance in technology.

- **First Generation (1951–57):** During the first generation, computers were built with vacuum tubes— electronic tubes that were made of glass and were about the size of light bulbs.

- **Second Generation (1958–63):** This generation began with the first computers built with transistors—small devices that transfer electronic signals across a resistor. Because transistors are much smaller, use less power, and create less heat than vacuum tubes, the new computers were faster, smaller, and more reliable than the first-generation machines.

- **Third Generation (1964–69):** In 1964, computer manufacturers began replacing transistors with integrated circuits. An integrated circuit (IC) is a complete electronic circuit on a small chip made of silicon (one of the most abundant elements in the earth's crust). These computers were more reliable and compact than computers made with transistors, and they cost less to manufacture.

- **Fourth Generation (1970–90):** Many key advances were made during this generation, the most significant being the microprocessor—a specialized chip developed for computer memory and logic. Use of a single chip to create a smaller "personal" computer (as well as digital watches, pocket calculators, copy machines, and so on) revolutionized the computer industry.

- **Fifth Generation (1991–2011 and beyond):** Our current generation has been referred to as the "Connected Generation" because of the industry's massive effort to increase the connectivity of computers. The rapidly expanding Internet, World Wide Web, and intranets have created an information superhighway that has enabled both computer professionals and home computer users to communicate with others across the globe.

This appendix provides you with a timeline that describes in more detail some of the most significant events in each generation of the computer age.

First Generation: The Vacuum Tube Age

1951 Dr. John W. Mauchly and J. Presper Eckert Jr. introduce the first commercially available electronic digital computer—the UNIVAC—built with vacuum tubes. This computer was based on their earlier ENIAC (Electronic Numerical Integrator and Computer) design completed in 1946.

1951–53 IBM adds computers to its business equipment products and sells over 1,000 IBM 650 systems.

1951 1952 1953 1954 1955 1956 1957

1957 Introduction of first high-level programming language—FORTRAN (FORmula TRANslator).

1952 Development team led by Dr. Grace Hopper, former U.S. Navy programmer, introduces the A6 Compiler—the first example of software that converts high-level language symbols into instructions that a computer can execute.

Second Generation: The Transistor Age

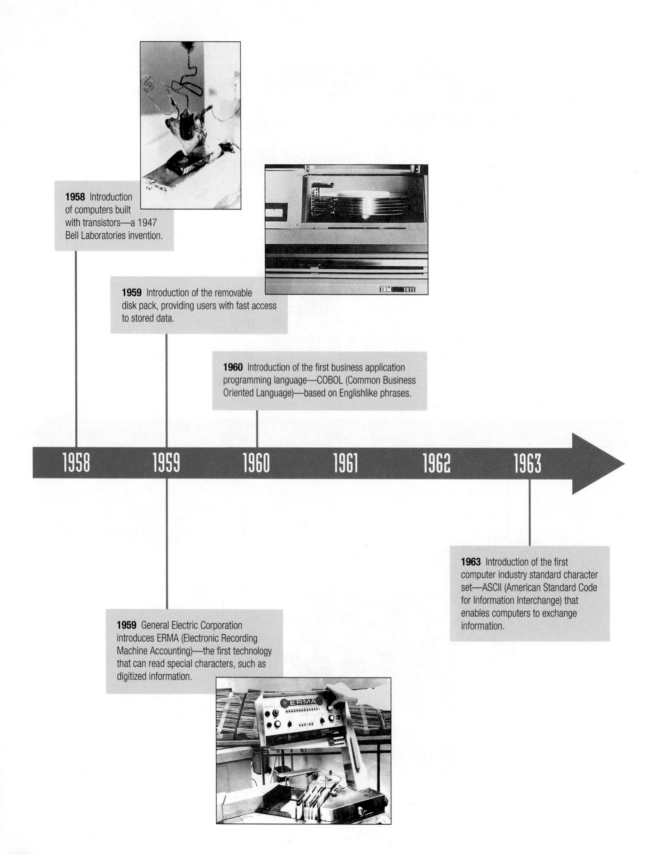

1958 Introduction of computers built with transistors—a 1947 Bell Laboratories invention.

1959 Introduction of the removable disk pack, providing users with fast access to stored data.

1960 Introduction of the first business application programming language—COBOL (Common Business Oriented Language)—based on Englishlike phrases.

1958　1959　1960　1961　1962　1963

1963 Introduction of the first computer industry standard character set—ASCII (American Standard Code for Information Interchange) that enables computers to exchange information.

1959 General Electric Corporation introduces ERMA (Electronic Recording Machine Accounting)—the first technology that can read special characters, such as digitized information.

Third Generation: The Integrated Circuit Age

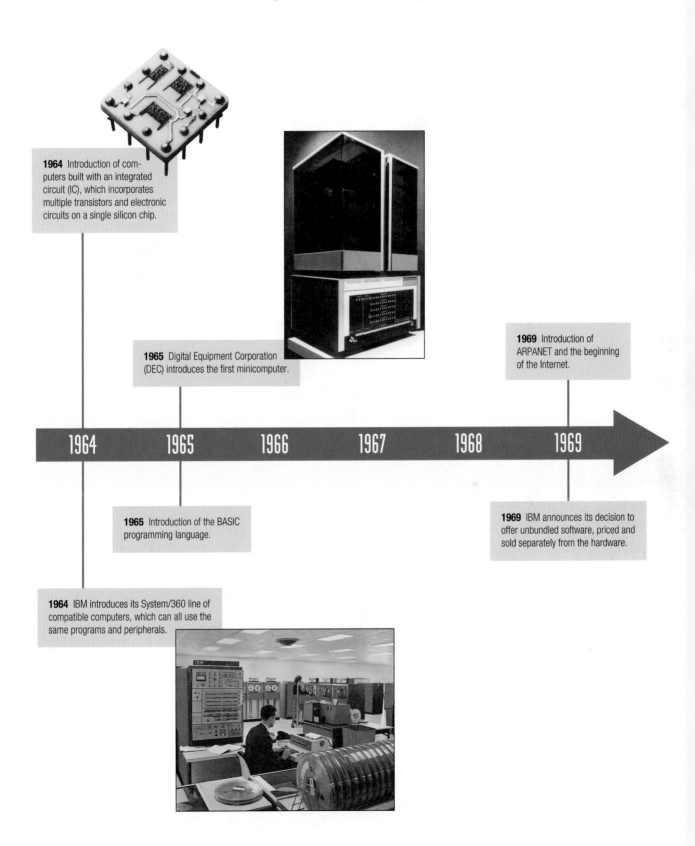

1964 Introduction of computers built with an integrated circuit (IC), which incorporates multiple transistors and electronic circuits on a single silicon chip.

1965 Digital Equipment Corporation (DEC) introduces the first minicomputer.

1969 Introduction of ARPANET and the beginning of the Internet.

1964 1965 1966 1967 1968 1969

1965 Introduction of the BASIC programming language.

1969 IBM announces its decision to offer unbundled software, priced and sold separately from the hardware.

1964 IBM introduces its System/360 line of compatible computers, which can all use the same programs and peripherals.

Fourth Generation: The Microprocessor Age

1970 Introduction of computers built with chips that used LSI (large-scale integration).

1975 First local area network (LAN)—Ethernet—developed at Xerox PARC (Palo Alto Research Center).

1977 Apple Computer, Inc., founded by Steve Wozniak and Steve Jobs, and Apple I introduced as an easy-to-use "hobbyist" computer.

1970   1971   1972   1973   1974   1975   1976   1977   1978   1979

1971 Dr. Ted Hoff of Intel Corporation develops a microprogrammable computer chip—the Intel 4004 microprocessor.

1975 The MITS, Inc., Altair becomes the first commercially successful microcomputer, selling for less than $400 a kit.

1979 Introduction of the first public information services—Compuserve and the Source.

1980 IBM asks Microsoft founder, Bill Gates, to develop an operating system—MS-DOS— for the soon-to-be-released IBM personal computer.

1981 Introduction of the IBM PC, which contains an Intel microprocessor chip and Microsoft's MS-DOS operating system.

1989 Introduction of Intel 486—the first 1,000,000-transistor microprocessor.

1980 1981 1982 1983 1984 1985 1986 1987 1988 1989 1990

1984 Apple introduces the Macintosh Computer, with a unique, easy-to-use graphical user interface.

1985 Microsoft introduces its Windows graphical user interface.

1990 Microsoft releases Windows 3.0, with an enhanced graphical user interface and the ability to run multiple applications.

Fifth Generation: The Age of Connectivity

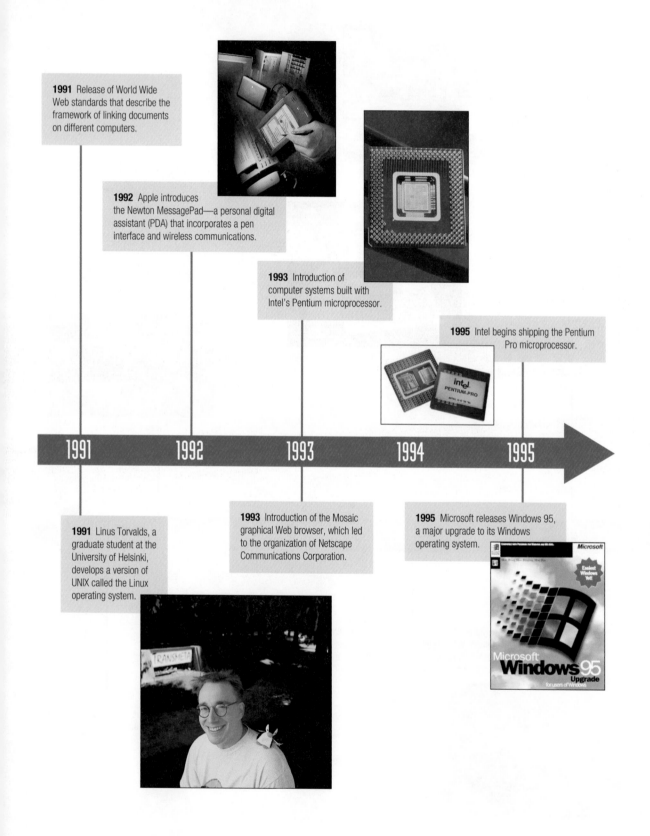

1991 Release of World Wide Web standards that describe the framework of linking documents on different computers.

1992 Apple introduces the Newton MessagePad—a personal digital assistant (PDA) that incorporates a pen interface and wireless communications.

1993 Introduction of computer systems built with Intel's Pentium microprocessor.

1995 Intel begins shipping the Pentium Pro microprocessor.

1991   1992   1993   1994   1995

1991 Linus Torvalds, a graduate student at the University of Helsinki, develops a version of UNIX called the Linux operating system.

1993 Introduction of the Mosaic graphical Web browser, which led to the organization of Netscape Communications Corporation.

1995 Microsoft releases Windows 95, a major upgrade to its Windows operating system.

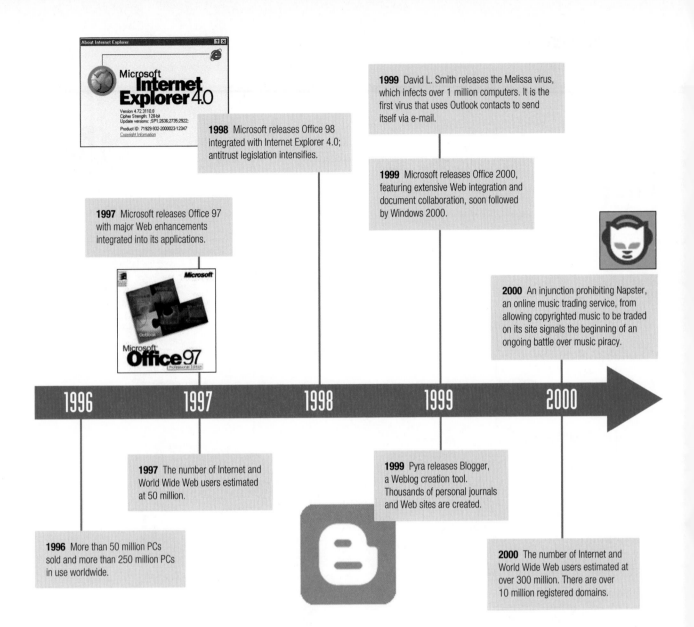

1998 Microsoft releases Office 98 integrated with Internet Explorer 4.0; antitrust legislation intensifies.

1999 David L. Smith releases the Melissa virus, which infects over 1 million computers. It is the first virus that uses Outlook contacts to send itself via e-mail.

1999 Microsoft releases Office 2000, featuring extensive Web integration and document collaboration, soon followed by Windows 2000.

1997 Microsoft releases Office 97 with major Web enhancements integrated into its applications.

2000 An injunction prohibiting Napster, an online music trading service, from allowing copyrighted music to be traded on its site signals the beginning of an ongoing battle over music piracy.

| 1996 | 1997 | 1998 | 1999 | 2000 |

1997 The number of Internet and World Wide Web users estimated at 50 million.

1999 Pyra releases Blogger, a Weblog creation tool. Thousands of personal journals and Web sites are created.

1996 More than 50 million PCs sold and more than 250 million PCs in use worldwide.

2000 The number of Internet and World Wide Web users estimated at over 300 million. There are over 10 million registered domains.

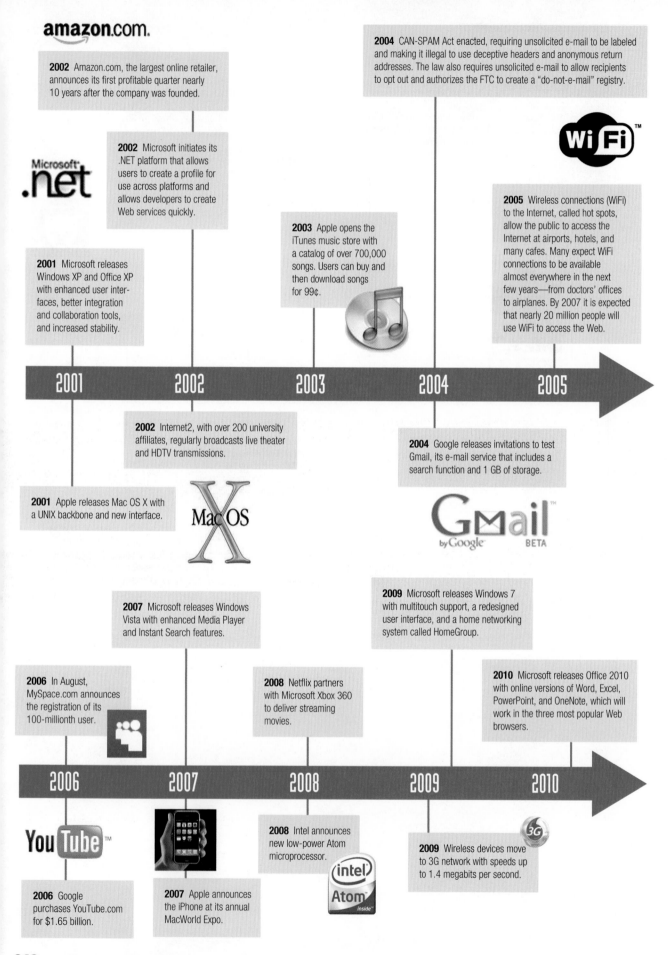

amazon.com.

2002 Amazon.com, the largest online retailer, announces its first profitable quarter nearly 10 years after the company was founded.

2004 CAN-SPAM Act enacted, requiring unsolicited e-mail to be labeled and making it illegal to use deceptive headers and anonymous return addresses. The law also requires unsolicited e-mail to allow recipients to opt out and authorizes the FTC to create a "do-not-e-mail" registry.

Microsoft .net

2002 Microsoft initiates its .NET platform that allows users to create a profile for use across platforms and allows developers to create Web services quickly.

2003 Apple opens the iTunes music store with a catalog of over 700,000 songs. Users can buy and then download songs for 99¢.

WiFi

2005 Wireless connections (WiFi) to the Internet, called hot spots, allow the public to access the Internet at airports, hotels, and many cafes. Many expect WiFi connections to be available almost everywhere in the next few years—from doctors' offices to airplanes. By 2007 it is expected that nearly 20 million people will use WiFi to access the Web.

2001 Microsoft releases Windows XP and Office XP with enhanced user interfaces, better integration and collaboration tools, and increased stability.

2001 2002 2003 2004 2005

2002 Internet2, with over 200 university affiliates, regularly broadcasts live theater and HDTV transmissions.

2004 Google releases invitations to test Gmail, its e-mail service that includes a search function and 1 GB of storage.

2001 Apple releases Mac OS X with a UNIX backbone and new interface.

Mac OS X

Gmail by Google BETA

2007 Microsoft releases Windows Vista with enhanced Media Player and Instant Search features.

2009 Microsoft releases Windows 7 with multitouch support, a redesigned user interface, and a home networking system called HomeGroup.

2006 In August, MySpace.com announces the registration of its 100-millionth user.

2008 Netflix partners with Microsoft Xbox 360 to deliver streaming movies.

2010 Microsoft releases Office 2010 with online versions of Word, Excel, PowerPoint, and OneNote, which will work in the three most popular Web browsers.

2006 2007 2008 2009 2010

You Tube

2008 Intel announces new low-power Atom microprocessor.

3G

2009 Wireless devices move to 3G network with speeds up to 1.4 megabits per second.

2006 Google purchases YouTube.com for $1.65 billion.

2007 Apple announces the iPhone at its annual MacWorld Expo.

intel Atom inside

342 The Evolution of the Computer Age

The Buyer's Guide How to Buy Your Own Microcomputer System

FOUR STEPS IN BUYING A MICROCOMPUTER SYSTEM

The following is not intended to make buying a microcomputer an exhausting experience. Rather, it is to help you clarify your thinking about what you need and can afford.

The four steps in buying a microcomputer system are presented on the following pages. We divide each step into two parts based on the assumptions that both your needs and the money you have to spend on a microcomputer may change.

STEP 1

What Needs Do I Want a Computer to Serve?

The trick is to distinguish between your needs and your wants. Sure, you *want* a cutting-edge system powerful enough to run every conceivable program you'll ever need. And you want a system fast enough to process them all at the speed of light. But do you *need* this? Your main concern is to address the following two questions:

- What do I need a computer system to do for me today?
- What will I need it to do for me in another year or two?

The questionnaire at the end of this guide will help you determine the answers to both questions.

Suggestions

Consider the type of computer most available on campus. Some schools favor Apple computers; others favor Windows-based computers. If you own a system that's incompatible with most computers on campus, you may be stuck if your computer breaks down.

Look ahead and determine whether your major requires a computer. Business and engineering students may find one a necessity; physical education and drama majors may not. Your major also may determine the kind of computer that's best. A journalism major may want a Windows-based notebook. An architecture major may want a powerful desktop Macintosh with a laser printer that can produce elaborate drawings. Ask your academic advisor for some recommendations.

Example

Suppose you are a college student beginning your sophomore year, with no major declared. Looking at the courses you will likely take this year, you decide you will probably need a computer mainly for word processing. That is, you need a system that will help you write short (10- to 20-page) papers for a variety of courses.

By this time next year, however, you may be an accounting major. Having talked to some juniors and seniors, you find that courses in this major, such as financial accounting, will require you to use elaborate spreadsheets. Or maybe you will be a fine arts or architecture major. Then you may be required to submit projects for which drawing and painting desktop publishing software would be helpful.

STEP 2

How Much Money Do I Have to Spend on a Computer System?

When you buy your first computer, you are not necessarily buying your last. Thus, you can think about spending just the bare-bones amount for a system that meets your needs while in college. Then you might plan to get another system later on.

You know the amount of money you have to spend. Your main concern is to answer the following two questions:

- How much am I prepared to spend on a computer system today?
- How much am I prepared to spend in another year or two?

The questionnaire at the end of this guide asks you this.

Visual Summary The Buyer's Guide: How to Buy Your Own Microcomputer System

NEEDS

What do I need a computer system to do for me today? In another year or two?

I WISH TO USE THE COMPUTER FOR:

	Today	1–2 years
Word processing—writing papers, letters, memos, or reports	❑	❑
Business or financial applications—balance sheets, sales projections, expense budgets, or accounting problems	❑	❑
Record keeping and sorting—research bibliographies, scientific data, or address files	❑	❑
Graphic presentations of business, scientific, or social science data	❑	❑
Online information retrieval to campus networks, service providers, or the Internet	❑	❑
Publications, design, or drawing for printed newsletters, architectural drawing, or graphic arts	❑	❑
Multimedia for video games, viewing, creating, presenting, or research	❑	❑
Other (specify): _____	❑	❑

BUDGET

How much am I prepared to spend on a system today? In another year or two?

I CAN SPEND:

	Today	1–2 years
Under $500	❑	❑
Up to $1,000	❑	❑
Up to $1,500	❑	❑
Up to $2,000	❑	❑
Up to $2,500	❑	❑
Over $3,000	❑	❑
(specify): _____		

Buying a Microcomputer System	
Step	**Questions**
1	*My needs:* What do I need a computer system to do for me today? In another year or two?
2	*My budget:* How much am I prepared to spend on a system today? In another year or two?
3	*My software:* What kind of software will best serve my needs today? In another year or two?
4	*My hardware:* What kind of hardware will best serve my needs today? In another year or two?

To help clarify your thinking about buying a microcomputer system, complete the questionnaire by checking the appropriate boxes.

SOFTWARE

What kinds of software will best serve my needs today? In another year or two?

The Application Software I Need Includes:

	Today	1–2 years
Word processing—Word, WordPerfect, or other (specify): _____	❏	❏
Spreadsheet—Excel, iWork's Numbers, or other (specify): _____	❏	❏
Database—Access, Paradox, or other (specify): _____	❏	❏
Presentation graphics—PowerPoint, Freelance, CorelPresentations, or other (specify): _____	❏	❏
Browsers—Mozilla Firefox, Apple Safari, Microsoft Internet Explorer, or other (specify): _____	❏	❏
Other—integrated packages, software suites, graphics, multimedia, Web authoring, CAD/CAM, other (specify): _____	❏	❏

The System Software I Need:

	Today	1–2 years
Windows 7	❏	❏
Windows Vista	❏	❏
Mac OS	❏	❏
UNIX	❏	❏
Other (specify): _____	❏	❏

HARDWARE

What kinds of hardware will best serve my needs today? In another year or two?

The Hardware I Need Includes:

	Today	1–2 years
Microprocessor—Celeron, Apple G4, other (specify): _____	❏	❏
Memory—(specify amount): _____	❏	❏
Monitor—size (specify): _____	❏	❏
Optical disc drive—CD-ROM, DVD-ROM (specify type, speed, and capacity): _____	❏	❏
Hard-disk drive—(specify capacity): _____	❏	❏
Portable computer—laptop, notebook, netbook, personal digital assistant (specify): _____	❏	❏
Printer—ink-jet, laser, color (specify): _____	❏	❏
Other—modem, network card, speakers, fax, surge protector (specify): _____	❏	❏

The Upgrader's Guide How to Upgrade Your Microcomputer System

If you own a microcomputer, chances are that your machine is not the latest and greatest. Microcomputers are always getting better—more powerful and faster. While that is a good thing, it can be frustrating trying to keep up.

What can you do? If you have lots of money, you can simply buy a new one. Another alternative is to upgrade or add new components to increase the power and speed of your current microcomputer. You probably can increase your system's performance at a fraction of the cost of a new one.

THREE STEPS IN UPGRADING A MICROCOMPUTER SYSTEM

The following is not intended to detail specific hardware upgrades. Rather, it is intended to help you clarify your thinking about what you need and can afford.

The three steps in upgrading a microcomputer system are presented on the following pages. Each step begins by asking a key question and then provides some suggestions or factors to consider when responding to the question.

STEP 1

Is It Time to Upgrade?

Almost any upgrade you make will provide some benefit; the trick is determining if it is worth the monetary investment. It is rarely practical to rebuild an older computer system into a newer model piece by piece. The cost of a complete upgrade typically far exceeds the purchase price of a new system. But if your system is just a piece or two away from meeting your needs, an upgrade may be in order.

Clearly defining what you hope to gain with an upgrade of some of your system's hardware will enable you to make the most relevant and cost-effective selections. Before deciding what to buy, decide what goal you hope to accomplish. Do you want to speed up your computer's performance? Do you need more space to save your files? Do you want to add a new component such as a DVD-RW drive?

Suggestions

A good place to start is to look at the documentation on the packaging of any software you use or plan to use. Software manufacturers clearly label the minimum requirements to use their products. These requirements are usually broken down into categories that relate to specific pieces of hardware. For instance, how much RAM (random access memory) does a new program require? How much hard disk space is needed? Keep in mind these ratings are typically the bare minimum. If your system comes very close to the baseline in any particular category, you should still consider an upgrade.

Another thing to investigate is whether there is a software solution that will better serve your needs. For instance, if you are looking to enhance performance or make more room on your hard disk, there are diagnostic and disk optimization utility programs that may solve your problem. In Chapter 5, we discuss a variety of utility programs, such as Norton SystemWorks, that monitor, evaluate, and enhance system performance and storage capacity.

Typical objectives of an upgrade are to improve system performance, increase storage capacity, or add new technology.

STEP 2

What Should I Upgrade?

Once you have clearly defined your objectives, the focus shifts to identifying specific components to meet those objectives.

Suggestions

If your objective is to improve performance, three components to consider are RAM, the microprocessor, and expansion cards. If your objective is to increase storage capacity, two components to consider are hard-disk drive and optical disc drive. If you are adding new technology, consider the capability of your current system to support new devices.

Performance

If you want to increase the speed of your computer, consider increasing the amount of RAM. In most cases, this upgrade is relatively inexpensive and will yield the highest performance result per dollar invested. How much your system's performance will increase depends on how much RAM you start with, the size of programs you run, and how often you run large programs.

Another way to increase speed is to replace your system's microprocessor. Processor speed is measured in gigahertz (GHz). This rating is not a direct measurement of how fast the processor works, but rather it gives you a general idea of how it compares to other processors. (Computing magazines such as *PC World* often publish articles comparing the relative effectiveness of different processors.) The concept behind a microprocessor upgrade is simple: A faster processor will process faster. This is often an expensive upgrade and not as cost-effective as increasing RAM.

If you are looking at upgrading for a specific type of application, perhaps an expansion card is your answer. Expansion cards connect to slots on the system board, provide specialized support, and often free up resources and increase overall system performance. For example, if you run graphics-intensive programs, such as a drafting program or a video game, a video-card upgrade may be a good buy. An upgraded video card can be used to support higher resolution displays, handle all video data, and speed up overall system performance.

Storage Capacity

It's not hard to know when it's time to upgrade your storage capacity. If you frequently have to delete old files to make way for new ones, then it is probably time for more space. A larger or an additional hard drive is usually the solution. Two things to consider when comparing new hard drives are (1) size, which is usually rated in gigabytes (GB) of data the drive can hold, and (2) seek time, which is a rating of the average time it takes the drive to access any particular piece of data.

If you are storing a lot of data that you no longer use, such as old term papers, you might consider adding a high-capacity floppy disk drive. This is usually cheaper and is a good way to archive and transport data. Access time is slower than from a hard drive, so this is an option best suited for infrequently used data or for backing up data.

New Technology

Perhaps you are not looking to modify existing hardware but would like to add a new device. Examples include large high-resolution monitors, DVD-RW drives, and high-speed printers.

The key consideration is whether the new device will work with your existing hardware. The requirements for these devices are typically printed on the outside packaging or available at the product's Web site. If not, then refer to the product's operating manuals. Obviously, if your current system cannot support the new technology, you need to evaluate the cost of the new device plus the necessary additional hardware upgrades.

STEP 3

Who Should Do the Upgrade?

Once you've decided that the cost of the upgrade is justified and you know what you want to upgrade, the final decision is who is going to do it. Basically, there are two choices. You can either do it yourself or pay for professional installation.

Suggestions

The easiest way, and many times the best way, is to have a professional perform the upgrade. If you select this option, be sure to include the cost of installation in your analysis. If you have had some prior hardware experience or are a bit adventurous, you may want to save some money and do it yourself.

Visit a few computer stores that carry the upgrades you have selected. Most stores that provide the parts will install them as well. Talk with their technical people, describe your system (better yet, bring your system unit to the store), and determine the cost of professional installation. If you are thinking of doing it yourself, ask for their advice. Ask if they will provide assistance if you need it.

If you decide to have the components professionally installed, get the total price in writing and inquire about any guarantees that might exist. Before leaving your system, be sure that it is carefully tagged with your name and address. After the service has been completed, pay by credit card and thoroughly test the upgrade. If it does not perform satisfactorily, contact the store and ask for assistance. If the store's service is not satisfactory, you may be able to have your credit card company help to mediate any disputes.

Visual Summary The Upgrader's Guide: How to Upgrade Your Microcomputer System

Upgrading a Microcomputer System	
Step	Questions
1	*Needs:* Is it time to upgrade? What do I need that my current system is unable to deliver?
2	*Analysis:* What should I upgrade? Will the upgrade meet my needs and will it be cost-effective?
3	*Action:* Who should do the upgrade? Should I pay a professional or do it myself?

NEEDS

Is it time to upgrade? What do I need that my current system is unable to deliver?

I Am Considering an Upgrade to:

❏ **Improve performance because**

  ❏ My programs run too slowly

  ❏ I cannot run some programs I need

❏ **Increase storage capacity because**

  ❏ I don't have enough space to store all my files

  ❏ I don't have enough space to install new programs

  ❏ I need a secure place to back up important files

  ❏ I'd like to download large files from the Internet

❏ **Add new technology**

  ❏ DVD-RW

  ❏ High-performance monitor

  ❏ Printer

  ❏ TV tuner card

  ❏ Enhanced video card

  ❏ Enhanced sound card

  ❏ Other _____

ANALYSIS

What should I upgrade? Will the upgrade meet my needs and will it be cost-effective?

I Will Improve:

❏ **Performance by**

  ❏ Adding random-access memory (RAM)

    Current RAM (MB) _____

    Upgrade to _____

    Cost $ _____

    Expected improvement _____

    Other factors _____

  ❏ Replacing the current microprocessor

    Current processor _____

    Upgrade processor _____

    Cost $ _____

    Expected improvement _____

    Other factors _____

  ❏ Adding an expansion card

    Type _____

    Purpose _____

    Cost $ _____

    Expected improvement _____

    Other factors _____

❏ **Storage capacity by**

  ❏ Adding a hard-disk drive

    Current size (GB) _____

    Upgrade size (GB) _____

    Cost $ _____

    Expected improvement _____

    Other factors _____

❏ Adding a Zip disk drive

Upgrade size (GB) _____

Cost $ _____

Type _____

Expected improvement _____

Other factors _____

❏ **Functionality by adding**

New technology _____

System requirements _____

Cost $ _____

Expected improvement _____

Other factors _____

To help clarify your thinking about upgrading a microcomputer system, complete the questionnaire by checking the appropriate boxes.

ACTION

Who should do the upgrade? Should I do it myself or should I pay a professional?

The Two Choices are:

❏ **Professional installation**

The easiest way, and many times the best way, is to have a professional perform the upgrade. If you select this option, be sure to include the cost of installation in your analysis. Pay with a credit card, and make sure your system is tagged with your name and address before you part with it.

❏ **Do-it-yourself installation**

If you have had some prior hardware experience or are a bit adventurous, you may want to save some money and do it yourself. Avoid touching sensitive electronic parts and be sure to ground yourself by touching an unpainted metal surface in your computer.

handles its own communications control. There is no host computer or file server.

Bus width: The number of bits traveling simultaneously down a bus is the bus width.

Business suite: *See* Productivity suites.

Business-to-business (B2B): A type of electronic commerce that involves the sale of a product or service from one business to another. This is typically a manufacturer–supplier relationship.

Business-to-consumer (B2C): A type of electronic commerce that involves the sale of a product or service to the general public or end users.

Button: A special area you can click to make links that "navigate" through a presentation.

Byte: Unit consisting of eight bits. There are 256 possible bit combinations in a byte and each byte represents one character.

C

Cable: Cords used to connect input and output devices to the system unit.

Cable modem: Allows all digital communication, which is a speed of 27 million bps.

Cable service: Service provided by cable television companies using existing television cables.

Cache memory: Area of random-access memory (RAM) set aside to store the most frequently accessed information. Cache memory improves processing by acting as a temporary high-speed holding area between memory and the CPU, allowing the computer to detect which information in RAM is most frequently used.

Capacity: Capacity is how much data a particular storage medium can hold and another characteristic of secondary storage.

Carder: Criminal who steals credit cards over the Internet.

Carrier package: The material that chips are mounted on which then plugs into sockets on the system board.

Cathode-ray tube (CRT) monitor: Desktop-type monitor built in the same way as a television set. The most common type of monitor for office and home use. These monitors are typically placed directly on the system unit or on top of a desk.

CD: *See* Compact disc.

CD-R: Stands for CD-recordable. This optical disc can be written to only once. After that it can be read many times without deterioration but cannot be written on or erased. Used to create custom music CDs and to archive data.

CD-ROM (compact disc–read only memory): Optical disc that allows data to be read but not recorded. Used to distribute large databases, references, and software application packages.

CD-RW (compact disc rewriteable): A reusable, optical disc that is not permanently altered when data is recorded. Used to create and edit large multimedia presentations.

Cell: The space created by the intersection of a vertical column and a horizontal row within a worksheet in a program like Microsoft Excel. A cell can contain text or numeric entries.

Cellular service: Links car phones and portable phones.

Center for European Nuclear Research (CERN): In Switzerland, where the Web was introduced in 1992.

Central processing unit (CPU): The part of the computer that holds data and program instructions for processing the data. The CPU consists of the control unit and the arithmetic-logic unit. In a microcomputer, the CPU is on a single electronic component called a microprocessor chip.

Character: A single letter, number, or special character, such as a punctuation mark or $.

Character effect: Changes the appearance of font characters by using bold, italic, shadow, and colors.

Character encoding standards: Assign unique sequence of bits to each character.

Chart: Displaying numerical data in a worksheet as a pie chart or a bar chart, making it easier to understand.

Checklist: In analyzing data, a list of questions helps guide the systems analyst and end user through key issues for the present system.

Child node: A node one level below the node being considered in a hierarchical database or network. *See* Parent node.

Chip: A tiny circuit board etched on a small square of sandlike material called silicon. A chip is also called a silicon chip, semiconductor, or integrated circuit.

Citation: The source of information used in developing a report.

Clarity: Indicated by the resolution, or number of pixels, on a monitor. The greater the resolution, the better the clarity.

Class: In an object-oriented database, classes are similar objects grouped together.

Client: A node that requests and uses resources available from other nodes. Typically, a client is a user's microcomputer.

Client/server network: Network in which one powerful computer coordinates and supplies services to all other nodes on the network. Server nodes coordinate and supply specialized services, and client nodes request the services.

Clip art: Graphic illustrations representing a wide variety of topics.

Clock speed: Also called clock rate. It is measured in gigahertz, or billions of beats per second. The faster the clock speed, the faster the computer can process information and execute instructions.

Coaxial cable: High-frequency transmission cable that replaces the multiple wires of telephone lines with a single solid-copper core. It is used to deliver television signals as well as to connect computers in a network.

Code: Writing a program using the appropriate computer language.

Code review: *See* Desk checking.

Coding: Actual writing of a computer program, using a programming language.

Cold boot: Starting the computer after it has been turned off.

Column: Using Microsoft Excel, for example, a vertical block of cells one cell wide all the way down the worksheet.

Combination key: Keys such as the Ctrl key that perform an action when held down in combination with another key.

Commercial database: Enormous database an organization develops to cover certain particular objects. Access to this type of database is usually offered for a fee or subscription. Also known as data bank and informational utility.

Common data item: In a relational database, all related tables must have a common data item or key field.

Common interest site: A site that brings together individuals that share common interests or hobbies.

Communication channel: The actual connecting medium that carries the message between sending and receiving devices. This medium can be a physical wire, cable, or wireless connection.

Communication device: Computer systems that communicate with other computer systems using modems. For example, it modifies computer output into a form that can be transmitted across standard telephone lines.

Communication system: Electronic system that transmits data over communication lines from one location to another.

Compact disc (CD): Widely used optical disc format. It holds 650 MB (megabytes) to 1 GB (gigabyte) of data on one side of the CD.

Compact disc–read only memory: *See* CD-ROM.

Compact disc rewriteable: *See* CD-RW.

Company database: Also called shared database. Stored on a mainframe, users throughout the company have access to the database through their microcomputers linked by a network.

Compiler: Software that converts the programmer's procedural-language program (source code) into machine language (object code). This object code can then be saved and run later.

Computer-aided design/computer-aided manufacturing (CAD/CAM) system: Knowledge work systems that run programs to integrate the design and manufacturing activities. CAD/CAM is widely used in manufacturing automobiles.

Computer-aided software engineering (CASE) tool: A type of software development tool that helps provide some automation and assistance in program design, coding, and testing. *See* Automated design tool.

Computer competency: Becoming proficient in computer-related skills.

Computer crime: Illegal action in which a perpetrator uses special knowledge of computer technology. Criminals

may be employees, outside users, hackers and crackers, and organized crime members.

Computer ethics: Guidelines for the morally acceptable use of computers in our society.

Computer Fraud and Abuse Act: Law allowing prosecution of unauthorized access to computers and databases.

Computer monitoring software: The most invasive and dangerous type of spyware. These programs record every activity made on your computer, including credit card numbers, bank account numbers, and e-mail messages.

Computer network: Communications system connecting two or more computers and their peripheral devices to exchange information and share resources.

Computer support specialist: Specialists include technical writers, computer trainers, computer technicians, and help-desk specialists who provide technical support to customers and other users.

Computer technician: Specialist who installs hardware and software and troubleshoots problems for users.

Computer trainer: Computer professional who provides classes to instruct users.

Computer virus: Destructive programs that can come in e-mail attachments and spam.

Concatenation structure: Logic structure in which one program statement follows another.

Connectivity: Capability of the microcomputer to use information from the world beyond one's desk. Data and information can be sent over telephone or cable lines and through the air so that computers can talk to each other and share information.

Consumer-to-consumer (C2C): A type of electronic commerce that involves individuals selling to individuals.

Content-markup language: Also known as markup language. Uses symbols, words, and phrases that instruct a computer on how to display information to the user. For example, HTML is a content-markup language used to display Web pages.

Content template: Includes suggested content for each slide in a PowerPoint presentation.

Contextual tab: A type of tab found in Microsoft Word that only appears when needed and anticipates the next operations to be performed by the user.

Control unit: Section of the CPU that tells the rest of the computer how to carry out program instructions.

Conversion: Also known as systems implementation; four approaches to conversion: direct, parallel, pilot, and phased. *See* Systems implementation.

Cookies: Programs that record information on Web site visitors.

Coprocessor: Specialized processing chip designed to improve specific computer operations, such as the graphics coprocessor.

Copyright: A legal concept that gives content creators the right to control use and distribution of their work.

Cordless mouse: A battery-powered mouse that typically uses radio waves or infrared light waves to communicate with the system unit. Also known as wireless mouse.

Cracker: One who gains unauthorized access to a computer system for malicious purposes.

Cryptographer: Designs, tests, and researches encryption procedures.

Cryptography: The science of disguising and revealing encrypted information.

Cybercash: *See* Digital cash.

Cylinder: Hard disks store and organize files using tracks, sectors, and cylinders. A cylinder runs through each track of a stack of platters. Cylinders differentiate files stored on the same track and sector of different platters.

Cynic: Individual who feels that the idea of using a microcomputer is overrated and too troublesome to learn.

D

Dashboard Widgets: A collection of specialized programs on the Mac OS X operating system that constantly updates and displays information such as stock prices and weather information.

Data: Raw, unprocessed facts that are input to a computer system that will give compiled information when the computer processes those facts. Data is also defined as facts or observations about people, places, things, and events.

Data administration subsystem: Helps manage the overall database, including maintaining security, providing disaster recovery support, and monitoring the overall performance of database operations.

Data bank: *See* Commercial database.

Data cube: A multidimensional data model. *Also see* Multidimensional database.

Data definition subsystem: This system defines the logical structure of the database by using a data dictionary.

Data dictionary: Dictionary containing a description of the structure of data in a database.

Data entry worker: Inputs customer information, lists, and other types of data.

Data flow diagram: Diagram showing data or information flow within an information system.

Data integrity: Database characteristics relating to the consistency and accuracy of data.

Data maintenance: Maintaining data includes adding new data, deleting old data, and editing existing data.

Data manipulation subsystem: Provides tools to maintain and analyze data.

Data mining: Technique of searching data warehouses for related information and patterns.

Data processing system (DPS): Transaction processing system that keeps track of routine operations and records these events in a database. Also called transaction processing system (TPS).

Data projector: Specialized device, similar to slide projector, that connects to microcomputers and projects computer output.

Data redundancy: A common database problem in which data is duplicated and stored in different files.

Data security: Protection of software and data from unauthorized tampering or damage.

Data warehouse: Data collected from a variety of internal and external databases and stored in a database called a data warehouse. Data mining is then used to search these databases.

Data worker: Person involved with the distribution and communication of information, such as secretaries and clerks.

Database: A collection of related information, like employee names, addresses, and phone numbers. It is organized so that a computer program can quickly select the desired pieces of information and display them for you.

Database administrator (DBA): Uses database management software to determine the most efficient way to organize and access data.

Database file: File containing highly structured and organized data created by database management programs.

Database management system (DBMS): To organize, manage, and retrieve data. DBMS programs have five subsystems: DBMS engine, data definition, data manipulation, applications generation, and data administration. An example of a database management system is Microsoft Access. *See* Database manager.

Database manager: Software package used to set up, or structure, a database such as an inventory list of supplies. It also provides tools to edit, enter, and retrieve data from the database.

Database model: Defines rules and standards for all data in a database. There are five database models: hierarchical, network, relational, multidimensional, and object-oriented. For example, Access uses the relational data model.

DBMS engine: Provides a bridge between the logical view of data and the physical view of data.

Debugging: Programmer's word for testing and then eliminating errors in a program. Programming errors are of two types: syntax and logic errors.

Decision model: The decision model gives the decision support system its analytical capabilities. There are three types of models included in the decision model: tactical, operational, and strategic models.

Decision support system (DSS): Flexible analysis tool that helps managers make decisions about unstructured problems, such as effects of events and trends outside the organization.

Decision table: Table showing decision rules that apply when certain conditions occur and what action should take place as a result.

Demand report: A demand report is produced on request. An example is a report on the numbers and types of jobs held by women and minorities done at the request of the government.

Demodulation: Process performed by a modem in converting analog signals to digital signals.

Denial of service (DoS) attack: A variant virus in which Web sites are overwhelmed with data and users are unable to access the Web site. Unlike a worm that self-replicates, a DoS attack floods a computer or network with requests for information and data.

Density: Refers to how tightly the bits (electromagnetic charges) can be packed next to one another on a floppy disk.

Design template: Provides professionally selected combinations of color schemes, slide layouts, and special effects for presentation graphics.

Desk checking: Process of checking out a computer program by studying a printout of the program line by line, looking for syntax and logic errors.

Desktop: The screen that is displayed on the monitor when the computer starts up. All items and icons on the screen are considered to be on your desktop and are used to interact with the computer.

Desktop computer: Computer small enough to fit on top of or along the side of a desk and yet too big to carry around.

Desktop operating systems: *See* Stand-alone operating system.

Desktop publisher: One who creates and formats publication-ready material.

Desktop publishing program: Program that allows you to mix text and graphics to create publications of professional quality.

Desktop system unit: A system unit that typically contains the system's electronic components and selected secondary storage devices. Input and output devices, such as the mouse, keyboard, and monitor, are located outside the system unit.

Device driver: Every device that is connected to the computer has a special program associated with it called a device driver that allows communication between the operating system and the device.

Diagnostic program: *See* Troubleshooting program.

Dialog box: Provides additional information and requests user input.

Dial-up service: Method of accessing the Internet using a high-speed modem and standard telephone lines.

Dictionary attack: Uses software to try thousands of common words sequentially in an attempt to gain unauthorized access to a user's account.

Digital: Computers are digital machines because they can only understand 1s and 0s. It is either on or off. For example, a digital watch states the exact time on the face, whereas an analog watch has the second hand moving in constant motion as it tells the time.

Digital camera: Similar to a traditional camera except that images are recorded digitally in the camera's memory rather than on film.

Digital cash: Currency for Internet purchases. Buyers purchase digital cash from a third party (a bank that specializes in electronic currency) by transferring funds from their banks.

Digital media player: Also known as digital music player; a specialized device for storing, transferring, and playing audio files.

Digital Millennium Copyright Act: Law that makes it legal for a program owner to make only his or her own backup copies of a software program. However, it is illegal for those copies to be resold or given away.

Digital music player: Also known as digital media player; a specialized device for storing, transferring, and playing audio files.

Digital rights management (DRM): Encompasses various technologies that control access to electronic media and files.

Digital signal: Computers can only understand digital signals. Before processing can occur within the system unit, a conversion must occur from what we understand (analog) to what the system unit can electronically process (digital). *See* Analog signal.

Digital subscriber line (DSL): Provides high-speed connection using existing telephone lines.

Digital subscriber line (DSL) service: Service provided by telephone companies using existing telephone lines to provide high-speed connections.

Digital versatile disc (DVD): A type of optical disc similar to CD-ROMs except that more data can be packed into the same amount of space. *Also see* DVD (digital versatile disc).

Digital video camera: Input device that records motion digitally.

Digital video disc: *See* DVD (digital versatile disc).

DIMM (dual in-line memory module): An expansion module used to add memory to the system board.

Direct access: A fast approach to external storage, provided by disks, where information is not in a set sequence.

Direct approach: Approach for systems implementation whereby the old system is simply abandoned for the new system.

Directory search: A search engine option that provides a directory or list of categories or topics to choose from, such as Arts & Humanities, Business & Economics, or Computers & Internet, that help you narrow your search until a list of Web sites appears.

Directory server: A specialized server that manages resources such as user accounts for an entire network.

Disaster recovery plan: Plan used by large organizations describing ways to continue operations following a disaster until normal computer operations can be restored.

Disk: *See* Floppy disk.

Disk caching: Method of improving hard-disk performance by anticipating data needs. Frequently used data is read from the hard disk into memory (cache). When needed, data is then accessed directly from memory, which has a much faster transfer rate than from the hard disk. Increases performance by as much as 30 percent.

Disk Cleanup: A Windows troubleshooting utility that eliminates nonessential files.

Disk Defragmenter: A Windows utility that optimizes disk performance by eliminating unnecessary fragments and rearranging files.

Display screen: *See* Monitor.

Distributed database: Database that can be made accessible through a variety of communications networks, which allow portions of the database to be located in different places.

Distributed processing network: System in which computing power is located and shared at different locations.

DO UNTIL structure: Loop structure in programming that appears at the end of a loop. The DO UNTIL loop means that the loop statements will be executed at least once. In other words, this program tells you to DO option one UNTIL it is no longer true.

DO WHILE structure: Loop structure in programming that appears at the beginning of a loop. The DO WHILE loop will keep executing as long as there is information to be processed. For example, DO option one WHILE (or as long as) option one remains true.

Document: Any kind of text material.

Document file: File created by a word processor to save documents such as letters, research papers, and memos.

Document scanner: Similar to a flatbed scanner except that it can quickly scan multipage documents. It automatically feeds one page of a document at a time through a scanning surface.

Document theme: Built-in sets of colors, fonts, and effects that can be quickly applied to an entire presentation.

Documentation: Written descriptions and procedures about a program and how to use it. *See* Program documentation.

Domain name: The second part of the URL; it is the name of the server where the resource is located. For example, www.mtv.com.

Domain name server (DNS): Internet addressing method that assigns names and numbers to people and computers. Because the numeric IP addresses are difficult to remember, the DNS server was developed to automatically convert text-based addresses to numeric IP addresses.

Dot-matrix printer: A type of printer that forms characters and images using a series of small pins on a print head. Used where high-quality output is not required.

Dot pitch: Distance between each pixel. The lower the dot pitch, the shorter the distance between pixels, and the higher the clarity of images produced.

Dots-per-inch (dpi): Printer resolution is measured in dpi. The higher the dpi, the better the quality of images produced.

Downloadable office suite: Office suite that is offered for free as downloadable software and then is stored on your desktop computer just like a traditional office suite.

Downloading: Process of transferring information from a remote computer to the computer one is using.

Drawing program: Program used to help create artwork for publications. *See* Illustration program.

Driver: *See* Device driver.

DS3: Provides support for very high-speed, all-digital transmission for large corporations.

DSL: *See* Digital subscriber line.

Dual-scan monitor: *See* Passive-matrix monitor.

DVD (digital versatile disc or digital video disc): Similar to CD-ROMs except that more data can be packed into the same amount of space. DVD drives can store 4.7 GB to 17 GB on a single DVD disc or 17 times the capacity of CDs.

DVD player: Also known as DVD-ROM drives. *See* DVD.

DVD–R (DVD recordable): A DVD with a write-once format that differs slightly from the format of DVD+R. Typically used to create permanent archives for large amounts of data and to record videos.

DVD+R (DVD recordable): A DVD with a write-once format that differs slightly from the format of DVD−R. Typically used to create permanent archives for large amounts of data and to record videos.

DVD-RAM (DVD random-access memory): A high-capacity, maximum-performance disc that allows the user to read the information, write over it, and erase the data if necessary. Used like a floppy disk to copy, delete files, and run programs. It has up to 8 times the storage capacity of a CD and also can be used to read CD and DVD formats.

DVD-ROM (DVD–read-only memory): Used to distribute full-length feature films with theater-quality video and sound. Also known as DVD players. Are read-only.

DVD–RW (DVD rewriteable): A type of reusable DVD disc that is more flexible than the DVD-RAM. DVD–RW is able to create and read CD discs along with creating and editing large-scale multimedia presentations.

DVD+RW (DVD rewriteable): Another DVD format to record and erase repeatedly. Able to create and read CD discs along with creating and editing large-scale multimedia presentations.

DVI (Digital Video Interface) port: A type of port that provides a connection to a digital monitor.

E

EBCDIC (Extended Binary Coded Decimal Interchange Code): Binary coding scheme that is a standard for minicomputers and mainframe computers.

E-book reader: Handheld, book-sized devices that display text and graphics. Using content downloaded from the Web or special cartridges, these devices are used to read newspapers, magazines, and books.

E-commerce: Buying and selling goods over the Internet.

E-learning: A Web application that allows one to take educational courses online.

E-mail: Communicate with anyone in the world who has an Internet address or e-mail account with a system connected to the Internet. You can include a text message, graphics, photos, and file attachments.

E-paper: Requires power only when changing pages, and not the entire time a page is displayed on the screen.

Economic feasibility: Comparing the costs of a new system to the benefits it promises.

Editing: Features that modify a document such as using a thesaurus, find and replace, or spell check.

Electronic commerce (e-commerce): Buying and selling goods over the Internet.

Electronic mail: Transmission of electronic messages over the Internet. Also known as e-mail.

Electronic paper: *See* e-paper.

Electronic profile: Using publicly and privately available databases, information resellers create electronic profiles, which are highly detailed and personalized descriptions of individuals.

Embedded operating system: An operating system that is completely stored within the ROM (read-only memory) of the device that it is in; used for handheld computers and smaller devices like PDAs.

Encryption: Coding information so that only the user can read or otherwise use it.

Encryption key: A binary number used to gain access to encrypted information.

End user: Person who uses microcomputers or has access to larger computers.

Enterprise storage system: Using mass storage devices, a strategy is designed for organizations to promote efficient and safe use of data across the networks within their organizations.

Entity: In an object-oriented database, a person, place, thing, or event that is to be described.

Erasable optical disc: Optical disc on which the disk drive can write information and also erase and rewrite information. Also known as CD-RW or compact disc rewriteable.

Ergonomic keyboard: Keyboard arrangement that is not rectangular and has a palm rest, which is designed to alleviate wrist strain.

Ethernet: Otherwise known as Ethernet bus or Ethernet LAN. The Ethernet bus is the pathway or arterial to which all nodes (PCs, file servers, print servers, Web servers, etc.) are connected. All of this is connected to a local area network (LAN) or a wide area network (WAN). *See* Bus network.

Ethernet cable: Twisted-pair cable commonly used in networks and to connect a variety of components to the system unit.

Ethernet port: A high-speed networking port that allows multiple computers to be connected for sharing files or for high-speed Internet access.

Ethics: Standards of moral conduct.

Exception report: Report that calls attention to unusual events.

Executive information system (EIS): Sophisticated software that can draw together data from an organization's databases in meaningful patterns and highly summarized forms.

Executive support system (ESS): *See* Executive information system.

Expansion bus: Connects the CPU to slots on the system board. There are different types of expansion buses such as industry standard architecture (ISA), peripheral component interconnect (PCI), accelerated graphics port (AGP), universal serial bus (USB), and FireWire buses. *See* System bus.

Expansion card: Optional device that plugs into a slot inside the system unit to expand the computers' abilities. Ports on the system board allow cables to be connected from the expansion board to devices outside the system unit.

Expansion slots: Openings on a system board. Users can insert optional devices, known as expansion cards, into these slots, allowing users to expand their systems. *See* Expansion card.

Expert system: Computer program that provides advice to decision makers who would otherwise rely on human experts. It's a type of artificial intelligence that uses a database to provide assistance to users.

ExpressCard: Technology replacing the PC Card to provide a direct connection to the system bus. *Also see* PC Card.

External data: Data gathered from outside an organization. Examples are data provided by market research firms.

External hard drive: Uses the same technology as an internal hard disk but is used primarily to complement an internal hard disk by providing additional storage. They are typically connected to a USB or FireWire port on the system unit and are easily removed.

Extranet: Private network that connects more than one organization.

F

Family Educational Rights Privacy Act (FERPA): A federal law that restricts disclosure of educational records.

Fax machine: A device for sending and receiving images over telephone lines.

Fiber-optic cable: Special transmission cable made of glass tubes that are immune to electronic interference. Data is transmitted through fiber-optic cables in the form of pulses of light.

Field: Each column of information within a record is called a field. A field contains related information on a specific item like employee names within a company department.

Fifth-generation language (5GL): Computer language that incorporates the concept of artificial intelligence to allow direct human communication.

File: A collection of related records that can store data and programs. For example, the payroll file would include payroll information (records) for all of the employees (entities).

File compression: Process of reducing the storage requirements for a file.

File compression program: Utility programs that reduce the size of files so they require less storage on the computer and can be sent more efficiently over the Internet. Examples of such programs are WinZip and Wizard.

File decompression: Process of expanding a compressed file.

File server: Dedicated computer with large storage capacity providing users access to shared folders or fast storage and retrieval of information used in that business.

File transfer protocol (FTP): Internet service for uploading and downloading files.

Filter: (1) A filter blocks access to selected Web sites. (2) A filter will locate or display records from a table that fit a set of conditions or criteria when using programs like Excel.

Find and replace: An editing tool that finds a selected word or phrase and replaces it with another. Click *edit*, *find*.

Firewall: Security hardware and software. All communications into and out of an organization pass through a special security computer, called a proxy server, to protect all systems against external threats.

FireWire bus: Operates much like USB buses on the system board but at higher speeds.

FireWire port: Used to connect high-speed printers, and even video cameras, to system unit.

Flash: An interactive animation program from Adobe that is usually full screen and highly dynamic, displaying moving text or complicated interactive features.

Flash drive: *See* USB drive.

Flash memory: RAM chips that retain data even when power is disrupted. Flash memory is an example of solid-state storage and is typically used to store digitized images and record MP3 files.

Flash memory card: A solid-state storage device widely used in notebook computers. Flash memory also is used in a variety of specialized input devices to capture and transfer data to desktop computers.

Flat-panel monitor: Or liquid crystal display (LCD) monitor. These monitors are much thinner than CRTs and can be used for desktop systems as well.

Flatbed scanner: An input device similar to a copying machine.

Floppy disk: Flat, circular piece of magnetically treated mylar plastic that rotates within a jacket. A floppy disk is 3½ inches and holds 1.44 MB of information. It is a portable or removable secondary storage device.

Floppy disk drive (FDD): A drive that stores data and programs by altering the electromagnetic charges on the disk's surface.

Folder: A named area on a disk that is used to store related subfolders and files.

Font: Also known as typeface, is a set of characters with a specific design.

Font size: The height of a character measured in points, with each point being ¹/₇₂ inch.

Form: Electronic forms reflecting the contents of one record or table. Primarily used to enter new records or make changes to existing records.

Format: Features that change the appearance of a document like font, font sizes, character effects, alignment, and bulleted and numbered lists.

Formula: Instructions for calculations in a spreadsheet. It is an equation that performs calculations on the data contained within the cells in a worksheet or spreadsheet.

Fourth-generation language (4GL): Task-oriented languages are designed to solve a specific problem and require little special training on the part of the end user.

Fragmented: Storage technique that breaks up large files and stores the parts wherever space is available in adjacent sectors and clusters.

Freedom of Information Act of 1970: Law giving citizens the right to examine data about them in federal government files, except for information restricted for national security reasons.

Friend: An individual on a list of contacts for an instant messaging server.

Friend-of-a-friend site: A site designed to bring together two people who do not know one another but share a common friend.

Frustrated: Person who feels it is an imposition to have to learn something new like computer technology.

Function: A built-in formula in a spreadsheet that performs calculations automatically.

Fuzzy logic: Used by expert systems to allow users to respond by using qualitative terms, such as *great* and *OK*.

G

Galleries: Feature of Microsoft Office 2007 that simplifies the process of making selections from a list of alternatives by replacing dialog boxes with visual presentations of results.

Game port: Were used to connect video game controllers and joysticks.

General ledger: Activity that produces income statements and balance sheets based on all transactions of a company.

Generations (of programming languages): The five generations are machine languages, assembly languages, procedural languages, problem-oriented languages, and natural languages. *See* Levels.

Global positioning system (GPS): Devices use location information to determine the geographic location of your car, for example.

GPU (graphics processing unit): *See* Graphics coprocessor.

Gramm-Leach-Bliley Act: A law that protects personal financial information.

Grammar checker: In word processing, a tool that identifies poorly worded sentences and incorrect grammar.

Graphical map: Diagram of a Web site's overall design.

Graphical user interface (GUI): Special screen that allows software commands to be issued through the use of graphic symbols (icons) or pull-down menus.

Graphics coprocessor: Designed to handle requirements related to displaying and manipulating 2-D and 3-D graphic images.

Graphics suite: Group of graphics programs offered at a lower cost than if purchased separately, like CorelDraw.

Grid chart: Chart that shows the relationship between input and output documents.

Groups: In Microsoft Word, each tab is organized into groups that contain related items.

Group decision support system (GDSS): System used to support the collective work of a team addressing large problems.

Guest operating system: Operating system that operates on virtual machines.

H

Hacker: Person who gains unauthorized access to a computer system for the fun and challenge of it.

Handheld computer: *See* Personal digital assistant (PDA) and Palm computers.

Handheld computer system unit: Smallest type of system unit, designed to fit into the palm of one hand.

Handwriting recognition software: Translates handwritten notes into a form that the system unit can process.

Hard disk: Enclosed disk drive containing one or more metallic disks. Hard disks use magnetic charges to record data and have large storage capacities and fast retrieval times.

Hardware: Equipment that includes a keyboard, monitor, printer, the computer itself, and other devices that are controlled by software programming.

HD DVD (high-definition DVD): A high-definition disc with a format similar to DVD with a much higher storage capacity. *Also see* DVD.

Head crash: When a read-write head makes contact with the hard disk's surface or particles on its surface, the disk surface becomes scratched and some or all data is destroyed.

Header: A typical e-mail has three elements: header, message, and signature. The header appears first and includes addresses, subject, and attachments.

Headphones: Audio-output devices connected to a sound card in the system unit. The sound card is used to capture as well as play back recorded sound.

Help: A feature in most application software providing options that typically include an index, a glossary, and a search feature to locate reference information about specific commands.

Health Insurance Portability and Accountability Act (HIPAA): A federal law that protects medical records.

Hexadecimal system (hex): Uses 16 digits to represent binary numbers.

Hi def (high definition) disc: The next generation of optical disc, which offers increased storage capacities.

Hierarchical database: Database in which fields or records are structured in nodes. Organized in the shape of a pyramid, and each node is linked directly to the nodes beneath it. Also called one-to-many relationship.

Hierarchical network: *See* Tree network.

High-capacity floppy disk: Also a 3½-inch floppy-disk cartridge. It is thicker than a floppy disk and requires a special drive. For example, Zip disks.

High Definition Multimedia Interface (HDMI): Port that provides high-definition video and audio, making it possible to use a computer as a video jukebox or an HD video recorder.

High-definition television (HDTV): All-digital television that delivers a much clearer and more detailed widescreen picture.

Higher level: Programming languages that are closer to the language humans use.

History file: Created by browser to store information on Web sites visited by your computer system.

Hits: The sites that a search engine returns after running a keyword search, ordered from most likely to least likely to contain the information requested.

Home network: LAN network for homes allowing different computers to share resources, including a common Internet connection.

Home software: *See* Integrated package.

Host: Also called a server or provider, is a large centralized computer.

Host operating system: Operating system that runs on the physical machine.

Household robot: Robot designed to vacuum or scrub floors, mow lawns, patrol the house, or simply provide entertainment.

HTML: *See* Hypertext Markup Language.

HTML editor: *See* Web authoring program.

Hub: The center or central node for other nodes. This device can be a server or a connection point for cables from other nodes.

Human resources: The organizational department that focuses on the hiring, training, and promoting of people, as well as any number of human-centered activities within the organization.

Hybrid network: A combination of different topologies.

Hyperlink: Connection or link to other documents or Web pages that contain related information.

Hypertext Markup Language (HTML): Programming language that creates document files used to display Web pages.

Icons: Graphic objects on the desktop used to represent programs and other files.

Identity theft: The illegal assumption of someone's identity for the purpose of economic gain.

IF-THEN-ELSE structure: Logical selection structure whereby one of two paths is followed according to IF, THEN, and ELSE statements in a program. *See* Selection structure.

IFPS (interactive financial planning system): A 4GL language used for developing financial models.

Illusion of anonymity: The misconception that being selective about disclosing personal information on the Internet can prevent an invasion of personal privacy.

Illustration program: Also known as drawing programs; used to create digital illustrations and modify vector images and thus create line art, 3-D models, and virtual reality.

Image editor: An application for modifying bitmap images.

Image gallery: Libraries of electronic images.

Immersive experience: Allows the user to walk into a virtual reality room or view simulations on a virtual reality wall.

Income statement: A statement that shows a company's financial performance, income, expenses, and the difference between them for a specific time period.

Individual database: Collection of integrated records used mainly by just one person. Also called microcomputer database.

Industrial robot: Robot used in factories to perform a variety of tasks. For example, machines used in automobile plants to do painting and polishing.

Information: Data that has been processed by a computer system.

Information broker: *See* Information reseller.

Information reseller: Also known as information broker. It gathers personal data on people and sells it to direct marketers, fund-raisers, and others, usually for a fee.

Information system: Collection of hardware, software, people, data, and procedures that work together to provide information essential to running an organization.

Information systems manager: Oversees the work of programmers, computer specialists, systems analysts, and other computer professionals.

Information technology (IT): Computer and communication technologies, such as communication links to the Internet, that provide help and understanding to the end user.

Information utility: *See* Commercial database.

Information worker: Employee who creates, distributes, and communicates information.

Infrared: Uses infrared light waves to communicate over short distances. Sometimes referred to as line-of-sight communication because light waves can only travel in a straight line.

Infrared Data Association (IrDA) port: A wireless mechanism for transferring data between devices using infrared light waves.

Ink-jet printer: Printer that sprays small droplets of ink at high speed onto the surface of the paper, producing letter-quality images, and can print in color.

Input device: Piece of equipment that translates data into a form a computer can process. The most common input devices are the keyboard and the mouse.

Instant messaging (IM): A program allowing communication and collaboration for direct, "live," connections over the Internet between two or more people.

Integrated circuit: *See* Silicon chip.

Integrated package: A single program providing functionality of a collection of programs but not as extensive as a specialized program like Microsoft Word. Popular with home users who are willing to sacrifice some advanced features for lower cost and simplicity.

Interactivity: User participation in a multimedia presentation.

Internal data: Data from within an organization consisting principally of transactions from the transaction processing system.

Internal hard disk: Storage device consisting of one or more metallic platters sealed inside a container. Internal hard disks are installed inside the system cabinet of a microcomputer. It stores the operating system and major applications like Word.

Internet: A huge computer network available to everyone with a microcomputer and a means to connect to it. It is the actual physical network made up of wires, cables, and satellites as opposed to the Web, which is the multimedia interface to resources available on the Internet.

Internet scam: Using the Internet, a fraudulent act or operation designed to trick individuals into spending their time and money for little or no return.

Internet security suite: Collection of utility programs designed to make using the Internet easier and safer.

Internet service provider (ISP): Provides access to the Internet.

Internet telephone: Low-cost alternative to long-distance telephone calls using electronic voice delivery.

Internet telephony: *See* Telephony.

Interpreter: Software that converts a procedural language one statement at a time into machine language just before the statement is executed. No object code is saved.

Intranet: Like the Internet, it typically provides e-mail, mailing lists, newsgroups, and FTP services, but it is accessible only to those within the organization. Organizations use intranets to provide information to their employees.

Intrusion detection system (NIDS): Using sophisticated statistical techniques to analyze all incoming and outgoing network traffic, this system works with firewalls to protect an organization's network.

Inventory: Material or products that a company has in stock.

Inventory control system: A system that keeps records of the number of each kind of part or finished good in the warehouse.

IP address (Internet Protocol address): The unique numeric address of a computer on the Internet that facilitates the delivery of e-mail.

IP telephony: *See* Telephony.

J

Java: Programming language for creating special programs like applets. *See* Applets.

JavaScript: A scripting language that adds basic interactivity to Web pages.

Joystick: Popular input device for computer games. You control game actions by varying the pressure, speed, and direction of the joystick.

K

Key: Another term for encryption key.

Key field: The common field by which tables in a database are related to each other. This field uniquely identifies the record. For example, in university databases, a key field is the Social Security number. Also known as primary key.

Keyboard: Input device that looks like a typewriter keyboard but has additional keys.

Keyboard port: Were used to connect keyboards to the system unit.

Keystroke logger: Also known as computer monitoring software and sniffer programs. They can be loaded onto your computer without your knowledge.

Keyword search: A type of search option that causes the search engine to compare your entry against its database and return with a list of sites, or hits, that contain the keyword you entered.

Kilobits per second (Kbps): Speed at which data is transferred.

Knowledge base: A system that uses a database containing specific facts, rules to relate these facts, and user input to formulate recommendations and decisions.

Knowledge-based systems: Programs duplicating human knowledge. It's like capturing the knowledge of a human expert and making it accessible through a computer program.

Knowledge work system (KWS): Specialized information system used to create information in a specific area of expertise.

Knowledge worker: Person involved in the creation of information, such as an engineer and a scientist.

L

Label: Provides structure to a worksheet by describing the contents of the rows and columns. *See* Text entry.

Land: *See* Lands and pits.

Lands and pits: Flat and bumpy areas, respectively, that represent 1s and 0s on the optical disc surface to be read by a laser.

Language translator: Converts programming instructions into a machine language that can be processed by a computer.

Laptop computer: *See* Notebook computer and Notebook system unit.

Laser printer: Printer that creates dotlike images on a drum, using a laser beam light source.

Legacy port: Was common on microcomputer systems to connect specific types of devices. They have largely been replaced by faster, more flexible ports such as the universal serial bus (USB).

Levels: Generations or levels of programming languages ranging from "low" to "high." *See* Generations (of programming languages).

Link: A connection to related information.

Linux: Type of UNIX operating system initially developed by Linus Torvalds, it is one of the most popular and powerful alternatives to the Windows operating system.

Liquid crystal display (LCD): A technology used for flat-panel monitors.

Local area network (LAN): Network consisting of computers and other devices that are physically near each other, such as within the same building.

Location: For browsers to connect to resources, locations or addresses must be specified. Also known as uniform resource locators or URLs.

Logic error: Error that occurs when a programmer has used an incorrect calculation or left out a programming procedure.

Logic structure: Programming statements or structures called sequence, selection, or loop that control the logical sequence in which computer program instructions are executed.

Logical operation: Comparing two pieces of data to see whether one is equal to (=), less than (<), or greater than (>) the other.

Logical view: Focuses on the meaning and content of the data. End users and computer professionals are concerned with this view as opposed to the physical view, with which only specialized computer professionals are concerned.

Loop structure: Logic structure in which a process may be repeated as long as a certain condition remains true. This structure is called a "loop" because the program loops around or repeats again and again. There are two variations: DO UNTIL and DO WHILE.

Low bandwidth: *See* Voiceband.

Lower level: Programming language closer to the language the computer itself uses. The computer understands the 0s and 1s that make up bits and bytes.

M

Mac OS: Operating system designed for Macintosh computers.

Mac OS X: Macintosh operating system featuring a user interface called Aqua.

Machine language: Language in which data is represented in 1s and 0s. Most languages have to be translated into machine language for the computer to process the data. Either a compiler or an interpreter performs this translation.

Magnetic card reader: A card reader that reads encoded information from a magnetic strip on the back of a card.

Magnetic-ink character recognition (MICR): Direct-entry scanning devices used in banks. This technology is used to automatically read the numbers on the bottom of checks.

Magnetic tape: To find specific information, you will have to go through the tape sequentially until that data comes up. On the other hand, using an audio compact disc, select the song and the disc moves directly to that song. Tape may be slow, but it is effective and a commonly used tool for backing up data.

Magnetic tape reel: Typically ½-inch wide and ½-mile long, this type of magnetic tape is used by mainframe computers due to its massive storage capacity.

Magnetic tape streamer: Device that allows duplication (backup) of the data stored on a microcomputer hard disk.

Mainframe computer: This computer can process several million program instructions per second. Sizeable organizations rely on these room-size systems to handle large programs and a great deal of data.

Maintenance programmer: Programmers who maintain software by updating programs to protect them from errors, improve usability, standardize, and adjust to organizational changes.

Malware: Short for malicious software.

MAN: *See* Metropolitan area network.

Management information system (MIS): Computer-based information system that produces standardized reports in a summarized and structured form. Generally used to support middle managers.

Many-to-many relationship: In a network database, each child node may have more than one parent node and vice versa.

Marketing: The organizational department that plans, prices, promotes, sells, and distributes an organization's goods and services.

Markup language: *See* Content-markup language.

Mass storage: Refers to the tremendous amount of secondary storage required by large organizations.

Mass storage devices: Devices such as file servers, RAID systems, tape libraries, optical jukeboxes, and more.

Mechanical mouse: Traditional and most widely used type of mouse. It has a ball on the bottom and is attached with a cord to the system unit.

Media: Media are the actual physical material that holds the data, such as a floppy disk, which is one of the important characteristics of secondary storage. Singular of media is medium.

Media center system unit: Use powerful desktop system hardware with specialized graphics cards for interfacing with televisions and other home entertainment devices.

Medium: *See* Media.

Medium band: Bandwidth of special leased lines, used mainly with minicomputers and mainframe computers.

Memory: Memory is contained on chips connected to the system board and is a holding area for data instructions and information (processed data waiting to be output to secondary storage). RAM, ROM, and CMOS are three types of memory chips.

Menu: List of commands.

Menu bar: Menus are displayed in a menu bar at the top of the screen.

Mesh network: A topology requiring each node to have more than one connection to the other nodes so that if a path between two nodes is disrupted, data can be automatically rerouted around the failure using another path.

Message: The content portion of e-mail correspondence.

Metasearch engine: Program that automatically submits your search request to several indices and search engines and then creates an index from received information. One of the best known is Dogpile.

Method: In an object-oriented database, description of how the data is to be manipulated.

Metropolitan area network (MAN): These networks are used as links between office buildings in a city.

Microblog: Publishes short sentences that only take a few seconds to write, rather than long stories or posts like a traditional blog.

Microcomputer: Small, low-cost computer designed for individual users. These include desktop, notebook, and personal digital assistant computers.

Microcomputer database: *See* Individual database.

Microprocessor: The central processing unit (CPU) of a microcomputer controls and manipulates data to produce information. The microprocessor is contained on a single integrated circuit chip and is the brains of the system.

Microwave: Communication using high-frequency radio waves that travel in straight lines through the air.

Middle management: Middle-level managers deal with control and planning. They implement the long-term goals of the organization.

MIDI: *See* Musical instrument digital interface.

Midrange computer: Also known as a minicomputer.

Minicomputer: Refrigerator-sized machines falling in between microcomputers and mainframes in processing speed and data-storing capacity. Medium-sized companies or departments of large companies use minicomputers.

Mistaken identity: When the electronic profile of one person is switched with another.

Mobile browser: Special browsers designed to run on portable devices.

Mobile robots: Robots that act as transports and are used for a variety of different tasks.

Modem: Short for modulator-demodulator. It is a communication device that translates the electronic signals from a computer into electronic signals that can travel over telephone lines.

Modem card: Also known as an internal modem, a card that allows distant computers to communicate with one another by converting electronic signals from within the system unit into electronic signals that can travel over telephone lines and other types of connections.

Modulation: Process of converting digital signals to analog signals.

Module: *See* Program module.

Monitor: Output device like a television screen that displays data processed by the computer.

Motherboard: Also called a system board; the communications medium for the entire system.

Mouse: Device that typically rolls on the desktop and directs the cursor on the display screen.

Mouse pointer: Typically in the shape of an arrow.

Mouse port: Was used to connect a mouse to the system unit.

Multicore chip: A new type of chip that provides two independent CPUs, allowing two programs to run simultaneously. *Also see* Central processing unit.

Multidimensional database: Data can be viewed as a cube having three or more sides consisting of cells. Each side of the cube is considered a dimension of the data; thus, complex relationships between data can be represented and efficiently analyzed. Sometimes called a data cube and designed for analyzing large groups of records.

Multifunctional devices (MFD): Devices that typically combine the capabilities of a scanner, printer, fax, and copying machine.

Multimedia: Technology that can link all sorts of media into one form of presentation, such as video, music, voice, graphics, and text.

Multimedia authoring programs: Programs used to create multimedia presentations bringing together video, audio, graphics, and text elements into an interactive framework. Macromedia Director, Authorware, and Toolbook are examples of multimedia authoring programs.

Multitasking: Operating system that allows a single user to run several application programs at the same time.

Multi-touch screen: Can be touched with more than one finger, which allows for interactions such as rotating graphical objects on the screen with your hand or zooming in and out by pinching and stretching your fingers.

Musical instrument digital interface (MIDI): A standard that allows musical instruments to connect to the system using MIDI ports.

N

Naive: People who underestimate the difficulty of changing computer systems or generating information.

National service provider: Internet service providers, such as America Online (AOL), that provide access through standard telephone or cable connections and allow users to access the Internet from almost anywhere within the country for a standard fee.

Natural language: Language designed to give people a more human connection with computers.

Netbook: A type of microcomputer that is smaller, lighter, and less expensive than a notebook computer.

Netbook system unit: Similar to notebook system units but smaller, less powerful, and less expensive.

Network: The arrangement in which various communications channels are connected through two or more computers. The largest network in the world is the Internet.

Network adapter card: Connects the system unit to a cable that connects to other devices on the network.

Network administrator: Also known as network manager. Computer professional who ensures that existing information and communication systems are operating effectively and that new ones are implemented as needed. Also responsible for meeting security and privacy requirements.

Network architecture: Describes how networks are configured and how the resources are shared.

Network attached storage (NAS): Similar to a file server except simpler and less expensive. Widely used for home and small business storage needs.

Network database: Database with a hierarchical arrangement of nodes, except that each child node may have more than one parent node. Also called many-to-many relationship.

Network gateway: Connection by which a local area network may be linked to other local area networks or to larger networks.

Network interface card (NIC): Also known as a network adapter card. They are used to connect a computer to one or more computers forming a communication network whereby users can share data, programs, and hardware.

Network operating system (NOS): Interactive software between applications and computers coordinating and directing activities between computers on a network. This operating system is located on one of the connected computers' hard disks, making that system the network server.

Network server: *See* Network operating system. This computer coordinates all communication between the other computers. Popular network operating systems include NetWare and Windows NT Server.

Node: Any device connected to a network. For example, a node is a computer, printer, or data storage device and each device has its own address on the network. Also, within hierarchical databases, fields or records are structured in nodes.

Notebook computer: Portable computer, also known as a laptop computer, weighing between 4 and 10 pounds.

Notebook system unit: A small, portable system unit that contains electronic components, selected secondary storage devices, and input devices.

Numbered list: Sequence of steps or topics on a page organized by numbers.

Numeric entry: In a worksheet or spreadsheet, typically used to identify numbers or formulas.

Numeric keypad: Enters numbers and arithmetic symbols and is included on all computer keyboards.

O

Object: An element, such as a text box, that can be added to a workbook, which can be selected, sized, and moved. For example, if a chart (object) in an Excel workbook file (source file) is linked to a word document (destination file), the chart appears in the word document. In this manner, the object contains both data and instructions to manipulate the data.

Object code: Machine language code converted by a compiler from source code. Object code can be saved and run later.

Object-oriented database: A more flexible type of database that stores data as well as instructions to manipulate data and is able to handle unstructured data such as photographs, audio, and video. Object-oriented databases organize data using objects, classes, entities, attributes, and methods.

Object-oriented programming (OOP): Methodology in which a program is organized into self-contained, reusable modules called objects. Each object contains both the data and processing operations necessary to perform a task.

Object-oriented software development: Software development approach that focuses less on the tasks and more on defining the relationships between previously defined procedures or objects.

Objectives: In programming, it is necessary to make clear the problems you are trying to solve to create a functional program.

Office automation system (OAS): System designed primarily to support data workers. It focuses on managing documents, communicating, and scheduling.

Office software suites: *See* Productivity suites.

Office suites: *See* Productivity suites.

One-to-many relationship: In a hierarchical database, each entry has one parent node, and a parent may have several child nodes.

Online: Being connected to the Internet is described as being online.

Online banking: A feature provided by banking institutions that allows customers to perform banking operations using a Web browser.

Online identity: The information that people voluntarily post about themselves online.

Online office suite: Office suite stored online and available anywhere the Internet can be accessed.

Online processing: *See* Real-time processing.

Online shopping: The buying and selling of a wide range of consumer goods over the Internet.

Online stock trading: Allows investors to research, buy, and sell stocks and bonds over the Internet.

Online storage service: Provide users with storage space that can be accessed from a Web site.

Operating system: Software that interacts between application software and the computer, handling such details as running programs, storing and processing data, and coordinating all computer resources, including attached peripheral devices. It is the most important program on the computer. Windows 7, Windows Vista, and Mac OS X are examples of operating systems.

Operational feasibility: Making sure the design of a new system will be able to function within the existing framework of an organization.

Operational model: A decision model that helps lower-level managers accomplish the organization's day-to-day activities, such as evaluating and maintaining quality control.

Operators: Operators handle correcting operational errors in any programs. To do that, they need documentation, which gives them the understanding of the program, thus enabling them to fix any errors.

Optical audio connection: Port used to integrate computers into high-end audio and home theatre systems.

Optical carrier (OC): Provide support for very high-speed, all-digital transmission for large corporations.

Optical-character recognition (OCR): Scanning device that uses special preprinted characters, such as those printed on utility bills, that can be read by a light source and changed into machine-readable code.

Optical disc: Storage device that can hold over 17 gigabytes of data, which is an equivalent of several million typewritten pages. Lasers are used to record and read data on the disc. The two basic types of optical discs are compact discs (CDs) and digital versatile or video discs (DVDs).

Optical disc drive: A disc is read by an optical disc drive using a laser that projects a tiny beam of light. The amount of reflected light determines whether the area represents a 1 or a 0.

Optical-mark recognition (OMR): Device that senses the presence or absence of a mark, such as a pencil mark. As an example, an OMR device is used to score multiple choice tests.

Optical mouse: A type of mouse that emits and senses light to detect mouse movement.

Optical scanner: Device that identifies images or text on a page and automatically converts them to electronic signals that can be stored in a computer to copy or reproduce.

Organic light-emitting diode (OLED): Has the benefits of lower power consumption and longer battery life, as well as possibilities for much thinner displays.

Organization chart: Chart showing the levels of management and formal lines of authority in an organization.

Organizational online storage: High-speed Internet connection to a dedicated remote organizational Internet drive site.

Output device: Equipment that translates processed information from the central processing unit into a form that can be understood by humans. The most common output devices are monitors and printers.

P

Packet: Before a message is sent on the Internet, it is broken down into small parts called packets. Each packet is then sent separately over the Internet. At the receiving end, the packets are reassembled into the correct order.

Pages: In Microsoft PowerPoint, another name for slides.

Page layout program: *See* Desktop publishing program.

Palm computer: Also known as a handheld computer. These systems combine pen input, writing recognition, personal organizational tools, and communications capabilities. They contain an entire computer system, including the electronic components, secondary storage, and input and output devices.

Parallel approach: Systems implementation in which old and new systems are operated side by side until the new one has shown it is reliable.

Parallel port: Used to connect external devices that send or receive data over a short distance. Mostly used to connect printers to the system unit.

Parallel processing: Used by supercomputers to run large and complex programs.

Parent node: Node one level above the node being considered in a hierarchical database or network. Each entry has one parent node, although a parent may have several child nodes. Also called one-to-many relationship.

Passive-matrix monitor: Monitor that creates images by scanning the entire screen. This type requires little energy but clarity of images is not sharp. Also known as dual-scan monitor.

Password: Special sequence of numbers or letters that limits access to information, such as electronic mail.

Payroll: Activity concerned with calculating employee paychecks.

PC Card: Also known as Personal Computer Memory Card International Association (PCMCIA) card. Credit card–sized expansion cards developed for portable computers.

PCI Express (PCIe): New type of bus that is 30 times faster than PCI bus.

PDA keyboard: Miniature keyboard for PDAs used to send e-mail, create documents, and more.

Peer-to-peer (P2P) network: Network in which nodes can act as both servers and clients. For example, one microcomputer can obtain files located on another microcomputer and also can provide files to other microcomputers.

People: End users who use computers to make themselves more productive.

Perception system robot: Robot that imitates some of the human senses.

Periodic report: Reports for a specific time period as to the health of the company or a particular department of the company.

Peripheral component interconnect (PCI): Bus architecture that combines the capabilities of MCA and EISA with the ability to send video instructions at speeds to match the microprocessor. PCI is a 32-bit or 64-bit speed bus that is over 20 times faster than an ISA bus.

Person-to-person auction site: A type of Web auction site where the owner provides a forum for numerous buyers and sellers to gather.

Personal area network (PAN): A type of wireless network that works within a very small area—your immediate surroundings.

Personal digital assistant (PDA): A device that typically combines pen input, writing recognition, personal organizational tools, and communication capabilities in a very small package. Also called handheld PC and palm computer.

Personal laser printer: Inexpensive laser printer widely used by single users to produce black-and-white documents.

Personal software: *See* Integrated package.

Phased approach: Systems implementation whereby a new system is implemented gradually over a period of time.

Phishing: An attempt to trick Internet users into thinking a fake but official-looking Web site or e-mail is legitimate.

Photo editor: *See* Image editor.

Photo printer: A special-purpose ink-jet printer designed to print photo-quality images from digital cameras.

Physical security: Activity concerned with protecting hardware from possible human and natural disasters.

Physical view: This focuses on the actual format and location of the data. *See* Logical view.

Picture elements: *See* Pixel.

Pilot approach: Systems implementation in which a new system is tried out in only one part of the organization. Later it is implemented throughout the rest of the organization.

Pit: *See* Lands and pits.

Pixel (picture elements): Smallest unit on the screen that can be turned on and off or made different shades. Pixels are individual dots that form images on a monitor. The greater the resolution, the more pixels and the better the clarity.

Pixel pitch: The distance between each pixel on a monitor.

Plagiarism: Representing some other person's work and ideas as your own without giving credit to the original source.

Plagiarist: Someone who engages in plagiarism.

Platform: The operating system. Application programs are designed to run with a specific platform. *See* Operating system.

Platform scanner: Handheld direct-entry device used to read special characters on price tags. Also known as wand reader.

Roller ball: *See* Trackball.

ROM: *See* Read-only memory.

Row: A horizontal block of cells one cell high all the way across the worksheet.

S

Sales order processing: Activity that records the demands of customers for a company's products or services.

Satellite: This type of communication uses satellites orbiting about 22,000 miles above the earth as microwave relay stations.

Satellite/air connection services: Connection services that use satellites and the air to download or send data to users at a rate seven times faster than dial-up connections.

Scam: A fraudulent or deceptive act or operation designed to trick individuals into spending their time and money for little or no return.

Schema: *See* Data dictionary.

Search engine: Specialized programs assisting in locating information on the Web and the Internet.

Search services: Organizations that maintain databases relating to information provided on the Internet and also provide search engines to locate information.

Secondary storage: Permanent storage used to preserve programs and data that can be retained after the computer is turned off. These devices include floppy disks, hard disks, magnetic tape, CDs, DVDs, and more.

Secondary storage device: These devices are used to save, backup, and transport files from one location or computer to another. *See* Secondary storage.

Sector: Section shaped like a pie wedge that divides the tracks on a disk.

Secure file transfer protocol (SFTP): *See* File transfer protocol.

Security: The protection of information, hardware, and software.

Selection structure: Logic structure that determines which of two paths will be followed when a program must make a decision. Also called IF-THEN-ELSE structures. If something is true, then do option one, or else do option two.

Semiconductor: Silicon chip through which electricity flows with some resistance.

Sequential access: An approach to external storage, provided by magnetic tape, where information is stored in sequence. *See* Magnetic tape.

Serial Advanced Technology Attachment (SATA): New type of bus used to connect magnetic and optical disc drives to the system board with far greater speed than other types of buses.

Serial port: Used to connect external devices that send or receive data one bit at a time over a long distance. Used for mouse, keyboard, modem, and many other devices.

Server: A host computer with a connection to the Internet that stores document files used to display Web pages.

Depending on the resources shared, it may be called a file server, printer server, communication server, Web server, or database server.

Shared laser printer: More expensive laser printer used by a group of users to produce black-and-white documents. These printers can produce over 30 pages a minute.

Sheet: A rectangular grid of rows and columns. *See* Spreadsheet or Worksheet.

Signature: Provides additional information about a sender of an e-mail message, such as name, address, and telephone number.

Silicon chip: Tiny circuit board etched on a small square of sandlike material called silicon. Chips are mounted on carrier packages, which then plug into sockets on the system board.

Slide: A PowerPoint presentation is made up of many slides shown in different views and presentation styles.

Slot: Area on a system board that accepts expansion cards to expand a computer system's capabilities.

Smart card: Card about the size of a credit card containing a tiny built-in microprocessor. It can be used to hold such information as personal identification, medical and financial knowledge, and credit card numbers. Information on this card is protected by a password, which offers security and privacy.

Smart phone: A type of cell phone that offers a variety of advanced functionality, including Internet and e-mail.

Snoopware: Programs that record virtually every activity on a computer system.

Social networking: Using the Internet to connect individuals.

Socket: Sockets provide connection points on the system board for holding electronic parts.

Software: Computer program consisting of step-by-step instructions, directing the computer on each task it will perform.

Software development: *See* Programming.

Software engineer: Programming professional or programmer who analyzes users' needs and creates application software.

Software environment: Operating system, also known as software platform, consisting of a collection of programs to handle technical details depending on the type of operating system. For example, software designed to run on an Apple computer is compatible with the Mac OS environment.

Software piracy: Unauthorized copying of programs for personal gain.

Software platform: *See* Software environment.

Software suite: Individual application programs that are sold together as a group.

Solid-state drive (SSD): Designed to be connected inside a microcomputer system the same way an internal hard disk would be, but contains solid-state memory instead of magnetic disks to store data.

Solid-state storage: A secondary storage device that has no moving parts. Data is stored and retrieved electronically directly from these devices, much as they would be from conventional computer memory.

Sony/Philips Digital Interconnect Format (S/PDIF): *See* Optical audio connection.

Sort: Tool that rearranges a table's records numerically or alphabetically according to a selected field.

Sound card: Device that accepts audio input from a microphone and converts it into a form that can be processed by the computer. Also converts internal electronic signals to audio signals so they can be heard from external speakers.

Source code: When a programmer originally writes the code for a program in a particular language. This is called source code until it is translated by a compiler for the computer to execute the program. It then becomes object code.

Spam: Unwelcome and unsolicited e-mail that can carry attached viruses.

Spam blocker: Software that uses a variety of different approaches to identify and eliminate spam or junk mail.

Speakers: Audio-output devices connected to a sound card in the system unit. The sound card is used to capture as well as play back recorded sound.

Specialized application: Programs that are narrowly focused on specific disciplines and occupations. Some of the best known are multimedia, Web authoring, graphics, virtual reality, and artificial intelligence.

Specialized search engine: Search engine that focuses on subject-specific Web sites.

Specialized suite: Programs that focus on specialized applications such as graphics suites or financial planning suites.

Speech recognition: The ability to accept voice input to select menu options, and to dictate text.

Spelling checker: Program used with a word processor to check the spelling of typed text against an electronic dictionary.

Spider: Special programs that continually look for new information and update the search servers' databases.

Spike: *See* Voltage surge.

Spotlight: An advanced search tool on the Mac OS X operating system for locating files, e-mail messages, and more.

Spreadsheet: Computer-produced spreadsheet based on the traditional accounting worksheet that has rows and columns used to present and analyze data.

Spy removal programs: Programs such as Spybot and Spysweeper, designed to detect Web bugs and monitor software.

Spyware: Wide range of programs designed to secretly record and report an individual's activities on the Internet.

Stand-alone operating system: Also called desktop operating systems; a type of operating system that controls a single desktop or notebook computer.

Star network: Network of computers or peripheral devices linked to a central computer through which all communications pass. Control is maintained by polling. The configuration of the computers looks like a star surrounding and connected to the central computer in the middle.

Stock photograph: Photographs on a variety of subject material from professional models to natural landscapes.

Storage area network (SAN): An architecture that links remote computer storage devices such as enterprise storage systems to computers so that the devices are available as locally attached drives.

Storage device: Hardware that reads data and programs from storage media. Most also write to storage media.

Strategic model: A decision model that assists top managers in long-range planning, such as stating company objectives or planning plant locations.

Strategy: A way of coordinating the sharing of information and resources. The most common network strategies are terminal, peer-to-peer, and client/server networks.

Structured program: Program that uses logic structures according to the program design and the language in which you have chosen to write the program. Each language follows techniques like pseudocode, flowcharts, and logic structures.

Structured programming techniques: Techniques consisting of top-down program design, pseudocode, flowcharts, and logic structures.

Structured query language (SQL): A program control language used to create sophisticated database applications for requesting information from a database.

Styles: A feature found in most word processors that quickly applies predefined formats.

Stylus: Penlike device used with tablet PCs and PDAs that uses pressure to draw images on a screen. A stylus interacts with the computer through handwriting recognition software.

Subject: Located in the header of an e-mail message; a one-line description used to present the topic of the message.

Supercomputer: Fastest calculating device ever invented, processing billions of program instructions per second. Used by very large organizations like NASA.

Supervisor: Manager responsible for managing and monitoring workers. Supervisors have responsibility for operational matters.

Surf: Move from one Web site to another.

Surge protector: Device separating the computer from the power source of the wall outlet. When a voltage surge occurs, a circuit breaker is activated, protecting the computer system.

Switch: The center or central node for other nodes. This device coordinates the flow of data by sending messages directly between sender and receiver nodes.

Syntax error: Violation of the rules of a language in which the computer program is written. For example, leaving out a semicolon would stop the entire program from working because it is not the exact form the computer expects for that language.

System: Collection of activities and elements designed to accomplish a goal.

System board: Flat board that usually contains the CPU and memory chips connecting all system components to one another.

System bus: There are two categories of buses. One is the system bus that connects the CPU to the system board. The other is the expansion bus that connects the CPU to slots on the system board.

System chassis: *See* System unit.

System flowchart: A flowchart that shows the flow of input data to processing and finally to output, or distribution of information.

System software: "Background" software that enables the application software to interact with the computer. System software consists of the operating system, utilities, device drivers, and language translators. It works with application software to handle the majority of technical details.

System unit: Part of a microcomputer that contains the CPU. Also known as the system cabinet or chassis, it is the container that houses most of the electronic components that make up the computer system.

Systems analysis: This second phase of the systems life cycle determines the requirements for a new system. Data is collected about the present system and analyzed, and new requirements are determined.

Systems analysis and design: Six phases of problem solving procedures for examining information systems and improving them.

Systems analysis report: Report prepared for higher management describing the current information system, the requirements for a new system, and a possible development schedule.

Systems analyst: Plans and designs information systems.

Systems audit: A systems audit compares the performance of a new system to the original design specifications to determine if the new procedures are actually improving productivity.

Systems design: Phase three of the systems life cycle, consisting of designing alternative systems, selecting the best system, and writing a systems design report.

Systems design report: Report prepared for higher management describing alternative designs, presenting cost versus benefits, and outlining the effects of alternative designs on the organization.

Systems development: Phase four of the systems life cycle, consisting of developing software, acquiring hardware, and testing the new system.

Systems implementation: Phase five of the systems life cycle is converting the old system to the new one and training people to use the new system. Also known as conversion.

Systems life cycle: The six phases of systems analysis and design are called the systems life cycle. The phases are preliminary investigation, systems analysis, systems design, systems development, systems implementation, and systems maintenance.

Systems maintenance: Phase six of the systems life cycle consisting of a systems audit and periodic evaluation.

T

T1: High-speed lines that support all digital communications, provide very high capacity, and are very expensive.

T3: Copper lines combined to form higher-capacity options.

Tab: Used to divide the ribbon into major activity areas, with each tab being organized into groups that contain related items.

Table (in database): The list of records in a database. Tables make up the basic structure of a database. Their columns display field data and their rows display records. *See* Field and Record.

Tablet PC: A type of notebook computer that accepts handwritten data, using a stylus or pen, that is converted to standard text and can be processed by a word processor program.

Tablet PC system unit: Similar to notebook system units. Two basic categories are convertible and slate. A stylus or pen is used to input data.

Tactical model: A decision model that assists middle-level managers to control the work of the organization, such as financial planning and sales promotion planning.

Tape cartridges: *See* Magnetic tape streamer.

Tape library: Device that provides automatic access to data archived on a large collection or library of tapes.

Task-oriented language: Programming language that is nonprocedural and focuses on specifying what the program is to accomplish. Also known as 4GLs or very high-level languages.

Technical feasibility: Making sure hardware, software, and training will be available to facilitate the design of a new system.

Technical writer: Prepares instruction manuals, technical reports, and other scientific or technical documents.

Telephone line: A transmission medium for both voice and data.

Telephone modem: Used to connect a computer directly to a telephone line.

Telephony: Communication that uses the Internet rather than traditional communication lines to connect two or more people via telephone.

Terminal server network: Network system in which processing power is centralized in one large computer, usually a mainframe. The nodes connected to this host computer are terminals, with little or no processing capabilities, or they are microcomputers running special software allowing them to act as terminals.

Text entry: In a worksheet or spreadsheet, a text entry is typically used to identify or label information entered into a cell as opposed to numbers and formulas. Also known as labels.

Thermal printer: Printer that uses heat elements to produce images on heat-sensitive paper.

Thesaurus: A word processor feature that provides synonyms, antonyms, and related words for a selected word or phrase.

Thin film transistor (TFT) monitor: Type of flat-panel monitor activating each pixel independently.

Third-generation language (3GL): *See* Procedural language.

Toggle key: These keys turn a feature on or off like the CAPS LOCK key.

Toolbar: Bar located typically below the menu bar containing icons or graphical representations for commonly used commands.

Top-down analysis method: Method used to identify top-level components of a system, then break these components down into smaller parts for analysis.

Top-down program design: Used to identify the program's processing steps, called program modules. The program must pass in sequence from one module to the next until the computer has processed all modules.

Top-level domain (TLD): Last part of an Internet address; identifies the geographical description or organizational identification. For example, using www.aol.com, the .com is the top-level domain code and indicates it is a commercial site. *Also see* Domain name.

Top management: Top-level managers are concerned with long-range (strategic) planning. They supervise middle management.

Topology: The configuration of a network. The four principal network topologies are *star, bus, ring,* and *hierarchical.*

Touch pad: Used to control the pointer by moving and tapping your finger on the surface of a pad.

Touch screen: Monitor screen allowing actions or commands to be entered by the touch of a finger.

Track: Closed, concentric ring on a disk on which data is recorded. Each track is divided into sections called sectors.

Trackball: Device used to control the pointer by rotating a ball with your thumb. Also called a roller ball.

Traditional cookies: Intended to provide customized service. A program recording information on Web site visitors within a specific site. When you leave the site, the cookie becomes dormant and is reactivated when you revisit the site.

Traditional floppy disk: A two-sided, high-density, 3½-inch disk with a capacity of 1.44 megabytes. *Also see* Floppy disk.

Traditional keyboard: Full-sized, rigid, rectangular keyboard that includes function, navigational, and numeric keys.

Transaction processing system (TPS): System that records day-to-day transactions, such as customer orders, bills, inventory levels, and production output. The TPS tracks operations and creates databases.

Transfer rate: Or transfer speed, is the speed at which modems transmit data, typically measured in bits per second (bps).

Transition: Used to animate how a presentation moves from one slide to the next.

Transmission control protocol/Internet protocol (TCP/IP): TCP/IP is the standard protocol for the Internet. The essential features of this protocol involve (1) identifying sending and receiving devices and (2) reformatting information for transmission across the Internet.

Tree network: Also known as a hierarchical network. A topology in which each device is connected to a central node, either directly or through one or more other devices. The central node is then connected to two or more subordinate nodes that in turn are connected to other subordinate nodes, and so forth, forming a treelike structure.

Trojan horse: Program that is not a virus but is a carrier of virus(es). The most common Trojan horses appear as free computer games, screen savers, or antivirus programs. Once downloaded they locate and disable existing virus protection and then deposit the virus.

Troubleshooting program: A utility program that recognizes and corrects computer-related problems before they become serious. Also called diagnostic programs.

Twisted pair: Cable consisting of pairs of copper wire that are twisted together.

Twitter: The most popular microblogging site that enables you to add new content from your browser, instant messaging application, or even a mobile phone.

TV tuner card: Contains TV tuner card and video converter changing the TV signal into one that can be displayed on your monitor. Also known as video recorder cards and video capture cards.

U

Unicode: A 16-bit code designed to support international languages, like Chinese and Japanese.

Uniform resource locator (URL): For browsers to connect you to resources on the Web, the location or address of the resources must be specified. These addresses are called URLs.

Uninstall program: A utility program that safely and completely removes unwanted programs and related files.

Universal instant messenger: An instant messaging service that communicates with any other messaging service programs.

Universal Product Code (UPC): A barcode system that identifies the product to the computer, which has a description and the latest price for the product.

Universal serial bus (USB): Combines with a PCI bus on the system board to support several external devices without inserting cards for each device. USB buses are used to support high-speed scanners, printers, and video-capturing devices.

Universal serial bus (USB) port: Expected to replace serial and parallel ports. They are faster, and one USB port can be used to connect several devices to the system unit.

UNIX: An operating system originally developed for minicomputers. It is now important because it can run on many of the more powerful microcomputers.

Uploading: Process of transferring information from the computer the user is operating to a remote computer.

USB drive: The size of a key chain, these hard drives connect to a computer's USB port enabling a transfer of files; has a capacity of up to 64GB.

User: Any individual who uses a computer. *See* End user.

User interface: Means by which users interact with application programs and hardware. A window is displayed with information for the user to enter or choose, and that is how users communicate with the program.

Utility: Performs specific tasks related to managing computer resources or files. Norton Utility for virus control and system maintenance is a good example of a utility. Also known as service programs.

Utility suite: A program that combines several utilities in one package to improve system performance. McAfee Office and Norton SystemWorks are examples.

V

Vector: Another common type of graphic file. A vector file contains all the shapes and colors, along with starting and ending points, necessary to recreate the image.

Vector illustration: *See* Vector image.

Vector image: Graphics file made up of a collection of objects such as lines, rectangles, and ovals. Vector images are more flexible than bitmaps because they are defined by mathematical equations so they can be stretched and resized. Illustration programs create and manipulate vector graphics. Also known as vector illustrations.

Very high-level languages: Task-oriented languages that require little special training on the part of the user.

VGA (Video Graphic Adapter) port: A type of port that provides a connection to an analog monitor.

Video editing software: Allows you to reorganize, add effects, and more to your video footage.

Videoconferencing system: Computer system that allows people located at various geographic locations to have in-person meetings.

Virtual environment: *See* Virtual reality.

Virtualization: A process that allows a single physical computer to support multiple operating systems that operate independently.

Virtualization software: Software that creates virtual machines.

Virtual keyboard: Display an image of a keyboard on a touch screen device. The screen functions as the actual input device, which is why the keyboard is considered virtual.

Virtual machine: A software implementation of a computer that executes programs like a physical computer.

Virtual memory: Feature of an operating system that increases the amount of memory available to run programs. With large programs, parts are stored on a secondary device like your hard disk. Then each part is read in RAM only when needed.

Virtual private network (VPN):   Creates a secure private connection between a remote user and an organization's internal network. Special VPN protocols create the equivalent of a dedicated line between a user's home or laptop computer and a company server.

Virtual reality: Interactive sensory equipment (headgear and gloves) allowing users to experience alternative realities generated in 3-D by a computer, thus imitating the physical world.

Virtual reality wall: An immersive experience whereby you are viewing simulations on a virtual reality wall in stereoscopic vision.

Virus: Hidden instructions that migrate through networks and operating systems and become embedded in different programs. They may be designed to destroy data or simply to display messages.

Voice over IP (VoIP):   Transmission of telephone calls over networks. *See also* Telephony.

Voice recognition system: Using a microphone, sound card, and specialty software, the user can operate a computer and create documents using voice commands.

Voiceband: Bandwidth of a standard telephone line. Also known as low bandwidth.

Voltage surge (spike):   Excess of electricity that may destroy chips or other electronic computer components.

VR: *See* Virtual reality.

W

WAN: *See* Wide area network.

Wand reader: Special-purpose handheld device used to read OCR characters.

Warm boot: Restarting your computer while the computer is already on and the power is not turned off.

Web: Introduced in 1992 and prior to the Web, the Internet was all text. The Web made it possible to provide a multimedia interface that includes graphics, animations, sound, and video.

Web auction: Similar to traditional auctions except that all transactions occur over the Web; buyers and sellers seldom meet face-to-face.

Web authoring: Creating a Web site.

Web authoring program: Word processing program for generating Web pages. Also called HTML editor or Web page editor. Widely used Web authoring programs include Macromedia Dreamweaver and Microsoft FrontPage.

Web-based applications: By using the Web to connect with an application service provider (asp), you can copy an application program to your computer system's memory and then run the application.

Web-based file transfer services: A type of file transfer service that uses a Web browser to upload and download files, allowing you to copy files to and from your computer across the Internet.

Web-based service: Web site that provides free access to programs that run within a browser window; for example, Google Apps.

Web bug: Program hidden in the HTML code for a Web page or e-mail message as a graphical image. Web bugs can migrate whenever a user visits a Web site containing a Web bug or opens infected e-mail. They collect information on the users and report back to a predefined server.

Web log: A type of personal Web site where articles are regularly posted.

Web page: Browsers interpret HTML documents to display Web pages.

Web page editor: *See* Web authoring program.

Web utilities: Specialized utility programs making the Internet and the Web easier and safer. Some examples are plug-ins that operate as part of a browser and filters that block access and monitor use of selected Web sites.

WebCam: Specialized digital video camera for capturing images and broadcasting to the Internet.

Webmaster: Develops and maintains Web sites and Web resources.

What-if analysis: Spreadsheet feature in which changing one or more numbers results in the automatic recalculation of all related formulas.

Wheel button: Some mice have a wheel button that can be rotated to scroll through information displayed on the monitor.

Wide area network (WAN): Countrywide and worldwide networks that use microwave relays and satellites to reach users over long distances.

Wi-Fi (wireless fidelity): Wireless standard also known as 802.11, used to connect computers to each other and to the Internet.

Wiki: A Web site that allows people to fill in missing information or correct inaccuracies on it by directly editing the pages.

Window: A rectangular area containing a document or message.

Windows: An operating environment extending the capability of DOS.

Windows 7: The newest version of the Windows operating system, released in 2009.

Windows Update: A utility provided in the Windows platform that allows you to update the device drivers on your computer.

Windows Vista: An upgrade to Windows XP with improved security, three-dimensional workspace, and filtering capabilities.

Wireless access point: Or base station. The receiver interprets incoming radio frequencies from a wireless LAN and routes communications to the appropriate devices, which could be separate computers, a shared printer, or a modem.

Wireless keyboard: Transmits input to the system through the air, providing greater flexibility and convenience.

Wireless LAN (WLAN): Uses radio frequencies to connect computers and other devices. All communications pass through the network's centrally located wireless receiver or base station and are routed to the appropriate devices.

Wireless modem: Modem that connects to the serial port but does not connect to telephone lines. It receives through the air.

Wireless mouse: *See* Cordless mouse.

Wireless revolution: A revolution that is expected to dramatically affect the way we communicate and use computer technology.

Wireless service provider: Provides Internet connections for computers with wireless modems and a wide array of wireless devices. They do not use telephone lines.

Wireless wide area network (WWAN) modem: *See* Wireless modem.

Word: The number of bits (such as 16, 32, or 64) that can be accessed at one time by the CPU.

Word processor: The computer and the program allow you to create, edit, save, and print documents composed of text.

Word wrap: Feature of word processing that automatically moves the cursor from the end of one line to the beginning of the next.

Workbook file: Contains one or more related worksheets or spreadsheets. *See* Spreadsheet.

Worksheet: Also known as a spreadsheet, or sheet; a rectangular grid of rows and columns used in programs like Excel.

Worksheet file: Created by electronic spreadsheets to analyze things like budgets and to predict sales.

Worm: Virus that doesn't attach itself to programs and databases but fills a computer system with self-replicating information, clogging the system so that its operations are slowed or stopped.

WYSIWYG (what you see is what you get) editors: Web authoring programs that build a page without requiring direct interaction with the HTML code and then preview the page described by the HTML code.

Z

Zombie: A computer infected by a virus, worm, or Trojan horse that allows it to be remotely controlled for malicious purposes.

Credits

Photo

p. 3	© Enamul Hoque/Rod Steele/Getty Images
p. 4 top left	© Sydney Shaffer/zefa/Corbis
p. 4 bottom	Microsoft product box shot(s) reprinted with permission from Microsoft Corporation.
p. 4 top right	Microsoft product box shot(s) reprinted with permission from Microsoft Corporation.
p. 5 left	© Willis Technology
p. 5 right	© Guy Crittenden/Getty Images
p. 7 top left	© ColorBlind Images/Getty Images
p. 7 bottom left	© AAGAMIA/Getty Images
p. 7 center	© Goodshoot/Punchstock
p. 7 right	© Ron Levine/Getty Images
p. 9 left	Microsoft screen shot reprinted with permission from Microsoft Corporation.
p. 11 top	Courtesy of IBM.
p. 11 center left	Courtesy of Apple.
p. 11 center middle	Courtesy of Apple.
p. 11 bottom left	© FURGOLLE/Image Point FR/Corbis
p. 11 bottom middle	Courtesy of Nokia.
p. 11 center right	Courtesy of Hewlett-Packard Company.
p. 11 bottom right	© PRNewsFoto/RadioShack Corporation
p. 12	© Willis Technology
p. 13 top	© Willis Technology
p. 13 bottom left	Courtesy of Samsung.
p. 13 bottom right	© Willis Technology
p. 15 top left	Courtesy of Apple.
p. 15 top center	Courtesy of Nokia.
p. 15 top right	Courtesy of LG Electronics.
p. 15 bottom left	© PRNewsFoto/Verizon Wireless
p. 15 bottom right	© PRNewsFoto/Verizon Wireless
p. 16	© Westend61/Getty Images
p. 17	© Colin Anderson/Getty Image
p. 18 left	© Sydney Shaffer/zefa/Corbis
p. 18 right	© AAGAMIA/Getty Images
p. 19 left	Microsoft product box shot(s) reprinted with permission from Microsoft Corporation.
p. 19 left	Microsoft product box shot(s) reprinted with permission from Microsoft Corporation.
p. 19 right	© Willis Technology
p. 24	Courtesy of Nokia.
p. 25	© Image Source/Getty Images
p. 26	© Huntstock/Getty Images
p. 29	© Colin Anderson/Getty Image
p. 51	© Peter Cade/Getty Images
p. 52	© Tom Ackerman/Getty Images
p. 53	© George Gutenberg/Beateworks/Corbis
p. 65	© Kheng Guan Toh/Veer
p. 84	Microsoft product box shot(s) reprinted with permission from Microsoft Corporation.
p. 85	Microsoft product box shot(s) reprinted with permission from Microsoft Corporation.
p. 88	© Stockbyte/Getty Images
p. 89	© Colin Anderson/Getty Image
p. 92	© Stockbyte/Getty Images
p. 101	© Design Pics/SuperStock
p. 102 top left	Courtesy of Adobe Systems Incorporated.
p. 102 bottom left	Courtesy of Adobe Systems Incorporated.
p. 102 center	Courtesy of Apple.
p. 102 right	Microsoft product box shot(s) reprinted with permission from Microsoft Corporation.
p. 105	Courtesy of Corel Corporation.
p. 112	© Chris Salvo/Getty Images
p. 113 top	© AP Photo/Steve Pope
p. 113 bottom	© Getty Images
p. 114 top	© Romilly Lockyer/Getty Images
p. 114 bottom	© Ciaran Griffin/Getty Images
p. 115	© John Lund/Getty Images
p. 118 top left	© Chris Salvo/Getty Images
p. 118 bottom	© AP Photo/Steve Pope
p. 118 top right	© Getty Images
p. 127	© Howard Grey/Getty Images
p. 129 left	© Sydney Shaffer/zefa/Corbis
p. 129 center	Microsoft product box shot(s) reprinted with permission from Microsoft Corporation.
p. 129 center	Microsoft product box shot(s) reprinted with permission from Microsoft Corporation.
p. 131 top	Courtesy of Research In Motion Limited.

p. 131 bottom	© Willis Technology
p. 143	© Thomas Barwick/Getty Images
p. 144	© Lucas Racasse/Getty Images
p. 145 left	Microsoft product box shot(s) reprinted with permission from Microsoft Corporation.
p. 155	© Photodisc/Getty Images
p. 157 top left	Courtesy of Apple.
p. 157 top right	Courtesy of Nokia.
p. 157 center left	Courtesy of Apple.
p. 157 center right	© FURGOLLE/Image Point FR/ Corbis
p. 157 bottom left	Courtesy of Hewlett-Packard Company.
p. 157 bottom right	© PRNewsFoto/RadioShack Corporation
p. 158 left	Courtesy of Hewlett-Packard Company.
p. 160	© Willis Technology
p. 161 top left	© Willis Technology
p. 161 top right	© Willis Technology
p. 161 bottom	© Willis Technology
p. 163	© Willis Technology
p. 165 left	© Willis Technology
p. 165 right	© Willis Technology
p. 166 left	© Willis Technology
p. 166 right	© Willis Technology
p. 167	© Willis Technology
p. 170	© Willis Technology
p. 172 top	© Willis Technology
p. 172 bottom left	© Willis Technology
p. 172 bottom right	© Willis Technology
p. 173	© Shalom Ormsby/Getty Images
p. 174	© Colin Anderson/Getty Image
p. 175 top left	Courtesy of Apple.
p. 175 top right	© Willis Technology
p. 175 bottom right	© Willis Technology
p. 176	© Willis Technology
p. 177	© Willis Technology
p. 185	© Blend Images/Getty Images
p. 187 top left	© John Lund/Paula Zacharias/ Getty Images
p. 187 top right	© AP Photo/Mark Lennihan
p. 187 bottom	© Willis Technology
p. 188 bottom	© Willis Technology
p. 189 top left	Courtesy of Microsoft Corporation.
p. 189 top right	Courtesy of Kensington Computer Products Group.
p. 189 bottom	© Jonnie Miles/Getty Images
p. 190 top left	© Photodisc/Getty Images
p. 190 top right	© Thinkstock Images/Getty Images

p. 190 bottom	© Dimitri Vervitsiotis/Getty Images
p. 191 left	© ColorBlind Images/Getty Images
p. 191 right	© Yamada Taro/Getty Images
p. 192 top left	© Ryan McVay/Getty Images
p. 192 right	Courtesy of Hewlett-Packard Company.
p. 192 bottom left	Courtesy of Logitech.
p. 193 left	© Getty Images
p. 193 right	© Phil Degginger/Getty Images
p. 194 top	© Junior Gonzalez/Getty Images
p. 194 bottom	© Royalty-Free/Corbis
p. 195 top left	© Beth Dixson/Getty Images
p. 195 top right	© Sullivan/Corbis
p. 198 top	Courtesy of Sony Electronics Inc.
p. 198 bottom	© Jose Luis Pelaez, Inc./CORBIS
p. 199 left	Courtesy of Sony Electronics Inc.
p. 199 right	Courtesy of Sony Electronics Inc.
p. 200	
p. 201	Courtesy of Amazon.com, Inc. Used with permission.
p. 203 top	Courtesy of Hewlett-Packard Company.
p. 203 bottom	Courtesy of Dell Inc.
p. 204	Courtesy of Hewlett-Packard Company.
p. 205	Courtesy of Apple.
p. 206	Courtesy of Linksys.
p. 207	© Justin Guariglia/Getty Images
p. 208	© Jason Reed/Ryan McVay/Getty Images
p. 209 left	© John Lund/Paula Zacharias/ Getty Images
p. 209 right	© Junior Gonzalez/Getty Images
p. 210	© Royalty-Free/Corbis
p. 210 right	Courtesy of Sony Electronics Inc.
p. 211 left	Courtesy of Hewlett-Packard Company.
p. 211 right	Courtesy of Linksys.
p. 219	© Digital Vision/Getty Images
p. 221	© Getty Images
p. 222	Courtesy of Iomega.
p. 223	Courtesy of Iomega.
p. 224 top left	© Willis Technology
p. 224 bottom left	© Willis Technology
p. 224 right	© Willis Technology
p. 225 left	© Willis Technology
p. 225 right	© Willis Technology
p. 227	Courtesy of Iomega.
p. 231	© Willis Technology
p. 232	Courtesy of Quantum Corporation.

p. 34 — Microsoft product screen shot(s) reprinted with permission from Microsoft Corporation.

p. 67 — Microsoft product screen shot(s) reprinted with permission from Microsoft Corporation.

p. 68 — Microsoft product screen shot(s) reprinted with permission from Microsoft Corporation.

p. 68–69 — Microsoft product screen shot(s) reprinted with permission from Microsoft Corporation.

p. 84 — Microsoft product screen shot(s) reprinted with permission from Microsoft Corporation.

p. 85 — Microsoft product screen shot(s) reprinted with permission from Microsoft Corporation.

p. 98 — © OSNews.com, 2010

p. 106 — Microsoft product screen shot(s) reprinted with permission from Microsoft Corporation.

p. 107 — Microsoft product screen shot(s) reprinted with permission from Microsoft Corporation.

p. 133 — Microsoft product screen shot(s) reprinted with permission from Microsoft Corporation.

p. 136–137 — Microsoft product screen shot(s) reprinted with permission from Microsoft Corporation.

p. 142 — Microsoft product screen shot(s) reprinted with permission from Microsoft Corporation.

p. 167–169 — Microsoft product screen shot(s) reprinted with permission from Microsoft Corporation.

p. 196–197 — Microsoft product screen shot(s) reprinted with permission from Microsoft Corporation.

p. 262 — Microsoft product screen shot(s) reprinted with permission from Microsoft Corporation.

p. 278 — Copyright, 2010 Internet.com All rights reserved. Reprinted with permission from http://www.internet.com.

p. 315, 325 — © ING Direct USA, 2008.

Subject Index

Metasearch engines, 44–45
Metropolitan area network (MAN), 259, 260
MFD, 206
MICR, 194
Microblog, 39–41
Microcomputers, 4, 11, 12–16
Microprocessor, 12, 13, 161–163
Microprocessor age (1970–90), 334, 338–339
Microprocessor chips, 162
Microsoft, 66
Microsoft Access, 79
Microsoft Office, 85
Microsoft Office Excel 2007, 74
Microsoft Office Word 2003, 67
Microsoft Office Word 2010, 70
Microsoft Sync, 195
Microsoft Works, 84
Microwave, 251, 252
MIDI, 171
Midrange computers, 10
Million bits per second (Mbps), 253
Minicomputers, 10
Mistaken identity, 285
Mobile browsers, 33
Mobile robots, 114
Modem, 14, 253
Modem cards, 165
Modulation, 253
Modulator-demodulator, 253
Monitor, 13, 198–200
Monitor resolution, 198
Motherboard, 160–161
Mouse, 12, 188–189
Mouse pointer, 188
Mouse port, 171
Mozilla Thunderbird, 34
Mozy, 231
MSN Messenger, 38
MSN Search, 44
Multi-touch screens, 190
Multicore chip, 162
Multifunctional devices (MFD), 206
Multimedia, 108–109
Multimedia authoring programs, 109
Multitasking, 130
Music player, 205
Musical instrument digital interface (MIDI), 171

N

Naive persons, 317
Nano processor, 163
NAS, 233
National service providers, 31
Natural hazards, 295
Navigation keys, 188
Net Nanny, 51
Netbook, 11, 156
Netbook system unit, 156, 157
Network, 16, 256–257
Network adapter cards, 165, 166
Network administrator, 16, 257, 269, 323

Network architecture, 260–267
Network attached storage (NAS), 233
Network configurations, 264
Network gateway, 258
Network interface card (NIC), 165, 166, 257
Network operating systems (NOS), 131, 257
Network security, 268
Network server, 131
Network strategies, 265–267
Network types, 260
NIC, 165, 166, 257
NIDS, 268
Node, 256
Norton Internet Security, 52
Norton SystemWorks, 138
NOS, 131, 257
Notebook computers, 11, 157, 172–173
Notebook system units, 156
Numbered lists, 71
Numeric entry, 74
Numeric keypad, 187, 188
Numeric representation, 159

O

Objectivity, 46
OC line, 254
OCR, 194
Office grapevine, 322
Office software suites, 85
Office suites, 85
OLED, 199
OMR, 194
On the Web explorations
    Adobe, 79
    artificial intelligence, 112
    e-mail service, 35
    encryption, 297
    ergonomic keyboards, 187
    flat-panel monitors, 199
    graphics programs, 104
    hard-disk space, 223
    HDTV, 200
    laser printer, 203
    Lotus, 82
    MFDs, 206
    microprocessors, 162
    Microsoft, 66
    multimedia authoring programs, 109
    password strength, 298
    privacy issues, 285
    Snort, 269
    system unit components, 160
    utility software, 139
    Web filtering programs, 51
    wireless home networks, 258
Online, 30
Online banking, 47
Online explorations. See On the Web explorations
Online identity, 289
Online job search, 331
Online office suites, 85
Online shopping, 47

Online stock trading, 47
Online storage services, 231
Operating systems, 9
    categories, 131–132
    features, 129–134
    Mac OS, 133
    UNIX/Linux, 133–134
    virtualization, 134
    Windows, 132
Optical audio connections, 171
Optical carrier (OC) line, 254
Optical-character recognition (OCR), 194
Optical disc drive, 227
Optical discs, 12, 13, 225–230
Optical-mark recognition (OMR), 194
Optical mouse, 189
Optical scanner, 191
Organic light-emitting diode (OLED), 199
Organizational networks, 267–269
Organizational online storage, 233
Organized crime, 292
Outlook, 34
Output, 198–208
    Amazon Kindle, 201
    audio-output devices, 205
    careers, 207
    combination input-output devices, 205–206
    defined, 198
    monitors, 198–200
    printers, 202–204
Output devices, 12
Outside users, 292

P

P2P network, 266, 267
Packetization, 255
Packets, 255
Page layout programs, 103
Pages, 82
PAN, 260
Parallel port, 171
Parallel processing, 162
Passive-matrix monitors, 199
Password strengths, 298
Passwords, 296
PayPal, 49
PC Cards, 166
PCI, 167
PCI Express (PCIe), 170
PCMCIA, 166
PDA keyboard, 187
PDAs, 11, 157
Peer-to-peer (P2P) network, 266, 267
People, 4, 5, 282–283
Perception system robots, 114
Performance enhancements, 223
Peripheral component interconnect (PCI), 167
Person-to-person auction sites, 48
Personal area network (PAN), 260
Personal digital assistants (PDAs), 11, 157

Software engineer, 16, 234, 323
Software environment, 132
Software piracy, 300
Software suite, 85
Solid-state drives (SSDs), 13, 224
Solid-state storage, 12, 13, 224–225
Sony/Philips Digital Interconnect Format (S/PDIF), 171
Sort, 79
Sorted, 81
Sound cards, 165
Spacebar, 188
Spam, 35
Spam blockers, 35
Speakers, 205
Specialization, 319
Specialized applications, 9, 66, 102–115
  artificial intelligence, 112–114
  audio/video, 105–108
  careers, 114
  digital video editing, 106–107
  graphics programs, 103–105
  knowledge-based (expert) systems, 113
  multimedia, 108–109
  robotics, 113–114, 115
  virtual reality, 112–113
  Web authoring, 109–112
Specialized ports, 171
Specialized search engines, 45
Specialized suite, 88
Specialty processors, 163
Speech recognition, 67, 68–69
Spelling, 70
Spelling checker, 71
Spiders, 43
Spike, 296
Spotlight, 133
Spreadsheet functions, 75
Spreadsheets, 73–78
Spy Doctor, 289
Spy removal programs, 289
Spy Sweeper, 289
Spyware, 287, 288
Spyware removal, 290–291
SSDs, 13, 224
Stand-alone operating systems, 131
Star network, 261, 264
Stock photographs, 104
Stock trading, online, 47
Storage. *See* Secondary storage
Storage area network (SAN), 234
Storage devices, 220
Strategy, 265–267
Styles, 71
Stylus, 190–191
Subject, 35
Supercomputers, 10
Surf, 32
Surge protector, 296
SVGA, 199
Switch, 256
Swivel screen, 158
SXGA, 199
System board, 160–161
System buses, 167
System chassis, 156

System software, 8–9, 66, 128–144
  careers, 143
  device drivers, 139–142
  operating systems, 129–134
  self-healing computers, 143–144
  utilities, 135–139
  virus protection/Internet security, 140–141
System unit, 12, 156–174
  bus lines, 167–170
  careers, 173
  electronic data/instructions, 158–160
  expansion slots/cards, 165–166
  memory, 163–165
  microprocessors, 161–163
  ports, 170–172
  power supply, 172–173
  system board, 160–161
  TV tuner cards/video clips, 168–169
  wearable computers, 174
System unit components, 158
Systems analyst, 323

T

T1 line, 254
T3 line, 254
Tables, 79, 80
Tablet PC system units, 156
Tablet PCs, 11, 156, 157
Tabs, 67
Tape cartridge, 232
Tape library, 233
TB, 164
TCP/IP, 255
Technical writer, 16, 207, 323
Technological failures, 295
Telephone line, 250
Telephone modem, 253
Telephony, 206
Telepresence, 270
Templates, 83
Terabyte (TB), 164
Terminal server network, 265, 267
Terminology, 352–375
Terrorists, 292–293
Text entries, 74, 76
TFT monitors, 199
Theft, 294, 295
Thermal printers, 204
Thesaurus, 70
Thin film transistor (TFT) monitors, 199
Thousands of bits (kilobits) per second (Kbps), 253
3G cellular networks, 254
TLD, 32
Toggle keys, 187–188
Toolbars, 66
Top-level domain (TLD), 32
Topology, 260
Torvalds, Linus, 133
Touch pads, 189
Touch screen, 190
Track, 136, 138, 221
Trackball, 189
Trading stocks, online, 47

Traditional cookies, 286–287
Traditional floppy disk, 231
Traditional keyboards, 187, 188
Traditional telephones-to-traditional telephone, 206
Transfer rate, 253
Transistor age (1958–63), 334, 336
Transitions, 82, 83
Translation, 208
Transmission control protocol/Internet protocol (TCP/IP), 255
Tree network, 261, 264
Trojan horses, 293
Troubleshooting programs, 135
TV tuner cards, 166
Twisted-pair cable, 250, 252
Twitter, 39–41

U

Unicode, 159
Uniform resource, 32
Uninstall programs, 135
Universal instant messenger, 38
Universal Product Code (UPC), 193
Universal serial bus (USB), 167
Universal serial bus (USB) port, 171
UNIX, 132, 133
UPC, 193
Upgrader's guide, 348–349
Uploading, 51
USB, 167
USB drives, 13, 225
USB port, 171
User interface, 66, 129
Utilities, 9, 128, 135–139
  Disk Cleanup, 137
  Disk Defragmenter, 136, 138
  Norton SystemWorks, 138
  suite, 88, 138–139
  Windows Vista search, 135
Utility software, 139
UXGA, 199

V

Vacation prize, 295
Vacuum tube age (1951–57), 334, 335
Vector, 104
Vector illustrations, 104
Vector images, 104
VGA port, 171
Video clip, 168–169
Video editing software, 105
Video Graphics Adapter (VGA) port, 171
Virtual environments, 112
Virtual keyboards, 187
Virtual machines, 134
Virtual memory, 164
Virtual private network (VPN), 268, 298
Virtual reality (VR), 112
Virtual reality wall, 113
Virtualization, 134
Virtualization software, 134

Virus protection, 106–107, 135, 140–141, 294
Viruses, 35, 138, 293
Voice over IP (VoIP), 206
Voice recognition systems, 195
Voiceband, 255
VoIP, 206
Voltage surge, 296
VPN, 268, 298
VR, 112

W

WAN, 259, 260
Wand readers, 193, 194
Warm boot, 130
Wearable computers, 174
Web, 16, 30–33
Web-accessible home appliances, 53
Web authoring, 109–112
Web authoring programs, 110
Web-based applications, 49–50
Web-based services, 49
Web bugs, 287
Web explorations. See On the Web explorations
Web filtering programs, 51
Web image galleries, 104
Web logs, 39
Web page, 32
Web page editors, 110
Web search, 43
Web site design, 110
Web site encryption, 298
Web utilities, 49
WebCam, 195, 196–197, 302
Webmaster, 16, 52, 323

What-if analysis, 75, 78
What you see is what you get (WYSIWYG) editors, 110
Wheel button, 188
Wide area network (WAN), 259, 260
WiFi, 251
WiFi standards, 251
Wiki, 42
Wikipedia, 42
Window, 66
Windows, 130, 132
Windows 7, 9, 132, 133, 134
Windows 98, 132
Windows 2000 Professional, 132
Windows Defender, 289
Windows Live Messenger, 196–197
Windows ME, 132
Windows Media Player, 50
Windows Movie Maker, 105
Windows Update, 142
Windows utilities, 135–137
Windows Vista, 132
Windows Vista search utility, 135
Windows XP, 132
Wireless access point, 259, 262
Wireless communication devices, 15
Wireless connections, 251
Wireless fidelity (WiFi), 251
Wireless keyboards, 187
Wireless LAN (WLAN), 259, 260
Wireless modems, 32, 254
Wireless mouse, 189
Wireless network encryption, 298
Wireless revolution, 16, 249
Wireless service providers, 32
Wireless wide area network (WWAN) modem, 254
WLAN, 259, 260

Word, 162
Word 2003, 67
Word 2010, 70
Word processors, 70–73
Word wrap, 70, 71
WordPress, 42
Workbook, 78
Workbook files, 73
Worksheet, 73, 74, 76
Worksheet files, 15
Worms, 293
Write once—CD-R, 227
Write-once DVD+R, 230
Writing files, 220
WWAN modem, 254
WYSIWYG editing, 111
WYSIWYG editors, 110

X

xDrive, 231
Xeon processor, 163
XGA, 199

Y

Yahoo!, 44
Yahoo Messenger, 38
YouTube, 228–229

Z

Zombies, 294